DATE DUE

OC 16 '00			
NO 6 '00			
NO 27 '00			
MR 27 '01			
MY 24 '01			
NO 14 01			
DE 4 '01			
FE 5 '03			
OC 1 '08			

DEMCO 38-296

Women in Middle

Eastern History

Women in Middle

Eastern History

Shifting Boundaries

in Sex and Gender

EDITED BY

NIKKI R. KEDDIE

BETH BARON

Yale University Press

New Haven and London

Designed by Sonia L. Scanlon.
Set in Palatino type by
The Composing Room of Michigan, Inc.
Printed in the United States of
America by Vail-Ballou Press,
Binghamton, New York.

Library of Congress
Cataloging-in-Publication Data

Women in Middle Eastern history :
  shifting boundaries in sex and gender/
  edited by Nikki R. Keddie and Beth Baron.
      p.   cm.
    Includes index.
    ISBN 0-300-05005-4 (cloth)
        0-300-05697-4 (pbk.)
    1. Women—Middle East—History.
I. Keddie, Nikki R.   II.   Baron, Beth.
HQ1726.5.W66   1992
305.42'0956—dc20   91-19665
                                                  CIP

The paper in this book meets the
guidelines for permanence and
durability of the Committee on
Production Guidelines for Book
Longevity of the Council on
Library Resources.
10 9 8 7 6 5 4 3 2

Contents

v

III Modern Turkey and Iran

IV The Modern Arab World

Preface

The need for a book of interpretive research papers regarding the history, and not just the current condition, of women in the Middle East has been evident for some time, but the possibility of producing a high quality and varied work depended on the existence of a critical mass of good scholars working on Middle Eastern women's history. Hence, even scholars whose works are not included in this volume have contributed to it. Scholars of Middle Eastern women's history have published and presented papers in many places, most notably in the annual meetings of the Middle East Studies Association and at the 1987 meeting of the Berkshire Conference on the History of Women, where a series of panels was organized by Margot Badran. Erika Friedl's, Mary Hegland's, and Paula Sanders's papers in this volume were rewritten from papers presented at that Berkshire conference.

Contributing in various ways to this volume have been Janet Afary, Marilyn Booth, Ken Cuno, Afaf Marsot, and Ruth Roded. In Great Britain, Albert Hourani, Anna Enayat, and Iradj Bagherzade gave us good advice about the manuscript and encouragement. Jane Bitar and the staff of the much-lamented Social Sciences Word Processing at UCLA retyped the entire manuscript in their usual exemplary fashion. Dean Paul Sherwin and the history department at City College, CUNY, gave invaluable support.

Charles Grench, Eliza Childs, Cynthia Carter Ayres, Linda Webster, and the others at Yale University Press did their usual excellent editorial job.

Aside from the listed technical help from CUNY and UCLA, this book, like most books edited or co-edited by Nikki Keddie, had no subvention and no advances. Nor was it based on a conference or invitational talks. This is mentioned only because many people think it is impossible to do an edited book without such prior support. While financial support is helpful, what is most needed is a vision, a cooperative spirit, and an open-minded flexibility and willingness to work by all involved, and this we had.

Organization of the Volume

BETH BARON

The chapters in this volume move from the distant to the more recent past, with those on the modern period arranged by region. Some periods and places receive more attention than others. Occasional clustering, based on a relative abundance of sources and of scholars in certain fields, provides depth as well as breadth for these societies, such as Mamluk and modern Egypt. The volume deals with major aspects of Middle Eastern women's history, and the theme of male and female boundaries runs throughout. The chapters, most written by historians or using a historical approach, suggest that gender boundaries in the Middle East have been neither fixed nor immutable.

Nikki Keddie introduces the volume with a survey of major questions in Middle Eastern women's history that emphasizes the Muslim majority. By sketching shifts in women's position from ancient to modern times, she helps to identify ideological and other problems in the field and to suggest useful directions for future research. Deniz Kandiyoti provides a comparative context for the Middle East, contrasting systems of male dominance in two regions that Islam crosses, the first in sub-Saharan Africa and the second in the Middle East and southern and eastern Asia. She finds that most women in the second region tacitly agreed to a family pattern she calls "classical patriarchy" in which they were subordinate as young brides in return for later benefits. Kandiyoti suggests that Middle Eastern gender relations have been influenced by a particular conjunction of classic patriarchy and Islam.

The next set of chapters looks at women and gender in the first centuries of Islam. Leila Ahmed documents the tension between two tendencies: a legal one, sometimes called orthodox, stressing gender inequalities and a spiritual, or unorthodox one based on ethical egalitarianism. The latter, expressed in Sufism and other unorthodox movements such as Qarmatism, gave greater scope and freedom to women. Yet the legal current prevailed, and with it a rigidification of gender boundaries. Denise Spellberg focuses on changing views of 'A'isha, Muhammad's favorite wife and a model for Muslim women. She shows how ninth-century historians used 'A'isha's defeat in the Battle of the Camel to point out the dangers of women's participation in government, effectively circumscribing women's political roles. Paula Sanders examines certain legal texts of Muslim jurists, mostly of the eleventh century, to see how they constructed gender. She selects the seemingly arcane but potentially dangerous problem of the ungendered, those who had both male and female reproductive organs—hermaphrodites. The ambiguity of hermaphrodites created a gray area in a world of bipolar divisions of male and female. In setting hermaphrodites into the social order by providing guidelines for ritual and behavior, medieval Muslim jurists reaffirmed gender boundaries and hierarchies.

The following cluster of chapters is set in the Mamluk period (1250–1517) in Egypt. Huda Lutfi shows how prescribed gender boundaries were broken in practice by medieval Cairene women. Extracting information on female behavior from a treatise by the fourteenth-century scholar Ibn al-Hajj, she finds that women shaped their habits and rituals according to their own needs and participated actively in public life, much to the chagrin of her scholar. Carl Petry sees gender as an important factor in shaping the strategies of the Mamluk elite for managing family property. Because of the endemic violence of Mamluk politics and the consequent high male mortality, women, whose chances of surviving were better, often became caretakers of estates and supervisors of trusts. In this way, they ensured family stability and class continuity, in turn augmenting their own status in Mamluk society. Jonathan Berkey describes how women pursued education through informal as opposed to institutional channels. Many specialized in transmitting hadith (Traditions), an endeavor that may have been permitted, according to Berkey, in part because it combined the skill of memorization with the advantage of age.

The chapters on the modern Middle East are grouped by region, starting with two on Ottoman and Turkish women. Donald Quataert argues that women played a crucial role in nineteenth-century Ottoman manufacturing, especially in handicraft, textile, and carpet production. By focusing on household economies and small workshops, he challenges the view that manufacturing and its labor force declined during this period. Quataert also finds that, with regional variation, many households showed flexibility in the division of labor. Nermin Abadan-Unat examines the educational and legal reforms of the Turkish Republic, assessing their impact on the position of women of various classes in Turkish society. She shows how Ataturk's secularizing path, unique to the region, has come under attack by Islamists, threatening to reverse earlier gains for women.

Regarding Iran, Erika Friedl has personally witnessed major social changes telescoped into decades in the tribal-rural Iranian community that she has studied for the past twenty years. She argues that overlapping and changing productive systems help to explain an increasing circumscription of women's roles and behavior. The relative freedom of many tribal-rural women has largely been based on socioeconomic necessity and is not deeply embedded in ideology. It is fragile and easily lost with changes in social circumstances, as the past two decades have shown. Mary Hegland looks at the public-private dichotomy as myth and ideology in a village. The myth obscures women's real political contributions, and the ideology functions to control women and their activities, creating a reservoir that can be tapped for appropriate political purposes.

The final section of the volume focuses on the Arab world. Judith Tucker attempts to recapture the female experience of the family in eighteenth- and nineteenth-century Palestine. Women could draw support and protection from family members to temper a husband's patriarchal control. Her evidence shows the importance of a number of different affective family relationships. The next chapter, set in late-nineteenth-century Algeria, echoes Ahmed's suggestion that mysticism gave women greater freedom. Julia Clancy-Smith examines the life of Lalla Zainab, an Algerian saint, mystic, and learned woman, documenting her struggle to succeed her father as head of a sufi lodge in the face of resistance from her cousin, who promoted his own claims, and French colonial officials, who backed the cousin. Zainab successfully defended her inheritance, drawing on her spiritual authority to transcend indigenous and foreign gender boundaries.

In the first of three chapters on modern Egypt, I sketch changing marital patterns among urban middle-class and upper-class Egyptians in the nineteenth and twentieth centuries. I argue that during this period the notion of marriage based on love and free choice began to displace the older ideal of arranged marriages. Virginia Danielson focuses on the lives of a group of Egyptian performers (among them Umm Kulthum) who dominated the music industry in the 1920s. These women demonstrated a high degree of autonomy in managing their careers, taking advantage of the opportunities that new technologies offered. In the final chapter of the volume, Cynthia Nelson probes the relationship of biographer and memoirist as she examines the life of Doria Shafik, an Egyptian feminist active in the 1940s and 1950s. Shafik fought for political equality for women before being placed under house arrest in 1957. Nelson argues that her feminism was grounded in indigenous culture and was not in opposition to Islam.

Each chapter provides insights into the past, opening new topics for consideration or encouraging reconsiderations of old ones. Together they improve our understanding of women and gender in Middle Eastern history. During the early centuries of Islam, once-fluid gender boundaries began to rigidify. Yet they were never impermeable, and in the Mamluk period seemed quite elastic as women of different backgrounds exercised relative autonomy. In modern times, shifting boundaries have mostly moved toward increased equality for women, but not always. Gender relations in the Middle East have proven dynamic, with women's spheres of action contracting and expanding at different moments and rates in response to a variety of factors, including women's acts and attitudes. Although the chapters within are concerned with far more than boundaries, gender boundaries and their changes over time provide one approach to illuminating the past and present of the Middle East.

Women in Middle

Eastern History

Introduction: Deciphering Middle Eastern Women's History

NIKKI R. KEDDIE

The position of women in the Middle East has aroused much interest, but serious scholarly work on Middle Eastern women's history has been limited, in comparison both with the study of women's history elsewhere and with the study of contemporary problems. Existing volumes of articles about women in the Middle East contain little that is historical. This is the first scholarly collection to stress Middle Eastern women's history, and it also includes the work of several social scientists whose theoretical perspectives are useful to the study of the past.

The relative neglect of women's history has occurred mainly because historians, unlike social scientists, cannot construct their own research projects based on people who can be directly observed, interviewed, or given questionnaires. Most historical work relies chiefly on written sources, which are heavily male oriented, and a great mass of documents needs to be unearthed or restudied with women's questions in mind.

Discussions of Middle Eastern women's history are also often ideologically charged. Such discussions may be wrenching ones for scholars who wish to overcome widespread prejudices against Islam, but not ignore the problems of Muslim women. One group denies that Muslim women, who comprise the great majority of women in the Middle East, are any more oppressed than non-Muslim women or argues that in key respects they have been less oppressed. A

Some of the material in this introduction was used in Nikki R. Keddie, "The Past and Present of Women in the Muslim World," *Journal of World History* 1, no. 1 (1990): 77–108. Where points differ, this text has priority. In addition to written sources, the chapter is based on wide travel, residence, and interviews in many Muslim countries.

second says that oppression is real but extrinsic to Islam; the Quran, they say, intended gender equality, but this was undermined by Arabian patriarchy and foreign importations. An opposing group blames Islam for being irrevocably gender inegalitarian. There are also those who adopt intermediate positions, as well as those who tend to avoid these controversies by sticking to monographic or limited studies that do not confront such issues. Some scholars favor shifting emphases away from Islam to economic and social forces.

Given the paucity of studies and the abundance of controversy, surveying major questions in the field might seem premature. It is perpetually too early to survey any field, but such surveys are vital for nonspecialists who wish to understand a field, and they help situate the field's problems and useful directions for research.

This chapter stresses the Muslim majority in Middle Eastern history, as do the chapters following, although research on minorities also exists. Differences between Muslims and non-Muslims concerning gender status are usually attributed mainly to the Quran, to early Muslim tradition and holy law. There are also other, including pre-Islamic, roots of difference. Differences between the Middle East and other cultures regarding gender relations were in most ways smaller in the past than in modern times. Muslim resistance to Western-sanctioned change is tied to a centuries-old hostility between the Muslim Middle East and the West, which has increased in modern times. The home has become a last line of defense against a West that has won out in political and economic spheres. So-called fundamentalists, or Islamists, see Western practices toward and views on women as part of a Western Christian and Jewish cultural offensive, accompanying political and economic offensives, and turn to their own traditions as a cultural alternative.

The origin of gender inequalities in the ancient Near East is disputed but it is known that hunter-gatherers and other pre-plow peoples are more egalitarian between genders than are people who have experienced the neolithic and agricultural revolutions. Technological developments that made possible a surplus, states, and ruling classes were accompanied by a greater division of labor, including class hierarchies and slavery, and encouraged the limiting of many urban women to domestic occupations. Class differences developed among women as well as among men, with some being slaves who filled menial or sexual roles, others who performed both nondomestic and domestic labor, and upper-class women who did not have to venture outside the home.[1] Veiling and seclusion developed in the pre-Islamic Near East and adjacent areas as markers for urban upper- and middle-class women, showing that they did not have to work and keeping them from strangers.

As women in ancient societies became more subordinate, often treated as property, many peoples developed myths about them as the source of evil and sexual temptation—dangerous and needing control. Once inheritance in the male line became important, female virginity and fidelity became central concerns. Males in most cultures were not required to be faithful, and male polygamy was often legal. Muslims note that female polygamy would raise doubts about fatherhood, which is unthinkable. Women had to be controlled largely to minimize their chances of contacts with outside men.

The guarding of women has been strong in Near Eastern and Mediterranean societies from ancient times. As many "Islamic" customs go back to the pre-Islamic Near East, something should be said about that before discussing Islam. In the first known reference to veiling, an Assyrian legal text of the thirteenth century B.C., it is restricted to respectable women and prohibited for prostitutes. From the first, veiling was a sign of status. Respectable Athenian women were often secluded, and veiling was known in the Greco-Roman world. Veiling and seclusion existed in pre-Islamic Iran and the Byzantine Empire, the two areas conquered by the first Muslims, though we do not know how widespread they were.[2]

A husband who had the means to keep his wife veiled and secluded showed that she was protected from advances and did not have to work or shop outside. Full veiling has been both a class phenomenon and an urban one. Early Muslims adopted veiling from conquered peoples, and both non-Muslims in Muslim societies and Mediterranean women in Christian societies were subject to many of the same forms of control and isolation from men. Mediterranean societies, Muslim and Christian, also had the same idea of the centrality of a man's honor, which lay chiefly in the purity of the women of his natal family.

Similarities in Mediterranean attitudes toward male-female relations are discussed by Germaine Tillion, who says that Mediterranean peoples favor endogamy, which increases the tendency to control women in tightly interrelated lineages. She notes that ancient Egyptians and Persians favored "incestuous" unions, whereas most Mediterranean peoples favor cousin marriage.[3] Building on Tillion, one could say that tribal groups, who are numerous among the Muslims of the Middle East, have special reasons to want to control women and to favor cousin marriage, and that the interaction of tribes with urban groups practicing seclusion added segregation to control.

The term *tribe* has been so misused that many, especially Africanists, avoid it. Whereas those who study Africa may justly react to a word misused to characterize groups with millions of people, there is a role for the word *tribe* in the Middle East. It translates terms in the main Middle Eastern languages that refer to contiguous groups claiming descent from

one ancestor. A tribe is a political-economic unit, and its leaders, generally chosen from one lineage, command more loyalty than the central
government, though they may now have little real power. In recent times
tribes tend to be strong when central governments are weak, and central
governments usually try to weaken tribes.

Tribes are not a primitive form of social organization. Pastoral nomadic
tribes, the most common in the Middle East, can evolve only after animals
are domesticated and there is a settled population with whom to trade
animal products for agricultural and urban ones. Cohesion requires
group decisions, which are facilitated in groups tied by kin. This favors
cousin marriage, as does the Islamic provision for female inheritance,
which encourages strategies to keep property in the lineage. Gertrude
Stern documents that Muslim Arabs increased cousin marriage after the
Quran required female inheritance.[4] When women inherit according to
Muslim law, there are clear advantages in cousin marriage. Certain familial controls may be tied to the prevalence of tribal structures. In other
areas, however, many tribes have strong and quite liberated women, and
veiling and seclusion are more urban than tribal phenomena. The interaction between tribal and urban controls on women was an important
influence on Middle Eastern gender relations.

The Quran was written in a context of different levels of sexual inequality among Arab tribes and in adjacent non-Arab empires. How it
affected the position of women is controversial.[5] The classic Muslim view
is that pre-Islamic Arabs lived in ignorance and barbarism and that the
divinely revealed Quran provided a great step forward on all questions.
Some scholars, however, have documented (especially in Arab poetry)
conditions of matriliny, greater activity for women, even on the battlefield, and freer divorce.[6] Such sources do indicate some matrilineal
and matrilocal customs, as well as freer divorce for women in certain
tribes, and a greater outspokenness and activity for many women than
became common after the rise of Islam, but we do not know how widespread these patterns were.

The Quran did bring in some reforms, however, including the outlawing of infanticide and the payment of the male dower to the bride, not to
her guardian. The Quran also prescribed female inheritance—half that of
a male heir—and women's control over their property (which was known
earlier, however, as seen in Muhammad's first wife, the merchant Khadija). Unfavorable features were free divorce for men but not for women
and polygamy for men (which already existed).

Although Islamic traditions say veiling and seclusion for all Muslim
women are in the Quran, this is a tendentious reading. One verse tells
women to veil their bosoms and hide their ornaments, later taken to

mean all except the hands, feet, and perhaps the face. This interpretation makes no sense, because if everything was to be veiled, there would be no point in ordering bosoms to be veiled separately. Another verse tells women to draw their cloaks tightly around them so they may be recognized and not annoyed. These are the only words generally taken to refer to veiling.

Other verses suggest seclusion for Muhammad's wives, and these stricter rules for an elite later spread, encouraged by the example of the conquered Near East, to the urban middle and upper classes. Later veiling was not, however, simply in emulation of the Prophet's wives. Nabia Abbott notes that Muhammad's veiling of his wives reflected the growing prosperity of the Muslim ruling group, enabling them to have servants and to keep women from nondomestic work, and also the Muslims' growing contact with surrounding societies where women were veiled.[7] As Muslim society became state centered and class divided like those of the surrounding and conquered peoples, many of their practices concerning women, appropriate to stratified social structures, and their reliance on family regulation to maintain social control were naturally also found appropriate by the Muslims.

The Quran gives men control of their wives, which extends to beatings for disobedience, and adulterers of both sexes are to be punished by lashing when there is either confession or four eyewitnesses to the act. Islamic law and tradition changed this to the far more severe punishment of stoning to death, but in practice women were often killed by their brothers and many escaped punishment.

Islamic practices about women are often said to be resistant to change because of their Quranic sanction, believed to be the word of God. This has some truth, but there has been much breaking and bending of Quranic admonitions throughout Muslim history. The Quran has been interpreted, against the meaning of its text, as enjoining veiling, whereas Quranic rules on adultery are rarely followed. Quranic inheritance rules were hard to follow in rural and nomadic societies, as daughters married out of the family, with only a minority marrying paternal first cousins. Land or flocks inherited by an out-marrying woman reduced the property of the patrilineal line. Hence means were found, in most rural and a minority of urban areas, to evade women's inheritance rights. Also, the general inheritance rules of the Quran were interpreted in a more patriarchal way by Islamic law.

In all these cases, later practice was more patriarchal than the Quranic text warrants. In general, the Quran was followed when it was not too inconvenient to men or to the patriarchal family to do so, and not followed when it was. This gives some basis to modern feminists and reformers who want to return to, and reinterpret, the Quran, although their interpretation sometimes moves as far in a new direction as the old one did in the opposite one. Islamic law and Traditions tended to stress and rigidify gender distinctions, seen as crucial to an ordered world, and went to great lengths to avoid gender ambiguities (see Sanders chapter in this volume).

Urban middle- and upper-class women, traditionally the most veiled and secluded, were also much more likely to inherit Quranically. This is a paradox only to a Westerner who reads back our concepts of women's rights into the past and thinks that "disadvantaged" veiled women should have fewer rights in other spheres. Urban residence in fact both made women's inheritance easier, by not involving flocks and fields, and encouraged veiling, because contact with unrelated strangers was more likely; also there were more middle- and upper-class women with more servants and slaves. Differences in class, place, and time meant that there was never one set of Muslim women operating under one set of rules.

A variety of historical and anthropological works contribute to the following overall picture of different female statuses: in general, rural and tribal women do not inherit as the Quran and Muslim law says they should, though "in return" they generally get permanent protection from their natal family, and in some cases their sons may get all or part of their share. Court records past and present suggest that urban women, however, usually do inherit and are willing and able to go to Islamic courts to protect their property rights, generally successfully. Sources also suggest that urban women have had more rights than agricultural-ists, although the great freedoms and powers of tribal nomadic women are also noted. These differences are accentuated by a class-difference pattern, with ruling class and upper-class women in both tribes and towns often notable for their powers and independence whereas poorer women were more dependent. Hence modern differences in styles of living between town, tribe, and countryside and between classes in town originate in earlier times and in continuing functional differences.[8]

This does not mean that the prescriptions of the Quran and Muslim law counted for little. The rules on polygamy, divorce, and child custody (to the father's family after a young age) were widely followed. If polyg-amy and divorce were less general than Westerners might imagine, they remained a threat to a wife. Divorce was generally common, but polyg-amy seems to have been a rare, mainly upper-class, custom.

The condition of most women seems to have been broadly comparable to that in the ancient Near East and the later Mediterranean and eastern and southern Asia (for a comparison across Asia, see Kandiyoti in this volume). Most women were valued mainly as producers of sons and were brought up to marry, produce children, and safeguard the family honor by not transgressing rules of sexual conduct and segregation. Most were married young in arranged marriages in which the husband's family had to pay a dower. This often included a delayed payment in case of divorce or death, which provided some protection for the wife when it was observed. Brides frequently lived in the husband's father's household, often with a menial position until the first son might be born. Young brides were often dominated by mothers-in-law more than by husbands, and they gained status mainly through their maturing sons. By the time the sons became adults their mother might be very powerful in the household, ready to dominate her sons' wives in turn.

This brief outline cannot suggest the variety and satisfactions that went along with the difficulties of women's lives. In the long preindustrial period when nuclear and extended families were the main productive units—whether in agriculture, herding, crafts, or trade—the organization of society around families and the superior power of dominant males and of male and female elders probably seemed natural to most people all over the world. It was only modern changes in economy, politics, and society that made these structures less functional and called them into question. Even before they were widely questioned, structures of male domination caused much suffering, however.

Dramatic differences between Muslims and non-Muslims came with nineteenth- and twentieth-century Muslim resistance to change, and with contemporary Islamic revivalism. Regarding gender relations, Islamism has no strict parallel in other civilizations, even though some practices in India and elsewhere indicate that the Muslim world is not the area of the worst atrocities toward women.

Whereas some scholars think the limitation of women's roles after the rise of Islam was due to borrowing from non-Muslims, others stress that this restriction began in Muhammad's time. The strongest women appeared at the beginning of Islam. Khadija, the merchant, who employed and married Muhammad, fifteen years her junior, was his first convert and helped him in every way. Muhammad's young wife 'A'isha, whom he married when she was a child and whose heedlessness of opinion sometimes caused trouble, exercised much power. After Muhammad's death she joined the coalition against Muhammad's son-in-law 'Ali and participated in the crucial battle against him.

If these figures were unparalleled in later generations, neither internal nor external forces were exclusively responsible. As Islamic society became more like the societies around it in stratification and patriarchy, it was natural to adopt their ways. Families wealthy enough to have slaves or servants could afford seclusion. Women often acquiesced in veiling and seclusion when to be less covered and to work outside were marks of low status.

Muslim women's lives have varied greatly by class, mode of production, time, and place. What generalizations one can make in a brief essay are partly based on Islamic laws and practices, even though their observation varied. Islamic law developed in the first few centuries of Islam, and recent scholarship has shown how much it reflected regional Middle Eastern customs—hence that much of it was in fact followed more in the Middle East than elsewhere, though far from all, is not surprising. There were four orthodox law schools, plus Shi'i schools, which differed on some points important to women. Regarding marriage, schools differed as to whether a virgin's consent was needed, or only that of her father or guardian. In all schools marriage is a contract, not a sacrament, and the man must provide materially for the wife and perform sexually. The wife must have sex whenever the husband wishes, but she has no material obligations. A man may divorce a wife by a thrice-pronounced declaration, whereas women can divorce only for specified causes, agreed to by a judge in court. Polygyny up to four wives was permitted, although the Quran says only if all are treated equally, which came to mean a norm of equal space and rotated sexual relations and overnight stays. Men were permitted concubines and female slaves, and their children's status was regulated. Another Shi'i practice goes back to pre-Islamic Arabia and seems to have been condoned by the Prophet, though it was outlawed for Sunnis by the caliph 'Umar. This is temporary marriage—a contract entered into for a definite period. As in all marriages there is a payment to the woman and children are legitimate. It flourishes especially in pilgrimage centers where men may come alone. It is wrong to consider it prostitution, and it has uses besides satisfying men's sexual desires.[9] Women are supposed to obey their husbands, and the Quran authorizes beating if they do not. This is one of several verses that has been reinterpreted by modernists.

Women could hold and manage any amount of property, although seclusion often made effective management difficult. Regarding the two-thirds or more of inheritance that followed fixed rules, women were supposed to receive half the share of men. In Shi'i law daughters without brothers inherited everything, whereas in Sunni law they generally got no more than half. In spite of the presumption of female inheritance by all schools, it was common for women not to inherit, especially land. This kept land from passing outside the paternal family. Partial compensation in the form of gifts or sustenance in case of divorce or widowhood was sometimes given to a woman who renounced inheritance. In addition, the institution of *waqf*, inalienable endowment, was sometimes used to endow descendants in the male line, thus avoiding both property division and female inheritance. Some waqfs, however, benefited women particularly, both as recipients and as guardians (see Petry in this volume).

Regarding the most effective form of birth control then known, coitus interruptus, most jurists and theologians allowed it, but some said it was licit only if the wife agreed, as she might want children or object to limiting her pleasure.[10] Some say the authorization of birth control came mainly because powerful men had slaves and concubines by whom they might not want children (see Ahmed in this volume).

As in many societies, particularly Mediterranean ones, the code of honor and shame has been central. A family's honor was seen as resting mainly on the purity of its girls and women, and shame lay in any aspersions cast on this. Purity meant not only virginity for girls and fidelity for wives, but also the impossibility that anyone should think or say these were in doubt. Neither girl nor wife should talk to an outside man. The ideal of segregation from gossip-provoking situations encouraged veiling and seclusion. Some wealthy families kept women from going out of the house except fully covered to see close relatives. In less wealthy families women might have to have some business interaction with men, but they were supposed to keep talk to a minimum and their eyes down. It seems that outdoor dress for the upper classes usually included a facial veil and loose covering for the body. Working, rural, and tribal women usually had no facial veil. Most women passed the greater part of their lives in homes, where they could wear and show off their more important clothing and ornaments. Fashion was important, and current reporters who are surprised that Arabian and Iranian women may wear jeans or miniskirts below their veils are really reporting nothing new, as Muslim women at home have long followed fashions, often ones from far away.

Honor and shame encouraged early marriage, as leaving a girl unmarried after puberty was seen as creating a situation in which she might be violated or impregnated. Mothers often played a greater role than fathers in finding a groom, and matchmakers were sometimes used. Paternal cousin marriage, which kept property in the patrilineal line, was favored. Despite this, only a minority of marriages were to paternal first cousins; even when this is claimed, investigation often shows a more distant relationship. This may have limited bad genetic effects from such marriages, although today many educated Muslims oppose cousin marriage for genetic reasons.

As in much of traditional Mediterranean Europe, that a girl and a man alone can be doing only one thing is widely assumed, and the girl is often punished. Traditional ideology assumes that a woman who behaves immodestly arouses uncontrollable urges in men. She is a cause of *fitna*, serious trouble, a word that also means revolt or civil war. Fathers, husbands, and brothers are given formal control over women and the family, as in many traditional societies, but observers often note the real power of women in the home and family.

In spite of formal and legal male dominance, Middle Eastern women followed a number of strategies to increase their sphere of power and freedom. Although men might control the quantity of sex, women had much control over its quality and the amount of pleasure the man had. Women controlled cooking, which many men found important, and they could keep the home neat or messy, noisy or tranquil, attractive or unattractive for the husband's visitors. Throughout Islamic history many rulers were ruled by their wives or mothers, and the same thing happened in many private homes. More equal husband-wife relations were also known. Women taught one another how to overcome formal inequalities, and the theoretical rules of Islamic law and the honor code were often not enforced.

Too little research has been done to provide a true history of how women fared over time in the Middle East. Here we can essay a few generalizations. There seem to be four periods that saw the greatest freedom of action for a significant number of Middle Eastern women: the earliest period of Islam; its first two centuries; the periods of nomadic and steppe-based rule (those of the Seljuks, Mongols, Mamluks, early Safavids); and the period of modern reform. In the first of these, the activities of Khadija and 'A'isha have been mentioned, and there were also many lesser powerful women, not to mention women who participated as aides in battle, or even fought (as they had in pre-Islamic times). The next period was more mixed (see Ahmed in this volume), but women continued to be important and powerful as queens, traditionists, and in mystical and sectarian religious movements. At the same time, however, slavery and class divisions were spreading. The invasions of Turkic and other military groups and nomads from the eleventh century on, and their rule over much of the Middle East, brought in, at least for the ruling classes and the nomads, more egalitarian treatment of women. Powerful women participated in rule in the Seljuk, Mongol, and Mamluk empires, where restrictions on women appear to have been lessened (see Petry and Berkey in this volume).

Through the centuries nonorthodox religious spheres have provided a forum for female power. Shi'ism has women mullas, and Sufi (mystic) orders include powerful and creative women leaders, and all had many women followers (see Ahmed, Clancy-Smith, and Lutfi in this volume).

Since the nineteenth century there have been modern, mainly legal and economic, reforms in the position of women, and the growth of reformist and feminist ideas. Although, as elsewhere, changes have been contradictory in their impact, the general trend thus far has been toward greater legal equality between the sexes and greater real equality among the urban Westernized middle and upper classes, although some in other classes have suffered.

Women's position, past and present, tended to become limited in times of economic contraction. At the very top, however, the role of women was determined most by court conditions. Where royal heirs were brought up within palace walls they might be subject to the influence of women or eunuchs. One example is the Ottoman Empire, where from the late sixteenth century potential heirs to the throne were kept from threatening the ruler by being immured in the harem. This greatly increased women's and eunuchs' influence on them, even after they came to rule. The negative phrase "harem rule" will probably have its revisionist historians, though it is probably true that sultans with experience of the outside world ruled better than those without. The influence of Ottoman queens and queen mothers, as with their lesser-known counterparts in Mamluk, Mongol, and Seljuk times, not to mention Safavid and Qajar Iran, shows how possible it was for women to exercise great power, given the right circumstances.

The common Western view of the harem has little relation to reality. The Arabic word *harim* does not have sexy connotations, but means the part of the house forbidden to men who are not close relatives. For the non-elite it mostly was not polygamous and had no slaves or concubines. The harem was where the indoor work of the family was planned and carried on, usually under the supervision of the wife of the eldest male. In polygamous households and those with servants and slaves, the activities of the harem were more complex, but it was not the den of idleness and voluptuousness depicted from their imaginations by Western painters. (Westerners who saw photographs of harems were disappointed to find the clothing and furniture to be in keeping with Victorian propriety, bearing no resemblance to the paintings of Delacroix.) The main work of household production, including its textiles and other crafts, and of reproduction, was done in the harem.[11]

Partly owing to difficulties of documentation, little study has been done of pre-modern working women, rural or urban, or of slaves. Slavery in Islam was rarely characterized by heavy gang labor, but was overwhelmingly either household or male military slavery. Muslims could not be enslaved, and so slaves were either war captives or purchased from among non-Muslims. Slaves were often sexually subject to their masters. Unlike those in the medieval West, their children were free. Some slaves rose very high—slaves could be queens—and many were freed by their masters. Although slavery was less onerous than, say, in the New World, it still entailed a lack of freedom and a sexual subjugation that were more severe than those experienced by free women. Slaves were often trained to be singers and dancers—professions that were not quite respectable in the Islamic world or in many other traditional areas.

Although it was suggested above that many tribes are highly concerned about the purity of lineage, in most other respects treatment of women among tribal peoples tends to be more egalitarian than among urbanites. It may be something about the long-term confluence of nomadic and urban cultures that helps explain Middle Eastern patterns of gender relations and controls. The greater gender egalitarianism of tribal peoples shows up among pre-Islamic and early Islamic Arab women, and among the Seljuks and Mongols in Iran, with their powerful women in government. Early European accounts and indigenous painting suggest that tribal women did not veil. The Safavids in Iran (1501–1722), who made Shi'ism Iran's state religion, came in supported by the military backing of Turkic nomadic tribes, and early Safavid miniatures are full of unveiled women. Italian travelers to Iran in those years wrote that women were shockingly exposed! By late Safavid times, the influence of the religious classes had grown, and women were increasingly veiled and secluded.

In recent decades, as veiling and seclusion were rejected by many modernists and feminists, and as local nationalisms grew, those who opposed veiling ascribed it to a different nationality from their own. Many Arabs say veiling was imposed on them by the Ottoman Turks. In fact, Turks began to veil only when they became assimilated in Islam, and if many Ottomans in Arab lands veiled this was mainly because ruling classes veiled, not because Turks in particular did. There is abundant evidence that widespread Arab veiling preceded the Ottomans, although it appears that pre-Ottoman Mamluk Egypt was freer in this respect than Ottoman Egypt. Iranian modernists often blame veiling on Arabs, and Turks on Arabs or Persians. As noted, veiling and seclusion are ancient Near Eastern customs, long adopted by all major language groups in the Middle East.

Some writers, reacting to Western hostility to veiling, deny its significance. Although veiling and seclusion do not prevent women from living varied and significant lives, they are parts of a system where males are dominant and females are to be controlled. The system affects even non-secluded women, who are expected to be modest and circumspect and are subject to sanctions if they transgress the rules. It is true that the overall system is more important than veiling as such.

The degree to which women follow the rules should not be exaggerated, however. Outside observers may see only heavily veiled shapes and assume that these women's lives are completely controlled by their menfolk. When seen from the inside, however, the same women may give quite a different impression. Thus two eighteenth-century Englishwomen wrote admiringly of the lives and freedom enjoyed by Ottoman ladies,[12] whereas their Western male colleagues reported no such views.

Various peoples have reported transgressions of the rules by Egyptian women (see Lutfi). Even in parts of the Middle East where Western influence is small, there have been recent reports of great independence on the part of women. These center on the Arabian peninsula and Berber-influenced North Africa, both areas of tribal strength. In the latter, among several signs of a freer position for women is the institution of the free woman, who may take lovers after divorce or widowhood without loss of respect or of opportunities for remarriage. In Arabia, where women are veiled and secluded, Leila Ahmed and Unni Wikan report deviant and independent behavior and views by women in the United Arab Emirates and Oman. Ahmed thinks that the relative success in organizing women to assert their rights in Marxist South Yemen owes much to the Arabian women's independence in views and action.[13] From both Yemen and Iran come reports of women's theater games in which male arrogance and other male cultural qualities are mercilessly mocked, and such mockery must have existed in the past. Egyptian women have also been noted for their independence from pre-Islamic times to the present, indicating that local traditions and conditions can be as important as tribal background in variability. Differences not only by country but among city, tribe, and countryside and between classes in degrees of women's independence have already been noted, and further research will surely show more variation. Women's independent attitudes are also expressed in folktales, popular poetry, and women's religious ceremonies.[14] Female religious leaders and ceremonies express women's initiative. It would be wrong, however, to ignore the widespread oppression and enforced subordination of women.

Changes in economy and society in the past two centuries, along with the Western cultural impact, brought about forces within Middle Eastern societies favoring changes in the conditions of women. At first this did not involve legal changes, but rather such things as women's education. Changes in Islamic law pertaining to women have met considerable resistance. Only the Catholics, of major religions, vie with the Muslims for tenacity regarding women's position and control of her body. Islamic conservatism as it affects family law comes partly from the prominence of laws on women in the Quran. Also, however, change concerning women was felt by Muslim men to be a final invasion in the last sphere they could control against aggressive infidels, once sovereignty and much of the economy had been taken over by the West. The need to guard women from the stares of the traditional Christian enemy has been documented since the French came to Egypt with Napoleon, and veiling increased as a reaction to their presence.[15]

In the past two centuries those Muslims who became Westernized tended to be those in the middle and upper classes who had profitable contacts with Westerners. For larger if less visible groups, Westernization was generally unpopular. The petty bourgeoisie and bazaar traders tended to support traditional Islamic ways. Modernizing liberals generally belonged to the higher social classes, whereas those who defended traditional ways appealed to the traditional small bourgeoisie.[16] The upper classes were in alliance with Westerners, but the small bourgeois classes competed with larger Western trade and tended to reject Western ways partly from a desire to defend their own position. Women were and are used in a game that is really more about politico-ideological questions, including relations with the West, than about women per se. The petty bourgeoisie in most Middle Eastern countries have stuck to essentially traditional positions on women. Some traditional bourgeois and lower-class women also prefer the old ways to being forced to obtain unpleasant and low-paying jobs.

Until recently battles for women's rights in the Middle East resulted in broadening those rights. The first names associated with those struggles were male, but from the beginning women too were involved. Public and independent activity for women's rights became widespread in the twentieth century (see Nelson in this volume).[17] These movements are only one aspect of complex changes that include those in marriage (see Baron), the family (Tucker), the economic role of women (Quataert), their social role (Abadan-Unat), their ability to be public figures (Danielson), and the like. Rural women have also undergone major transformations, often becoming more stratified and more secluded, but sometimes also more political (see Hegland and Friedl chapters). Modernization has had contradictory results in the Middle East and elsewhere, and whereas some women's positions have changed for the better, some poorer women have suffered from modernization's economic effects, becoming more, rather than less, restricted; having to work in unhealthful and poorly paid positions; and often removed from the community security of rural life. Veiling and seclusion spread in the countryside among the status conscious as they declined among Westernized city dwellers, and women's roles were sometimes limited by the economic effects of Western contacts. These contradictions have been reflected in conflicting women's attitudes on modernization versus tradition.

Although the success of reform was tied to economic and social changes, its immediate problems were often ideological; mainly, what attitude to take toward the holy law. A few, notably the reforming Turkish ruler Ataturk, took a secular position, legislating substantial legal equality for women on the basis of European law. Far more widespread have been modernist interpretations of the Quran and Islamic law. Attachment to these is strong not only because they are sacred texts, but also for identity vis-à-vis the West. There is an impetus to ground arguments in Islam, even for many who are privately secularists.

Varied modernist arguments have some widespread features. One is that the Quran has several meanings, with its literal one for its own time, and later interpretations to be made by modernists. Some stress the "spirit of the Quran," which is said to be egalitarian (largely true), and argue that several passages show that rights and egalitarianism were intended for women. There has been much reinterpretation of key verses. Modernists hold that the Quran opposes polygamy, because it says the conditions for it cannot be met. Various passages are seen to mean male-female equality, as the Quran sees them as equal believers and often explicitly addresses both men and women.

Reformists usually refer to the earliest sources—the Quran and selected Traditions about Muhammad—and reject most later interpretation. Subsequent Islamic law is rightly seen as more patriarchal than the Quran. If the Quran is reinterpreted, law can be reshaped. Such new interpretations could end polygamy and improve women's rights.

Reformist arguments arose partly because of a rapidly changing economy and society that was undergoing the influence of the capitalist and imperialist West. As in the West, the rise of capitalism and of paid jobs created new positions in the labor market for women, who had worked chiefly in the household economy. In the Middle East early demand was for nurses, midwives, doctors for women, and teachers. Demand soon spread to low-paid factory and white-collar work (see Quataert). As elsewhere, the development of capitalist relations had a contradictory impact on different women. Putting women in the paid labor force could change rules about sexual segregation, although not always. Some popular-class women became more restricted than before (see Friedl). Wealthier families, in contact with Westerners, saw advantages in women's education and participation in the wider world. Women's education was favored by reformists to improve child rearing and to prepare some women for jobs. The first arguments said that women's education would improve the rearing of sons, but women and men soon argued for women's rights. Although steps toward women's education, jobs, and freedom met resistance, until recently change was in the direction of greater equality.

Women's schools and women's or mixed universities were built in almost every Muslim country; new jobs were opened; and laws were reformed almost everywhere. The most radical reforms were those of Ataturk in Turkey. He took the unique path of adopting Western codes that outlawed polygamy and created substantial legal equality for women. Women got the vote in Turkey earlier than in France and Italy. Turkey was able to move radically owing to long contact with the West; to its experience of long, gradual reform; because Islamic leaders were discredited after World War I; and also due to Ataturk's huge popularity, as a leader who, uniquely in the Middle East, had taken territory back from Western powers (see Abadan-Unat). The next most thorough reforms, outside Eastern Europe, were in Tunisia and Marxist South Yemen. In Tunisia, Habib Bourguiba's Personal Status Code of 1956 outlawed polygamy on Muslim reformist grounds and created substantial legal equality for women, while retaining a few Islamic features and male privileges. In South Yemen polygamy is allowed in a very few circumstances, but family law is otherwise egalitarian, and as important, women's organizations were encouraged to carry out education and propaganda.[18] Elsewhere legal reform is more limited, but significant. In spite of Islamist agitation there has until now been little retreat in reform except in Iran and, on a few matters, in Pakistan.

The main thrust of legal reform where it is not egalitarian is to place restrictions on divorce, polygamy, and age of marriage, often by means of Islamic precedents and often by making men justify divorce or polygamy to the courts. This is in line with a modern trend to put personal and family matters increasingly under state control and reduce the power of Islamic courts. Reforms are, however, called Islamic, and Islamic courts generally keep some power. Equally important, women's roles in education, politics, and most parts of the work force have continued to grow.

Since World War II, a number of trends have undermined liberal reformism and encouraged Islamic revival. Among these are: (1) the growing cultural gap between the Westernized elite and the majority; (2) the growth in the power of the West and of Israel; (3) socioeconomic dislocations resulting from rapid urbanization, oil-backed modernization, and growing income distribution gaps; and (4) disillusionment with the failures of Westernized rulers and theories in the Middle East. The gap between the elite and the masses has created two cultures in the Middle East. Elite cultures tend to be Western-oriented, with young people getting a Western-style education and having little contact with the traditional bourgeoisie or the masses. Sometimes the two speak different languages, as in North Africa. The popular classes identify much more with Islam than the elite does. Among students and migrants from rural or small-town Islamically oriented backgrounds who migrate to overcrowded cities, alienation and Islamic revival are strong. It is also strong among some urban groups who stress identity and anti-imperialism.

Western consumer goods and experts are more evident than ever. Most important to Islamism, Western cultural influence is pervasive—in consumption, the media, and all cultural forms. Although many of these are items of choice, the backlash of rejection of Western cultural dominance is not surprising. Also, Israel is widely seen as a Western bastion of neocolonialism, bringing further reactions against pro-Western leaders and ways.

Socioeconomic dislocations, reinforced by fluctuations in oil income, include rapid urbanization, with the rich but rarely the poor getting richer; the problems of migrants; and the breakdown of accustomed family and rural ways. Islamism provides a social cement that appears familiar in the face of new problems.

Disillusionment with postcolonial governments that had nationalist and Westernizing, not Islamic, ideologies has focused on the Pahlavis in Iran, Anwar Sadat in Egypt, the National Liberation Front in Algeria, and Bourguiba in Tunisia. Nationalist and Western ideologies were discredited among many attracted instead by new visions of Islam, with major implications for women. Islam had the advantage of familiarity and of not having ruled recently, which could have discredited it.

Modern Islamic revivalism has roots in the Egyptian Muslim Brethren founded in 1928 and in the work of Abu al-A'la Maududi for Islamic government in Muslim India. Islamism grew after World War II, and especially after the 1967 Arab defeat by Israel and the 1973 oil price rise, with its resultant economic and social dislocations. In advocating state enforcement of Islamic law Islamism is innovating, as traditional Muslim states since the development of Islamic law have not applied it as states or in a centralized, codified way. What is demanded is novel, a modern centralized theocracy, using many modern economic and technical means, sometimes renamed.

Islamist movements are populist in appeal, stressing the rights of the oppressed and the socially egalitarian nature of the Quran. They are far from egalitarian about women, however, and take what they see as the Islamization of women's role as a touchstone of Islam. This is partly because matters affecting women make up much of the legislation in the Quran, and also because a return to Quranic injunctions on dress, polygamy, and so forth is a highly visible way to show one is a good Muslim. Dress is a symbol of Islamist beliefs, and the dress adopted by Islamist women is almost as important as a badge of ideology as it is a means to modesty or seclusion. In fact, Islamist women are not secluded from the world, but are found heavily among students, young working women, and the like, and are also engaged in political activity. The dress of most Islamist women also is not traditional, but newly fashioned.

There is separation of the sexes among Islamists. This is part of an ideology that can be stated, in terms familiar to the American past, as one of "separate but equal." Islamists often say that men and women are equal, but have different capacities according to their different roles. They stress the importance of homemaking and child rearing, and are divided on whether women can work provided it does not interfere with child rearing.[19] Practices in Islam that are unequal are justified as based on men's and women's different natures and needs. Polygamy is seen as better than the West's prostitution and mistresses, and early marriage as better than Western-style promiscuity. (Many Western ways shock strict Muslims just as many Muslim ways shock Westerners.) As in the former U.S. Supreme Court separate but equal doctrine for blacks, however, separation, in fact, means inferior rights—whether in education, work, or the family. The real strains of recent decades encourage nostalgia for an idealized past, including its sexual roles.

Though in most countries the leading Islamists tend to have partly Westernized educations, this was not true of Khomeini's clerical group in Iran, who took a hard line on reversing reforms concerning women. Other governments with Islamic claims, like those of Sudan, Saudi Arabia, Pakistan, and Libya, have been less absolute in their approach to women. And in Algeria, Pakistan, and Egypt threats of Islamist legislation have been a catalyst to mobilize women against this. Iran today is becoming less strict about women, but other countries are becoming more restrictive.

Islamist movements have had an appeal for some women, especially among students in some faculties and among the traditional classes. In Iran more women demonstrated for Khomeini than against him. Elsewhere Islamist women are also active and organized. Islamists encourage women's participation in many spheres. Many women have chosen to wear Islamic dress, and one of the reasons they give is that it keeps men from bothering them in street or social contacts. Islamic dress is again a badge—here saying that this is a serious respectable woman who should not be touched or annoyed.

Other aspects of Islamism that appeal to many women include their frequent women's circles and organizations, where women discuss important matters in all-woman surroundings that are not intimidating. They are also encouraged to undertake propaganda activities. Girls and women whose parents or husbands do not normally let them out allow them to go to mosque meetings, and some even reject proposed marriage partners on the grounds that they are not good Muslims.[20]

Many Islamist women experience protection and respect. The legal reforms in Muslim countries affected chiefly the elite, so that for many women Islamism may not seem a step backward and may even restore recently lost protections. Those who had experienced benefits, however, often suffer under Islamist rule or pressures. Hence there are radically different views about Islamism, often and understandably voiced and acted on with vehemence.

Feminists disagree about whether they should continue trying to interpret Islam in reformist ways or rather should stand foursquare for secularization, saying that Islam should be a matter for private belief and worship only. This is one of the key problems for Middle Eastern feminists today, extending from Pakistan's influential Women's Action Forum to the arguments among Middle Eastern women in many journals, including the *New Left Review*.[21] Those who stress the reinterpretation of Islam hope to meet some of the cultural needs of ordinary women, including Islamists, but their opponents say they are prolonging the repressive life and practices of political Islam.

A few modernists in a sense combine the two positions, presenting an Islam that does not require following Quranic practices regarding women. One Egyptian scholar claimed that the legal parts of the Quran were intended only for the lifetime of the Prophet. And a small group of Sudanese say that only the Meccan suras of the Quran (which have religious rather than legal content) and not the legalistic Medinan ones are valid after the Prophet.[22] Such views are rejected by most Muslims today, but they could fare better in the future.

Islamist trends will not necessarily continue strong far into the future. Khomeini was able to appeal to various kinds of discontented people, but once in power he aroused discontent. Even where Islamists do well in elections, many elements of a protest vote are involved. The Islamist phase of the 1970s and 1980s may continue, but it seems unlikely in radical form to outlive widespread experience with so-called Islamic governments. Only Iran in the Middle East to date has repealed major legislation favorable to women, although women's groups in Egypt and Pakistan have had to struggle to forestall major changes, which could still occur there or elsewhere.

Economic realities bring women in the Middle East more and more into the labor force and the public sphere, and this continues, despite Islamist trends. Yet women's legal struggles today are mostly defensive. Both the feminists who are convinced that Islamic theory must be reinterpreted in their cause and those who say that this approach will only play into the hands of anti-feminists are trying to find the most promising way to bring back a situation in which women's rights may be actively furthered. It may be that both the Islamic reformist and the secularist path can contribute to this, especially if they concentrate more on the needs and desires of popular-class women. And although the study of history is not simply a pragmatic exercise, understanding the reasons for the positions of women in the near and distant past can also help to formulate how those positions might be changed.

Notes

1. The wide literature on these subjects includes Guity Nashat, "Women in the Ancient Middle East," in *Restoring Women to History* (Bloomington, Ind.: Organization of American Historians, 1988); Gerda Lerner, *The Creation of Patriarchy* (New York: Oxford University Press, 1986); and Karen Sacks, "Engels Revisited: Women, the Organization of Production, and Private Property," in *Women, Culture, and Society*, ed. Michelle Zimbalist Rosaldo and Louise Lamphere (Stanford: Stanford University Press, 1974).

2. Nashat, "Women in the Ancient Middle East," discusses ancient Near Eastern practices and influences. See also Lois Beck and Nikki Keddie, eds., *Women in the Muslim World* (Cambridge: Harvard University Press, 1978), 21, 32 n. 12.

3. Germaine Tillion, *Le harem et les cousins* (Paris: Seuil, 1966).

4. Gertrude Stern, *Marriage in Early Islam* (London: Royal Asiatic Society, 1939).

5. On this issue, see especially Leila Ahmed, "Women and the Advent of Islam," *Signs* 11 (1986): 665–91.

6. Works that stress women's power but have been criticized by more recent scholarship are W. Robertson Smith, *Kinship and Marriage in Early Arabia* (Cambridge: Cambridge University Press, 1885), and W. Montgomery Watt, *Mohammad at Medina* (Oxford: Clarendon, 1956). More limited reports of women's independence are largely based on pre-Islamic poetry found in the collection *al-Aghani*.

7. Nabia Abbott, *Aishah, the Beloved of Mohammad* (Chicago: University of Chicago Press, 1942).

8. See Shahla Haeri, *Law of Desire: Temporary Marriage in Shi'i Iran* (Syracuse: Syracuse University Press, 1989).

9. Among many sources, see Judith E. Tucker, *Women in Nineteenth-Century Egypt* (Cambridge: Cambridge University Press, 1985); the articles of Martha Mundy on Yemen; and *Embassy to Constantinople: The Travels of Lady Mary Wortley Montagu*, ed. and comp. Christopher Pick, with an introduction by Dervla Murphy (London: Century, 1988). Elizabeth N. Macbean Ross, *A Lady Doctor in Bakhtiari Land* (London: Leonard Parsons, 1921), shows leading tribal women managing lands, flocks, and accounts during their husbands' long absences. Recent literature shows how often urban women went to court and defended their legal and property rights and stresses the independence of many tribal women, but indicates less independence for the rural and urban popular classes. These findings have not been coordinated, however, and some authors take a single group as typical of women as a whole.

10. B. F. Musallam, *Sex and Society in Islam* (Cambridge: Cambridge University Press, 1983).

11. See Afaf Lutfi al-Sayyid Marsot, "The Revolutionary Gentlewoman," in *Women in the Muslim World*, ed. Beck and Keddie; and Sarah Graham-Brown, *Images of Women: The Portrayal of Women in the Photography of the Middle East, 1860–1950* (New York: Columbia University Press, 1988).

12. See the citation in R. C. Jennings, "Women in Early Seventeenth Century Ottoman Judicial Records: The Sharia Court of Anatolian Kayseri," *Journal of the Economic and Social History of the Orient* 28 (1975): 53–114 (56–57 n. 5).

13. Unni Wikan, *Behind the Veil in Arabia* (Baltimore: Johns Hopkins University

Press, 1982); Leila Ahmed, "Feminism and Feminist Movements in the Middle East, A Preliminary Exploration: Turkey, Egypt, Algeria, People's Democratic Republic of Yemen," *Women's Studies International Forum* 5, no. 2 (1982): 153–68. The women I met in North Yemen, externally a country of heavy veiling and seclusion, included the following, all of whom were typical according to the Yemeni specialist who accompanied me: a woman who said that the best thing that could occur in a pregnancy was miscarriage, and that it was best to have no children; three women who said that the longer their migrant husbands stayed away the better; and a woman who had left her husband and returned to her family and was then bargaining conditions for her return. In addition, many of Yemen's divorced and married women are known to have had affairs. Such conditions are not limited to tribally based societies, as indicated as early as Lady Mary Montagu's reports on upper-class women's freedoms in Turkey in the early eighteenth-century; but specialists who compare southern Arabia and certain other tribal areas with other parts of the Middle East note "liberated" features that seem to owe nothing to Westernization.

14. Claudie Feyein, *A French Doctor in the Yemen*, trans. Douglas McKee (London: R. Hale, 1957), esp. p. 191; Lila Abu-Lughod, *Veiled Sentiments* (Berkeley: University of California Press, 1986); and the chapters by Vanessa Maher, Daisy Hilse Dwyer, and Erika Friedl in *Women in the Muslim World*, ed. Beck and Keddie.

15. Nada Tomiche, "The Situation of Egyptian Women in the First Half of the Nineteenth Century," in *Beginnings of Modernization in the Middle East*, ed. W. R. Polk and R. L. Chambers (Chicago: University of Chicago Press, 1968).

16. Juan R. Cole, "Feminism, Class, and Islam in Turn-of-the-Century Egypt," *International Journal of Middle East Studies* 19 (1981): 387–407.

17. On twentieth-century feminist movements, see Ahmed, "Feminism"; Eliz Sanasarian, *The Women's Rights Movement in Iran* (New York: Praeger, 1982); Azar Tabari and Nahid Yeganeh, eds., *In the Shadow of Islam: The Women's Movement in Iran* (London: Zed, 1982); and Margot Badran, "Dual Liberation: Feminism and Nationalism in Egypt, 1870s–1925," *Feminist Issues* 8, no. 1 (1988): 15–34.

18. Maxine Molyneux, "Legal Reform and Socialist Revolution in Democratic Yemen: Women and the Family," *International Journal of the Sociology of Law* 13 (1985): 147–72.

19. Many statements by Islamist leaders against women's working are cited in Yvonne Y. Haddad, "Islam, Women, and Revolution in Twentieth Century Arab Thought," *Muslim World* 74 (1984): 137–60. My interviews with Tunisian, Egyptian, and other Islamist women, however, show that many of them work or expect to work, even if they sometimes justify it as less than ideal. Haddad's article also includes the results of interviews in several countries. There has been a considerable literature on Islamist women, including such authors as Fadwa al-Guindi, Afaf Marsot, Nesta Ramazani, John Alden Williams, and others. See also Sherifa Danielle Zuhur, "Self-image of Egyptian Women in Oppositionist Islam" (Ph.D. diss., University of California, Los Angeles, 1990).

20. See Nikki R. Keddie, "The Islamist Movement in Tunisia," *Maghreb Review* 11, no. 1 (1986): 26–39.

21. Mai Ghoussoub, "Feminism—or the Eternal Masculine—in the Arab World," *New Left Review* 161 (1987): 3–18; Reza Hammami and Martina Rieker,

"Feminist Orientalism and Orientalist Marxism," *New Left Review* 170 (1988): 93–106; Mai Ghoussoub, "A Reply to Hammami and Rieker," *New Left Review* 170 (1988): 108–9.

22. See especially Mahmoud Mohamed Taha, *The Second Message of Islam*, translated with an introduction by Abdullahi Ahmed An-Na'im (Syracuse: Syracuse University Press, 1987), and Abdullahi Ahmed An-Na'im, *Toward an Islamic Reformation* (Syracuse: Syracuse University Press, 1990).

2

Islam and Patriarchy:

A Comparative Perspective

DENIZ KANDIYOTI

In contrast to the growing body of historical scholarship on gender relations in the West, the question of women in Muslim societies has remained closely tied to a predominantly ahistorical consideration of the main tenets of Islamic religion and their implications for women. This has been attributed by some to the more general shortcomings of Middle Eastern historiography, namely the lingering influence of orientalism and an idealist bias that presents historical facts as flowing directly from ideology.[1] In the case of scholarship on women, these tendencies have been compounded by a high degree of confusion between polemical and analytical goals. There is a continuing output of exegetical writing by Muslim scholars, many of whom identify themselves as feminists.[2] This writing typically tries to establish Islam's compatibility with the emancipation of women. The favored sources of such works continue to be the Quran, the hadith, and the lives of prominent women in early Islam. There is a clear attempt to resuscitate early Islamic history and the holy text in order to formulate an indigenous feminist project, or at the very least to encourage more progressive reading of the texts that are regularly invoked by traditionalists to justify the status quo. That feminists and traditionalists are equally concerned with appropriating the "true" message of Islam indicates that all parties believe it to be the only legitimate ideological terrain on which issues pertaining to women can be debated. I will not discuss the adequacy or merits of this position, but merely point out that it has been one of the tendencies giving a longer lease of life to ahistorical approaches to the question of women in Muslim societies.[3]

There is, on the other hand, a vigorous body of scholarship that locates women as historical and political actors firmly in the context of temporal processes of socioeconomic transformation.[4] Most work in this genre does not necessarily privilege Islam as an analytic category, but inserts gender into broader discourses about social transformation or the various theoretical paradigms of different social science disciplines. At one extreme of this spectrum, one finds studies that are barely distinguishable from work on women and development in any other part of the Third World. The specificity of Muslim women's subordination, if any, and the possible role of Islamic ideology and practice in reproducing it are thus lost from view. This leads to a paradoxical situation whereby Islam sometimes appears to be all there is to know, and at other times to be of little consequence in understanding the condition of women, or more broadly, gender relations in Muslim societies.

I argue in this chapter that this is in part because we have not found adequate ways of talking about the articulation between Islam and different systems of male dominance,[5] which are grounded in distinct material arrangements between the genders but are rather imprecisely labeled with the blanket term *patriarchy*. Indeed, the literature confirms that different systems of male dominance, and their internal variations according to class and ethnicity, exercise an influence that inflects and modifies the actual practice of Islam as well as the ideological constructions of what may be regarded as properly Islamic. Religious practice is necessarily influenced by the history of productive and reproductive relations between the genders, as reflected in the workings of different indigenous kinship systems. It may be, and has been argued, that the spread of Islam has expedited the demise of varied local systems in favor of a more uniformly patriarchal mode, with an emphasis on patrilineality and patrilocality, and with characteristic modes of control of female sexuality and spatial mobility.[6] This does not, however, justify the use of imprecise expressions such as "Muslim patriarchy"[7] to denote the sexual asymmetries encountered in contexts as varied as those of a Bedouin tribe, a Hausa village, or an upper-class harem in Cairo or Istanbul. We therefore need to examine critically the concept of patriarchy itself, before moving on to a more detailed consideration of its usefulness for an understanding of gender relations in Muslim societies.

PATRIARCHY: A PROBLEMATIC CONCEPT

Although a brief incursion into feminist theory cannot do justice to the complex debates generated around the term *patriarchy*,[8] I will attempt a sketchy outline of some contemporary developments in its usage.

Radical feminists were the first to initiate a fairly liberal usage of the term to apply to almost any form or instance of male dominance. Since patriarchy defined in those terms was an all-pervasive, virtually timeless phenomenon, its manifestations could be sought anywhere, although the symbolic and psychic spheres were singled out as privileged areas of investigation. In spite of numerous modifications and reworkings within radical feminism, patriarchy was by and large allocated to the ideological sphere, with a material basis in the division of labor between the sexes (and in particular the facts of reproductive biology).[9]

In the case of Marxist or socialist feminism, the concept has a somewhat different history. It emerged as a residual category, because forms of exploitation and oppression based on gender proved singularly recalcitrant to reduction to other forms (such as those based on race and class). In those terms, what could not be explained through the workings of capital could be put down to the logic of a related but distinct system with its own laws of motion, namely that of patriarchy. However, the degree of analytic independence assigned to the category of patriarchy, as distinct from capitalism or the class system, could be quite variable, as indeed was the degree of commitment to a systematic consideration of the relations between the two.[10] Nonetheless, this position had advantages in that patriarchy was acknowledged to have a material basis in the social relations between the sexes, which are in turn subject to historical transformations. The emphasis on the reciprocal relations between types and systems of production, the sexual division of labor, and age and gender hierarchies meant that the psychodynamics and cultural constructions of gender could be historicized, and at least in principle, more adequately theorized. In practice, however, most of the debate remained centered on the effects of industrial and postindustrial capitalism on gender relations, with relatively fewer attempts to establish linkages within a broader comparative perspective.

The ways in which such linkages were theorized have in addition been quite diverse. Some concentrated on establishing empirical associations between types of production, kinship systems, and indicators of women's status. Ester Boserup, for instance, made a distinction between male and female farming systems, relating them to population density, technology, and type of cultivation.[11] Female farming systems, most prevalent in sub-Saharan Africa, are characterized by abundant land, low population density, shifting cultivation, and the use of the hoe as a farming implement. Apart from tasks like clearing the land for cultivation, food production is primarily the responsibility of women, who, according to Boserup, have a high degree of mobility and the ability to market their surplus to support themselves and their children. Male farming systems, more characteristic of Asia, are prevalent under conditions of higher population density, the necessity to increase productivity, and the use by men of draught animals and the plow. Plow agriculture is prevalent in areas of private ownership where a landless class whose labor may be hired exists. Ideally, the women of landed households are released from agricultural work in the fields and confined to domesticity, often actually secluded as a symbol of prestige and family honor (as in Muslim veiling or the purdah system). They increasingly come to depend on men for both economic support and symbolic shelter.

Germaine Tillion, in her analysis of codes of honor and female modesty in the Mediterranean, argues that these phenomena may in fact be of more recent origin than suspected and may have evolved as a reaction to the threat posed to endogamous tribal societies, which form the backbone of the post-neolithic ancient world, by outside forces, particularly by an expanding urban civilization.[12] She sees the customs and practices related to the seclusion of women as results of the incomplete evolution and degeneration of tribal society and of the structures of defense it erected to maintain its integrity. Islamic rules are incidental to this process, as evidenced by the very selectivity with which they are applied, ignored, or circumvented. For instance, women are either altogether deprived of their inheritance rights when these threaten tribal property and solidarity, or when they are accorded such rights, they are tightly monitored through strict controls over marriage alliances and their spatial mobility. Thus the apparent irony behind the fact that veiled urban women have property rights whereas their unveiled rural sisters, whose contribution to subsistence is typically higher, are deprived of them, disappears. Although Tillion is quite clear about the material forces underpinning tribal endogamy, the process of erosion of such structures through contact with city values and exposure to other civilizational influences (operating through changes in mentality and outlook) remains more nebulous.

Jack Goody followed up Boserup's typology by relating women's contribution to production with kinship systems and modes of inheritance.[13] He notes the empirical association between plow agriculture, male farming, diverging devolution (that is, bilateral inheritance), and monogamy, all characteristic of Eurasia, which stand in contrast to Africa, where female predominance in hoe cultivation is accompanied by homogenous inheritance (matrilineal or patrilineal), polygyny, and bridewealth. This approach has been criticized for trying to explain differences in kinship patterns between very broadly defined regions through ahistorical reference to technological and ecological variations and for trying to understand kinship and systems of production solely in terms of property relations.[14]

At a more general level, approaches to women's subordination stressing their modes of contribution to subsistence were criticized for their "productivist" bias. It was argued that ultimately the position of women could not be explained in terms of participation in production, which could be extremely variable, but could be better understood with reference to their roles in reproduction.[15] Some even turned the productivist argument on its head by suggesting not only that women's status was not predicated on their roles in production but also that productive roles may in fact themselves be defined and limited by the kinds of reproductive tasks assigned to women at different junctures of capital accumulation.[16] Thus Lourdes Beneria and Gita Sen argued in their critique of Boserup that the crucial distinguishing features of African and Asian farming do not reside in the tools used—the hoe or the plow—but in the forms of appropriation of land, surplus, and women's reproductive capacities.[17] They proposed an analysis based on the dual concepts of accumulation and reproduction, it being understood that there are systematic connections between different phases of accumulation, class formation, and gender relations.[18]

Where did these developments leave the concept of patriarchy? To the extent that efforts were made to relate it to processes of accumulation, it became increasingly insubstantial and was often reduced to an epiphenomenon of the workings of capital. The allocation of productive and reproductive tasks between the sexes is frequently presented as functional to the maintenance of a cheap labor force, with gender ideologies merely acting to justify the existing division of labor. In spite of strenuous attempts at disentangling the workings of patriarchy from those of capitalism and the wish to grant the former some analytic autonomy,[19] a great deal was said about the laws of motion of capitalism whereas those of patriarchy have at best remained nebulous and vague. This is partly due to the often implicit assumption that there is such a thing as a unitary and universal system that we may call patriarchy, and that the differences in the character of women's subordination concretely encountered are merely the outcome of different expressions or stages of the same system.[20] This has resulted in an overly abstract and monolithic conception of male dominance, which obfuscates rather than reveals the intimate inner workings of different gender arrangements.

I have proposed elsewhere that a useful point of entry for the identification of different systems of male dominance may be found through analyses of women's strategies in dealing with them.[21] I have argued that women strategize within a set of concrete constraints that reveal and define the blueprint of what I term the *patriarchal bargain*[22] of any given society, which may exhibit variations according to class, caste, and ethnicity. These patriarchal bargains exert a powerful influence on the shaping of women's gendered subjectivity and determine the nature of gender ideology in different contexts. They also influence both the potential for and the actual forms of women's active or passive resistance. Most important, patriarchal bargains are not timeless or immutable entities, but are susceptible to historical transformations that open up new areas of struggle or renegotiation of the relations between genders.

By way of illustration, I will contrast two systems of male dominance, rendered ideal-typical for the purposes of discussing their implications for women. I use these ideal types as heuristic devices that necessarily simplify more complex reality, but can be fleshed out and expanded with comparative, empirical content. These two types are based on examples from sub-Saharan Africa and from the Middle East and southern and eastern Asia. My aim is to highlight a continuum ranging from less corporate forms of householding, involving the relative autonomy of mother-child units evidenced in sub-Saharan polygyny, to the more corporate male-headed entities prevalent in the regions identified by James Caldwell as the "patriarchal belt."[23] Against this background, I will explore the extent to which Islam cut across different systems of male dominance and the possibility that gender relations in the Middle East are influenced by a particular conjunction between Islam and the system I identify as "classic patriarchy." Finally, I will speculate on the impact of contemporary social transformations on patriarchal bargains and gender ideologies.

AUTONOMY AND PROTEST: SOME EXAMPLES FROM SUB-SAHARAN AFRICA

As I reviewed the literature on women in agricultural development projects in sub-Saharan Africa, my own background, as a woman born and raised in Turkey, left me totally unprepared for what I found.[24] This literature was rife with instances of women's resistance to attempts to lower the value of their labor, and more significant, women's refusal to allow the total appropriation of their production by their husbands.

Whenever new agricultural schemes provided men with inputs and credit, and the assumption was made that as heads of household they would have access to their wives' unremunerated labor, problems seemed to develop. In the Mwea irrigated rice settlement in Kenya, where women were deprived of access to their own plots, their lack of alternatives and their total lack of control over men's earnings made life so intolerable to them that wives commonly deserted their husbands.[25] In Gambia, in yet another rice-growing scheme, the irrigated land and the credit were made available to men, even though it was the women who traditionally grew rice in tidal swamps and there was a long-standing practice of men and women cultivating their own crops and controlling the produce. Women's customary duties with respect to labor allocation to common and individual plots protected them from demands by their husbands that they provide free labor on men's irrigated rice fields. Men had to pay their wives wages or lend them an irrigated plot to have access to their labor. In the rainy season, when women had the alternative of growing their own swamp rice, they created a labor bottleneck for men, who simply had to wait for the days on which women did not go to their own fields.[26] Pepe Roberts also illustrates the strategies used by women to maximize their autonomy in the African context.[27] Yoruba women in Nigeria negotiate the terms of their farm-labor services to their husbands while they aim to devote more time and energy to the trading activities that will enable them to support themselves. Hausa women in Niger, whose observance of Islamic seclusion reduces the demands husbands can make on their services (an important point to which we shall return), allocate their labor to trade, mainly the sale of ready-cooked foodstuffs.

In short, the insecurities of African polygyny for women are matched by areas of relative autonomy that they clearly strive to maximize. Men's responsibility for their wives' support, although normative in some instances, is in actual fact relatively low. Typically, it is the woman who is primarily responsible for her own and her children's upkeep, including meeting the costs of their education, with varying degrees of assistance from her husband. Women have little to gain and a lot to lose by becoming totally dependent on husbands, and quite rightly resist projects that tilt the delicate balance they strive to maintain.

Documentation of a genuine trade off between women's autonomy and men's responsibility for their wives can be found in some historical examples. Kristin Mann suggests that despite the wifely dependence entailed by Christian marriage, Yoruba women in Lagos accepted it with enthusiasm because of the greater protection they thought they would receive.[28] Conversely, men in contemporary Zambia resist the more modern ordinance marriage, as opposed to customary marriage, because it burdens them with greater obligations for their wives and children.[29] A form of conjugal union in which the partners may openly negotiate the exchange of sexual and labor services seems to lay the groundwork for more explicit forms of bargaining. Commenting on Ashanti marriage, Katherine Abu singles out as its most striking feature "the separateness of spouses' resources and activities and the overtness of the bargaining element in the relationship."[30] Polygyny, and in this case, the continuing obligations of both men and women to their own kin, does not foster a notion of the family or household as a corporate entity.

Clearly, there are important variations in African kinship systems with respect to forms of marriage, residence, descent, and inheritance rules, which are grounded in complex historical processes, including different modes of incorporation of African societies into the world economy.[31] Nonetheless, it is within a broadly defined Afro-Caribbean pattern that we find some of the clearest instances of noncorporateness of the conjugal family both in ideology and in practice, which informs marital and marketplace strategies for women.

It is therefore particularly interesting to see how Islam, which privileges patrilineal bonds and clearly enjoins men to take full responsibility for the support of their wives, acts on gender relations in different African contexts. Enid Schildkrout's study of secluded Hausa women in Kano, Nigeria, suggests that a typically West African pattern of high economic activity and relative autonomy of women persists within a family structure defined by Islamic values concerning the sexual division of labor.[32] She relates how women are able to subvert the idealized structure of the domestic economy through the control they exercise over the labor of their children, which makes it possible for them to trade in cooked foods without having direct contact with the marketplace. Their seclusion obviously restricts their mobility so that they are dependent on manipulating the limited resources their husbands provide for consumption and diverting them to their own productive ends. However, this also puts limits on the services husbands may expect from their wives, as they cannot rely on them as a source of support and are thus at least in theory expected to be the providers. Schildkrout suggests that the widespread adoption of purdah in Kano is possible precisely because women have the ability to play active economic roles while participating in the myth of their total dependence on men. To the extent that this ability is predicated on their control over children's labor, however, it will be increasingly jeopardized as the latter are absorbed by the modern educational system and become unavailable as domestic labor. Ultimately, the structure of all but the wealthiest families in Islamic West Africa may be challenged by such contemporary changes.

In Mette Bovin's work on the Manga women in Bornu, Niger, she detects signs of actual female resistance to Muslim institutions in spite of nine hundred years of "Islamization."[33] Islam in Bornu grafted itself on an older matrilineal system with different pre-Islamic marriage rules, which were superseded but not totally eradicated by a Muslim patrilineal system. Bovin suggests that it is women who maintain and transmit this pre-Islamic cultural heritage, through their struggle to enforce the matrilineal principle, the actual result being a kind of bilateral system. Pre-Islamic influences are also apparent in traces of totemism in women's rituals, the existence of independent statuses for women, and women's vocabulary, which unlike men's does not include Arabic words. It is as though Islamic rules were being negotiated by participants with diverging gender interests, the women stubbornly clinging to aspects of the pre-Islamic system that may have been more empowering.

One does not have to accept this particular interpretation of pre-Islamic survivals to concede a more general and rather obvious point. There may or may not be a good fit between Islamic injunctions concerning kinship and marriage and local pre-Islamic customs and practices. In the latter case, not only local kinship patterns and ideologies are modified but often the practice and interpretation of Islam itself. Presenting women as active participants in this process of reinterpretation and cultural negotiation exercises a corrective influence on depictions of Muslim women as passive victims of patriarchal domination. It is no accident, moreover, that it is in sub-Saharan Africa that we encounter the clearest instances of women's resistance, since they frequently involve the safeguarding of existing spheres of autonomy.

SUBSERVIENCE AND MANIPULATION: WOMEN UNDER CLASSIC PATRIARCHY

The foregoing examples of women's resistance stand in stark contrast to women's accommodations to the system I call classic patriarchy. The clearest instances of classic patriarchy are found in the geographical area that includes North Africa, the Muslim Middle East (including Turkey, Pakistan, and Iran), and southern and eastern Asia (specifically India and China).[34]

The key to the reproduction of classic patriarchy lies in the operations of the patrilocally extended household, which is also commonly associated with the reproduction of the peasantry in agrarian societies.[35] Even though demographic and other constraints may have curtailed the actual predominance of three-generational patrilocal households, there is little doubt that they represented a powerful cultural ideal. It is plausible that the emergence of the patriarchal extended family, which gives the senior man authority over everyone else, including younger men, is bound up in the incorporation and control of the family by the state,[36] and in the transition from kin-based to tributary modes of surplus control.[37] The implications of the patrilineal-patrilocal complex for women are not only remarkably uniform but also entail forms of control and subordination that cut across cultural and religious boundaries, such as those of Hinduism, Confucianism, and Islam.

Under classic patriarchy, girls are given away in marriage at a very young age into households headed by their husband's father. There they are subordinate not only to all the men but also to the more senior women, especially their mothers-in-law. The extent to which this represents a total break with their own kin group, and consequent isolation and hardship, varies in relation to the degree of endogamy in marriage practices. Michael Meeker in his comparison between the rural Arabs of the Levant and the Black Sea Turks draws our attention to the different structuring of conceptions of honor among them and its possible relation to the degree of endogamy they favor in marriage.[38] Among the Turks, he finds much lower rates of endogamy, and that the husband is directly and principally responsible for a woman's honor. Among the rural Arabs of the Levant, there is much greater mutuality among affines, and a woman's natal family retains both an interest and an active involvement in protecting a married daughter's honor. As a result, a Turkish woman's traditional position may more closely resemble the status of the "stranger-bride" of pre-revolutionary China than that of an Arab woman, whose position in the patriarchal household may be somewhat attenuated by endogamy and recourse to her natal kin.

Lila Abu-Lughod, in her study of the Awlad 'Ali, Bedouins of the Western Desert in Egypt, draws attention to the tension that marriage creates in an ideological system in which agnation is given clear priority as a basis for affiliation, and suggests that one resolution of this tension may be sought in a preference for patrilateral parallel-cousin marriages.[39] She comments on the preferential treatment that wives from the same patrikin as their husbands receive and on their greater sense of security. Unni Wikan in her study of Oman indicates quite perceptively that although in principle men subscribe to the ideal of cousin marriage and agnatic loyalties, in practice they strive to stay clear of such unions.[40] Marrying a stranger enhances the control of the husband by reducing accountability to related in-laws and ensures the wife's exclusive dependence on him.

Under classic patriarchy women frequently have no claim on their father's patrimony, whether the prevalent marriage payment is brideprice or dowry. Their dowries do not qualify as a form of premortem inheritance since they are transferred directly to the bridegroom's kin and do not take the form of productive property, such as land.[41] In the case of the *mahr* (brideprice), the proportion retained by the bride's father and that returned to her in the form of valuables can be extremely variable, despite explicit provision that part of the mahr belongs to her. Likewise, women's access to and control over property can vary a great deal. There is substantial historical evidence that women in the Middle East did own and control property, especially if they were urban and middle or upper class.[42] There is equally widespread evidence that the patrilineage expropriates them if productive property takes the form of land or flocks and if their inheritance rights threaten the economic integrity of the family or tribal unit. Thus whether they are members of Muslim, Hindu, or Confucian communities, young brides often enter their husband's household as effectively dispossessed individuals, who can establish their place in the patriliny only by producing male offspring.

A woman's life cycle in the patrilocally extended family is such that the deprivation and hardship she may experience as a young bride are eventually superseded by the control and authority she will have over her own daughters-in-law. The powerful postmenopausal matriarch thus is the other side of the coin of this form of patriarchy. The cyclical nature of women's power and their anticipation of inheriting the authority of senior women encourages a thorough internalization of this form of patriarchy by the women themselves. Subordination to men is offset by the control older women have over younger women. Women have access to the only type of labor power they can control, and to old-age security, however, through their married sons. Since sons are a woman's most critical resource, ensuring their lifelong loyalty is an enduring preoccupation. Older women have a vested interest in the suppression of romantic love between youngsters to keep the conjugal bond secondary and to claim their sons' primary allegiance. Young women have an interest in circumventing and possibly evading their mother-in-law's control. There are culturally specific examples of how this struggle works to the detriment of the heterosexual bond,[43] but there are striking similarities in the overall pattern. In the case of Muslim societies, Fatima Mernissi emphasizes the role of Islamic ideology, which posits the primacy of the male believer's relationship with God, treating all other involvements, especially passionate and exclusive relationships with women, as diversionary if not positively subversive.[44] Although this ideology may indeed constitute a local contributory factor, there is little doubt that what is being played out in the mother-son-bride triangle forms a central structural component of a much broader patriarchal scenario.

The class or caste impact on classic patriarchy produces additional complexities. Among the wealthier strata, the withdrawal of women from nondomestic work is frequently a mark of status institutionalized in such seclusion and exclusion practices as the purdah system and veiling. The women who are thus restricted nonetheless share in the privileges of their class through greater access to and control over property, more leisure, and eventually better access to education. For the women of poorer strata, who can ill afford to observe this cultural ideal, the ideology of seclusion and dependence on men still exercises a powerful influence that severely restricts the range of options available to them. Judith Tucker's data on nineteenth-century Egypt suggest that the strongly interventionist state policies of the Muhammad 'Ali period resulted in women's recruitment into public works, state-run industries, and expanding sectors of health and education.[45] Yet at the same time she draws our attention to how women's independent access to income could result in losses on the family front, as when women in certain kinds of employment were legally deprived of the right of guardianship of their children. Ultimately, women's access to resources is mediated through the family. In situations where the observance of restrictive practices is a crucial element in the reproduction of family status, women will resist breaking the rules, even if observing them produces economic hardship. I would therefore agree with Maria Mies's analysis of the lacemakers of Narsapur, India, about whom she observes that the ideology of their domesticity keeps them working at home, for extremely low wages, even though they are producing for the world market.[46] In this instance, ideology acts as a material force that results in a lucrative export commodity produced by conveniently cheap labor.

Women in areas of classic patriarchy thus are often unable to resist unfavorable labor relations in both the household and the market, and frequently adhere as far and as long as they possibly can to rules that result in the devaluation of their labor. The cyclical fluctuations of their power position, combined with status considerations, result in their active collusion in the reproduction of their own subordination. They frequently adopt interpersonal strategies that maximize their security through manipulation of the affections of their sons and husband. As Margery Wolf's insightful discussion of the Chinese uterine family suggests, this strategy can even result in the aging male patriarch losing power to his wife.[47] Even though these individual power tactics do little to alter the structurally unfavorable terms of the overall patriarchal script, women become experts at maximizing their own life chances.

This creates the paradoxical situation noted by Kay Anne Johnson, who comments on female conservatism in China: "Ironically, women through their actions to resist passivity and total male control, became participants with vested interests in the system that oppressed them."[48] One also gains important insights into women's investment in existing gender arrangements through ethnographic studies of the Middle East. Some suggest that far from producing subjective feelings of oppression, this willing participation enhances women's sense of control and self-worth. Wikan, for instance, depicts Omani women in the following terms: "Indeed many of the constraints and limitations imposed on women, such as the *burqa* [veil], restrictions of movement and sexual segregation, are seen by women as aspects of that very concern and respect on the part of the men which provide the basis for their own feeling of assurance and value. Rather than reflecting subjugation, these constraints and limitations are perceived by women as a source of pride and a confirmation of esteem."[49]

The survival of the moral order of classic patriarchy, as well as the positioning of male versus female and young versus old, however, is grounded in specific material conditions. Changes in these conditions can seriously undermine the normative order. As expressed succinctly by Mead Cain, S. R. Khanan, and S. Nahar, it is both the key and the irony of this system that "male authority has a material base, while male responsibility is normatively controlled."[50] Their study of a village in Bangladesh offers a striking example of the strains placed by poverty on bonds of obligation between kin and, more specifically, on men's fulfillment of their normative obligations toward women. Martin Greeley also documents the growing dependence of landless households in Bangladesh on women's wage labor, including that of married women, and discusses the ways in which the stability of the patriarchal family is thereby undermined.[51]

In a purely analogical sense, patriarchal bargains, like scientific paradigms,[52] can be shown to have a normal and a crisis phase, which challenges our very interpretation of what is going on in the world. Thus during what we might call the normal phase of classic patriarchy, there were always large numbers of women who were in fact exposed to economic hardship and insecurity. They were infertile and had to be divorced, or orphaned and without recourse to their natal family, or unprotected because they had no surviving sons or, even worse, had ungrateful sons. They were merely considered "unlucky," however, anomalies and accidental casualties of a system that otherwise made sense. It is at the point of breakdown that every system reveals its internal contradictions and often forces participants in the system to take up new and seemingly contradictory ideological positions.

THE DEMISE OF PATRIARCHAL BARGAINS: RETREAT
INTO CONSERVATISM OR RADICAL PROTEST?

The material bases of classic patriarchy crumble under the impact of new market forces, capital penetration in rural areas,[53] and processes of economic marginalization and immiseration. Although there is no single path leading to the breakdown of this system, its consequences are fairly uniform. The domination of younger men by older men and the shelter of women in the domestic sphere were the hallmarks of a system in which men controlled some form of viable joint patrimony in land, animals, or commercial capital. Among the propertyless and the dispossessed, the necessity of every household member's contribution to survival turns men's economic protection of women—which is central to Muslim men's claims to primacy in the conjugal union—into a myth.

The breakdown of classic patriarchy results in the earlier emancipation from their fathers of younger men and their earlier separation from the paternal household. Whereas this process implies that women escape the control of mothers-in-law and head their own households at a much younger age, it also means that they themselves can no longer look forward to a future surrounded by subservient daughters-in-law. For the generation of women caught in between, this transformation may represent genuine personal tragedy, since they have paid the heavy price of an earlier patriarchal bargain, but are not able to cash in on its promised benefits. Wolf's statistics on suicide among women in China suggest a clear change in the trend since the 1930s, with a sharp increase in the suicide rates of women over forty-five, whereas previously the rates were highest among young women, especially new brides.[54] She relates this change explicitly to the emancipation of sons and their new chance to escape familial control in their choice of spouse, which robs the older woman of her power and respectability as mother-in-law.

In the case of Muslim societies, Mernissi comments on the psychologically distortive effects of the discordance between deeply ingrained images and expectations of male-female roles and the changing realities of everyday life. "The wider the gap between reality and fantasy (or aspiration), the greater the suffering and the more serious the conflict and tension within us. The psychological cost is just barely tolerable. The fact that we cling to images of virility (economic power) and femininity (consumption of the husband's fortune) that have nothing whatever to do with real life contributes to making male-female dynamics one of the most painful sources of tension and conflict."[55] This tension is documented through an analysis of "sexual anomie" in contemporary Morocco, in which she stresses primarily men's frustration and humiliation at being unable to fulfill their traditional role and the threat posed by women's greater spatial mobility and access to paid employment.

The breakdown of classic patriarchy may be equally threatening to women, however, who often resist the process of change because they see the old normative order slipping away from them without any empowering alternatives. In a broader discussion of women's interests, Maxine Molyneux suggests that this may not be put down merely to "false consciousness" but to the possibility that changes realized in a piecemeal fashion "could threaten the short-term practical interests of some women, or entail a cost in the loss of forms of protection that are not then compensated for in some way."[56]

Thus when classic patriarchy enters a crisis, many women may continue to pressure men to live up to their obligations and will not, except under the most extreme circumstances, compromise the basis for their claims by stepping out of line and losing their respectability. Their passive resistance takes the form of claiming their half of this particular patriarchal bargain—protection in exchange for submissiveness and propriety, and a confirmation that male honor is indeed dependent on their responsible conduct.

The response of some women who have to work for wages in this context may be an intensification of traditional modesty markers, such as veiling. Often, through no choice of their own, they are working outside the home and are thus "exposed"; they must now use every symbolic means at their disposal to signify that they continue to be worthy of protection. It is significant that Khomeini's exhortations to keep women at home found enthusiastic support among many Iranian women, despite the obvious elements of repression. The implicit promise of increased male responsibility restores the integrity of their original patriarchal bargain in an environment where the range of options available to women is extremely restricted. Younger women adopt the veil, Farah Azari suggests, because "the restriction imposed on them by an Islamic order was therefore a small price that had to be paid in exchange for the security, stability and presumed respect this order promised them."[57] That this promise has proven to be illusory is strongly suggested by Haleh Afshar's review of social policies under the Islamic Republic.[58] She nonetheless acknowledges a large support base among the poor and working classes. Fadwa El Guindi's analysis of young women taking up the veil in Egypt also speaks of women's concern with retaining respectability and a measure of "untouchability" now that they are present in public spaces in growing numbers.[59]

It would be simpleminded to single out Islam as unique in fulfilling this soothing and restorative function. There is evidence from non-Muslim societies that retreat into social and religious conservatism is one of the possible responses to changes that seem to threaten the moral order, especially when they present challenges to existing gender arrangements. At the ideological level, broken bargains seem to instigate a search for culprits, a hankering for the certainties of a more traditional order, or a more diffuse feeling that change might have gone either too far or badly wrong. The familism of the New Right and the anti-feminist movement in the West thus have been interpreted by some as an attempt to reinstate an older patriarchal bargain, with feminists providing a convenient scapegoat on whom to blame the loss of family values, intimacy, and community.[60] What makes conservative Islamic discourse even more compelling is that it often associates moral decay with contamination by foreign, generally Western values, and assigns women a privileged role in restoring the lost authenticity of the community of believers. This anti-imperialist, populist discourse constructs women upholding Muslim values as radical militants rather than mere traditionalists, adding a significant new dimension to female reaction in the Muslim world. What unites female conservatism in the West with Muslim women's militancy in the Middle East, however, is the common perception that the furtherance of women's gender interests lie in the restoration of an original patriarchal bargain that afforded them protection and dignity.

I have argued here that one of the major weaknesses in our theorizing about women in the Middle East stems from a conflation of Islam, as ideology and practice, with patriarchy. This conflation is encouraged by monolithic and essentialist conceptions of both Islam and patriarchy. In search of an alternative, I presented case materials illustrating women's strategies and coping mechanisms as a means of capturing the nature of patriarchal systems in their cultural, class specific, and temporal concreteness. I have tried to show how two ideal-typical systems of male dominance could provide different base lines from which women negotiate and strategize, and how each affects the potentialities of their resistance and struggles.

Islam cuts across these ideal types and extends well beyond them (as in the case of Southeast Asian societies). Even though Islam brings its own prescriptions to bear on gender relations in each context, it nonetheless achieves different accommodations with the diverse cultural complexes it encounters. That the core areas of Islamic civilization have historically coincided with areas of classic patriarchy has tended to obscure these variations, and encouraged a confusion between the assumed workings of Islam and those of a specific type of patriarchy.

The different political projects of modern nation-states, the specificities of their nationalist histories, and the positioning of Islam vis-à-vis diverse nationalisms also account for deep and significant variations in policies and legislation affecting women.[61] These variations find concrete expression in the degree of access that women have to education, paid employment, social benefits, and political participation.

There is, nonetheless, a sense in which Islam in the contemporary world may be promoting a homogenization of ideology and practice concerning women, the family, and gender relations. This political Islam speaks to the gap created by the breakdown of patriarchal bargains and to the turmoil and confusion created by rapid and often corrosive processes of social transformation. The extensive "ideologization" of the sphere of family and gender relations is itself, however, a historical phenomenon of fairly recent origin that cannot be imputed to Islam itself.

It should be clear that these different levels at which I have invoked Islam—kinship systems, the state, and political ideologies—cannot be conflated and must be kept analytically distinct. We should now be moving toward finely grained historical analyses of how they intersect, interact, and change.

Notes

1. Nikki R. Keddie, "Problems in the Study of Middle Eastern Women," *International Journal of Middle East Studies* 10 (1979): 225–40; Judith E. Tucker, "Problems in the Historiography of Women in the Middle East: The Case of Nineteenth-Century Egypt," *International Journal of Middle East Studies* 15 (1983): 321–36.

2. Nawal al-Saadawi, "Women and Islam," in *Women and Islam,* ed. Azizah

al-Hibri (Oxford: Pergamon, 1982), 193–206; Azizah al-Hibri, "A Study of Islamic Herstory," in *Women and Islam*, 207–20; Fatima Mernissi, *Le harem politique* (Paris: Albin Michel, 1987).

3. For critical views on this question, see Azar Tabari, "The Women's Movement in Iran: A Hopeful Prognosis," *Feminist Studies* 12 (1986): 343–60; Mai Ghoussoub, "Feminism—or the Eternal Masculine—in the Arab World," *New Left Review* 161 (1987): 3–18.

4. Lois Beck and Nikki Keddie, eds. *Women in the Muslim World* (Cambridge: Harvard University Press, 1978); Judith E. Tucker, *Women in Nineteenth-Century Egypt* (Cambridge: Cambridge University Press, 1985); Elizabeth W. Fernea, ed., *Women and the Family in the Middle East* (Austin: University of Texas Press, 1985); UNESCO, *Social Science Research and Women in the Arab World* (London: Frances Pinter, 1984).

5. We have likewise not paid enough systematic attention to the articulation between Islam, nationalism, and different state-building projects in the Middle East. On this question, see Deniz Kandiyoti, ed., *Women, Islam and the State* (London: Macmillan, 1991).

6. Leila Ahmed, "Women and the Advent of Islam," *Signs* 11 (1986): 665–91.

7. Mervat Hatem, "Class and Patriarchy as Competing Paradigms for the Study of Middle Eastern Women," *Comparative Studies in Society and History* 29, no. 4 (1987): 811–18.

8. This discussion will not be representative of the broader debate on the question of the origins and causes of women's subordination. On the question of origins, see Gerda Lerner, *The Creation of Patriarchy* (New York: Oxford University Press, 1986). A useful collection of essays may be found in Michelle Zimbalist Rosaldo and Louise Lamphere, eds., *Women, Culture, and Society* (Stanford: Stanford University Press, 1974). This work introduces the public-private dichotomy, which has been particularly influential, as well as contested, in analyses of women in the Middle East. See chapters by Friedl and Hegland in this volume.

9. For two very different materialist accounts, see Shulamith Firestone, *The Dialectic of Sex* (London: Women's Press, 1979), and Christine Delphy, *The Main Enemy* (London: Women's Research and Resource Centre, 1977).

10. As in Zillah Eisenstein, "Developing a Theory of Capitalist Patriarchy," in *Capitalist Patriarchy and the Case for Socialist Feminism*, ed. Zillah Eisenstein (New York: Monthly Review Press, 1979), 5–40; Roisin McDonough and Rachel Harrison, "Patriarchy and Relations of Production," in *Feminism and Materialism*, ed. Annette Kuhn and Ann Marie Wolpe (London: Routledge and Kegan Paul, 1978), 11–41; Heidi Hartmann, "The Unhappy Marriage of Marxism and Feminism: Towards a More Progressive Union," in *Women and Revolution*, ed. Lydia Sargent (London: Pluto, 1981), 1–41; Michele Barrett, *Women's Oppression Today* (London: Verso, 1980).

11. Ester Boserup, *Women's Role in Economic Development* (London: George Allen and Unwin, 1970).

12. Germaine Tillion, *The Republic of Cousins* (London: Al Saqi, 1983).

13. Jack Goody, *Production and Reproduction* (Cambridge: Cambridge University Press, 1976).

14. Ann Whitehead, "Review of Jack Goody's *Production and Reproduction*," *Critique of Anthropology* 3, nos. 9–10 (1977): 151–59; Karen Sacks, *Sisters and Wives: The Past and Future of Sexual Equality* (Westport, Conn.: Greenwood, 1979).

15. Felicity Edholm, Olivia Harris, and Kate Young, "Conceptualizing Women," *Critique of Anthropology* 3, nos. 9–10 (1977): 101–30.

16. Lourdes Beneria, "Reproduction, Production and the Sexual Division of Labour," *Cambridge Journal of Economics* 3, no. 3 (1979): 203–25.

17. Lourdes Beneria and Gita Sen, "Accumulation, Reproduction and Women's Role in Economic Development: Boserup Revisited," *Signs* 7 (1981): 279–98.

18. There have been many variations on this theme. See, for instance, Maria Mies, *Patriarchy and Accumulation on a World Scale* (London: Zed, 1986).

19. As in Sargent, ed., *Women and Revolution*, and Barrett, *Women's Oppression Today*.

20. Hence the host of such imprecise formulations as "state" patriarchy versus "private" patriarchy, Muslim patriarchy, and so on.

21. Deniz Kandiyoti, "Bargaining with Patriarchy," *Gender and Society* 2, no. 3 (1988): 274–90.

22. This term is intended to indicate the existence of set rules and scripts regulating gender relations, to which both genders accommodate and acquiesce, yet which may nevertheless be contested, redefined, and renegotiated.

23. James C. Caldwell, "A Theory of Fertility: From High Plateau to Destabilization," *Population and Development Review* 4 (1978): 553–77.

24. Deniz Kandiyoti, *Women in Rural Production Systems: Problems and Policies* (Paris: UNESCO, 1985).

25. John Hanger and Jon Moris, "Women and the Household Economy," in *Mwea: An Irrigated Rice Settlement in Kenya*, ed. Robert Chambers and Jon Moris (Munich: Weltforum, 1973), 209–44.

26. Janet Dey, "Gambian Women: Unequal Partners in Rice Development Projects," in *African Women in the Development Process*, ed. Nici Nelson (London: Frank Cass, 1981), 109–22.

27. Pepe Roberts, "The Sexual Politics of Labour in Western Nigeria and Hausa Niger," in *Serving Two Masters*, ed. Kate Young (New Delhi: Allied Publishers, 1989), 27–47.

28. Kristin Mann, *Marrying Well: Marriage, Status and Social Change among the Educated Elite in Colonial Lagos* (Cambridge: Cambridge University Press, 1985).

29. Monica Munachonga, "Income Allocation and Marriage Options in Urban Zambia," in *A Home Divided: Women and Income in the Third World*, ed. Daisy Dwyer and Judith Bruce (Stanford: Stanford University Press, 1988), 173–94.

30. Katherine Abu, "The Separateness of Spouses: Conjugal Resources in an Ashanti Town," in *Male and Female in West Africa*, ed. Christine Oppong (London: George Allen and Unwin, 1983), 156–68.

31. Jane I. Guyer and Pauline E. Peters, eds., *Conceptualizing the Household: Issues of Theory and Policy in Africa*, special issue of *Development and Change* 18 (1987).

32. Enid Schildkrout, "Dependence and Autonomy: The Economic Activities of Secluded Hausa Women in Kano, Nigeria," in *Women and Work in Africa*, ed. Edna G. Bay (Boulder, Colo.: Westview, 1982), 55–81.

33. Mette Bovin, "Muslim Women in the Periphery: The West African Sahel," in *Women in Islamic Societies*, ed. Bo Utas (London: Curzon, 1983), 66–103.

34. I am excluding not only Southeast Asia but also the northern Mediterranean, despite important similarities in the latter concerning codes of honor and the overall importance attached to the sexual purity of women, because I want to restrict myself to areas where the patrilocal-patrilineal complex is dominant. Thus societies with bilateral kinship systems such as Greece, in which women do inherit and control property and whose dowries constitute productive property, do not qualify in spite of important similarities in other ideological respects. This is not to suggest, however, that an unqualified homogeneity of ideology and practice exists within the geographical boundaries indicated. There are critical variations within the Indian subcontinent, for example, that have dramatically different implications for women. For these, see Tim Dyson and Mick Moore, "On Kinship Structures, Female Autonomy and Demographic Behavior," *Population and Development Review* 9 (1983): 35–60. Conversely, even in areas of bilateral kinship, there may be instances in which all the facets of classic patriarchy, namely property, residence, and descent through the male line, may coalesce under specified circumstances. See Bette Denich, "Sex and Power in the Balkans," in *Women, Culture, and Society*, ed. Rosaldo and Lamphere, 243–62. What I am suggesting is that the most clear-cut and easily identifiable examples of classic patriarchy are found within the boundaries indicated in the text.

35. Eric Wolf, *Peasants* (Englewood Cliffs, N.J.: Prentice Hall, 1966).

36. Sherry Ortner, "The Virgin and the State," *Feminist Studies* 4 (1978): 19–36.

37. Eric Wolf, *Europe and the People without History* (Berkeley: University of California Press, 1982).

38. Michael Meeker, "Meaning and Society in the Near East: Examples from the Black Sea Turks and Levantine Arabs," *International Journal of Middle East Studies* 7 (1976): 383–422.

39. Lila Abu-Lughod, *Veiled Sentiments* (Berkeley: University of California Press, 1986).

40. Unni Wikan, *Behind the Veil in Arabia* (Baltimore: Johns Hopkins University Press, 1982).

41. Ursula Sharma, *Women, Work and Property in North West India* (London: Tavistock, 1980).

42. Ronald C. Jennings, "Women in Early Seventeenth Century Ottoman Judicial Records: The Sharia Court of Anatolian Kayseri," *Journal of the Economic and Social History of the Orient* 28 (1975): 53–114; Haim Gerber, "Social and Economic Position of Women in an Ottoman City, Bursa, 1600–1700," *International Journal of Middle East Studies* 12 (1980): 231–44; Tucker, *Women in Nineteenth-Century Egypt*.

43. Abdelwahab Boudhiba, *Sexuality in Islam* (London: Routledge and Kegan Paul, 1985); Kay Anne Johnson, *Women, the Family and Peasant Revolution in China* (Chicago: University of Chicago Press, 1983); Margery Wolf, *Women and the Family in Rural Taiwan* (Stanford: Stanford University Press, 1972).

44. Fatima Mernissi, *Beyond the Veil* (London: Al Saqi, 1985).

45. Tucker, *Women in Nineteenth-Century Egypt*.

46. Maria Mies, "The Dynamics of the Sexual Division of Labour and Integra-

tion of Women into the World Market," in *Women and Development: The Sexual Division of Labour in Rural Societies*, ed. Lourdes Beneria (New York: Praeger, 1982), 1–28.

47. Wolf, *Women and the Family in Rural Taiwan*.

48. Johnson, *Women, the Family and Peasant Revolution in China*, 21.

49. Wikan, *Behind the Veil in Arabia*, 184.

50. Mead Cain, S. R. Khanan, and S. Nahar, "Class, Patriarchy and Women's Work in Bangladesh," *Population and Development Review* 5 (1979): 408–16.

51. Martin Greeley, "Patriarchy and Poverty: A Bangladesh Case Study," *South Asia Research* 3 (1983): 35–55.

52. Thomas S. Kuhn, *The Structure of Scientific Revolutions* (Chicago: University of Chicago Press, 1970).

53. Deniz Kandiyoti, "Rural Transformation in Turkey and Its Implications for Women's Status," in *Women on the Move: Contemporary Changes in Family and Society* (Paris: UNESCO, 1984), 17–30.

54. Margery Wolf, "Women and Suicide in China," in *Women in Chinese Society*, ed. Margery Wolf and Roxane Witke (Stanford: Stanford University Press, 1975), 111–41.

55. Mernissi, *Beyond the Veil*, 149.

56. Maxine Molyneux, "Mobilization without Emancipation? Women's Interests, the State and Revolution in Nicaragua," *Feminist Studies* 11 (1985): 227–54.

57. Farah Azari, "Islam's Appeal to Women in Iran: Illusion and Reality," in *Women of Iran: The Conflict with Fundamentalist Islam*, ed. Farah Azari (London: Ithaca Press, 1983), 1–71.

58. Haleh Afshar, "Behind the Veil: The Public and Private Faces of Khomeini's Policies on Iranian Women," in *Structures of Patriarchy*, ed. Bina Agarwal (London: Zed, 1988), 228–47.

59. Fadwa El Guindi, "Veiling Infitah with Muslim Ethic: Egypt's Contemporary Islamic Movement," *Social Problems* 8 (1981): 465–85.

60. Janet S. Chafetz and Anthony G. Dworkin, "In the Face of Threat: Organized Antifeminism in Comparative Perspective," *Gender and Society* 1 (1987): 33–60; Deborah Rosenfelt and Judith Stacey, "Second Thoughts on the Second Wave," *Feminist Studies* 13 (1987): 341–61; Judith Stacey, "Sexism by a Subtler Name? Postindustrial Conditions and Postfeminist Consciousness in the Silicon Valley," *Socialist Review* (November 1987): 7–28.

61. Kandiyoti, ed., *Women, Islam and the State*; see also Deniz Kandiyoti, "Emancipated but Unliberated? Reflections on the Turkish Case," *Feminist Studies* 13 (1987): 317–38.

The

First

Islamic

Centuries

3 Political Action and Public Example:

'A'isha and the Battle of the Camel

DENISE A. SPELLBERG

'A'isha bint Abi Bakr (d. A.D. 678) lived a long and controversial existence within the nascent Islamic community. Acknowledged in the earliest Arabic texts as the favorite wife of the Prophet Muhammad, 'A'isha was accorded a special status that derived primarily from the privileges of her marriage to the founder of Islam. Her ascribed status, however, was also affected by her actions after her husband's death. Indeed, as she herself recounted, her married state lasted only nine years. At eighteen, 'A'isha became a widow.[1] Her involvement in the first Islamic civil war culminated with her participation in the Battle of the Camel (656). 'A'isha's political action resulted in the creation of a problematic female public example. After the Battle of the Camel, 'A'isha continued to be revered as the favorite wife of the Prophet, but her actions as a widow provoked criticism.

This chapter examines 'A'isha bint Abi Bakr as a model for other Muslim women. The depiction of 'A'isha was negatively affected by her participation in the struggle for political succession. The debate over 'A'isha's political activity is directly linked in the earliest Arabic texts with larger issues concerning the place of women in early Islamic society and their access to political power. To define 'A'isha's impact as a public and political figure, therefore, is also to come to terms with the nature of her influence on the Islamic community as it sought to determine the place of all women in society.

There has been much scholarly debate concerning the position of women in Arabia before and after the rise of Islam. To ascertain how 'A'isha bint Abi Bakr fits the cultural configuration engendered by Islam, it is necessary to outline briefly the major Western scholarly arguments concerning the position of women during this transitional period. Such a survey, although suggestive, is to date more divisive than conclusive. The thesis of W. Robertson Smith that pre-Islamic, or *jahiliyya*, society was matriarchal has been challenged successfully in this century by such scholars as W. Montgomery Watt and Gertrude Stern.[2] Watt has distinguished both patrilineal and matrilineal tendencies in pre-Islamic customs.[3] However, more recent analyses of the same body of ninth-century Arabic texts, the earliest sources available for the pre-Islamic era, have resulted in three quite different interpretations of the impact of Islam on women. Barbara Freyer Stowasser argues that "the majority of pre-Islamic women appear to have lived in a male dominated society in which their status was low and their rights were negligible."[4] Her overall assessment of the transition from the jahiliyya to the Islamic period underscores her perception of the more positive standing women found in the new Muslim community, where "both social status and the legal rights of Muslim women were much improved."[5] Nabia Abbott by contrast, depicts the Prophet Muhammad as a reformer who "strove successfully for the improvement of the economic and legal status of all Moslem women," while at the same time leaving "woman forever inferior to man, placing her one step below him."[6] Abbott asserts that certain new Islamic institutions, such as the seclusion decreed in the Quran for the wives of the Prophet, resulted in an eventual negative restructuring of the role of Muslim women "into one of passivity and submissiveness comparable to that already imposed" on neighboring Jewish and Christian women.[7] Suggesting that Abbott's thesis rests on the implicit assumption of "misinterpretation by later generations," Leila Ahmed states that the Islamic impact on pre-Islamic social and political norms was inexorable and eradicated "those elements of activeness and independence to be found in the women of the first Muslim society."[8] Unlike Abbott, Ahmed believes that Islam was not misinterpreted, but that the more positive conditions for women's participation that had existed in pre-Islamic society were "superseded and transformed" by Islam in ways detrimental to women.[9] As Ilse Lichtenstadter states, "pre-Islamic Arab women played a part in the life of their tribe and exercised an influence which they lost only later in the development of Islamic society."[10] Lichtenstadter and Ahmed both agree that a wider variety of participation was available to women in the pre-Islamic era. Ahmed argues that "even if only fleetingly" women before Islam pursued many roles, which included priestesses, warriors, leaders of rebellions, and nurses on the battlefield.[11] Through the examination of the earliest written Arabic sources concerning 'A'isha's participation in battle and politics, this chapter suggests that her actions reflected both pre-Islamic and Islamic components. The depiction of 'A'isha as a public and political figure reflected the nuances of a society in transition.

The Prophet Muhammad changed the institution of marriage and with it the basic relationship between the sexes. His own wives, of whom 'A'isha was the most beloved, received an exalted status in Islamic society, one that set them apart from ordinary women, conferring on them the unique title "Mothers of the Believers." In the Quran 33:32, the wives of the Prophet are described as "not like any other women." The need for modesty was greater for the Mothers of the Believers than for other women, since an attack on their honor was also an attack on the Prophet. The directives in the Quran concerning both seclusion and the veil are specifically addressed to the wives of the Prophet. The Mothers of the Believers were regarded as models for all Muslim women in much the same way Muslim men looked to the example of the Prophet.[12]

Muhammad married at least twelve women.[13] Marriage conferred on his many wives a prestige at once separate and singularly potent. The number of wives taken by the Prophet has been the subject of much speculation by non-Muslim scholars who have often judged these marriages as a form of self-indulgence. The actions of the Prophet, generated in a world where polygyny was common, were not merely personal, however, but were part of a social and political program. Muhammad changed the institution of marriage by replacing more flexible pre-Islamic options with the Quranic injunction that no man take no more than four wives. As Lichtenstadter's work demonstrates for the pre-Islamic period, tribal alliances were cemented through matrimony.[14] In binding significant Muslim families together, Muhammad also employed the Islamic institution of marriage to ensure the unity of the community.

All of Muhammad's wives were widows, except 'A'isha. Marriage to the Prophet in many cases provided these widows with their sole means of support after the death of their husbands. As demonstrated by M. E. Combs-Schilling, however, Muhammad's marriages were not merely a means of providing simple social welfare for the widows of his fledgling religious community.[15] The Prophet utilized marriage to forge major political alliances. The importance of this policy was demonstrated even after his death. Marriage, the giving and taking of women, in both the pre-Islamic and Islamic periods provides the true "tie that binds."[16] Each of the first five caliphs, the temporal political successors to the Prophet after his death, was bound to him through marriage. These men either gave their daughters to the Prophet in marriage or married Muhammad's daughters. Combs-Schilling asserts that "the Muslim community used Muhammad's decision making concerning political alliances solidified through marriages as a guide to which men were worthy to rule."[17] The marriage of 'A'isha bint Abi Bakr serves as the first case in point, linking her father, Abu Bakr, who would become the first caliph of Islam, to the Prophet. 'A'isha's political interests and status within the Islamic community were prestigious on two counts, for her father and her husband were the most prominent men of their time. Indeed, the first civil war in Islamic society exemplifies not just a dispute over the leadership of the community, but also the attempt by Muslims to define their loyalty to those who could demonstrate the closest relationship to the Prophet. 'A'isha took the field as the representative of a political marriage alliance, one enhanced by the Prophet's preference for her during his lifetime. 'A'isha, Mother of the Believers, and daughter of the first caliph, Abu Bakr, opposed the fourth caliph, 'Ali, the representative of a marital union with the Prophet's daughter Fatima. After the death of the Prophet, the Islamic community was directed for forty-eight years (632–80) by men connected to him through marriage.

The Battle of the Camel was the major military conflict in the first *fitna* (civil war) in Islamic society. The fitna was precipitated by the murder of the third caliph, 'Uthman, who like his predecessors was linked to the Prophet Muhammad through marriage. 'A'isha's involvement in the politics leading to 'Uthman's assassination is extensively documented, particularly in the early chronicles, where her political motivation is the object of debate.[18] The dispute ended with a battle near Basra in which 'A'isha, together with Talha and al-Zubair, two of Muhammad's Companions, were defeated by 'Ali ibn Abi Talib, first cousin and son-in-law of the Prophet and the fourth caliph of Islam. The battle, referred to in ninth-century Muslim sources with the pre-Islamic phrase *Yaum al-Jamal*, "the Day of the Camel," immortalized 'A'isha's presence in a closed litter atop her camel.

The first civil war provided 'A'isha with an opportunity to participate directly in the affairs of the Islamic state. Her closeness to the Prophet during his lifetime, the result of her preferential status among his wives as the *habiba* (favorite), had given her tremendous prestige within the Muslim community, which even the Prophet's death could not obliterate. Men followed her, a woman, into battle together with two male Companions of the Prophet, an event that suggests not just her prestige, but her power. How much of 'A'isha's motivation and conduct in politics reflects pre-Islamic norms? Most important, could her military and political participation be reconciled with the emerging role of women in Islam?

What did 'A'isha's role in the first civil war mean in seventh-century terms? This question is significant because the first written sources dealing with the Battle of the Camel date from the ninth century, not the seventh. Thus nearly one hundred and fifty years of oral transmission formed the basis of the first Arabic texts of the ninth century. The reliability of these sources, which include politically inspired accounts, remains the object of intense controversy in modern scholarship.[19] Yet the most obvious political anachronisms may be as valuable as those attributed to seventh-century originators because such anachronisms may reflect later eighth- and ninth-century observations. Watt suggests that a major problem in ninth-century sources is reflected by the process of "tendential shaping."[20] He proposes, in reviewing accounts of such "external acts" as the Battle of the Camel, that the acts are not the most likely object of distortion, but rather the qualities and motivations attributed to the major actors in them. As Watt observes with reference to the Battle of the Camel, "nobody denies that 'A'ishah left Medina shortly before the murder of the caliph 'Uthman, but whether her motives were honourable, dishonourable, or neutral is vigorously debated."[21] Here Watt advocates that the "modern historian . . . largely discount allegation of motives" in sources.[22] Yet the very aspect of the sources that Watt believes should be ignored may be the most valuable for analyzing 'A'isha's depiction as a reflection of the emergence of Islamic social norms concerning women. Even if they are the product of eighth- or ninth- rather than contemporary seventh-century accounts, the depiction of 'A'isha's motivations together with observations about her personal qualities best represents the variety of Muslim attitudes concerning her participation in the first civil war. Indeed, although the accounts attributed to 'A'isha herself concerning the motivation for her actions may reflect "tendential shaping," they should be understood as the product of an ongoing dispute within the Muslim community that shaped the past and defined its implicit significance for the future.

Did 'A'isha break pre-Islamic or Islamic precedent by participating directly in battle? In pre-Islamic times, women participated in tribal warfare on the Arabian peninsula. With the advent of Islam women did not relinquish their place on the battlefield. Many women fought alongside the Prophet Muhammad, and the instances of "such participation can be found literally by the dozens."[23] Indeed, even after the Battle of the Camel, women fought for both the fourth caliph 'Ali and his opponent Mu'awiyya at Siffin.[24] Nor is there any Quranic verdict on women's place on the battlefield, whether in a military or a supportive role. 'A'isha did not fight in the engagement, but served rather as a standard and a spur for her troops, many of whom fell defending her. 'A'isha's participation appears, initially, not to have prevented other Muslim women from gaining combat access. In yet another pre-Islamic aspect of the Battle of the Camel, the heaviest fighting took place around 'A'isha's camel, where her supporters made a final effort to defend her. In the pre-Islamic era, tribal Arabs often placed their women near the area of combat as an incentive to achieve victory or defeat in death.[25] It was the risk to 'A'isha's life that precipitated the bloody last stand of her partisans. Indeed, one of the accusations lodged by 'Ali's supporters against

'A'isha's male companions was that they had "exposed" the wife of the Prophet to the threat of death in battle.[26]

The Quran likewise does not forbid women from exercising direct political rule. In the one instance in the Quran where a woman rules she is faulted not for her inability to govern, but for her ignorance of true faith. The queen of Sheba on her throne is described in verse 27:23 as a commanding figure of truly regal bearing: "I found a woman ruling over them, and she had been given [an abundance] of all things, and hers is a mighty throne." Her kingdom was governed by consensus. Men were consulted, although the queen retained the final right of decision. Abbott has argued that this verse, revealed at Mecca, predates the strictures Muhammad later imposed on his wives at Medina.[27] She further stresses that the part of the Quran in which Sheba figures was revealed "before personal reasons led Muhammad to seclude his women."[28] Moreover, Abbott adds in a conjectural vein, he "had no definite intention of categorically disqualifying all women from state service and condemning any or all their efforts in that direction."[29] The injunctions that served, by extension, to condemn women's action in politics is the famous verse 33:33, which commands the wives of the Prophet to stay in their homes.

Taken as a whole, ninth-century references to 'A'isha's role in the first civil war may be divided thematically into negative appraisals of rule by women, predictions of doom, censure, humor, and regret. These varied categories reflect the Muslim community's range of response to 'A'isha's persona as defined by her participation in the Battle of the Camel. In all but the first two categories 'A'isha is the object of both praise and blame. This oppositional coupling of reactions, often found in the same account, reflects the difficulty the entire community had in coming to grips with 'A'isha's participation in the battle. In this process a significant dimension of 'A'isha's legacy became fixed.

A series of ninth-century traditions concerning the relation of women to government are recorded in the hadith collections of al-Bukhari (d. 870) and Ibn Hanbal (d. 855). Ultimately, these traditions link 'A'isha with generally negative appraisals of women and rule by predicting the evil outcome of 'A'isha's involvement in the Battle of the Camel. The role played by 'A'isha in these sources does not end with the ninth century, but continues to evolve in the chronicles of the tenth century and various later works of different genres. The elaboration of such themes over time suggests the centrality of 'A'isha to the debate over the relation of women to Islamic government.[30] The problems of assessing 'A'isha's role in the determination of women's participation in Islamic government expose underlying assumptions about all women.

The discussion of women and rule in ninth-century sources is often introduced by traditions that present the defects of women as the greatest fitna, "source of temptation or chaos."[31] Another meaning of *fitna* is a trial whereby an individual must choose between good and evil, which is how the term is used in the Quran.[32] In ninth-century traditions, the Prophet stated that there would be "no fitna more harmful to men than women."[33] Women are here equated with a definition of dangerous female sexuality. *Fitna*, as noted above, is also the political term for civil war. Although 'A'isha is never directly linked with *fitna* as a definition for women, by virtue of her gender she implicitly participates in the connotations of the term as they applied to all women in ninth-century tradition. When the definition of women as fitna is coupled with 'A'isha's participation in the Battle of the Camel, the private and public definitions converge. 'A'isha, at once personifies the worst inclinations of her gender and, by extension, the ill effects resulting from female participation in politics. In a similar vein, ninth-century hadith also note the predominance of women as inhabitants of hell.[34] The same source also implies that the cause of female overrepresentation in the fires of hell is lack of *'aql* (reason). This serious defect is presumably one from which no member of the gender may escape. These misogynistic observations provide the context for the critical ninth-century assessment of 'A'isha's foray into politics in the Battle of the Camel.

'A'isha's participation in the battle is used to warn against all women's involvement in affairs of state in a tradition that features her co-wife, Umm Salama. According to al-Ya'qubi's (d. 897) version, as 'A'isha was leaving for the Battle of the Camel, Umm Salama reminded her that "the support of the religion does not depend upon the exertions of women."[35] Umm Salama, a staunch supporter of 'Ali, was considered by later Shi'i Muslims to be Muhammad's favorite wife. The antagonism between 'A'isha and Umm Salama reflects not just their differing personalities, but also the political divisions rife within the Prophet's own household after his death.

The predictions of doom that originated in the ninth century in relation to the Battle of the Camel concern the disastrous consequences resulting from female rule. The two hadith that mention this concern are part of a larger number of traditions that described how the Prophet, on hearing that a woman ruled Sasanian Iran, said: "A people who place women in charge of their affairs will never prosper."[36] A woman named Boranduxt did rule Iran circa 630–31, but we know little of her short reign for good or ill, except that she ruled long enough to be immortalized on coins.[37] Only one variation of these traditions contained in Ibn Hanbal directly mentions 'A'isha. In this account, the Prophet is said to have uttered strong warnings about females, stating that "men perish if they obey women."[38] Enhancing the impact of his words was their utterance "while his head rested on 'A'isha's breast."[39] The outcome of the Battle of the Camel and the role of 'A'isha in it were at once seemingly predicted, but, more pointedly, condemned. In the context of this hadith, 'A'isha cannot even be defended, for at the time the observation was allegedly made, she had as yet done nothing to bear out the Prophet's prognostications. Al-Bukhari recorded the Prophet's prediction about women generally and then concluded, with ninth-century hindsight, that Muhammad's words must have been spoken in reference to the Battle of the Camel.[40]

References to the Battle of the Camel that censure 'A'isha in Ibn Sa'd (d. 845) and al-Baladhuri (d. 892) are not narrated on her authority. The majority of the accounts depict a similar incident: an unnamed man censures 'A'isha on the day of the battle by attacking her reputation and is publicly rebuked by a Companion of the Prophet and supporter of 'Ali, the eminent 'Ammar Ibn Yasir. That 'A'isha is defended by her enemy, a supporter of 'Ali for the position of caliph as well as in battle, emphasizes her prestige within the community as a whole. Ibn Sa'd's account offers one perspective: "A man attacked 'A'isha's reputation on the Day of [the Battle of] the Camel. The people agreed with him. Then 'Ammar said, 'What's this?' They replied, 'A man vilified 'A'isha.' Then 'Ammar said to him, 'Silence your disgraceful clamor. Are you attacking the beloved of the Prophet of God? She is his wife in heaven!' "[41]

This tradition reflects 'A'isha's prestige as the favorite wife of the Prophet, which in this instance represented an implicit defense of her actions. This defense was made even more forceful when uttered by a supporter of 'Ali who, in emphasizing 'A'isha's previous status as the favorite wife, reminded her accusers that her place in heaven was assured. The incident also served as a warning to later audiences that 'A'isha's prestige, built on Muhammad's preference for her, could not be obliterated by her actions after his death. The honor of the Prophet's wife must be maintained, in spite of the independent actions of his widow. The accusation is dismissed, but no defense against the specifics of the assault of 'A'isha's reputation is recorded. By the nature of its subject, the account also preserved a current of ridicule and derision regarding 'A'isha's involvement in the Battle of the Camel.

The broader implications of 'A'isha's direct involvement in the political contests of the Islamic community are better captured in al-Bukhari's hadith on 'A'isha's *fada'il* (superior qualities). Again, the element of praise is apparent in the author's decision to include this account. Yet although the theme offers 'A'isha her due in prestige as the wife of the Prophet "in this world and the next," al-Bukhari's version provides a new setting and motivation for 'Ammar's loyalty to 'Ali: "When 'Ali sent 'Ammar and al-Hasan to Kufa to call upon them [the inhabitants] to fight [against 'A'isha], 'Ammar made a speech. He said, 'I know that she is his [the Prophet's] wife in this world and the next, but Allah puts you to test [whether] to be His followers or hers.'"[42] Here the Kufans were urged to support 'Ali by the partisan 'Ammar, who in deference to the Prophet gives 'A'isha her prestigious due. There appears to be little doubt in 'Ammar's plea, however, about whose cause is the righteous one. 'Ali's followers are also supporters of the divine will. 'A'isha, although praised, is thus faintly but distinctly damned in spite of her future access to heaven, for to follow 'A'isha is to fail Allah's test.

A unique type of reference to 'A'isha's role in the battle employed humor to underscore the criticism of the Prophet's wife. Al-Baladhuri offers the following tradition:

> 'A'isha needed something so she sent [a message] to Ibn [Abi] 'Atiq saying, "Send your mule," so that she could ride it on an errand. He said to her messenger, and he [Ibn Abi 'Atiq] was an idle joker, "Say to the Mother of the Believers, 'By God, we have not yet gotten over the shame of the Day of [the Battle of] the Camel, are you not too exhausted to give us the Day [of the Battle] of the Mule?'"[43]

The point of the jest relies on the play of words and images. When the mule is substituted for the camel, the idea of a battle so-named becomes ludicrous. It is doubtful, however, that even an "idle joker" would address 'A'isha with such scorn and sarcasm. The anecdote, despite its humorous context, was a pointed accusation of 'A'isha's wrongdoing.

Two ninth-century sources depict 'A'isha expressing regret for her actions in the Battle of the Camel. Ibn Qutaiba (d. 889) included an account in which 'A'isha apparently overheard unidentified men glorifying the Battle of the Camel, although whose role or what side they were supporting is not revealed. She urged them to desist, stating that there had been enough *siyah* (outcry) regarding that *fashal* (fiasco).[44] Regret should not be confused with remorse, for 'A'isha's feelings as represented in these traditions nowhere signify repentance. The account may be read as regret defined in terms of a desire to disassociate herself from the defeat, rather than from participation in the battle. In short, the passage is suggestive, but not conclusive, and represents a unique instance within the ninth-century corpus of observations about 'A'isha.

The hadith in Ibn Sa'd's biographical dictionary that comes closest to an outright confession is the one in which 'A'isha, on her deathbed, reveals her own perspective about her actions after the Prophet's death and their consequences: "'A'isha said about the time of her death, 'I caused wrongdoing after the Prophet. So they should bury me with the [other] wives of the Prophet.'"[45] The implications of this admission of regret about the Battle of the Camel are that her burial site should not be special. Instead of being buried with the Prophet, beneath her own house, 'A'isha denies any privileged status and asserts that she is to be buried like any other wife of Muhammad.

'A'isha's role in the Battle of the Camel, as depicted in ninth-century sources, reveals a range of reactions, a variety of Muslim responses to a controversial event in the history of the early Muslim community. 'A'isha and her participation in the Battle of the Camel were perceived as a flawed ideal. The first fitna marked the beginning of Islamic political strife and, with it, the legacy of varied responses to 'A'isha's historical personality.

It has been suggested by Abbott that 'A'isha's loss at the Battle of the Camel prompted the exclusion of women from public life.[46] Although it is true that 'A'isha never again joined directly in the Islamic struggle for political succession after her defeat in the first civil war, that her example alone stopped all other women from similar political forays is unlikely. Abbott's appraisal of 'A'isha can be disputed on two separate counts. First, 'A'isha was at best a participant, not the leader of the opposition to 'Ali. Immediately after her defeat other Muslim women fought in the second civil war, as they had fought before and after the advent of Islam. Second, her political actions represent at once a convergence and a clash of pre-Islamic practice and Islamic strictures. 'A'isha derived her power as a political figure from her relationship to two men: her father and her husband. 'A'isha's unique position was derived from a truly Islamic prestige and for that very reason her new exemplar status provided the basis for her censure. The role of the wives of the Prophet had been outlined by the revelations of the Quran, but not tested in the lives of the women to whom it applied. By taking the battlefield, by assuming a role as a political figure after the death of her husband, 'A'isha challenged the Islamic restrictions placed on the Mothers of the Believers, restrictions that did not inhibit the actions of any other seventh-century Arab women. Her defeat, coupled with her influential status, definitively circumscribed the sphere of her role as a political figure. It could be argued that 'A'isha's defeat assured that the Mothers of the Believers, the most prominent group of women in the first Islamic community, remained outside the political arena. Thus while the men closest to the Prophet vied for political leadership, the potential for the women closest to him to follow the same course was obstructed by divine revelation and the defeat of the Prophet's favorite wife, 'A'isha.

As mentioned earlier, however, the political fate of the Mothers of the Believers was not necessarily the destiny of all seventh-century Muslim women. Neither 'A'isha nor the Quranic injunction directed at the wives of the Prophet to stay secluded set a precedent for all women. More likely, the definition of women in general as expressed in ninth-century hadith extended and refined the idea that women were basically flawed and dangerous to the maintenance of political order. The revealing application of the term *fitna* to women between the eighth and early ninth centuries signaled an end to the options of all Muslim women in political affairs.

In the tenth-century account of al-Mas'udi (d. 956), 'A'isha's example as a political figure summoned a decidedly negative response. When Zubaida, wife of the famed Abbasid caliph Harun al-Rashid (d. 809), heard the news of her son's death in a civil war, she was urged to follow 'A'isha's example. She declined, saying: "It is not for women to seek vengeance and take the field against warriors."[47] She then went into mourning and seclusion. Zubaida's response depicts 'A'isha as an unworthy political model for women.

The Battle of the Camel prompted a defense of 'A'isha, who retired to private life after her defeat in the first civil war. 'A'isha's retreat from public life has been perceived as representative of the future limited role of all women in the Islamic community.[48] Yet 'A'isha's defeat also signaled a new stage in her participation in the Islamic community, for she retained a different source of prestige: her knowledge of the faith. Although 'A'isha's image would be successfully manipulated to confirm the danger of female participation in government, her powerful memory and authority in matters crucial to the Islamic community, ranging from methods of worship to medicine, ensured her praise among Sunni Muslims.

Notes

1. Muhammad Ibn Sa'd, *al-Tabaqat al-kubra* (Beirut: Dar Sadir, 1958), 8:62.

2. W. Robertson Smith, *Kinship and Marriage in Early Islam* (Cambridge: Cambridge University Press, 1885); Gertrude Stern, *Marriage in Early Islam* (London: Royal Asiatic Society, 1939); W. Montgomery Watt, *Muhammad at Medina* (Oxford: Clarendon, 1956).

3. Watt, *Muhammad at Medina*, 272–89.

4. Barbara Freyer Stowasser, "The Status of Women in Early Islam," in *Muslim Women*, ed. Freda Hussain (New York: St. Martin's, 1984), 15.

5. Ibid.

6. Nabia Abbott, "Women and the State in Early Islam," *Journal of Near Eastern Studies* 1, no. 1 (1942): 107. She cites Quran 2:228 and 4:34. See *The Glorious Qur'an*, trans. M. M. Pickthall (New York: Muslim League, 1977). Pickthall's version is used throughout this chapter.

7. Abbott, "Women and the State," 107.

8. Leila Ahmed, "Women and the Advent of Islam," *Signs* 11 (1986): 690, 691.

9. Ibid., 691.

10. Ilse Lichtenstadter, *Women in Ayyam al-Arab* (London: Royal Asiatic Society, 1935), 81.

11. Ahmed, "Women and the Advent of Islam," 691.

12. Reuben Levy, *The Social Structure of Islam*, 2d ed. rev. (London: Cambridge University Press, 1975), 126.

13. Watt, *Muhammad at Medina*, 395–99.

14. Lichtenstadter, *Women in Ayyam al-Arab*, 65.

15. M. E. Combs-Schilling, *Sacred Performances: Islam, Sexuality, and Sacrifice* (New York: Columbia University Press, 1989), 69–72.

16. Ibid., 69.

17. Ibid., 72.

18. For the debate over 'A'isha's motivations in ninth-century sources, see Ahmad Yahya al-Baladhuri, *Ansab al-ashraf*, ed. S. D. F. Goitein (Jerusalem: Jerusalem University Press, 1936), 5:341–63; and Abu Ja'far Muhammad b. Jarir, *Ta'rikh al-rusul wa'l-muluk* (Leiden: E. J. Brill, 1898), 6:3000–3130.

19. On the subject of the authenticity of early hadith, see G. H. A. Juynboll, *Muslim Tradition: Studies in Chronology, Provenance and Authorship of Early Hadith* (Cambridge: Cambridge University Press, 1983); and Ignaz Goldziher, *Muslim Studies*, ed. S. M. Stern and trans. C. R. Barber and S. M. Stern (London: George Allen and Unwin, 1971).

20. W. Montgomery Watt, *Muhammad at Mecca* (Oxford: Oxford University Press, 1953), xiv.

21. Ibid.

22. Ibid.

23. Abbott, "Women and the State," 118.

24. Abu 'Umar Ahmad Ibn 'Abd al-Rabbihi, *al-'Iqd al-farid* (Cairo: n.p., 1876), 4:158.

25. Lichtenstadter, *Women in Ayyam al-Arab*, 43.

26. Abu al-Hasan 'Ali b. Husain al-Mas'udi, *Muruj al-dhahab wa ma'adin al-jauhar* (Beirut: Dar Sadir, 1965), 2:367.

27. Abbott, "Women and the State," 120.

28. Ibid.

29. Ibid.

30. See Denise A. Spellberg, "Nizam al-Mulk's Manipulation of Tradition: 'A'isha and the Role of Women in Islamic Government," *Muslim World* 78, no. 2 (1988): 111–17.

31. E. W. Lane, *Arabic-English Lexicon* (reprint, Cambridge: Islamic Texts Society, 1984), 2:2335–36.

32. For this usage, see Quran 37:61.

33. For example, see Abu Ahmad 'Abd Allah Isma'il al-Bukhari, *Kitab al-jami' al-Sahih*, ed. M. Krehl (Leiden: E. J. Brill, 1864), 2:419; and Ahmad Ibn Hanbal, *Musnad* (Cairo: n.p., 1895), 3:22. The most recent discussion is by Fatima Mernissi, *Beyond the Veil: Male-Female Dynamics in a Modern Muslim Society* (Cambridge, Mass.: Schenkman, 1975).

34. Al-Bukhari, *al-Sahih*, 3:419.

35. Ahmad b. Abi Ya'qub b. Ja'far b. Wahb b. Wadih al-Ya'qubi, *Ta'rikh*, ed. M. Houtsma (Leiden: E. J. Brill, 1883), 2:209.

36. Ibn Hanbal, *Musnad* 5:38.

37. See Robert Gobl, *Sasanian Numismatics* (Brunswick: Klinkhardt and Biermann, 1971).

38. Ibn Hanbal, *Musnad* 5:45.

39. Ibid., 48.

40. Al-Bukhari, *al-Sahih* 4, pt. 1, 376–77.

41. Ibn Sa'd, *al-Tabaqat* 8:65.

42. Al-Bukhari, *al-Sahih* 2:447.

43. Al-Baladhuri, *Ansab* 1:421.

44. Abu Muhammad 'Abd Allah Ibn Muslim Ibn Qutaiba, *'Uyun al-akhbar* (Cairo: n.p., 1930), 1:108.

45. Ibn Sa'd, *al-Tabaqat* 8:74.

46. Abbott, "Women and the State," 120–21.

47. 'Ali ibn al-Husain al-Mas'udi, *Les prairies d'or* (Paris: Imprimerie Impériale and Imprimerie Nationale for the Société Asiatique, 1970), 6:485–86.

48. Ahmed, "Women and the Advent of Islam," 690.

4

Early Islam and the Position of Women:

The Problem of Interpretation

LEILA AHMED

The message of Islam as instituted by Muhammad's teachings and practice comprehended two tendencies that were in tension with each other.[1] Patriarchal marriage and male dominance were basic components of the institution of marriage as established by Muhammad in the first Islamic society, and yet Islam preached an ethical egalitarianism as a fundamental part of its broader spiritual message. Some sects chose to give primacy to the ethical dimension of the Islamic message. They regarded the regulations put into practice by Muhammad as bearing primarily on that immediate social context and period, and thus not necessarily binding on Muslims at all times in all societies. This, however, was not the position taken by orthodox Islam in the Umayyad and Abbasid periods, crucial in Muslim history because the elaborations of scriptures and of laws during this time have ever since been regarded as the founding defining texts of Islam.

Orthodox Islam, in rendering the Islamic message into scriptures and into an elaborate legal code, chose to view the regulations and practices put into effect by Muhammad as the fundamentals of the message and as binding on all Muslims. The ethical injunctions enjoining fair treatment of women were aspects of the Islamic message by and large not heard, at least as reflected in the body of the law as it took shape in this age. Had the ethical dimension of Islam been heard, it would have tempered the articulation of the law and we might today have a far more humane and egalitarian Islamic law regarding women. But the period as a whole, and in particular the Abbasid age, was an unpropitious one for

Portions of this chapter appear in somewhat different form in *Women and Gender in Islam: Historical Roots of a Modern Debate* (Yale University Press, 1992).

women. In the context of the age's mores with respect to women—the decline in their position following Islam's expansion beyond the borders of Arabia and the degradation of the very notion and definition of *woman* at the level of the elite—the egalitarian dimension of Islam would have been an exceedingly difficult one to hear.

Quranic precepts consist mainly of broad, general propositions chiefly of an ethical nature, rather than specific legalistic formulations. As legal scholars have pointed out, as a legislative document the Quran raised many problems and by no means provided a simple and straightforward code of law.[2] On the contrary, the specific content of the laws derivable from the Quran depended greatly on the interpretation that legists chose to bring to it and the elements of its complex utterances they chose to give weight to. As an example of this intrinsic complexity or ambiguity and of the crucial role played by interpretation, legal historians cite the Quranic references to polygyny. Polygyny, up to a maximum of four wives, is expressly permitted by the Quran, but at the same time husbands are enjoined to treat co-wives equally and if they fear they will be unable to do so, to marry only one wife. The legal base of marriage and of polygyny would differ profoundly depending on whether the ethical injunction to treat wives impartially was judged to be a matter of legislation or left purely to the individual man's conscience.[3]

The formation of Islamic law took place over several centuries and by a variety of processes. During Muhammad's lifetime he was judge of the community and interpreter of the general provisions of the divine revelation. On his death the responsibility for interpreting Quranic precepts, and translating that interpretation into practical decisions, devolved on the caliphs who immediately succeeded him. The difficulties of interpreting and rendering ethical ideas into law were compounded by the Arabs' rapid acquisition of vast foreign territories. With the establishment of the capital of the empire of the Umayyads (661–750) in Damascus the Arab rulers adopted the administrative machinery of the Byzantine rulers they had succeeded, which facilitated the assimilation of foreign concepts into the still developing and essentially rudimentary apparatus of Islamic law. Government-appointed judges, who initially combined the role of judge with that of administrator, tended to apply local laws (which varied throughout the territories) informed by their own understandings of Quranic precepts. Disparities soon arose among regions. In Medina, for example, a woman could not contract a marriage on her own account but had to be given in marriage by a guardian, whereas in Kufa the law gave her the right to contract her own marriage without the intervention of a guardian.[4] Differences of interpretation of Quranic injunctions also arose. One judge ruled that the Quranic injunction to "make a fair provision" for divorced wives should be interpreted as having a legalistic dimension and that therefore such a payment to the wife was obligatory. Another judge, however, hearing a similar case ruled that the Quranic injunction was directed only at the husband's conscience and was not legally binding.[5]

Over the course of the Umayyad period local laws were modified and elaborated by Quranic rules and "overlaid by a corpus of administrative regulations and infiltrated by elements of foreign systems."[6] Growth was haphazard and brought together heterogeneous materials, and the Quranic elements were largely submerged.

Scholars of religion began to voice their views as to the standards of conduct that would express the Islamic ethic. Grouping together in fraternities in the last decades of the Umayyad period and critical of the Umayyad legal establishment, they formed the early schools of law. When the anti-Umayyad Abbasids came to power (750–1250), these legal schools were recognized and sponsored by the new state and as a result developed rapidly.[7] The legal doctrines they propounded became, with state sponsorship and the appointment of representatives of the schools of law to the judiciary and as government advisers, the practice of the courts. The piecemeal review of local practice began in light of the principles the scholars believed to be enshrined in the Quran. Originating in the personal reasoning of individual scholars, a body of Islamic doctrine gradually formed, which as time passed gained authority.[8] The development and elaboration of legal doctrine and of juridical procedures continued into the ninth century, with some variation between the decisions of different regions. The Kufan school of law, for example, formed in an environment influenced by the Sasanid sense of the importance of class, developed the doctrine that required a husband to be the social equal of his wife's family, a doctrine that formed no part of the law as it developed in Medina.[9] By the tenth century the body of Sunni Muslim legal thought and practice achieved final formulation in four schools of law, representing in part the different regional origins of the schools and named after major legal proponents—the Hanafi, the Shafi'i, the Hanbali, and the Maliki. The body of law and of legal thought embodied in the writings of those four schools was recognized as absolutely authoritative, partly through the application of a juridical principle that had gained general acceptance, that of *ijma'* (consensus). According to this principle the unanimous agreement of the qualified jurists on a given point had a binding and absolute authority. Such agreement, once reached, was deemed infallible and to contradict it became heresy.[10] Although theoretically an earlier consensus could be repealed by a later generation with a similar consensus, because of the authoritativeness with which the existent body of law was now invested, such a possibility became highly unlikely. Further discussion was precluded, not only of points that were the subject of consensus, but also of matters on which the jurors had agreed to differ.

In the early tenth century Muslim jurisprudence formally recognized the body of already formulated legal opinion as final. The duty of the jurist henceforth was to "imitate" his predecessors, not to "originate" doctrine. Thus the whole body of the law as it had evolved during the first three centuries in effect was consecrated as the complete and infallible expression of divine law. Even though, as Noel Coulson points out, "the great bulk of the law had originated in customary practice and in scholars' reasoning . . . and [the development] of classical theory . . . was the culmination of a process of growth extending over two centuries," traditional Islamic belief came to hold that the law as articulated in this literature was operative from the beginning. "The elaboration of the law," Coulson writes, "is seen by Islamic orthodoxy as a process of scholastic endeavour completely independent of historical or sociological influences."[11] Consequently, the vision of society developed by the men of this period, and their understanding of the relations that should pertain between men and women, was established as the ultimate and infallible articulation of the Islamic notion of justice, which has, ever since, been imposed as finally binding on Muslims.

The claim is (and must be, if the body of legal thought as a whole is affirmed as representing the correct and infallible articulation in legal form of the ethical formulations of the Quran) that the different schools of law are essentially in agreement and that variations among them are only on matters of insignificant detail. Some of these "insignificant" differences in interpretation, however, result in laws profoundly different in their consequences for women. Whereas all schools agree that marriage may be unilaterally terminated extrajudicially by the male, Maliki law differs from the other three schools as to women's right to obtain judicial divorce. Hanafi law, for example, permits it only on the grounds of sexual impotence, but Maliki law allows a woman to petition on grounds of desertion, failure to maintain her, cruelty, sexual impotence (even after the consummation of the marriage), and if the husband is afflicted with a chronic or incurable disease detrimental to her.[12] The differences for women obviously are fundamental. Similarly, Hanafi law differs radically from the other three in its view of marriage contracts, and of women's right to stipulate such terms as that the husband may not take a second wife. The other three schools consider men's right to unilateral divorce and their right to marry as many as four wives to be of the essence of marriage, and therefore elements that may not be altered by the specific contractual agreements entered upon by man and wife. The Hanafi school, however, considered that the Quranic utterances on polygyny, for instance, were permissive, not mandatory, and that for a man to have only one wife is therefore not contrary to the essence of marriage; the spouse's agreement to this (or other matters) in the contract is consequently valid and enforceable.[13]

Such differences make plain that the ethical injunctions on marriage in the Quran are open to radically different interpretations, even by individuals who share the assumptions, worldview, and perspective on the nature and meaning of gender typical of Muslim society in the Abbasid period. That groups of male jurists were able, in spite of the unquestioning androcentrism and misogyny of the age, to interpret the Quran as enabling women to bind men to monogamy and to obtain divorce in a broad range of oppressive situations is itself important. It suggests that a reading by a less androcentric and less misogynist society, one that gave greater ear to the ethical injunctions of the Quran, could have elaborated (and could still reelaborate) a law that radically altered women's position for the better. If, for example, the two dissenting doctrines just mentioned had been the view of the majority (and thus formed the basis of general legal practice in Islamic countries rather than that of a minority), they (particularly in combination) could have fundamentally altered women's status in marriage.

Nor were those two the only (though quite fundamental) points on which jurists of the day revealed the androcentric assumptions of their society in their interpretation of the Quran, while at the same time failing to give legal form to its ethical injunctions. The reflections of two modern legal scholars on this matter are worth quoting in full:

[A] considerable step—a process of juristic development extending over more than two centuries—separates the Quran from the classical formulation of Islamic law. . . . The modicum of explicit Quranic legal rulings on the status of women were naturally observed, but outside this the tendency was to interpret the Quranic provisions in the light of the prevailing standards. . . . In particular, the general ethical injunctions of the Quran were rarely transformed into legally enforceable rules, but were recognized as binding only on the individual conscience.

Thus, for example, a husband was never required to show that he had any reasonable or proper motive before exercising his power to repudiate his wife. And while the Quran might insist upon impartial treatment of co-wives in polygamous unions, classical Islamic law did not elevate this requirement into any kind of legal restriction upon the husband's entrenched right to have four wives. The result was that the Quranic provisions concerning women's status and position in the family were dissipated and largely lost.[14]

The rulings the jurists developed on women's rights in matters of sexuality, contraception, and abortion, outlined by Basim Musallam in his important book *Sex and Society in Medieval Islam,* are interesting. In contrast to the laws regulating marriage, those governing contraception and abortion appear remarkably liberal in the measure of control they allowed women in preventing and terminating pregnancy, and thus might be taken superficially as remarkably free of androcentric bias. In fact (as I have argued in detail elsewhere), though such laws did permit women to exercise some control in preventing and terminating pregnancy, when the broad legal environment of which they were a part is taken into account, these laws also may be seen as entirely in harmony with an androcentric perspective.[15] As such, they were part of a legal system that permitted polygyny and concubinage and that also stipulated, on the basis of clear Quranic rulings, that males were economically responsible for their offspring. If a man's concubine bore him a child, the concubine could not thereafter be sold and she became legally free at his death; her child became the man's legal heir along with children born to his wives. Given this system, it was economically to men's advantage that women not bear many children, and that concubines not bear any children, since if they did they ceased to be a profitable investment. And in a system that permitted polygyny and unrestricted divorce and concubinage, a woman who did not give birth would present no hardship for the man since he had the options of divorcing her, of taking another wife without divorcing her, or of taking a concubine. Although sexual and other services were wifely duties according to the law, child bearing was not. Oral culture, both in contemporary and earlier Muslim societies, in contrast, placed heavy stress on women's generative capacity. To reproduce was economically to women's advantage: for slaves it was a passport to freedom and for wives it bound up the husband's emotional, sexual, and monetary resources and thus lessened his ability to take on more women. Arguably, then, oral culture expressed women's interests just as the law expressed men's.

The problem of interpretation and of the biases and assumptions that a particular age brought to its readings and renderings of a text is relevant beyond the founding texts of Islamic legal thought. With respect to the central texts at the core of the edifice of orthodox Islam, interpretation again played a vital but more hidden role.

Interpretation is of necessity part of every act of reading or of inscribing a text. According to orthodox Islam the text of the Quran represents the exact words recited by Muhammad. This view holds that the Quran was perfectly preserved in oral form from the beginning and was written down during Muhammad's lifetime or shortly thereafter, when it was "collected" and arranged for the first time by his Companions. The orthodox account of the process is that a complete written text was made after Muhammad's death in the reign of the first caliph, Abu Bakr (632–34), and that the authoritative version was established during the reign of the third caliph, 'Uthman (644–56). A dispute between Syrian and Iraqi troops as to the correct recitation of the Quran prompted 'Uthman to compile a single authorized version. Obtaining Hafsa's collection, he commissioned four prominent Meccans to make a copy following the dialect of the Quraish. When the process was complete, 'Uthman sent copies to the major centers and ordered other versions destroyed. This was done everywhere except in Kufa, where for a time the Kufans refused to destroy their version. Eventually, however, 'Uthman's text became the canonical version and the final consonantal text. The fully vocalized version was established in the tenth century.[16]

Some Quranic scholars have asserted that the Quran is not in the Quraish dialect. In addition, a number of other elements suggest that the process by which Muhammad's recitations were transformed from oral materials to written text was not as seamless as orthodox accounts declare.[17] For one thing, as these accounts themselves indicate, a number of different versions were evidently in circulation at the time of the compiling of the canonical version, including one sufficiently different for the Kufans to reject that version. There is also the element of uncertainty arising sheerly from the material conditions attending the inscription of a text in this place and period. In addition to the rough nature of the materials (such as animal bones) used to note down Quranic verses during Muhammad's lifetime, the Arabic letters used at this point were incomplete. The dots necessary to distinguish between the consonants were lacking, for example, so that in a group of consonants two or more readings were possible. Deciding which reading was correct based on these notations and on oral memories that orthodox belief also admits were divergent, a process not finalized according to orthodox statements until at least fifteen years and many foreign conquests after Muhammad's death, was itself an act of interpretation. Similarly, deciding which vocalization was to be the canonical one with respect to a text in which only consonants were written (a process not finalized until the tenth century) could itself importantly alter meaning, and thus such decisions also were interpretative.[18] As one important study of Muslim inheritance law has recently shown, in deciding between variant readings and finalizing one of two mutually exclusive readings as authoritative, the theologians and legists of the day were already choosing meanings from the perspective of their own environment, meanings fundamentally different from those connoted by the same phrases in the early Muslim environment.[19]

The role of interpretation in the preservation and inscription of the Quran is, however, suppressed in orthodox doctrine, and the belief that the text is precisely as Muhammad recited it is itself a tenet of orthodox faith. To question whether the body of consecrated Islamic law represents the only possible legal interpretation of the Islamic vision is surrounded with awesome interdictions. That its central texts do embody acts of interpretation is precisely what orthodoxy is most concerned to conceal and erase from the consciousness of Muslims. This is understandable, because the authority and power of orthodox religion, whose interests were closely bound up in the Abbasid period with those of the ruling elite and the state, depended on its claim to a monopoly of "truth," by declaring its version of Islam absolute and all other interpretations heresies.

Various other interpretations of the Islamic vision, however, from the start developed and counterposed their readings to that of orthodoxy, even as it gained firm control and denounced alternative visions as heretical. Among those that posed radically different interpretations were the Qarmati and Sufi movements, which both drew many adherents from the underclass. The Qarmati movement, a radical variety of Isma'ili Shi'ism, and the Sufi movement in some of its more radical aspects were declared heretical and persecuted until the former was entirely eradicated and the latter shorn of its more radical dimensions. Movements of political and religious dissent often also entailed different understandings of the social dimension of Islam, including matters directly affecting women, as was true of the early Kharijite movement. Divergent and, as will be suggested, oppositional views to those of the orthodox on a comprehensive range of matters, religious, political, and social, were rooted in a reading of Islam that differed fundamentally from that of the orthodox. Both Sufism (in its more radical form) and the Qarmati movement emphasized Islam's ethical, spiritual, and social teachings as its essential message. They believed that the regulations Muhammad put into effect in his society, and even his own practices, were above all ephemeral aspects of Islam, relevant primarily to a particular society at a certain stage in its history. Again, therefore, the issue is difference of interpretation, not in the sense of understanding particular words or passages in the text, but more radically, pre-textually or supra-textually, in the sense of how to "read" Muhammad's acts and words and how to construe their relation and import to history. Was the import of the Islamic moment a specific set of ordinances, or the initiation of an impulse toward a juster and more charitable society? The Sufi and Qarmati movements are of specific interest in the present context because both broadly opposed the politics and religion of the dominant culture, including, the evidence suggests, its view of women.

Sufism was a movement in which pietism, asceticism, and mysticism were dominant elements. Possibly originating in the days of Muhammad, it gained ground and developed importantly in particular during the first three or four centuries of Islam, that is, coterminous with state-supported orthodox Islam. Sufism had political dimensions, being a form of dissent and of passive opposition and resistance both to the government and to established religion. Its oppositional relation to the society and ethos of the dominant is evident in the values enunciated as fundamental to its vision. Asceticism, the renunciation of material goods and of money not earned by the labor of one's own hands and in excess of one's daily needs, and the emphasis on celibacy (though not an invariable requirement), precisely reverse the materialism, exploitation of the labor of others, and unbridled sexuality that were enshrined in the mores and way of life of orthodox society. Sufi emphasis on the inner and spiritual meaning of the Quran, and the underlying ethic and vision it affirmed as opposed to the letter of the text and law, similarly countered the letter-bound approach of orthodoxy.

A number of elements in Sufism strongly suggest that the Sufi ethos countered that of the dominant society with respect also to their gender arrangements and their view of women. From early on the Sufis counted women among those importantly contributing to their tradition and included such women as Rabi'a al-'Adawiyya (d. 801) among the ranks of the most elect of spiritual leaders. Moreover, Sufi tales and legends incorporate elements that suggest a rejection of the values of the dominant society with regard to women.

The narratives about Rabi'a al-'Adawiyya, for instance, most of which are clearly legendary, exemplify distinctly countercultural elements with respect to ideas about gender. The notion underlying all male-female interaction in the dominant society, that biology and sexuality govern relations between the sexes, for example, is clearly repudiated by one short Sufi narrative. In it, the highly esteemed Sufi leader Hasan al-Basri (d. 728) declares, "I passed one whole night and day with Rabi'a speaking of the Way and the Truth, and it never passed through my mind that I was a man nor did it occur to her that she was a woman, and at the end when I looked at her I saw myself as bankrupt [i.e. as spiritually worth nothing] and Rabi'a as truly sincere [that is, rich in spiritual virtue]."[20] The tale also reverses the dominant society's valuation of male over female, by representing not merely any man but one of the most revered male Sufi leaders describing himself as "bankrupt" compared with a woman of truly superior merits. This theme is amplified in many such short narratives that depict Rabi'a surpassing her male colleagues in intellectual forthrightness and percipience as well as in spiritual powers. In another tale, again featuring Hasan al-Basri, he approaches Rabi'a, who is sitting on a bank with a number of contemplators. Throwing his carpet on the water, Hasan sits on it and calls to Rabi'a to come and converse with him. Rabi'a, understanding that he wants to impress people with his spiritual powers, throws her prayer carpet into the air, flies up to it, and sitting there says, "Oh Hasan, come up here where people will see us better." Hasan is silent, because it is beyond his power to fly. "Oh Hasan," Rabi'a then says, "that which you did a fish can do . . . and that which I did a fly can do. The real work [for the saints of God] lies beyond both of these."[21] Other tales show her similarly surpassing prominent male Sufi figures. One relates how, when Rabi'a is making her pilgrimage to Mecca, the Ka'ba rises up and comes forward to meet her. Observing this, Rabi'a comments, "What have I to do with the house, it is the Lord of the house I need." Meanwhile an eminent fellow Sufi, Ibrahim ibn Adham, also making the pilgrimage to Mecca, takes many years to reach his destination because he repeatedly stops piously to perform ritual prayers. Arriving at Mecca and seeing no Ka'ba, he thinks his eyes are at fault, when a voice informs him that the Ka'ba has gone forth to meet a woman. When Rabi'a and the Ka'ba then both appear, Rabi'a informs Ibrahim (who is consumed with jealousy that the Ka'ba has so honored her) that whereas he crossed the desert with formal ritual prayers, she came in inward prayer. In addition to showing her outdoing men, the tale shows her gently undercutting the formalism and literalness of orthodox religion and the trappings of piety, just as does a remark attributed to Rabi'a about another Sufi, Sufyan al-Thauri. "Sufyan would be a [good] man," she says, "if only he did not love the Traditions."[22]

Although such narratives perhaps capture some qualities exemplified by the historical Rabi'a, doubtless they are mainly of a legendary nature. Given their dates, for instance, it is highly unlikely that Hasan and Rabi'a ever met, let along enjoyed the above exchanges. The legendary nature of such stories gives them greater weight as exemplars of Sufi thought, in that they are not merely records of happenings but rather narrative structures deliberately devised to express thoughts. And among those thoughts is that women may excel over even the ablest of men and may be men's teachers in the domain of the spiritual, and that interactions between men and women on the intellectual and spiritual plane far exceed in importance their sexual interactions. This is not to suggest that all Sufi men were non-sexist, or even that Sufi literature did not incorporate some of the misogynist elements present in its broad environment.[23] The argument here is simply that it did include elements rejecting misogyny and transcending definitions of human beings based on biology.

Other details in the legends about Rabi'a suggest reasons besides the spiritual that women might be drawn to Sufism. According to biographical legend, for example, Rabi'a was either a slave or a servant of very poor origin until her master released her from service after he woke one night to see a light, the light of saintliness, shining over her head and illuminating the entire house. Rabi'a then retired into the desert; she later returned to practice, for a time, the profession of flute player. Thereafter, in the words of Margaret Smith, Rabi'a's twentieth-century biographer, the extant material "gives a clear idea of a woman renouncing this world and its attractions and giving up her life to the service of God."[24] Although Smith focuses on Rabi'a's spiritual concerns, Rabi'a's class background is worth taking note of, as is the fact that a female slave or servant scarcely had the option of renouncing many worldly attractions. Sufism, it is clear, offered the possibility of a life of independence and autonomy otherwise certainly impossible for women, particularly women of Rabi'a's class. Tales in which Rabi'a rejects offers of marriage from numerous admiring Sufi companions similarly emphasize her autonomy and capacity to remain free of any male authority. Although it was impossible for women according to orthodox mores, Sufism enabled a few women to enjoy such autonomy. To say this is not to cast doubt on or belittle Rabi'a's mysticism, but only to recognize it as a complex and comprehensive response to her society and its mores. As mystic, Rabi'a's major contribution is regarded as having been the emphasis on the centrality of the love of God to mystical experience.[25] She declared, according to legend, that her love of God was such that it allowed no room even for love of Muhammad. Among the most famous tales is that of her carrying a torch and a ewer through the streets of Basra, intent on setting fire to paradise and pouring water on the flames of hell in order, Rabi'a explained, that those two veils would disappear from the eyes of believers and they come to love God for His beauty and not out of fear of hell or desire for paradise.[26]

Much less is known regarding Qarmati views about women, but they, too, appear to have departed fundamentally from the prescriptions in orthodox Islamic society pertaining to the proper relations between men and women. Qarmati writings have not survived, and so one cannot base investigations of their beliefs and practices on their own accounts. The movement, which was distinctly one with roots and followers among the underclass, challenged the Abbasid regime militarily and for a time even succeeded in establishing an independent republic. It was eventually eradicated and its writings destroyed or lost. Nearly all the available information about its activities and society comes from the pens of unsympathetic observers who were supporters of the Abbasid regime.

The Qarmati movement saw itself, like other movements of dissent, as representing the true realization of the Islamic message, opposed to the misinterpretations of Islam and the corruptions practiced by the dominant society. Accounts of their society depict them as advocates of communal property. Qarmati missionaries are described, for example, as organizing villagers and inviting them to bring to a central place all they owned by way of "cattle, sheep, jewelry, provisions"; thereafter no one owned anything and the goods were redistributed according to people's needs. "Every man worked with diligence and emulation at his task in order to deserve high rank by the benefit he brought. The woman brought what she earned by weaving, the child brought his wages for scaring away birds."[27] In the republic they established, property was communal and was administered by a central committee, which ensured that all had their housing, clothing, and food needs taken care of. Some writers asserted that the Qarmatis also treated women as communal property. Contemporary scholars, however, suggest that this view represents the writers' misperception of what they witnessed—which was so different from the practices regarding women of their own society. The evidence adduced in support of their accusation was that Qarmati women were not veiled, that both sexes practiced monogamy, and that women and men socialized together. These and similar practices apparently led the writers to believe that the Qarmatis were "debauched" and "obscene"; they themselves of course came from societies in which the "unobscene" norm among the elite was for men to keep, and relate sexually to, women by the dozen.[28]

Thus Islam in this period was interpreted in ways, often representing the interest and vision of different classes, that implied profoundly different societies, including the arrangements and attitudes governing the relationship between the sexes. The dissent and the "heresies" dividing the society were concerned not so much with obscure theological points (as orthodox history generally suggests) as with the social order and the values inscribed in the dominant culture. The uniformity of interpretation and the generally minimal differences characterizing the versions of Islam that were to survive thus do not reflect unanimity of understanding. Rather, they represent the triumph over its rivals of the Abbasid state and of the religious and social vision it sponsored at this crucial formative moment in history.

One figure in particular deserves mention in the context of the concept of woman and of the feminine in the formative Islamic ages, both for this countercultural understanding of Islam with respect to women and because he is probably unique among major Muslim scholars and philosophers in regarding women sympathetically. Ibn al-'Arabi (1165–1240), whose intellectual stature and range arguably surpass al-Ghazali's, was born in Murcia, Spain. In his youth he studied under Sufi masters in his native land, including two women, Shams, Mother of the Poor, and Nunah Fatima bint al-Muthanna. He said of Shams that "in her spiritual activities and communications she was among the greatest" and described miracles performed by Nunah Fatima, with whom he studied when she was in her nineties. He helped build her a hut of reeds.[29] Ibn al-'Arabi instructed his daughter in theology, and she apparently was able to answer theological questions when scarcely a year old; he wrote movingly of her joy on seeing him after an absence. (The extent to which the different mores of Arab Spain, where Ibn al-'Arabi came to maturity, shaped his attitude to women is certainly an important question and one that has yet to be explored.)

Ibn al-'Arabi was persecuted as a heretic a number of times. On at least one occasion the "heresy" he committed that outraged the orthodox was in connection with his statements about women. His poem *Turjuman al-ashwaq* (The interpreter of longing), for example, centers on the figure of a young woman he met in Mecca. He wrote that she was "learned and pious, with an experience of spiritual and mystic life," and that but for "paltry souls . . . predisposed to malice, I should comment here on the beauty of her body as well as her soul." The memory of "the grace of her mind and the modesty of her bearing" and the "unwavering friendship" she offered him become the sources of inspiration in his poem, the central metaphor of which (as in Dante's work two centuries later) is that the young woman (Nizam) is the earthly manifestation of Sophia, the divine wisdom that his soul craves.[30] The notion of divinity in the female face was profoundly offensive to the orthodox, and the antagonism the poem earned Ibn al-'Arabi led him later to write a commentary to the work asserting that its meaning was entirely spiritual and allegorical. Ibn al-'Arabi continued to develop in his thought the notions of the feminine dimension of the divine and the complementarity of the sexes. Among such notions were the idea that Adam was the first female, because Eve was born from his inside, and that Mary, by generating Jesus, became the second Adam.[31] Again using Adam and Eve as metaphor, Ibn al-'Arabi wrote of God drawing forth from Adam "a being in his own image, called woman, and because she appears to him in his own image, the man feels a deep longing for her, as something which years for itself."[32] Moreover, Ibn al-'Arabi construed the creative Breath of Mercy, a component of the Godhead itself, as feminine.[33] Although he was subjected to hostility during periods of his life, the intellectual power evidenced in his prodigious literature was such that he is widely acknowledged as a major Muslim thinker.

The moment in which Islamic law and scriptural interpretation were elaborated and cast into the forms that were to be considered authoritative to our own day was a singularly unpropitious one for women. The mores and heritage of Ummayad and, in particular, of Abbasid society were, with respect to women, deeply negative. They played a significant part in the extent to which the elaboration of the law would be weighted against women, first by determining that Islam's broad propositions instituting male dominance in marriage would be emphasized and given legal articulation, rather than its broad ethical injunctions emphasizing justice and fairness. Second, they led to interpretations of those propositions that in their specificities were the least favorable systematically to women. The minority legal opinions on women's right to divorce and to stipulate conditions in their contracts indicate that even in this androcentric age a reading of Islam that was fairer to women was possible; unsurprisingly, in a society in which women were deeply devalued this fairer reading was not favored by the majority of the legists of the day. Similarly, the example of the Sufis and the Qarmatis indicates that there were different ways of reading the Islamic moment and text from those of the dominant culture, and that such readings had important implications for the conceptualization of and the social arrangements around issues of gender.

These findings obviously are relevant to the issues being debated today in Muslim societies, given in particular the trend to interpret and apply classical Muslim law yet more rigidly to women and in all ways, societally and governmentally, to endorse the orthodox Islamic vision of woman. Now that women in unprecedented and ever-growing numbers are forming part of the intellectual community in Muslim countries, perhaps—as they are already reclaiming the right, not enjoyed for centuries, of attending the mosques—these veins of thought will be reopened and the process of the creation of Islamic law will be brought into question.

Notes

1. See Leila Ahmed, *Women and Gender in Islam: Historical Roots of a Modern Debate* (New Haven: Yale University Press, 1992), chap. 6.
2. N. J. Coulson, *A History of Islamic Law* (Edinburgh: Edinburgh University Press, 1964), 10–11, 17.
3. Ibid., 18–19.
4. Ibid., 30.
5. Ibid., 30–31.
6. Ibid., 34. The summary of the history of Islamic law in the following pages is based on Coulson's account in his *History,* chaps. 1–3, and on Joseph Schacht's *An Introduction to Islamic Law* (Oxford: Clarendon, 1964), chaps. 4–10.
7. Coulson, *History,* 36–37.
8. Ibid., 39.
9. Ibid., 49.
10. See Coulson, *History,* 77–78; Schacht, *Introduction,* 28–30.
11. Coulson, *History,* 85.
12. Ibid., 97.
13. Noel J. Coulson, *Conflicts and Tensions in Islamic Jurisprudence* (Chicago: University of Chicago Press, 1969), 25–30.

14. Noel J. Coulson and Doreen Hinchcliffe, "Women and Law Reform in Contemporary Islam," in *Women in the Muslim World*, ed. Lois Beck and Nikki Keddie (Cambridge: Harvard University Press, 1978), 38.

15. See B. F. Musallam, *Sex and Society in Islam* (Cambridge: Cambridge University Press, 1983); and Leila Ahmed, "Arab Culture and Writing Women's Bodies," in *Feminist Issues* 9, no. 1 (1989): 41–55.

16. See *Encyclopaedia of Islam*, s.v. "al-Kur'an" (5:400–432, 464).

17. Theodor Noldeke, *Geschichte des Qorans*, ed. F. Schwally, 3 vols. in 1 (Leipzig, 1909; reprint, Hildesheim: G. Olms, 1961), ii, 57–62.

18. See *Encyclopaedia of Islam*, s.vv. "al-Kur'an" and "Kira'a" (5:127–28).

19. See David S. Powers, *Studies in Qur'an and Hadith: The Formation of the Islamic Law of Inheritance* (Berkeley: University of California Press, 1986).

20. Cited in Margaret Smith, *Rabi'a the Mystic and Her Fellow Saints in Islam* (Cambridge: Cambridge University Press, 1928), 14.

21. Ibid., 36.

22. Ibid., 9, 16.

23. Annemarie Schimmel observes that Sufism was ambivalent toward women, noting, for example, that even the title of the Persian mystical poet Sana'i's poem *Banat al-na'sh* (Daughters of the bier) "points by its very name to the fact that daughters are better on a bier than alive." She notes further that some male Sufis "were absolutely antagonistic to or disinterested in women, even to the point that they would not touch food cooked by a woman," and that "early Islamic asceticism and the mystical writings based on these ascetic ideals were as inimical to women as is any ascetic movement in the world of religion, be it medieval Christianity or early Buddhism. It was easy for the Muslim ascetics of the eighth and ninth centuries to equate woman and *nafs*, the 'lower self that incites to evil' . . . since the word *nafs* is feminine in Arabic. Furthermore, as they saw in woman, as it were, the *nafs* principle personified they also represented (like their Christian colleagues) the word as a hideous ghastly old hag." *Mystical Dimensions of Islam* (Chapel Hill: University of North Carolina Press, 1975), 426, 428; Schimmel, "Women in Mystical Islam," in *Women and Islam*, ed. Azizah al-Hibri (New York: Pergamon, 1982), 146. Schimmel does grant, however, that Sufism was more favorable to women than other branches of Islam were.

24. Smith, *Rabi'a*, 9.

25. A. J. Arberry, *Muslim Saints and Mystics* (London: Routledge and Kegan Paul, 1979), 51.

26. This story made its way to medieval Europe, where in one text the account as Schimmel reports it is accompanied by an illustration of an oriental woman with a torch and a ewer. See Schimmel, "Women in Mystical Islam," 147.

27. Cited in Bernard Lewis, *The Arabs in History* (London: Arrow, 1958), 109. See also Ibn al-Jauzi, "Kitab al-muntathim fi ta'rikh al-muluk wa'l-ummam," in *Akhbar al-qarammita fi al-Ahsa', al-Sham, al-'Iraq, al-Yaman*, 2d ed. (Damascus: Dar Hassan, 1982), 255–72.

28. For a discussion of this, see M. J. De Goeje, "Carmatians," *Encyclopedia of Religion and Ethics* (New York: Charles Scribner's Sons, 1961); and *Mémoire sur les Carmathes du Bahrain et les Fatimides* (Leiden: E. J. Brill, 1886).

29. *Sufis of Andalusia: The Ruh al-quds and al-Durrat al-fakhirah of Ibn 'Arabi,*

translated with introduction and notes by R. W. J. Austin (London: George Allen and Unwin, 1971), 142–43.

30. Henry Corbin, *Creative Imagination in the Sufism of Ibn 'Arabi,* trans. Ralph Manheim (Princeton: Princeton University Press, 1969), 137–39.

31. Ibn al-'Arabi, *The Bezels of Wisdom,* translated with an introduction by R. W. J. Austin (New York: Paulist Press, 1980), 35; see also Fazlur Rahman, *Islam,* 2d ed. (Chicago: University of Chicago Press, 1979), 146.

32. Ibn al-'Arabi, *Bezels,* 274.

33. R. W. J. Austin, "The Feminine Dimensions in Ibn 'Arabi's Thought," *Journal of the Muhyiddin Ibn 'Arabi Society* 2 (1984): 5–14.

Gendering the Ungendered Body:

Hermaphrodites in Medieval Islamic Law

PAULA SANDERS

No aspect of life in medieval Islamic societies was free from considerations of sex.[1] The boundary between male and female was drawn firmly and was deeply embedded both in views of the cosmos and in social structures. The most visible expression of this boundary, the social segregation of men and women, was only a particularly concrete demonstration of the notion that male and female were opposites, and that an ordered human society depended on maintaining boundaries that had been ordained by God.

Men and women not related by blood or marriage lived in separate, but intersecting, spheres. Interaction between them was understood to be both necessary and inevitable, but it was permissible and desirable only under carefully controlled and rigidly prescribed circumstances. The most desirable of these circumstances is expressed by the institution of *nikah*, often narrowly translated as "marriage." Nikah and *zina* (unlawful intercourse) constitute the two fundamental categories of possible interaction between unrelated men and women in the social world. These categories rest upon the existence of the male-female boundary, and therefore even zina, in some sense, affirms that boundary while threatening others.[2]

Violation of those permitted relationships promised not

I am grateful to the friends and colleagues whose comments on various versions of this chapter and whose discussions with me on the topic have been invaluable: Natalie Zemon Davis, Fatma Muge Gocek, Monica Green, Susan Lurie, Shaun Marmon, Leslie Peirce, Kevin Reinhart, and Everett Rowson. I also thank Marilyn Sanders, M.D., for assistance with modern medical literature on human hermaphroditism. Kevin Reinhart of Dartmouth College is preparing an edition of al-Asnawi's *Idah al-mushkil* from a manuscript in the Zahiriyya Library in Damascus (private communication, 3 Sept. 1990).

only social disruption, but disorder on a much larger (and perhaps unseen) scale. Those disruptions could be caused not only by actual violations of taboos, but even by the suggestion that such violations had occurred. The false accusation of adultery (*qadhf*, often translated simply as "slander"), for example, is one of only five crimes for which the Quran prescribes punishment.[3] The broad Quranic concepts concerning licit and illicit relationships, as well as modesty, pertain equally to men and to women, but they were interpreted primarily in terms of the dangers that women's disruptive sexuality present to an ordered society.

Men and women were socialized into this world of relations, which assumed that men and women must interact, that they must interact in prescribed ways, and that interaction in other ways threatened the social order and had to be guarded against at all costs. The question of one's maleness or femaleness was a crucial factor in determining what kinds of protection against social disorder needed to be employed. Although men and women presumably bore equal responsibility for such illicit relations, that responsibility was construed in terms of certain assumptions about the natures of men and women. Men were considered susceptible to seduction and the actors, whereas women were considered to be both seductresses (that is, tempting men to act in certain destructive ways) and the recipients of the men's acts.[4]

Furthermore, the relations and dangerous possibilities rested on assumptions about the responsibilities of men to prescribe behaviors and set limits for women, who were considered to be their inferiors. If the spheres of men and women intersected, they were also established in a clear hierarchy that placed men above women. Although women were considered to be the equals of men before God, this spiritual egalitarianism did not imply a similar egalitarianism in the social world. This was the social context in which the Quranic verses stating that "men are a degree above women" and that "men are the managers of the affairs of women" were to be understood.[5]

Women were presumed to be the major site of social disorder (*fitna*) by medieval jurists and commentators as well as in popular literature. But even the notion of the potentially dangerous sexuality of women, of the ever-present threat of fitna, was relational. Although the danger was located among women, it was not their being that represented disorder, but the possibilities of their illicit relationships with men.[6]

Under these circumstances, a person who fit neither of the available categories presented a serious dilemma in a society where the boundary between male and female was drawn so clearly and was so impenetrable. In this respect, medieval Islam differed from medieval and early modern European societies, where the boundary between male and female was more permeable and where the troubling possibility of the mixing of sexes did exist.[7]

Not all boundaries in medieval Islamic societies were as impermeable as that between male and female. There were other, equally fundamental boundaries in Islamic societies that also involved hierarchies: Muslim and non-Muslim, free and slave. But these boundaries could be crossed. One's fundamental category could be changed by conversion or manumission. The sexual boundary was different, since it could not be crossed legitimately simply by an act of will.[8]

What did medieval Muslims do when confronted with a person whose sex was unknown? In societies that took for granted that everyone was either male or female, what place if any was there for the hermaphrodite, who seemed to fit neither category? For occasionally children were born or individuals encountered who did not fall into these two categories, whose anomalies in sexual physiology made it impossible to determine whether the person was male or female.[9]

The biological process of sex determination, according to medieval Muslim natural philosophers and physicians, required the domination or precedence of the semen of one parent over the other. Whereas it was assumed that women were created from man (that is, from Adam's rib) and inferior in most respects, they were considered biologically equal in human reproduction. Both male and female shared equally the power of generation, because both were believed to contribute semen to the reproduction of the child. Semen was regarded as a complex substance that came from all parts of the body, which explained why children resembled their parents.[10] The child would have the sex of the parent whose semen dominated. Ibn al-Qayyim al-Jauziyya attributed this domination to conditions of heat or cold in the womb, as well as to the relative strength or weakness of the semen contributed by each parent.[11]

This theory of generation as advanced in medical texts intersected with Quranic doctrines of creation. There was a deep coherence between Quran, commentary, and scientific literature on this subject. In particular, the preference for the Hippocratic-Galenic over the Aristotelian tradition seems to have been due largely to its consistency with the classical Islamic understanding of the Quranic doctrine of creation. Similarly, the medical assumption that there were two sexes was consistent with the interpretation of the Quranic verse "we have created of everything a pair" (51:49), which was clearly understood by the commentators to refer to male and female.[12]

The insistence on the two sexes of male and female and the articulation of this assumption in the theory of generation found its way even into lexicography. The medieval lexicon *Lisan al-'Arab*'s discussion of the term *dhakar* (meaning, among other things, "male" and "penis") states: "If the [seminal] fluid of the man dominates the [seminal] fluid of the woman, they will produce a male child. If the [seminal] fluid of the male precedes the [seminal] fluid of the female, she will bear a male child, if God wills." If the semen of neither parent dominated, the child would be a her-maphrodite.[13] Although the jurists were confident that every person had a true sex—known at least, or perhaps only, to God—discovering what that sex was remained a human dilemma subject to the limitations of human knowledge. The first concern of the jurists was to assign sex to such a person, usually an infant born with ambiguous genitalia.[14]

One jurist stated simply, "If the child has a vulva (farj) and a penis (dhakar) then it is a hermaphrodite (khuntha)." Other lawyers and medi-eval lexicographers defined the khuntha as one who has "what is proper to both men and to women," "what is proper to both the male and the female," or "neither what is proper to the male or to the female."[15] This last condition, according to al-Sarakhsi, was the gravest form of du-biousness (ishtibah); he was describing a child who was neither male nor female, excreting from its navel (surratuhu).

Al-Sarakhsi told his readers further that "the two characteristics [having what is male and female] are not combined in one person, be-cause they are dissimilar by way of being contradictory." Nowhere in these texts is there even the slightest suggestion that a khuntha is both a man and a woman. Human beings had to be either male or female; some-times they seemed to be neither, but they could not be both. The difficulty lay in establishing a place for the hermaphrodite until its primary set of organs could be determined, that is, the set of organs that had legal value and to which sex would be attributed.

The basic rule in establishing the sex of the child was al-hukm li'l-mabal (the judgment is attributed to the urinary orifice). This principle can be traced to pre-Islamic Arabian custom. It was also established in hadith that "the inheritance is awarded to the urinary orifice" (al-mirath li'l-mabal), that is, the sex of the child was determined by the mabal. Al-Sarakhsi explained further:

> The division between male and female at birth is manifest in the [urinary] organ ['ala] . . . at the time of separation of the child from the mother, the use [manfa'a] of that organ is urination; other uses of the organ occur after that . . . but the primary use [al-manfa'a al-asliyya] of the organ is that it is the urinary orifice [mabal, lit. "place of urination"]. So if it urinates from the mabal of men, the organ of division is in its [the male urinary orifice] jurisdiction [that is, the child is male], this being so even if the other has a larger aperture in the body. And if it urinates from the mabal of women, then that is the [primary] organ [the one to which sex is attributed].[16]

If the distinction could be made on this basis at birth, the sex of the child was determined and the additional organs accorded the status of "defect" ('aib). In other words, the presence of the extra organs was recognized as an objective reality, but these extra organs were assigned no legal value. Once relegated to the status of 'aib, or defect, they could be removed surgically.[17]

If, however, the child urinated from both of the orifices, then the one from which the urine proceeded first was primary.[18] If it urinated from both simultaneously, some said that primacy would be awarded to the organ from which the greater quantity of urine proceeded.[19] Abu Ja'far al-Tusi, the Shi'i jurist, added another criterion: "If the onset of urination from [the mabals] is simultaneous, then [the sex of the child] is considered on the basis of the one that urinates last."

Other alternatives were offered: "Some say to count the ribs, and if they are equal in number then it is a woman; if they are unequal, it is a man. And some say to consider it on the basis of the inclination of its nature." This is the only instance where anything other than strictly biological measures were suggested to determine the sex of a khuntha; it does not reflect the conventional juridical wisdom on such matters.

If the sex of the child could not be determined by these conventional methods, it remained in a state of dubiousness (ishtibah) or ambiguity (ishkal) until the onset of puberty. Puberty (bulugh, idrak) in Islam is determined by the appearance of signs ('alamat) that indicate sexual maturity. For a man, these are intercourse using the penis, the appearance of facial hair, and nocturnal emissions; for a woman, they are the growth of the breasts, the onset of menstruation, vaginal intercourse, conception, and lactation.[20]

For a khuntha, the appearance of any one of these signs would nullify the dubiousness or ambiguity. Such a sign determined both sex and the attainment of sexual majority. Furthermore, the hermaphrodite was not disabled by the ambiguity surrounding its sex in reporting the appearance of these signs. Its claims of puberty were accepted just like those of a normal child, because no one else could know about it. In this sense, the hermaphrodite benefited from the general ambiguity surrounding childhood. Since children are not considered to be sexual beings in Islam, the rules of modesty or other precautions aimed at preventing illicit sex between adults do not apply to them. Their sex is known, but they are not part of the social-sexual world of adults. They are, in a word, unsocialized.

But Islamic jurists recognized that the period immediately preceding puberty was different. The prepubescent adolescent (murahiq) was neither child nor adult; it hovered around the frontier of sexuality in a way that was troubling because of this ambiguity. Jurists were often unsure whether particular precautions regarding modesty, for example, ought to be imposed on the adolescent. Reaching puberty lifted the cloud of ambiguity that covered all children and adolescents. It was a small step to exploit and extend this ambiguity to the khuntha.

The condition of ambiguity was presumed to be temporary. Manifestation of any one of the signs of puberty removed the ambiguity permanently. Once the sex of a person had been established, that judgment was irreversible, regardless of any evidence that might be produced to the contrary.[21] The system aimed at providing every possible opportunity for establishing the true sex of the child. Nonetheless, it was possible that none of the signs of puberty ('alamat) would appear. In this case, said al-Quduri, the khuntha was ambiguous (*mushkil*).[22]

Khuntha mushkil was the technical legal term for a hermaphrodite who had passed the age at which puberty normally occurs without manifesting any of its signs.[23] Its sex could not be determined. The mushkil label was a difficult one to contest, once applied, because of the same legal principle of precedence that allowed the jurists to insist on the permanence of sex once it had been assigned. In that case, after the determination of male sex based on a nocturnal emission, the appearance of such contradictory evidence as the growth of breasts had no legal consequence. By the same reasoning, the admission that one was unable to determine sex prevented the hermaphrodite from asserting later that it had reached puberty. Now jurists had to contend with the tension between their desire to determine the sex of every human being with certainty, and the caution that was demanded in attributing sex.

Although Islamic jurists could not establish the true sex of the khuntha mushkil, they nonetheless had to incorporate it into the adult social world in which everyone was either male or female. They had to assign the khuntha mushkil to one of these categories in order to either prescribe or proscribe, because the rules for men and women were different.

This process, as opposed to establishing true sex, I would call *gendering*. I have invoked this most modern of terms with the full awareness that it is anachronistic. But feminist scholarship has created new meanings for what was once simply a grammatical term. Gender goes beyond biological definitions of sex (although these are also cultural constructions). It is embedded in the social understanding of what constitutes maleness or femaleness, as well as the social implications and consequences of being male or female.[24] I use the word *gendering* to describe the strategies by which medieval Muslim jurists constructed the khuntha mushkil—an unsexed, ungendered, and therefore unsocialized being—as a social person in terms of traditional categories of sex.

In doing this, they changed their focus from the true sex of the individual to the prescriptions for whole categories (male and female). This

process, in turn, reaffirmed those categories and maintained the boundary between male and female while retaining the emphasis on male and
female in relation to one another. This strategy was possible not because
new categories were invented, but by virtue of the structure of Islamic
law itself. If sex was not arranged on a continuum for medieval Muslims,
the moral universe encoded in Islamic law was. There were only two
poles for sex: male and female. But all behavior fell somewhere on a scale
of religious qualifications that included five categories: obligatory, recommended, neutral, reprehensible, and forbidden. Under certain circumstances, reprehensible behavior might be preferred when the alternative
was committing a forbidden act. In determining which course of action to
take, jurists employed another fundamental principle of law: precaution
(*ihtiyat*), denoting the choice of a course of action that is founded on
certainty rather than uncertainty.

The possibilities of the khuntha being a man or a woman had to be
considered with respect to every variation that is tied to sex. Decisions
were often based on procedural rules not directly related to sex. Depending on the situation, jurists might be informed by a different hierarchy of
concerns in negotiating the gender of the hermaphrodite. The negotiation of gender was not invariably difficult or complicated. Gendering
seems to have been least problematic when it involved segregation and
where spatial relations clearly reflected sexual hierarchy. In these circumstances, the simple arrangement of male above female could be exploited
to grant the hermaphrodite an intermediary position.

These concerns informed the discussions of where the hermaphrodite
should stand in prayer (*salat*). Prayer is a daily obligation. Numerous
occurrences can invalidate a person's prayer, in which case the prayer
must be repeated, just as missed prayer must be made up at another time.
Men and women may pray in the same room, but the rows of men must
always precede the rows of women. This is a clear case of segregation and
the spatial expression of male supremacy. Where should the khuntha
mushkil stand in prayer? In Friday prayer, between the rows of men and
the rows of women:

> It should stand behind the men and in front of the women as a
> precaution, because if it is a man standing among the rows of wom-
> en, his own prayer is invalid; and if it is a woman standing among
> the rows of men, then the prayers of those men on her right, her
> left, and behind her will be invalid. An adolescent is, in this, like a
> mature adult. But if the khuntha is in the rows of men, in front of
> the women, we are certain of the validity of its [own] prayer. If it
> stands among the women, however, we prefer that it repeat the

prayers, because the obligatory nature of prayer for [a man] is well-established, while the non-fulfillment of this duty is doubtful.

This is a perfect example of the way the boundary and the hierarchy were preserved: the validity of the hermaphrodite's own prayer and of those of the other congregants was assured by its segregation, and by standing between the rows of men and women, it neither threatened the superior status of men nor was it threatened with an inferior position. Should it turn out to be a man, he would simply constitute the last row of men; should it turn out to be a woman, she would be the first row of women. The hierarchy expressed in the spatial relation of men and women in prayer also applied to the dead:

> When a khuntha mushkil dies and is prayed over with a man and a woman, the man is placed right next to the *imam* [prayer leader], the khuntha next, and the woman following the khuntha, in considera-tion of their position in life . . . and if they are buried in a common grave due to some extenuating circumstance, there is no objection [provided that] a partition of dirt is made between the bodies. The man faces the *qibla* [direction of Mecca], followed by the khuntha, and then the woman, because facing the qibla is an honor, so the man should be closest to it.

In these two cases, the concern with maintaining both the boundary and the sexual hierarchy intersected with another concern that informed the negotiation of the jurists: protecting the male domain from intrusion. Every precaution was taken to ensure against violating any existing boundaries: the supremacy of male over female was always asserted, and the superior position of the khuntha to women in prayer and burial customs was a way of maintaining the hierarchy in which men were, in relation to women, the superior party. When in doubt, the rule seemed to be to accord the inferior status to hermaphrodites. What was important was that access to the higher status of men be successfully protected. The rules assured that no hermaphrodite would attain the status accorded to men unless it could be demonstrated that he was, indeed, a man.

These same concerns also informed the distribution of inheritance shares. Inheritance in Islam is governed by the rules laid down in the Quran and elaborated by the later jurists. It is basically a modification of agnatic succession, amended to include women and spouses.[25] The Is-lamic law of inheritance developed and elaborated the principle that a hermaphrodite inherits in the same proportions as the female, because it must accept the lesser status of the two. If a father died leaving a son and also a hermaphrodite, the wealth was divided among them in three shares: two for the son and one for the khuntha, for the khuntha was treated as a female.

But the jurists worried that others might try to exploit the ambiguity of the hermaphrodite's sex for their own advantage. Because of the interdependence of men and women in matters relating to family life (such as marriage and inheritance), the social fact of the khuntha's sex had important implications for other people, particularly relatives. The sex of the khuntha would affect the shares of its own blood relations, as in the case of a man who died leaving a wife and two children, one of whom was a khuntha. "Then the khuntha died after its father, and so the mother claimed this to be a son, urinating from where boys urinate. The accepted opinion is the word of the son, because the mother claims an excess in her inheritance by claiming him [the khuntha] to be a son, whereas the [other] son has no excess to gain, so his word is accepted with an oath."[26] Presumption operated in favor of the son's claim, because he had nothing to gain from determining the sex of the child. The mother, however, stood to gain by establishing the khuntha as a male child, from whom she could inherit. Determining sex was important because the relationships of the living to the khuntha were not altered by the fact of death.

There were other fundamental concerns. Numerous problems in gendering hermaphrodites revolved around the issue of modesty.[27] Many prescriptions for dress, demeanor, and segregation are based on this concept of modesty, called in Arabic sitr al-'aura, literally, "covering [one's] nakedness." The exhortation to preserve modesty applies equally to men and women in Islam, but the various law schools have diverging definitions of what constitutes the 'aura for men and women, and they usually emphasize women's responsibility. When the concerns of jurists were centered on sitr al-'aura, the hermaphrodite was almost always gendered as female.

In the absence of any clear hierarchical concerns, and given the complicated matrix of concerns around modesty, the difficulties of negotiating gender often required invoking other frontiers. Jurists might, for example, exploit the recognized category of the adolescent, who is not always required to adhere to prescriptions for adults, to resolve a question about the necessity of veiling in prayer. Al-Sarakhsi concluded that a khuntha should be veiled while praying: "If it is a man, his being veiled is not forbidden in prayer, and if it is a woman, she is obliged to be veiled in her prayer." If it prayed without a veil, the adult khuntha was required to repeat the prayer, because of the possibility that it was a woman. But if it prayed without a veil before reaching puberty, it need not repeat the prayer, because an adolescent female (murahiqa) is not obliged to wear the veil when praying.

Jurists were not able to exploit another frontier—death—in negotiating gender around the question of sitr al-'aura. When discussing the ritual ablutions and burial shrouds of the khuntha, they unanimously advocated precautionary veiling in the interests of modesty. Al-Sarakhsi reminds us also that what applied to the khuntha in lifetime with respect to sitr al-'aura applied equally in death. It is clear from this text that the restraints on relationships between men and women that exist in life are neither abolished nor neutralized by death. The boundary remains as firm for the dead as for the living, and the taboos that govern the relationships between men and women while they are alive govern also that between the living and the dead:

> If it dies before reaching puberty, but while approaching it, neither a man nor a woman should perform the *ghusl* [the major ritual ablution, involving a full bath] on it, but rather should perform the *tayammum* [ritual ablution using clean sand or dust instead of water, to be substituted for the ghusl only under special conditions]. This is because of the principle that gazing upon the 'aura is forbidden and this prohibition is not lifted in death. . . . If it is mushkil—that is, having no sex or its not being known whether it is a male or female—perform the tayammum. This is an extenuating circumstance because there is no one who can perform the ghusl on it. . . . This is parallel to the case of a woman who dies among men when there is no other woman; in such a case, the tayammum is performed. The case of the khuntha is like this. If the person performing the tayammum is a woman, there is no need for a rag [covering her hand]; likewise if it is a man who is related on the mother's side in the forbidden degree. But if he is unrelated to her, the tayammum must be performed with a rag [wrapped around the hand]. It is permitted to look at the face, and to expose it to the arms only, because it might be a woman and in this case, precautions must be taken with respect to those things that are [ordinarily] founded upon precaution, namely [to prevent] looking at the 'aura.

Al-Sarakhsi also recommended that the khuntha be buried like a girl, because this is closest to the sitr. Women are shrouded in more layers than men, but these excess layers are permitted for men when buried under special circumstances. Dubiousness of sex is one of those.

Even insisting that modesty be a priority did not preclude complications in negotiating gender in every situation. The requirements for dress for men and women making the pilgrimage (*hajj*) are, according to some schools of law, contradictory and raise the specter of committing two equally forbidden acts. [28] In the case of a khuntha past adolescence, some Hanafi jurists were confounded, because "a man in *ihram* [a state of ritual purity marked by putting on special clothes at the beginning of the pilgrimage] may not wear seamed clothing, while a woman in ihram is obliged to wear seamed clothing and is prohibited from going without a waistband and cloak." Had the risk involved a choice between committing a reprehensible act or a forbidden one, the judgment might well have been different. Al-Sarakhsi admitted that he did not know the answer because each possibility is equally forbidden. The hierarchy of human activities manifest in the scale of religious qualifications helps negotiate gender only when the two possibilities are not equally forbidden.

But some jurists resolved the problem by returning to the issue of modesty. They suggested that the khuntha dress as a woman because this is closer to the sitr, and her status in a state of ihram is founded on sitr, just as it is at other times. Moreover, al-Shaibani maintained, a man can wear seamed clothing during his ihram when there are extenuating circumstances ('udhr, lit. "excuse"), and "dubiousness of the matter of its sex is one of the gravest [extenuating] circumstances."

Protecting against violations of the prescriptions for modesty could create difficulties even in trying to determine the true sex of the khuntha mushkil. Jurists could invoke another boundary to mitigate the complicated circumstances, of slavery. The legal position of the female slave as the sexual property of her master permitted the negotiation of gender without the risk of violating the rules of modesty.[29]

> It is reprehensible [makruh] for a man or a woman to inspect [the khuntha] until he reaches puberty and the matter of his sex is cleared up, because the adolescent is in the position of the pubescent with respect to the obligation of sitr al-'aura. A person of one sex looking at a person of the opposite sex is not permitted. . . . Whether a man or a woman examines him, there is [still] the suspicion of looking at [the nakedness] of a person of the opposite sex (nazr khilaf al-jins). Instead, a slave girl who is knowledgeable in these matters is bought for him from his own money to examine him, so that he owns her by means of actual purchase. If the khuntha is a woman, then the person looking is a member of the same sex (nazr al-jins ila al-jins) and if it is a man, then it is a slave [mamluka] looking at her master.

That the determination of sex should have been in the hands of someone who, in every other respect, was a disprivileged person is remarkable. Slaves, for example, could not give testimony in an Islamic court. In spite of its legal implications and importance, the determination of true sex apparently took place outside the formal structures both of law and of medicine. Physicians do not seem to have been participants in this process.[30] Because it was permissible for a slave to look at her master, a khuntha was circumcised by a slave girl purchased for him either from his own funds or, if he was indigent, from the funds of the public treasury.[31]

The notion that the sex of the khuntha was a social concern was reinforced by the commitment of funds from the *bait al-mal* (public treasury) to buy the slave girl. The funds of the treasury were to be used for the public good, and what could be more in the interests of the public good than the knowledge of whether someone was male or female? The establishment of sex was not only important to determine the legal status of the khuntha, but also had implications for the position of others within the community. Even a single individual whose sex was not known threatened the social order. The sex of one person was inevitably tied to the status of others.

Whereas conditional gendering worked to preserve social order in many instances, establishing the true sex of the khuntha mushkil was the only remedy under other circumstances. This, as we have seen, was often impossible. If the sex of the khuntha could not be determined, some matters, including the status of other people, simply had to be held in abeyance.

> If it is said: if the first child you bear is a boy, you are divorced; or, to a slave, if the first child you bear is a girl, you are free, and then they each bear a khuntha mushkil, neither the divorce nor the manumission takes place until the child's sex has been determined, because whatever is contingent upon a condition cannot be carried out as long as the condition does not actually exist. With ishkal, the existence of the condition is not a certainty. This is parallel to the case where someone says: If I don't enter so-and-so's house, then his slave is free, and then he dies without it being known whether or not he entered. [In this case,] the manumission does not take place.[32]

Here, fulfilling the condition depended on establishing the sex of the child. Sometimes, however, the problem could be solved by employing a formula that allowed for both possibilities:

> If a man says, "All of my male slaves are free" or "All of my female slaves are free" and he has a slave who is a khuntha, the khuntha is not free until the matter of his sex has been determined. But if the master says the two statements together, then the khuntha is freed, because if they are combined then one of the two must apply to him; if they are pronounced separately, then it is not certain [whether or not it applies to the khuntha], whereas servitude is a certainty. Likewise, if a man says [to his wife], "If I buy a male slave, then you

are divorced," and he buys a khuntha, she is not divorced. But if he makes the two statements together ["If I buy a male slave or female slave, then you are divorced"] then she is divorced by the purchase of the khuntha because of the certainty of the condition.

The punishment of crimes like slander (*qadhf*) and theft was relatively simple, because the penalties did not differ for men and women, so the ambiguity of the khuntha's condition was irrelevant. But when the khuntha was the object of slander, the situation was quite different. The form of the accusation then depended on the sex of the accused.

A man slandering a khuntha is not subject to the *hadd* (Quranically prescribed punishment) because he is in the position of someone who slanders a lunatic or a *ratqa'* (a woman who is physically incapable of having intercourse). The slanderer deserves the punishment by virtue of relating a man to an act that he perpetrates, and by relating a woman to having made possible the perpetration of an act committed by someone other than her. Because of the ambiguity of the sex of the khuntha, the reason [for the punishment] cannot be determined: it is known which of the two acts the slanderer is attributing to the khuntha. If it is attribution of the perpetration of the act, and the khuntha is really a woman, then he has attributed an impossibility to her and thus stands in the position of a person who slanders a lunatic or a ratqa'. If he attributed it to making possible the commission of the act, and the khuntha is a man, it is something in whose domain he is powerless, and this does not call for the hadd. So it is not possible to undertake inflicting the hadd punishment while the matter of the khuntha's sex is ambiguous.

The analogy between the khuntha and the lunatic or idiot was not intended to reflect on the supposed intellectual capacity of the khuntha, but rather to demonstrate the impossibility of establishing precisely on what grounds the accusation was being made. In Islamic law, the exact terms of an accusation are essential to determining guilt or innocence. The nature of the accusation of zina is determined by the sex of the accused adulterer. Men are accused of perpetrating the act, women of being the parties who allow the action. The structure of these accusations reveals, in fact, that medieval Muslim jurists constructed sexuality differently for men and women. The concern of the jurists was to preserve not only the categories of male and female, but also a particular understanding of what those categories meant and implied. They wanted to preserve biological difference, but they understood that difference to have social meanings.[33]

This concern about the social implications of sex is nowhere clearer than in the reasoning displayed in a discussion of the legal validity of the marriage of a khuntha.[34] The validity of the marriage of a khuntha whose father had married it to a man or a woman could not be determined until its true sex was discovered. This was not, as we might think, because of concerns about inheritance, incest taboos, or modesty. It was because, as al-Sarakhsi states, the male entered marriage as a *malik* (owner), whereas the female became *mamluka* (owned) by virtue of marriage. This short statement communicates powerfully not only the necessity of knowing who is male or female, but what it means socially to be male or female. "If it manifests [at puberty] the signs ['alamat] of men and its father had previously married it to a woman, then [that] nikah is regarded as being valid from the time the father contracted it, because it has become clear that his action coincided with the actual status of the khuntha . . . but if the father had married it to a man and it then manifested the signs of male puberty, then it has become clear that the action did not coincide with the khuntha's actual status, and the nikah is null."[35]

What does al-Sarakhsi mean when he talks about the action coinciding with the actual status of the khuntha? That "actual status" is not merely the biological fact of one individual's sex, but the more important categorical fact that all men enter marriage as possessors and all women as possessions. The difficulty thus rests not only in the apparent sexual contradiction and impossibility of two men marrying each another, but also in the related social fact that two people cannot both enter a marriage as owners. One must enter as the malik (owner), one as the mamluka (owned). And this means that one must be male and one female.

With marriage, an institution founded on the fundamentally sexual relationship between men and women, the separate concerns that the jurists dealt with came together. Questions of sexual hierarchy, as we have just seen, of the protection of the male domain, modesty, and incest taboos, all converged. Sometimes, as with a question of modesty, the relationship established by marriage between husband and wife permitted the jurists to negotiate gender without risking violation of any taboo. Although the marriage of a khuntha to a woman, for example, could not be regarded as valid as long as the sex of the khuntha was unknown, it was still considered to be *mustaqim*, meaning that it did not involve anything forbidden. The jurists reasoned that if the khuntha turned out to be a woman, this meant only that two members of the same sex had seen one another and that the marriage itself was merely a blunder. If it turned out to be a man, this constituted the gaze of a woman upon her husband, and there was no prohibition against that.

The jurists were more concerned, however, that a marriage might violate the incest taboos. The prohibition of affinity could be established by a man kissing an adolescent girl, for example, in which case her mother and sisters would be forbidden to him in marriage. The rule extended to hermaphrodites, and the jurists were careful not to allow the possibility of contracting a marriage that might violate these taboos. "If a man kisses [the hermaphrodite] with lust, then he may not marry the khuntha's mother until the status of its sex has been determined. Because if it is female, his kissing her after [she] reaches adolescence establishes the prohibition of their becoming related by marriage, and the mother would be forbidden to him. This is the prevailing opinion, because it is preferable to forgo nikah with a woman who is permitted to him than to engage in nikah with a woman who is forbidden to him."

Yet the continual attempts to normalize the khuntha also intersected with a conservative thrust within Islamic law that attempts to preserve marriages. If a khuntha married a woman and failed to have intercourse with her, the same rules applied as would to an impotent man—that is, no action could be taken to dissolve the marriage until a period of one year had passed. This delay was intended as a waiting period to see whether the impediment to intercourse was temporary or permanent.[36]

What is striking about the laws concerning marriage of the hermaphrodite is the complete absence of the anxiety about homosexuality that pervades the European texts on hermaphroditism. Where early modern Europeans agonized over the dangers of homosexual activity in a union involving a hermaphrodite, medieval Muslims had other concerns: incest taboos and modesty. Although homosexuality is disapproved in Islam, it does not seem to have been a part of the hierarchy of concerns informing the negotiation of gender in law.[37]

If medieval Muslim jurists had an overriding anxiety, it was not any of the particular concerns—incest taboos, modesty, segregation, or even hierarchy—that organized their negotiation of gender, but maintaining the gendered integrity of their world as a whole. Their received view of the world was as a place with only two sexes, male and female. In this, medieval Muslims were closer to modern Americans than, say, to the ancient Greeks.[38] Their interpretation of the khuntha mushkil was embedded in this bipolar view of the world. A person with ambiguous genitalia or with no apparent sex might have been a biological reality, but it had no gender and, therefore, no point of entry into the social world: it was unsocialized.

In this world where everyone had to be gendered, a person without gender could not be socialized. Such a person could not participate in ritual, in itself a profoundly communal and social activity, until it had been artificially gendered. Hermaphrodites were usually gendered in the world of ritual as female.

An ungendered person could not enter into the gendered world of marriage and kinship: one was a son or a daughter, a brother or a sister, a husband or a wife. This is not to say that medieval Muslims denied the biological tie between a hermaphrodite and a blood relation any more than the biological fact of ambiguous sex. Rather, it means that this bond could not be interpreted and could not be invested with social meaning unless it was gendered. The social implications of ties of blood or milk depended on whether one was male or female, just as the very existence of a familial tie could depend on gender. This is why, for example, the jurists insisted that a man not marry the mother or sisters of a khuntha he had kissed. If the khuntha was female, that act created a relationship of affinity that prohibited marriage; if it turned out to be male, no such relationship existed. In either case, the man had kissed the khuntha, but the interpretation of that act as having social consequences or not, as constructing a relationship or not, was entirely dependent on gender.

Sex and gender were social matters with implications for whole groups—especially because of the complex familial and household networks that characterized medieval Islamic societies. The presence of one ungendered person, as we have seen, could compel an entire network to hold in abeyance questions of marriage, inheritance, and relation to one another. Even the efforts by the jurists to normalize the hermaphrodite in order to permit the continued formation of marital ties, for example, could not be entirely successful. Ultimately, the interpretation of those relationships was suspended until the sex of the hermaphrodite was known. In this world, the ungendered person was not only unsocialized, but could desocialize everyone else by compelling them to suspend the normal formation of social and familial ties.

I have tried to demonstrate how the ungendered body was unsocialized and the strategies that jurists used to gender and therefore socialize the body in the case of hermaphrodites. By doing this, they permitted them to carry out the daily business of life and death: prayer, pilgrimage, burial, marriage, inheritance, manumission. Even when decisions had to be held in abeyance, the fundamental categories of male and female and the social embodiment of those categories were preserved. What was at stake for medieval Muslims in gendering one ungendered body was, by implication, gendering the most important body: the social body.

Notes

1. There is a growing literature on sex and sexuality in Islamic societies. See Abdelwahab Bouhdiba, *Sexuality in Islam* (London: Routledge and Kegan Paul, 1985), and the collection *Society and the Sexes in Medieval Islam,* ed. Afaf Lutfi al-Sayyid-Marsot (Malibu, Calif.: Undena, 1979).

2. On the laws concerning unlawful intercourse, see Joseph Schacht, *Introduc-*

tion to Islamic Law (Oxford: Oxford University Press, 1964), 178ff. See also, for an analysis in terms of sexuality, Bouhdiba, *Sexuality in Islam*, 14–18, 32.

3. On *hadd* (Quranically prescribed punishments), see Schacht, *Islamic Law*, 178–87.

4. The best-known example of these two qualities is the story of Joseph and Zulaika (the Quranic version of the biblical story of Potiphar's wife, but different in a number of important ways). The Quranic version is in Sura 12 (Joseph); the biblical version in Genesis 39. Bouhdiba, *Sexuality in Islam*, 20–29, has an interesting analysis of the story and of a sequel to the story in Islamic tradition.

5. Quran 2:228, 4:38.

6. On women as fitna, see the numerous references compiled by Bouhdiba, *Sexuality in Islam*, 118ff. See also the provocative argument about the structure of male desire in Islamic societies by Fatna Sabbah, *Woman in the Muslim Unconscious* (Oxford: Pergamon, 1984). This attitude is expressed in the well-known Prophetic tradition, "I have not left any disorder (fitna) more damaging to men than women," cited widely in the hadith (Traditions) collections and lexicographies; see *Lisan al-'Arab*, s.v. "f-t-n."

The term *fitna* has a wide range of meanings in medieval Arabic and Islamic societies, where it refers to the civil wars of the early Islamic state and can mean either a political or a social threat to the internal order of the Islamic community. But it can also mean any sort of disruption or distraction from one's love of God: children, because of the numerous demands they make, are sometimes seen as a source of fitna. See, for example, the references collected by Aliah Schliefer, *Motherhood in Islam* (Cambridge: Islamic Academy, 1986), an interesting example of a modern Islamist study based on Quran and hadith.

7. On hermaphrodites in early modern Europe, see Lorraine Daston and Katharine Park, "Hermaphrodites in Renaissance France," *Critical Matrix* 1, no. 5 (1985): 1–19, and the numerous references cited there. On sexuality in general, see Danielle Jacquart and Claude Thomasset, *Sexuality and Medicine in the Middle Ages* (Oxford: Polity Press, 1988), and Ian Maclean, *The Renaissance Notion of Women* (Cambridge: Cambridge University Press, 1980).

8. There were, however, numerous ways to violate the boundary, including homosexual acts, adultery, transvestism, sodomy, and bestiality. These are labeled as abominations in the Quran and are punishable in different degrees of severity. Ritual impurity, incurred by such emission of fluids and discharges from the body as menstrual blood, semen, urine, and feces, constitutes another violation. But this impurity can be removed by performing ritual ablutions. Ritual impurity, as distinct from abominations, can be incurred even while engaged in licit sexual activities. For example, the act of sexual intercourse itself does not render one ritually impure, but rather the discharge of semen.

There were also men of altered sex in Islam. Eunuchs were particularly important in political and military affairs and are best known popularly as the ubiquitous guards of the harems. Eunuchs were created by castration outside the lands of Islam, and their legal status was clearly defined; they were slaves. Caliphs and sultans assembled large corps of personal guards composed entirely of eunuchs. Eunuchs have been studied primarily in the context of their military functions in the Mamluk corps by David Ayalon; see "The Eunuchs in the Mamluk Sultanate," in *The Mamluk Military Society* (London: Variorium Reprints, 1979), no. 3, and "The Eunuchs of Islam," in *Jerusalem Studies in Arabic and Islam* (Jerusalem: Magnes Press, 1979), 67–124. See also *Encyclopaedia of Islam,* new ed., s.v. "khasi."

For an entirely new approach to eunuchs as a distinct social group, see Shaun Elizabeth Marmon, "Eunuchs of the Prophet: Space, Time and Gender in Islamic Society" (Ph.D. diss., Princeton University, 1990).

9. Hermaphroditism is defined medically as a physical condition in which reproductive organ tissues from both sexes are present in a single individual. The true hermaphrodite has both ovarian and testicular tissue; the external genitalia usually have an essentially male or ambiguous appearance. Daston and Park, "Hermaphrodites in Renaissance France," 19 n. 56, cite an estimate of the current incidence of human hermaphroditism as 1:25,000 births.

There is a large medical literature on sexual differentiation and human hermaphroditism and the criteria to be used in sexing hermaphrodites. For two examples of this literature, separated by nearly two decades, see John Money, Joan G. Hampson, and John L. Hampson, "An Examination of Some Basic Sexual Concepts: The Evidence of Human Hermaphroditism," *Bulletin of the Johns Hopkins Hospital* 97 (1955): 301–19, and John Money and Anke A. Ehrhardt, *Man and Woman, Boy and Girl* (Baltimore: Johns Hopkins University Press, 1972). The second work is widely regarded in the medical community as the definitive statement on the heredity versus environment question on the development of sexual differentiation and identification. The book, which approaches this problem using studies of hermaphrodites and pseudohermaphrodites, is notable for its absolute insistence on gendering children as either male or female. It is a fascinating document of American bipolar attitudes toward sexual differentiation. Although Money and Ehrhardt chronicle the powerful influence of environment on sexual differentiation, they do not question the categories of male and female, nor do they analyze the ways in which American culture has constructed these categories. For a different approach that deals with the cultural construction of gender, see n. 24, below.

10. See B. F. Musallam, *Sex and Society in Islam* (Cambridge: Cambridge University Press, 1983), chap. 3.

11. Ibn al-Qayyim al-Jauziyya, *Tuhfat al-maudud bi-ahkam al-maulud* (fourteenth century; Damascus: Dar al-Kutub al-'Ilmiyya, 1971); also available in numerous inexpensive Cairo editions. See also 'Arib b. Sa'id al-Katib al-Qurtubi (eleventh century), *Kitab khalq al-janin wa-tadbir al-habala wa'l-mauludin* (Arabic with French translation, Le livre de la génération du foetus et le traitement des femmes enceintes et des nouveau-nés), chap. 4, p. 24 (Arabic); p. 32 (French).

12. The coherence between these various genres within the Islamic tradition has been meticulously reconstructed by Musallam, *Sex and Society.* For this interpretation of Quran 51:49, see al-Tabarsi, *Jawami' al-Jami'* (Beirut: Dar al-Adwa', 1985), 2:606–8, and the *Tafsir al-Jalalain* (Beirut: Dar al-Kutub al-'Ilmiyya, n.d.), 684.

13. Ibn Manzur, *Lisan al-'Arab,* s.v. "dh-k-r."

14. The legal material for this study is drawn largely from eleventh-century sources. One of the longest discussions of hermaphrodites is found in *al-Mabsut* of al-Sarakhsi (d. 1090), a lengthy encyclopaedic compendium of Hanafi law, one of

the four orthodox schools. Two other Hanafi texts, *al-Mukhtasar* of al-Quduri (d. 1036) and *al-Hidaya* of al-Marghinani (d. 1196), although much shorter, corroborate al-Sarakhsi. A fourth text, *al-Mabsut fi fiqh al-imamiyya* of Abu Ja'far al-Tusi (d. 1067), is a Shi'i work. The minor variations in al-Tusi's text result from slight differences in methodological principles between Sunni and Shi'i law; they do not reflect a different conception of the hermaphrodite. See Peter Freimark, "Zur Stellung des Zwitters in rabbinischen und islamischen Recht," *Zeitschrift der Deutschen Morgenländischen Gesellschaft* 120 (1970): 84–102. A more extensive study of the development of the law on hermaphrodites is Agostino Cilardo, "Historical Development of the Legal Doctrine Relative to the Position of the Hermaphrodite in the Islamic Law," *The Search* 7 (1986): 128–70. See also the few paragraphs devoted to hermaphrodites in Jean-Paul Charnay, *L'ambivalence dans la culture arabe* (Paris, 1967), 184–85. Thanks to Fedwa Malti-Douglas for this reference.

15. Edward Lane, *Arabic-English Lexicon*, s.v. "khanatha"; *Lisan al-'Arab* and *Muhit al-Muhit*, s.v. "khanatha"; al-Quduri, *al-Mukhtasar*; al-Sarakhsi, *al-Mabsut*. In *Muhit al-Muhit*, we find a fascinating use of the term *khuntha* applied to a particular grammatical case: "Some grammarians call [the word] to which the *ya' al-mutakallim* [a grammatical marker of the first person] is added 'khuntha,' claiming that it is not *mu'rab* [desinentially inflected] because it follows the *kasra* [one of the short vowels of Arabic] before the *ya'* and is not *mabni* [ending indeclinably] because of the absence of one of the reasons of indeclinability. This is like a person who is neither male nor female." In Arabic grammar a basic distinction is made between words that can be inflected and those that are indeclinable. Thus the comparison between a word that is neither declinable nor indeclinable and a person who is neither male nor female is an apt one.

16. The hadith is transmitted by Najm al-din b. Hafs al-Nafasi, *Talibat al-Talaba fi al-istilahat al-fiqhiyya* (Baghdad, A.H. 1211), 171, a twelfth-century dictionary of legal terms. See also al-Tusi, *al-Mabsut*, 114. All block quotations, unless otherwise noted, are from al-Sarakhsi, *al-Mabsut* (Beirut, 1986), vol. 30, chapters "K. fara'id al-khuntha" and "Kitab al-khuntha," 91–114.

17. This was the suggestion of Avicenna in his *Canon* (al-Qanun), vol. 2, bk. 3, p. 603. I am grateful to Basim Musallam for the reference.

18. Al-Sarakhsi based this on the legal principle of "the preponderance of precedence in the event of opposition or equivalence." In defining sex, as in determining the proper course of action in any given circumstance, previously established legal principles were applied. No new principles of law were introduced to accommodate the khuntha.

19. The Hanafi jurists Abu Yusuf and Muhammad al-Shaibani accepted this, but Abu Hanifa rejected the argument on two counts: first, because the quantity of urine indicated the width of the *makhraj* (the mabal, the urinary orifice) and no consideration was given to that; second, because large or small quantity would be manifest in the urine itself, not the mabal, which was the distinguishing organ. These opinions were reported also by al-Quduri and al-Marghinani.

20. See *Encyclopaedia of Islam*, new ed., s.v. "baligh."

21. As al-Sarakhsi said, if sex was attributed to the khuntha on the basis of urination from one of the mabals and it then urinated from the other one, the

judgment "is not changed by urination from the other organ." He likened this person to a man who presented evidence for his marriage to a woman and was awarded the judgment, or to a judgment made about the lineage of a child on the basis of certain evidence. The presentation of different evidence after the judgment would not reverse it, following from the legal principle of "the preponderance of precedence in the event of opposition or equivalence."

22. On one occasion, however, al-Sarakhsi mentioned that if none of the signs appeared, the absence of breasts would indicate (legally) that it was a man. This attribution of male sex on the basis of the absence of breasts is unique among these texts.

23. The terms *mushkil* and *ishkal* are both derived from the triliteral root *sh-k-l.* As used in the texts, *ishkal* seems to be a general term for ambiguity and is interchangeable with *ishtibah* (dubiousness), whereas *mushkil* seems to be a technical legal term as well as a general term.

24. There is a large literature on the cultural construction of gender. Readers will find a good introduction to the topic in Sherry Ortner and Harriet Whitehead, *Sexual Meanings: The Cultural Construction of Gender and Sexuality* (Cambridge: Cambridge University Press, 1981). See also Caroline Walker Bynum, Steven Harrell, and Paula Richman, eds., *Gender and Religion: On the Complexity of Symbols* (Boston: Beacon, 1986). The introduction by Bynum is particularly useful. On gender in historical analysis, see Joan W. Scott, "Gender: A Useful Category of Historical Analysis," *American Historical Review* 91 (1986): 1053–75. These works all provide excellent introductions and voluminous references in the notes.

25. See Schacht, *Islamic Law,* 169–75, for a brief introduction to the topic.

26. When no clear evidence could be presented in a case, judges were permitted to extract oaths from the parties involved. For a clear explanation of legal procedure, including the presentation of testimony by witnesses and the use of oaths, see Schacht, *Islamic Law,* 188–98, and *Encyclopaedia of Islam,* new ed., s.v. "da'wa" (action at law), "kadi." Determining who is the plaintiff and who the defendant in a case is particularly important in Islamic law because the rules of evidence and presumption are different for the two parties. This determination was often the crux of a particular case.

27. Modesty, and the related issues of segregation and veiling, have received much attention recently from feminist scholars. See Valerie J. Hoffman-Ladd, "Polemics on the Modesty and Segregation of Women in Contemporary Egypt," *International Journal of Middle East Studies* 19 (1987): 23–50; and Fatima Mernissi, *Beyond the Veil: Male-Female Dynamics in a Modern Muslim Society* (Cambridge, Mass.: Schenkman, 1975).

28. When a Muslim pilgrim reaches the point at which he or she crosses over into the territory approaching Mecca, the site of the Ka'ba, he or she enters a state of ritual purity. No sexual relations are allowed at any time and special attire must be donned by both men and women. See *Encyclopaedia of Islam,* new ed., s.v. "ihram," for details.

29. For an excellent introduction to the topic of female slavery in Islam, see Shaun Marmon, "Concubinage, Islamic," in *Dictionary of the Middle Ages.* The master's sexual rights over his female slave, although broad, were not unlimited.

The same prohibitions regarding incest applied to the master and female slave as to husband and wife.

Gender difference is fundamental to the different conception in Islamic law of male and female slavery. Unlike the male slave, the female slave's primary role was sexual. The formula "Your sexual organ is free" thus functioned legally to manumit a female slave, but not a male slave.

30. In medieval and early modern Europe, physicians were integral to the process of determining sex. See Datson and Park, "Hermaphrodites in Renaissance France."

31. See Ibn al-Qayyim al-Jauziyya, *Tuhfat al-maudud bi-ahkam al-maulud*, which includes a long chapter on circumcision.

32. Divorce upon the fulfillment of a specific condition is permitted, though discouraged, in Islam. See Schacht, *Islamic Law*, 163–66.

33. This is not to say that they thought, as modern feminism does, that the science of biology itself was socially or culturally constructed, but that they considered the boundary between male and female to be important because it implied a difference in social anatomy.

34. Concluding a marriage contract in the presence of witnesses is the only legal act required in constituting a marriage in Islam. There are impediments to marriage that result from close blood or milk ties, and so marriage is forbidden with any of the incest-forbidden relatives (*maharim*), with the maharim of one's wet nurse, or with women who are related to each other in forbidden degrees by consanguinity, affinity, or fosterage.

Marriage contracts may be concluded on behalf of minors by their guardians or fathers, and these marriages are consummated when the children reach puberty. Even without consummation, however, these are valid marriages and establish the rights of inheritance between husband and wife. All of these rules apply equally to the khuntha.

35. Determining whether the marriage was defective or null affected the possible inheritance by either spouse.

36. This conservative tendency with respect to marriage must be taken into consideration when trying to understand the divorce laws. The popular conception that divorce by repudiation is accomplished in Islam easily or without consequences is misleading. Although technically possible, it is disapproved of, and numerous Prophetic Traditions (hadiths) denounce the practice.

37. The available material on homosexuality in Islam is limited at present. The basic legal position is outlined in the article "liwat" in *Encyclopaedia of Islam*, new ed. References are ordinarily scattered; see James A. Bellamy, "Sex and Society in Islamic Popular Literature," in al-Sayyid-Marsot, *Society and the Sexes*, 36–40; S. D. Goitein, "The Sexual Mores of the Common People," ibid., 59–60, who mentions the cult of the ephebes among the Jewish intelligentsia of Muslim Spain; and the more expanded discussion in Goitein, *A Mediterranean Society: The Jewish Communities of the Arab World as Portrayed in the Documents of the Cairo Geniza* (Berkeley and Los Angeles: University of California Press, 1988), vol. 5, chap. X.B.5, "Sex." John Boswell, *Christianity, Social Tolerance, and Homosexuality* (Chicago: University of Chicago Press, 1980), 194ff., compares medieval Islamic and Christian attitudes.

38. For a fascinating discussion of the common-sense view of different cultures

toward intersexuality, see Clifford Geertz, "Common Sense as a Cultural System," in his *Local Knowledge: Further Essays in Interpretive Anthropology* (New York: Basic Books, 1983), 80–84, and Robert Edgerton, "Pokot Intersexuality: An East African Example of the Resolution of Sexual Incongruity," *American Anthropologist* 66, no. 6, pt. 1 (1964): 1288–99.

II

The

Mamluk

Period

6

Manners and Customs of Fourteenth-Century Cairene Women: Female Anarchy versus Male Shar'i Order in Muslim Prescriptive Treatises

HUDA LUTFI

> Some of our worthy ancestors [*al-salaf*] may God be pleased with them said: "A woman is permitted three exits: one to the house of the husband when she is married to him; one when her parents die; and one when she is carried to her grave." By God, listen to this *salafi* advice, and observe the kind of chaos and corruption caused by women's frequent exits nowadays.
> —Ibn al-Hajj

Egyptian Mamluk society in the mid-fourteenth century enjoyed relative economic prosperity and political stability.[1] Like other medieval societies, however, it experienced a large share of poverty and physical pain. Both rich and poor suffered from sickness, premature death, and low life expectancies. In response to the hazards of recurrent diseases and plagues, contemporary medical practices were largely supplemented by popular superstitious belief in the power of amulets, holy relics, and preservatives to bring about effective escape or relief from such common disasters. Here, the all-important role of the dead or living *sufi* (mystic) saint was sustained by popular belief that saint and shrine pilgrimage could cure poverty and sickness and relieve the stressful conditions of daily life. Hence saint shrines in urban communities to which pilgrims, especially women, brought their supplications became ubiquitous. Daily routines and human difficulties also were transcended through the celebration of numerous religious festivities and tomb-visiting rituals, which became characteristic features of everyday female life in Egyptian cities.

I should like to thank Lila Abu-Lughod for the valuable remarks she made on this chapter.

In their prescriptive literature and sermons, Muslim salafi scholars made heavy and repeated attacks on these popular religious customs.[2] Indeed, the scattered knowledge we have of such popular practices is primarily due to these Muslim scholars, who denounced them as harmful innovations (bid'a). This is not to say that all religious scholars struggled against these popular practices. In his prescriptive treatise al-Madkhal, Ibn al-Hajj repeatedly blamed religious scholars (ulama) for the religious ignorance of the masses.[3] Appalled by the corrupt practices of the commoners (al-'awamm) and the vile habits of women, as well as by the indifference and decadence of the Egyptian religious scholars, in his four-volume treatise Ibn al-Hajj painstakingly demonstrated to his religious colleagues the preponderance of innovations and abominations in Egyptian Mamluk society, reminding them repeatedly of their sacred religious duty to order the good and forbid the evil. Like a good Muslim scholar, Ibn al-Hajj took on himself the task of writing a treatise that would expose and denounce these popular practices, prescribing proper shar'i (legal) rules in their place. Our scholar typically viewed any form of behavior not enjoined by the Quran and without precedence in the sunna of the Prophet and his companions to be a vile bid'a that should be stamped out.

He especially deplored the immodest mingling of men and women on any religious or social occasion. Ibn al-Hajj, like other salafi scholars, saw a clear division between the public domain of men and the private domain of women. Neither should intrude into the other, and women's proper place should be restricted to the private space of the household. Ibn al-Hajj's firm belief in the exclusion of women from the outside world of men was informed by a sexual ideology that viewed the presence of the female body as threatening to the order of the male world. Accordingly, any infringement of these spatial restrictions was considered by Ibn al-Hajj to be an act promoting anarchy or chaos.

Nowhere can we better document the fear of the female so typical of most formal Islamic discourse than in Ibn al-Hajj's treatise. In a revealing statement, he tells us how the feminine should be viewed as the symbol of corruption, defying shar'i order: "The origin of all chaos and corruption in society is one of three things: neglecting the advice of religious scholars on matters regarding proper Muslim behavior; the infiltration of base customs and traditions to the extent that they become the accepted religious practices; and acceptance of the opinion of those whom the Lawgiver, may God be pleased with him, has regarded as lacking in religion and reason [that is, women]."[4] Ibn al-Hajj thus attributed the chaos in society to the prevalence of female ways. If we examine his cultural biases, we see that he considered women to combine all three causes of social anarchy: they are ignorant because they do not seek religious knowledge; they are carriers of vile traditions; and this is due to their mental and physical deficiencies. In reiterating this view through-out his treatise, Ibn al-Hajj quotes the notorious tradition attributed to the Prophet: "You are lacking in mind and religion."[5] He tells us that men are less vulnerable to religious ignorance, not only because they are inher-ently superior in mind and body, but because "men have more frequent contact with religious scholars than women. This is so because women are secluded and have been reared in ignorance, hence they are more prone to adopt innumerable vile habits contrary to the shari'a."[6] To rid women of their ignorance, Muslim religious scholars must dedicate more time to the task of educating them. Ironically, Ibn al-Hajj, who was partic-ularly rigid about the rules of female exit, made an exception here: "It is the duty of the husband to inform his wife of the relevant religious rules when she is ignorant of them, but if he was ignorant of them himself, he should seek someone to teach him, or he should permit her to go out to seek her religious education."[7]

Like other Muslim religious and historical literature, Ibn al-Hajj's writ-ings were inspired by a pious mentality that correlated the prevalence of unislamic practices to the inevitable occurrence of disasters, as a sign of divine wrath.[8] Hence he warns Egyptian Muslims, especially women, that if they continue to indulge in their unislamic practices and extrava-gances they are bound to bring down Allah's punishment. This mentality seems to have been exaggerated when women were involved, for they were often chosen as easy scapegoats by religious scholars and rulers in order to control female public behavior and explain away the real causes behind political crises and catastrophes. We are told, for example, that during the famine and plague of A.D. 1438 the Mamluk sultan Barsbay conferred with the religious scholars about the causes behind these catas-trophes, and they agreed that the primary cause was the appearance of women in the streets. A decree was immediately issued ordering women to stay home![9]

But it was the earlier government of the Fatimid caliph al-Hakim that was known for its notorious hostility to women's independence and mobility outside their private spatial boundaries. The Mamluk historian al-Maqrizi makes repeated references to al-Hakim's decrees forbidding women to go out, and it is no coincidence that these anti-women state injunctions were issued at times of crisis: droughts, famines, plagues, and inflation. Women were ordered to stay home and were forbidden to walk in the markets, to visit tombs of relatives or saints, and to go to public baths; shoemakers were forbidden to make shoes for women.[10] After much search for any sign of female protest against these measures of state control, I found only a short anecdotal reference to an incident that supposedly took place in response to al-Hakim's hostility toward women. We are told that "one day the inhabitants of the Egyptian capital came across an effigy made in the image of a veiled woman holding a piece of paper insulting and cursing al-Hakim because he forbade women from walking in the streets."[11] For Ibn al-Hajj, it was not simply women's manners and vile habits that needed to be strictly controlled to save the moral integrity of the Muslim community; he considered commoners and religious minorities, whose corrupting habits should be fought by good Muslims, also to be social elements of chaos.[12]

To the feminist social historian, Ibn al-Hajj's treatise is important in two respects. First, it allows us to explore the discrepancy between theoretical and actual restrictions on women. Throughout his treatise Ibn al-Hajj systematically demonstrates the existing discrepancies between the ideal and the real in medieval Egyptian society, showing that prescriptive religious literature should not necessarily be taken as a reflection of reality. Lower- and middle-class Egyptian Muslim women seem to have paid little attention to the religious restrictions prescribed in this literature. Egyptian women participated actively in public life and devised strategies that enabled them to do so. Two classic female strategies that appear to have been commonly used were the denial of sexual pleasure to and the threat of separation from a husband who tried to exercise control over a strong-willed wife. Cultural and religious restrictions, however, did influence female behavior, most evident in modest dress and in the efforts to separate women from men physically. Second, in denouncing the existing manners and customs of Egyptian Muslims, Ibn al-Hajj inadvertently provides the historian with impressive data on the everyday life of Egyptian men and women in the cities of Cairo and Misr. Most interesting is his focus on the details concerning the lives of ordinary and obscure people in Egyptian Mamluk society, which are systematically ignored in the historical literature. But to what extent can we rely on Ibn al-Hajj's historical data? This is a difficult question, since most of the information he gives cannot be found elsewhere in the historical literature. Recognizing that Ibn al-Hajj's description reflects the viewpoint of a Muslim religious scholar who looked upon women's behavior as dangerous, we can nevertheless read his account against the grain to make it reveal a description of Cairo life of the period, a picture corroborated by other accounts, like that of al-Maqrizi.

The researcher faces a challenge in trying to make sense of the scattered and irregular data found in *al-Madkhal*. Working to discover and reconstruct the female experience in medieval Muslim culture, I use gender as the central category of analysis, according to which historical data are reconstructed and refocused. What did Cairene women do in their daily life? What was the nature of male-female interaction? Besides these important questions, the conception of the opposition between the public and private domains is used to clarify our understanding of the female experience, and to show how far women abided by the restrictive rules of space. Working with *al-Madkhal* as a prescriptive treatise may also aid us in examining the use of gender to impose order and stability in a Muslim society. Here, women were typically viewed as perpetuators of anarchy, whose power needed to be broken by the shari'a.

Like other medieval urban cultures, Egyptian Muslim culture viewed the basic role of women to be within the boundaries of the household, caring for the family and managing household matters. Among the middle and upper-middle classes, this view was reinforced by an ideology of strict segregation, where the female was asked not to overstep her spatial boundaries. Ibn al-Hajj was a strong protagonist of this view, as is evident in his bitter criticism of urban Egyptian women, who did not adhere strictly to these rules: women belonging to the lower, middle, and upper-middle orders were often seen crossing the private boundaries of the home into the public world of men. In this regard, our scholar repeatedly admonishes the Egyptian man, be it husband, father, brother, or religious scholar, to prevent anarchic behavior by women on the street: he explains to them the rules of going out (*adab al-khuruj*) according to the sunna. A woman should go out only for a necessity, and if she does, she should go in long and unattractive garments. If women walk in the streets, they should walk close to the walls of houses, in order to make way for men. In accordance with the Prophet's saying, Ibn al-Hajj admonishes men to make the road difficult and narrow for women, and he exclaims: "Look how these norms have been neglected in our days. . . . She goes out in the streets as if she were a shining bride, walking in the middle of the road and jostling men. They have a manner of walking that causes the pious man to withdraw closer to the walls, in order to make way for them. Other men, however, would jostle and humor them deliberately."[13] Heedless of such warnings, women went to the markets to purchase their needs, and they seem to have done that regularly on two important market days: the *suq* (market) of Cairo on Mondays, and the suq of Misr on Sundays.[14] The favorite spots of women were the jeweler's shop, that of the cloth merchant, and that of the shoemaker. According to Ibn al-Hajj's description, women would sit in shops for several hours, conversing and humoring the shop owners, hoping for a good bargain.[15] In this regard, a long piece of advice is delivered to the shopkeeper, warning him of female corrupting behavior:

> And he must be careful when a woman comes to buy something, to look at her behavior, for if she was one of those women dressed up in delicate clothes, exposing her wrists, or some of her adornments, and speaking in a tender and soft voice, he should leave the selling transaction and give her his back until she leaves the shop peace-

fully. . . . This is a great affliction nowadays, for one rarely sees the shop of the cloth merchant without the presence of women dressed in delicate clothes which expose their adornment, and behaving as if they were with their husbands, or members of their family.[16]

To secure their household needs, women of the city also dealt with male peddlers who facilitated selling and buying transactions in residential areas distant from the market. Even though Ibn al-Hajj praises the peddler for transporting necessities to the women in their houses, thus protecting the *harim* (wives) of Muslims, he criticizes women's casual behavior in dealing with these peddlers.[17] The transport of such important items as water, milk, oil, flour, and flax entailed regular visits to homes, which in turn must have led to the development of some degree of familiarity between the peddler and his female client.[18] Ibn al-Hajj insists that rules should be followed: women should not be alone with a peddler; should not come to the door unveiled, as was their custom; and should not get involved in long arguments over selling and buying.[19] "And it is a great wonder that many of their men, who are supposed to be superior in mind and piety, arrive to their houses to find the peddler of flax, or whatever, discussing with their women matters regarding buying and selling. And the men do not forbid what is going on . . . and their answer to this is to say: 'I do not accuse my wife of anything, because I trust her and do not believe that infidelity crosses her mind.'"[20] In defense of their casual behavior, middle- and upper-middle-class women produced a typical class argument: to these women, such men were of an inferior status and therefore ineligible as sexual partners.[21] To this argument Ibn al-Hajj retorts: "They invent their own rules, arguing that men such as the flax seller and the water-carrier are not men to be ashamed of . . . they are not ashamed of slaves or commoners either, because they view them as being too inferior in status. This attitude has become widespread among many women nowadays."[22]

Within their private households, women came into constant contact with neighbors and relatives of both sexes. Ibn al-Hajj admonishes men to forbid women from socializing together, as they customarily do, for fear that they will corrupt one another. Moreover, he criticizes women's free mingling with male relatives and neighbors, thus breaking the rules of sexual segregation within the household: "They constantly mingled with male cousins and neighbors, they would joke and converse with one another in isolation; as for the male and female neighbors, and those raised together since childhood, you cannot find much difference in female treatment between the husband and these men, except in sexual matters."[23]

In the daily household scene, women seem to have been holders of power in domestic affairs. To denounce their un-shar'i ways, Ibn al-Hajj relates some of their daily habits in the house. He expresses great suspicions regarding the common practice of Cairene women whereby the wife reserves for the husband his special food and eating utensils, which are not to be used by other members of the family. Our scholar considered this contrary to the sunna, which requires that eating meals should be an occasion shared by the whole family, but he also feared that the practice was a subterfuge by which women could perform magical artifices against their unpliable husbands.[24] Female superstitious beliefs also added special significance and order to women's daily chores and practices. "On each day they performed specific chores that could not be undertaken on other days, and they believed that any infringements of these arrangements might bring about bad luck." On Saturdays, for example, women would not purchase or cook fish, buy soap or wash clothes, or go to the public bath. Sunday was a day of rest; women performed no domestic chores on that day. These customs, Ibn al-Hajj remarks, were copied from Jews and Christians and were hence unislamic. On Wednesdays, milk was not allowed to be purchased; on Mondays, Tuesdays, and Thursdays, women performed the necessary domestic chores and purchased necessities for the household. On Fridays, they rested from spinning and combing flax, probably to spend more time with their families when the men were off from work as well.[25]

Believing that the performance of specific domestic practices on special religious occasions would bring about prosperity and health for their families, Cairene women followed these practices closely. The purchasing and burning of incense, for example, was a must on the feast of 'Ashura; they believed this to bring blessing for the whole year, cure sickness, and ward off the evil eye.[26] Similarly, women bought milk on the eve of the Islamic new year to ensure household prosperity. On equinoctial occasions, both men and women, relatives and neighbors, picked camomile flowers, reciting magical formulas while cutting the plants. Wrapped in paper dyed with saffron, the camomile was then kept in a box in the house to bring affluence to all family members.[27] Another domestic tradition, practiced by some women, was the refusal to do any housecleaning during the absence of a male member of the family, in the belief that if they did, the traveler might never return.[28] These and other female daily habits most probably were carried over from Egyptian or Coptic traditions, which Ibn al-Hajj considered harmful innovations, but which may have served the important function of giving women a feeling of more security and control over their daily lives.

In addition to their regular domestic chores as mothers and wives, lower-class Cairene women, especially the older ones, contributed a significant service to the households of the middle and upper-middle classes: they safeguarded the rules of sexual segregation and the boundaries of female territory, so valued by Muslim cultural norms. Ironically, Ibn al-Hajj, who repeatedly criticizes Egyptian women for being out too often in the streets, commends the services that female peddlers contributed in protecting the chastity of the harim: "And there must be female peddlers to pass by houses in order to carry the dough to the baker, so as to protect the harim of the Muslims."[29] Lower-class women performed other valuable services to the harims of urban households: they were the official mourner (*al-na'iha*), the undertaker (*al-ghasila*), the midwife (*al-qabila*), the barber (*al-sani'a*), the bath attendant (*al-ballana*), and the experienced female doctor.[30] Uninhibited by the strict rules of female segregation, these women moved around in the public space of men. We are told that they even used the precincts of mosques to sell their yarn, shouting and bargaining with their male dealers for a better price. Ibn al-Hajj complains that the women abused the sanctity of the mosque, "for the house of Allah is not a place for selling goods, or a place to bring children who will defile its purity."[31]

Throughout *al-Madkhal*, Ibn al-Hajj stresses repeatedly that the Muslim man should be responsible for the proper shar'i behavior of his females, and he complains that in actuality women were left unguided and unrestricted, inventing and following their own ways.[32] He says that these unislamic manners can be observed in the female customs associated with wedding celebrations, divorces, eating, sexual habits, rituals of purity, modes of dress and adornment, birth and death rituals, as well as in social and religious festivities. "As for what they did in wedding ceremonies, do not ask about the innumerable violations that they invented, for what they invented in childbirth is a drop in a bucket, compared to what they do in marriage ceremonies."[33] Unfortunately, Ibn al-Hajj gives us only a few details of what women did in marriage celebrations. Women indulged in excessive gaiety, producing their trilling cries of joy, clapping, dancing, and singing to the beats of the tambourine.[34] Moreover, wedding celebrations involved drinking wine, listening to unveiled female singers, and the presence of unveiled women during the festivities.[35]

Of divorce practices prevalent in urban Egyptian society, Ibn al-Hajj mentions only those that violated the shari'a. He severely criticizes the widespread practice of repeated divorces, exceeding the Islamic legal limit of three consecutive divorces permitted to the husband. He says that certain men performed the function of a *muhallil* (husband of convenience) for a fixed period and fee, after which the wife could go back to her former but real husband.[36] According to Ibn al-Hajj, mother, daughter, and granddaughter solicited the services of the same muhallil in order to go back to their respective husbands, who had divorced them three consecutive times. "Here is yet another example of female chaotic behavior, which defies all the rules of the shari'a, for how can it be that mother, daughter and granddaughter are permitted to marry the same man."[37] When disputes between husband and wife got too complicated, women resorted to the help of the judge, who held his court in the precincts of the quarter's mosque. Prior to the court hearing, women waited inside the mosque, discussing their cases with their agents and husbands. Here again, Ibn al-Hajj states that women overstepped their boundaries, "for the mosque is surely not a place for marital squabbles."[38] Divorced or widowed women were more vulnerable, because of their repeated exploitation by the male witnesses testifying to their marriage contracts. Ibn al-Hajj tells us that a widow was often forced to pay the witness any sum he demanded so that he might agree to testify as to the correct sum of her deferred dowry.[39]

When it came to sexual matters, Ibn al-Hajj placed the onus on the man, not the woman, for the female was viewed as a passive body that needed to be sexually satisfied by the man. Contrary to the common habit of sleeping in ordinary clothes, he advises both man and wife to sleep in the nude, as indicated in the sunna.[40] This, he argues, gives pleasure to the woman and allows for greater sexual gratification. Ibn al-Hajj criticizes the sexual attitude of the Egyptian man, who commonly approaches his wife without warning and achieves his sexual satisfaction without paying attention to her sexual desires. Sunni precedent requires sensitivity in sexual matters from the husband. Ibn al-Hajj states that although female sexuality is stronger than that of the male, it is difficult for the man to sense her sexual desire because of her *haya'* (modesty). But the wife's desire, he argues, can be sensed from her special adornments: her makeup, perfume, and finery. Ibn al-Hajj also severely condemned the common practice of anal sex. According to the sunna, this is almost equivalent to the sin of homosexuality.[41] Moreover, anal sex gives no satisfaction to the wife, thus leaving her sexually ungratified, which in turn makes her a potential sexual threat. The main concern of Ibn al-Hajj here was that female sexuality left unsatisfied within the boundaries of marriage would result in sexual chaos in Muslim society; therefore, the woman's sexual desires must be satisfied within marriage.

Both husbands and wives apparently practiced the habit of conjuring the mental image of a beloved during the sexual act and imagining the beloved, and not the spouse, to be their sexual partner. Ibn al-Hajj believed this practice to be tantamount to adultery, which would inevitably lead to much sexual chaos. He blamed the practice on the mingling between men and women in Egyptian urban society and on the habit of indulging in sexual talk in male and female gatherings.[42] He describes another sexual behavior that seems to have been commonly practiced by some Egyptian wives: "This is an ugly and base habit; when the wife comes to bed, she takes something from the husband, most probably in addition to her *nafaqa* (legal allowance), which varies according to his financial situation, and is paid as a bed fee (*haqq al-firash*)."[43] If we accept what Ibn al-Hajj tells us about the sexual insensitivity of husbands, however, we can perhaps understand why some wives demanded a "bed fee" before going to bed with their husbands.

Female rituals of purity were a subject of great concern to our scholar, and in Islamic culture these are given much importance because they are closely related to female sexuality and religiosity. The sunna of the Prophet prohibited sexual intercourse and demanded abstention from religious obligations during the period of menstruation. Resumption of sexual intercourse and religious duties after termination of the menstrual period then entailed an elaborate and formal ritual of purification. Ibn al-Hajj viewed the ritual of female purity with utmost seriousness, and to correct the faulty and confused rituals of purity practiced by Cairene women, he wrote two long sections on the proper rituals of purity to be followed by men and women.[44] Our scholar observes that Egyptians in general did not really care about religious formalities, but more about worldly matters. Both men and women were to blame: "It is a wonder to see that most of them pay a thousand to buy a house or to build one themselves, but they do not bother to build a space for ablution, let alone washing. . . . The women encourage the men to neglect this duty, as though it was a conspiracy between them."[45] As a result, says Ibn al-Hajj, a woman does not have the place or utensils to perform her proper ablutions after the sexual act or menstruation. Furthermore, women who were too shy to go to the public bath to perform their ablutions ended up neglecting their religious duties of fasting and praying.[46] Ibn al-Hajj argues, however, that even women who performed their rituals of ablution did so in a faulty manner. Some women, for example, believed that the menstrual period lasted for one week, and whether the blood disappeared or not, they proceeded to perform their ablution ritual and resumed their religious duties and normal sexual relations. Ibn al-Hajj considered this a heretical practice, for it contradicted the rules of Allah and his Prophet, and a Muslim was in danger of losing his religion if he had sexual intercourse with a menstruating woman. Equally condemned was the common female practice of purification in which the woman waited until her menstrual blood disappeared, on the following day bought her soap, the day after washed her clothes, and on the third day performed her ablution and prayers. According to Ibn al-Hajj, such a practice allowed women to waste two days of prayers.[47] He further criticized the ignorance of women who went to the public baths to perform their major ritual of ablution without performing the ritual of pronouncing *al-niyya al-shar'iyya* (the shar'i intention), which should accompany the act of ablution. İbn al-Hajj also severely criticized the common female belief that a woman could not attain purity after menstruation unless she washed the interior of her vulva. This was not only contradictory to the sunna, he states, but was also sexually corrupting because it encouraged the woman to touch a highly excitable area of her body.[48]

Women, we are told, were also inconsistent when it came to rituals of purity during the obligatory fast. Some went on fasting in spite of their menstruation, arguing that it was more difficult to make up their lost period of fasting at a time when everybody else was eating normally. Others broke their fast for the first three days of their menstrual period only, claiming that after the third day fasting becomes obligatory, despite the presence of menstrual blood. Furthermore, women who fasted during menstruation did not always perform their regular prayers. "And when I ordered one of the women to perform her prayers, she exclaimed, 'do you find me an old woman?' As if prayers were not an obligation on the young." Ibn al-Hajj even criticized women who adopted stricter but not necessarily Islamic measures of purity, as they went so far as to restrain themselves from touching food or coming near the pantry.[49]

Female nudity in the public baths also upset Ibn al-Hajj: "When women performed their ablution, Muslim, Jewish and Christian women pranced about the place naked, and women there are so bold as to scold the more timid females who wished to cover from the navel to the knees."[50] To prevent such chaotic female behavior, women were told not to perform their major ritual of purity in the public bath, but to perform it instead in their homes. Typically, Ibn al-Hajj considered all these female chaotic practices a result of the ignorance of women, who seem to have been continually inventing their own religious rituals to suit their daily patterns of work and socializing.

Muslim prescriptive literature viewed the female body primarily as the repository of male sexual pleasure, and hence a source of *fitna* (temptation) that should be concealed; Ibn al-Hajj's treatise is no exception. Hence, female clothes were seen to serve the crucial function of concealment. Properly concealed, women might cease to be a threat to the social order. Yet female clothes were also viewed as serving the function of adornment for the husband's sexual pleasure. Thus, in contrast to men, women were legally permitted to use such luxurious items of adornment as gold, silver, and silk: "For it is as the *hadith* stated, they are deficient in mind and religion, and therefore, they are permitted to use silk, gold, silver and other such items because of their *nuqsan* [deficiency]. As for the man, he is the repository of perfection, God has perfected and adorned him, so he is not allowed to indulge in the adornment permitted to those who are deficient." Men were also warned not to emulate women in their mode of dress lest they become effeminate: dress style should enhance the segregation between the sexes.[51] Ibn al-Hajj's descriptions of female modes of dress in Cairo give us an insight into how women actually dressed there, and to what extent Cairene women abided by the Islamic rules of female dress. The basic female dress in Cairo was the long and loose *thaub* or *qamis* (chemise), under which long and baggy *sirwals* (baggy trousers) were worn; the head and neck were normally covered by long and ample headcloths. But Ibn al-Hajj tells us that instead of the wide and ample clothes that were designed to conceal the contours of the female body, Cairene women wore a tight and short chemise, which defined the body and was contrary to the prescribed shar'i dress. "Women wore the short and tight chemise which only reached the knees; as for the trousers, worn under the chemise, these were worn far below the navel, exposing that part to the eye, unless the upper garment was made of thick and ample material."[52] But it seems that women wore their trousers only outside the house; at home they wore just the chemise. Ibn al-Hajj considered this to be defying the shari'a, which prohibits the woman from exposing the forbidden parts of her body to anyone but her husband. The wide short sleeves were another bid'a invented by Cairene woman. Ibn al-Hajj exclaims, "if a woman is dressed in this manner, and she raises her arms, her underpits and her breasts are exposed, which is the behavior of wicked women who wish to expose their bodies in public (*al-mutabarrijat*)."[53] Equally criticized were women who stood on the roof-tops, dressed in the short chemise without trousers. Ibn al-Hajj also condemned the fashionable '*imama* (turban), for it was not only ugly but contrary to the shari'a as well, because it concealed the woman's beauty from her husband and prevented her from performing her proper ablutions.

Ibn al-Hajj tells us that the female body most desired by men was the voluptuous and fleshy body, and to secure male attention Cairene women seemed to work hard at nurturing a plump body. To do so, some women abstained from Ramadan fasting; some families went so far as to discourage their young unmarried daughters from fasting in order to attract more male suitors. Ibn al-Hajj states that female obsession with corpulence led some women to indulge in incessant eating, even if they were not hungry. In addition to wasting food, our scholar complains, some of these women became so obese that they could no longer perform their prayers or ablutions properly.[54] Ibn al-Hajj criticized such practices of female adornment as painting the eyebrows and tattooing the skin because they too interfered with the proper performance of rituals of ablution. As for the removal of facial hair and splitting and filing teeth to render them white, we are told that these should not be performed by a male barber, as was normally done: "A strange man should not be permitted to touch the lips and face of a woman because it leads to corrupting behavior."[55] Ibn al-Hajj did not criticize such practices because he opposed female adornment, for he stressed the importance of the wife's duty to adorn herself for her husband. Alas, this was not the case among most Cairene women: "At home she usually dresses in her worst clothes, pays no attention to her looks, and leaves her hair uncombed. She allows herself to be in such a state of dirt and sweat that her husband shuns her. . . . But when she goes out she dresses in her best clothes. Adorned and perfumed, she puts on her jewelry, wearing her ankle-bracelet over her sirwal."[56] Competition in female adornment was most intense when women went to the public bath. There women would take their expensive clothes and jewelry to show off after they were finished with their bath. Ibn al-Hajj complains bitterly because of the numerous problems that ensued between husband and wife—she demanding that he should buy her expensive clothes to match those of her female friends. We are told that the situation could become complicated, particularly if the husband could not afford the expensive tastes of his wife.

The common but significant event of childbirth was and still is a cause of much celebration among Egyptian families and particularly among women. In medieval Egyptian society, where female fertility was highly prized and child mortality was often acute, a successful delivery was naturally celebrated with the utmost joy and publicity. The event inspired a host of rituals, all aimed to bring good health and fortune to the baby and the mother, as well as joy to the whole family. Typically, Ibn al-Hajj launched severe attacks on these female innovations, which he found to be meaningless, extravagant, and without precedent in the Muslim sunna. He was, therefore, unhappy to see men contributing to and participating in these wicked rituals: "And men do not scold them, on the contrary, they seem to be pleased with all this, and encourage it. This is also true of the religious scholars and mystics, they also celebrate this in their homes, and invite people for the celebrations."[57]

During the process of delivery and the festivities consequent on the birth of the child, the midwife played the leading role. Ibn al-Hajj, obsessed as he was with female impurities, warned husbands of the un-shar'i practices of the midwife, who touches the baby and its clothes with hands soiled by the impure blood of delivery. "And they do worse than this, they smear the baby with the impure blood on their fingers, explaining that it is good for this and that." If the midwife was dealing with a difficult delivery, she would mix soft bread with mouse stools and stuff it into the mouth of the mother, claiming that this would help ease the pain.[58]

When the baby was born, loud and long-drawn-out shrills were heard everywhere in the house, as a manifestation of female joy. Music, dancing, and an atmosphere of gaiety followed, and a variety of special dishes was served to the family and neighbors of the community. This, Ibn al-Hajj tells us, went on for seven days; every time a woman came to express her congratulations, the song and dance would start all over again. To publicize the happy event, trumpets and pipes were blown in front of the house door, inviting neighbors and friends to participate in the joyful atmosphere. Our scholar remarks that these practices were so ingrained in people's daily lives that they considered them as important as religious rituals.

Ritual celebrations on the seventh day after delivery (*al-subu'*) were especially important, as they signified the safe passage of the newly born into the world.[59] An atmosphere of feasting was created by the women of the house; various kinds of rich sweet dishes were served to visitors and friends, and whole dishes of nuts and candies were readily available around the house.[60] On the eve of the subu', women of the family participated in various rituals reserved for the occasion. Items of special meaning were collected and placed near the baby's head. In the morning, some of these items were offered to relatives, neighbors, and the poor, in order to bring *baraka* (blessing) for the baby. Another important ritual, performed before removal of the umbilical cord and aimed to bring benediction for the baby, was to wrap its head with a cloth on which the Quranic verse of Yasin was written with saffron. For protection against illness, the important ritual of the umbilical cord was attended by all the newborn babies of the neighborhood. Some mothers kept the knife used on the occasion close to the baby's head, and carried it while they worked around the house. This went on for forty days and was believed to protect the mother against the evil spirits. The subu' festivities culminated in a joyous ceremony in which mother, baby, midwife, female relatives, and friends participated. Candles were lit, and the mother, elegantly dressed in new clothes, marched close to the midwife, who carried the baby in a tour all over the house. Meanwhile, a woman relative walked in front of the midwife with a plate of salt mixed with cumin and saffron, which she sprinkled right and left over the participants. Incense, prepared specially for the ritual, was burned to ward off the evil spirits and to protect mother and child against disease. For this happy occasion, the father bought new clothes for all members of the family and new furnishings for the house, adding to the spirit of joy and renewal.[61]

Like those of childbirth, death and funerary rituals were given great importance by women in Cairo. Historically, ancient Egyptian death rituals were known to have been quite elaborate and complicated, undertaken primarily for the spiritual welfare of the deceased soul and to ease the adjustment necessary to accommodate the event of death.[62] Some of these rituals may have been carried over to later historical periods, since both the Coptic and Islamic religions, like ancient Egyptian religions, emphasize the importance of life after death. Women followed these ancient traditions more closely than men. Ibn al-Hajj denounced the numerous "innovations" in this area, and by way of guidance he devoted a long section to proper shar'i rituals of death.

When death befell a family member, the women of the household, especially those closest to the dead person, confronted the event with rituals of rejection. Social and religious inhibitions were little regarded, and the women gave vent to their sorrow and pain in a most vehement way: "Women expose their faces and spread their hair, they blacken both face and body, and lament and wail in loud, shrieking voices. They heap earth on their heads, and place chains around their necks, and stain their houses in black."[63] The most important funerary ritual was the process of body purification. In the case of female corpses, this task was undertaken by a woman specialist (al-ghasila). Ibn al-Hajj describes the dramatic scenario that occurred when the women of the house saw the ghasila approaching the house: "When the ghasila enters the house, the women give vent to a loud scream (al-saiha al-'uzma); they pour insults and beatings on her. The ghasila, aware of this female tradition, is on her guard, and tries to hide from them. They shout at her, 'you are the face of calamity,' and in response, she says, 'I have seen the calamity in your house.' Eventually, they allow her to perform the washing ritual, and in turn, she admonishes them, and reminds them that death is God's will."[64] Following the meticulous cleansing of the body, the ghasila recites formulas of praise for the dead soul, which are followed by the ritual of shrouding the corpse. Contrary to the Islamic tradition, which leaves the face uncovered, Egyptians shrouded the whole body from head to toe, just as their ancient ancestors did.[65]

After the body was properly shrouded, it was moved from the house to the bier, and here another farewell female shriek was heard as members of the family stood by to see the corpse leave the house. The *imam* (prayer leader) of the closest mosque then usually led a collective prayer, in which men and women prayed for the comfort and peace of the dead soul. This was followed by a lengthy funeral procession, in which religious and Quranic chanting was performed. "Walking behind their men, women performed their usual ritual of collective wailing and shrieking. They walk about oblivious of proper female modesty, striking their faces in lamentation."[66]

On the morning following the death, men and women of the family usually went for lengthy visits to the tomb of their dead relative, using the house inside the graveyard for lodging. Food offerings formed an important part of Egyptian funerary rituals, and women of the family cooked food for three consecutive nights after the death. On the third evening special rituals of commemoration took place around the tomb. Baffled by these feastlike practices, Ibn al-Hajj remarks that they seemed more like wedding celebrations than death rituals. Male and female relatives and friends congregated to feast on a large variety of food and to listen to Quranic reciters and mystical chantings. In addition, male and female preachers were hired to relate admonishing stories to this audience.[67]

A period of intensive mourning followed, and it was the women of the family who mourned most passionately. During the mourning period immediately after the death, close female relatives of the deceased stayed home to receive condolences from female relatives and friends. A *na'iha* (professional wailer) was hired to intensify the atmosphere of mourning in the house: leading female relatives and friends to the beats of the tambourine, the wailer orchestrated a powerful scene of lamentation. Ibn al-Hajj informs us that women indulged in these scenes, in defiance of the shari'a, for several days and nights after the death.[68] Mourning continued for at least one year, during which the women of the family wore black, the color of sorrow, and abstained from all forms of adornment. After the year of mourning was over, women prepared for the period of dissolving sorrow (*fakk al-huzn*). This meant that they could go to the public bath, apply henna stain, and use other female embellishments.[69]

This did not mean that women forgot their dead. In the hope of finding comfort and relief from their daily problems, women spent a great deal of time visiting the tombs of their dead relatives and favorite saints. Tomb visiting was also an important aspect of religious festivities; on those occasions men and women spent all morning and most of the afternoon in the company of their dead relatives or favorite saints.[70] Ibn al-Hajj denounced women's tomb visiting, and he quotes a Prophetic tradition supporting his view: "God curses women who visit tombs."[71] Being opposed to women's crossing forbidden boundaries outside their homes, he viewed their frequent visiting of tombs as a cause of great evil and corruption: "Observe, may God forgive us and forgive you, what the women have invented in connection with these visits. They have allocated for each shrine a specific day of the week, so that most of their weekdays are used to obtain their wicked desires. . . . On Mondays, they visit the shrine of al-Husain; on Tuesdays and Saturdays, they visit al-Sayyida Nafisa; Thursdays and Fridays were dedicated to visiting the tombs of other holy saints and the tombs of their dead."[72] Ibn al-Hajj was very critical of Cairene women's conduct on the way to and from the cemeteries, because they violated all the shar'i rules of sexual segregation. We are told that to reach the cemeteries, women hired the services of a donkey owner who was willing to make the round trip. As the woman rode behind the man on the donkey, much touching occurred between the two people: "Her hands would be on his shoulder, and his hand would be on her thighs, talking to one another as though they were husband and wife."[73] Here Ibn al-Hajj remarks that whereas the feminine nature inclines toward chaotic and corrupt behavior, men are expected to take corrective measures to control the behavior of their women. But Cairene men disappointed him repeatedly: "The strange thing is that the husband and other men see all this and know of it, but do little about it. Even though this female behavior entails the forbidden, all those people who watch are silent; they make no comments, and do not even display any signs of Islamic jealousy (*ghaira islamiyya*)." In spite of the threats of a pious husband, however, the wife insisted on having her own way. We are told that if the husband tried to stop his wife from visiting the tombs, she would refuse, threatening him with separation or denial of sexual pleasures. The dispute could lead to enmity and beating and ultimately reach the judge's court.[74]

Tomb visiting was most popular on the eve of Friday, especially during the full moon. Men and women often went to the cemeteries on Thursday evenings, spent all of Friday there, and returned on Saturday. Spending the night in the cemeteries was usually facilitated by the presence of houses within the precincts of graveyards; a tradition that Ibn al-Hajj found ugly and corrupting. Tomb visiting was also favored on special religious feasts.[75] During these visits, lights and fire were kindled and the Quran was chanted. Women sang and played the tambourine, and both men and women joined to dispel the darkness of death, receiving comfort from the presence of the dead soul.[76] At the end of their visits men and women would open an individual dialogue with the dead saint or relative, telling him or her their problems and asking for assistance in fulfilling their needs.[77]

Cairene women also enjoyed participating in popular religious festivals. These became so popular that the ruling elite found it important to participate in their celebration.[78] Ibn al-Hajj mentions many of these festivals, both Coptic and Muslim, and in doing so denounced the corrupt manners of Cairenes.[79] During these festivals, women mingled with men in the mosques, the streets, and the precincts of the cemetery. Ibn al-Hajj found women's presence in the mosques most offensive. "Women should be isolated in a place distant from men, contrary to what happens today. They mingle with men, and on feast days you find the mosque crowded with women."[80] On these religious occasions, sufi orders held intense public celebrations, in which women and men participated. However, private celebrations were also held separately for both men and women. The female sessions, privately held in a home, were normally orchestrated by a female sufi (*shaikha*) who led the women in their collective experience of chanting, clapping, dancing, and playing music. In addition, the shaikha preached and told stories to her female audience: "The shaikha was also an interpreter of God's book, she interprets and relates stories of prophets, adds and deletes, often committing blatant blasphemies with nobody to correct or guide her. I have been told that she did so in the house of one of the respectable religious scholars, and no one corrected her; on the contrary, they were generous with her."[81] Women also apparently could be initiated into sufi orders headed by women shaikhas. Some of these shaikhas required their female initiates to wear the sufi woolen garb and to free themselves from matrimonial bonds. Viewing these female practices as contrary to the shari'a, Ibn al-Hajj demanded that the shaikha be reprimanded and her ways reformed: "But alas, many respected scholars speak of her virtues, praise her, and invite her to perform the *dhikr* [mystical practice] in their congregations, and even visit her in her house. As for the other shaikhas who do not wear the woolen garments, they commit more vile imperfections that are too many to enumerate and too ugly to mention."[82] In other *maulids* (religious birthday feasts), the female sufis headed by their shaikha would recite the Quran and perform the dhikr collectively before male sufi groups. Moreover, men and women belonging to some popular sufi orders seem to have established bonds of fraternity. "These orders establish covenants of fraternity between men and women without disapproving or hiding it . . . they went so far as to tolerate women sitting close to men, claiming that they are the spiritual children of their shaikh, and once women became the spiritual sisters of men they did not need to veil themselves from them."[83] Dhikr sessions held by the more popular sufi orders during the various maulids were less restricted by rules of sexual segregation; women behaved more freely among the sufis, throwing off their veils of modesty when they were around their holy men. The visit of sufi orders during maulids initiated a communal spiritual atmosphere among the inhabitants of the quarter. Uttering shrills of joy, women would go out unveiled to welcome the men of Allah and to offer them free food and accommodations. In the evenings, men and women from the quarter engaged in a collective spiritual dance inspired by sufi singing and chanting. Predictably, Ibn al-Hajj disapproved strongly of these sufi aberrations.

In addition to the numerous Muslim and Coptic festivals in which Cairene women participated, the city of Cairo offered many other opportunities for social entertainment: lush parks, scenic sites by the banks of the river, and pleasant boat rides.[84] According to Ibn al-Hajj's and al-Maqrizi's descriptions, the favorite spots of recreation were the scenic sites built by the shores of the Nile and the ponds of the city. Men, women, and families spent their recreation days enjoying the open air and the water. We are told that women went on donkeys to these spots, where they would promenade or swim.[85] Nile boat rides seem to have been the most popular form of recreation among Cairenes, notorious for indulgence in fun and pleasure. Ibn al-Hajj expressed his anger concerning women's presence in the midst of what he considered to be a corrupt atmosphere: "As witnessed by all, riding in boats involved more corruption than riding on donkeys, and hence does not need to be described in detail. As for the outings of men and women to the barrages, and what takes place there, it is too much for the ear to hear and for the eye to see."[86] Ibn al-Hajj resented female presence in the parks of Cairo, because he considered public parks as places for male outings and recreation where women should not be seen. Nonetheless, women went to the parks in their best adornments, and together with male members of the family they spent their day "listening to music and recitals of love poetry which softens the hearts of men and women."[87]

The most common form of female entertainment among upper-middle- and upper-class women was viewing public events, such as religious festivities and everyday street events, from behind their laced window screens or from house rooftops. There are numerous descriptions in *al-Madkhal* of the female custom of watching the panorama of the outside male world from behind their screens. Even this form of female modesty aroused Ibn al-Hajj's anger, for he complained that women sat by the windows dressed in their best clothes and that their sight was a source of temptation for the men who gazed at them. Also, women hiding behind their screens, eagerly watching the weekly sufi gatherings and listening attentively to the young and handsome male singers, were tempted by male beauty, which could jeopardize marital relations.

Our scholar was not content to bar women from going out shopping, socializing, visiting tombs, and sharing in public festivities; he demanded that women should be completely concealed from the eyes of men: "All doors, windows and roofs should be shut. And they should be forbidden to look outside when men were out"; only thus could women's corrupting and chaotic behavior be checked.[88] Ibn al-Hajj reminds us finally that only if a strict demarcation between male and female territory is guarded can shar'i order prevail in the Muslim community.

The historical evidence on Cairene women gleaned from Ibn al-Hajj's treatise demonstrates the gap between prescriptive literature and the existing reality of women's everyday life. This literary genre should be viewed primarily as an "ideal" that Muslim male scholars tried to prescribe for their societies to bring about an ideal Islamic order, which they saw as lacking in reality. In trying to impose this shar'i order, Ibn al-Hajj showed how Cairenes in general, and women in particular, deviated from it. Women wielded power in their immediate surroundings; they shaped their daily habits and religious rituals according to their own needs in the Cairene urban context. This is most evident in the way they scheduled and organized their wide-ranging domestic chores, as well as their daily outings into the public domain of the market, the shrine, the cemetery, the mosque, and the park. Even in religious rituals, which were more rigidly defined by the religious scholars, Cairene women adapted rituals of purification, fasting, and prayer to suit their daily patterns of domestic life.

Even though female life revolved around important domestic affairs, like marriage, childbirth, death, and social and religious festivities, this does not mean that women were housebound. Working-class women, in addition to their regular domestic work, performed all the necessary female-related services for upper- and middle-class women, thus obtaining some economic leverage and a greater mobility in the public domain. Exclusive female gatherings occupied much time, and must have given women the opportunity for intense and meaningful socializing outside their homes. This can be seen in frequent female visiting, childbirth festivities, mourning periods, and sufi sessions, which were held separately from those of men. Women not only were able to hold their dhikr sessions separately, but they could also be initiated into women's sufi orders headed by a female sufi. This is not to say that Cairene women were completely segregated from the male world, for women interacted with men on a daily basis: on their trips to the cemetery and to the market, in shops, in the precincts of shrines and mosques, as well as in sufi gatherings. As Ibn al-Hajj tells us, Cairene women were too easygoing in their behavior with "foreign" men.

Unlike the stereotypical submissive and obedient wife, the Cairene women depicted by Ibn al-Hajj were strong willed and defiant of male and shar'i authority. They often used classical female strategies to obtain what they desired from recalcitrant husbands. Ibn al-Hajj repeatedly mentions threats of separation or withdrawal of sexual services as the primary weapons wives used to break down their husbands' resistance. These strategies were complemented by two institutionalized practices, which may have given the woman greater leverage in her relationship with her man: her frequent use of the judge's court to ensure her legal rights and her demand of a "bed fee" for her sexual services.

Notes

1. See Ira M. Lapidus, *Muslim Cities in the Later Middle Ages* (Cambridge: Harvard University Press, 1967). A close reading of al-Maqrizi's *al-Khitat al-maqriziyya*, written in the fifteenth century, reflects the author's nostalgia for the prosperity of the previous century; the Halabi edition, 2 vols. (Cairo, n.d.), hereafter *Khitat*.

2. Medieval male-authored legal, ethical, philosophical, mystical, and medical treatises form a rich literary body that needs to be explored from a new perspective. This cultural heritage defines for us the social and religious values and norms

in Muslim societies, and it continues to inspire modern religious scholars who wish to perpetuate an Islamic ideal order as prescribed by Islamic patriarchal values.

3. Ibn al-Hajj's full name was Abu 'Abd Allah ibn Muhammad al-'Abdari al-Fasi. He was born in Fez, Morocco, and died in Cairo in A.H. 737/A.D. 1336–37. He composed several religious treatises, the most important of which is the one under study: *al-Madkhal ila tanmiyat al-a'mal bi tahsin al-niyyat* (An introduction to the development of deeds through the improvement of intentions), 4 vols. (Cairo: Al-Matba'a al-Misriyya, 1929), hereafter *al-Madkhal.*

4. *Al-Madkhal* 4:104.

5. Ibid., 1:146, 241.

6. Ibid., 3:282.

7. Ibid., 1:274, 276.

8. See *Khitat* 2:5, 367–68.

9. A. S. Sa'd, *Social and Economic History of Egypt* (in Arabic) (Beirut, 1979), 489.

10. *Khitat* 2:287. In a study of the popular Islamic writings on women, recently published in Egypt, I analyzed Muslim male attitudes to women. The paper was delivered at a conference organized by the Arab Women Solidarity Association, Cairo, 1986.

11. Khitat 2:102.

12. *Al-Madkhal* 3:127.

13. Ibid., 1:244–45.

14. Ibid., 2:17–18.

15. Ibid., 4:32–34.

16. Ibid., 4:32.

17. Ibid., 4:101.

18. Cairene peddlers still come to the houses to sell their merchandise to housewives.

19. *Al-Madkhal* 4:101–2.

20. Ibid., 4:103.

21. Ibid., 4:102, 180.

22. Ibid., 4:103.

23. Ibid., 4:103–4.

24. Ibid., 1:216.

25. Ibid., 1:278, 279.

26. The feast of 'Ashura became a popular religious feast of mourning during the Fatimid period. It commemorates the day Husain, the grandson of the Prophet Muhammad, was martyred. After the Fatimids, the Sunni Ayyubids celebrated 'Ashura as a feast of joy; see *Khitat* 1:431, and Edward William Lane, *Manners and Customs of the Modern Egyptians* (London: Aldine, 1954), 434–39.

27. *Al-Madkhal* 1:277, 279.

28. Ibid., 2:67.

29. Ibid., 4:199.

30. Ibid., 3: 232, 246, 290, 4:105, 114.

31. Ibid., 2:226–27.

32. Ibid., 2:168.

33. Ibid., 3:288.

34. Ibn al-Hajj often refrains from describing details that are too well known, or too vile to describe. More-detailed descriptions of wedding celebrations can be culled from Mamluk literary sources; see F. Amin, *Egyptian Society as Portrayed by Mamluk Literature* (in Arabic) (Cairo: Dar al-Ma'arif, 1982), 254, 297.

35. *Al-Madkhal* 1:162–63.

36. Most schools of Islamic law will allow a thrice-divorced woman to remarry her ex-husband, but only after she temporarily takes a new husband (al-muhallil).

37. *Al-Madkhal* 2:61.

38. Ibid., 2:227.

39. Ibid., 2:161.

40. Ibid., 2:169, 1:183.

41. Ibid., 2:191, 192–94.

42. Ibid., 2:195–96.

43. Ibid., 2:169.

44. Ibid., 2:175–77, 1:211, 276.

45. Ibid., 1:169–70.

46. Ibid., 2:170.

47. Ibid.

48. Ibid., 1:213–14.

49. Ibid., 2:62, 68.

50. Ibid., 2:172.

51. Ibid., 1:140–46 (quotation on p. 146).

52. Ibid., 1:241–45. See also *Khitat* 2:323; the *hisba* manuals, which provide the market supervisor (*al-muhtasib*) with the shar'i rules of commercial transactions and moral behavior, are replete with references to female dress and conduct in the markets.

53. *Al-Madkhal* 1:243–44.

54. Ibid., 2:60, 63.

55. Ibid., 4:105.

56. Ibid., 1:168.

57. Ibid., 2:287, 185.

58. Ibid., 3:283.

59. Ibid., 3:287. The subu' rituals are still widely practiced all over Egypt, especially among the lower-middle classes and in rural areas.

60. Ibid., 3:292.

61. Ibid., 3:290–91.

62. On ancient Egyptian funerary rituals, see C. J. Bleeker, *Egyptian Festival Enactments of Religious Renewal* (Leiden: E. J. Brill, 1967), 124–38.

63. *Al-Madkhal* 3:233.

64. Ibid., 3:246.

65. Ibid., 3:242.

66. Ibid., 3:250, 277.

67. Ibid., 3:278–79.

68. Ibid., 3:235.

69. Ibid., 3:281.

70. See Bleeker, *Egyptian Festival Enactments*, 124–38.

71. *Al-Madkhal* 1:25.

72. Ibid., 1:269.

73. Ibid., 1:267.

74. Ibid., 1:266, 269.

75. Ibid., 1:268. It is a common practice among present-day Egyptian families to visit the tombs of their dead on feast days.

76. Ibid., 1:268, 2:17, 309, 310, 311.

77. Ibid., 2:312.

78. This is especially true of the Fatimid period, during which the caliphs participated in many religious festivals; see *Khitat* 1:387–88, and 490–96. For a more detailed description of festivals during the Mamluk period, see ibid.

79. On Islamic festivals, see *al-Madkhal* 1:283–85, 290–312; on Coptic festivals, see ibid., 2:49–60. It is interesting to note here that, much to the annoyance of Ibn al-Hajj, Egyptian Muslims also participated in Coptic festivals. On Coptic festivals during the Fatimid and Mamluk periods, see *Khitat* 1:264–69.

80. *Al-Madkhal* 1:287, 289.

81. Ibid., 2:12.

82. Ibid., 2:141.

83. Ibid., 3:200.

84. For more details on recreation sites in Mamluk Cairo, see *Khitat* 2:125, 130–32, 144, 152, 162.

85. *Al-Madkhal* 1:270.

86. Ibid., 1:272.

87. Ibid., 1:271.

88. Ibid.

7

Class Solidarity versus Gender Gain: Women as Custodians of Property in Later Medieval Egypt

CARL F. PETRY

On A.H. 22 Jumada I 884/A.D. 11 August 1479, the foremost chronicler of the later Mamluk period in Egypt and Syria, Ibn Iyas, provided the following obituary notice for Khawand (princess) Zainab, wife of Sultan Inal (857–65/1453–61):

> She was among the most noble of princesses in rank. She enjoyed such prestige during the reign of her husband that she administered state affairs, influencing both appointments and dismissals. She commanded wide respect, and possessed a substantial fortune. She married only al-Ashraf Inal, who himself took no other wife. Upon his [Inal's] death, al-Zahir Khushqadam [865–72/1461–67] subjected her to several confiscations, extorting vast sums of money. Yet despite these adversities, the princess retained her honor and maintained her status until her death, at more than eighty years of age. Truly, she was among the notables of her time.[1]

To observers superficially acquainted with medieval Islamic societies, such an entry might seem unusual. Given traditional concepts about the status of women under Islamic law, overt references to a seasoned ruler consulting his wife on state policy would imply a level of mutual respect inconsistent with either Quranic injunction or long-standing social practice.[2] But although few royal spouses may have wielded the political influence exercised by Khawand Zainab, many certainly enjoyed her status. Indeed, as historians probe the sources that describe the urban society of Egypt and Syria during the Ayyubid and Mamluk periods (566–922/1171–1517), they soon discover a remarkable degree of parity between men and women who belonged to the ruling elite. Although sharp divisions in public roles and postures distinguished the two sexes, these do not appear to have created any appreciable differences in status. No dimension of this elite's activity more vividly illustrates this situation than the assignment of custodianship over property and the endowment of charitable trusts. Class identity combined with pragmatic necessity to promote the mutual supervision of estates by men and women, certified by elaborate legal procedure. Quite often, women were chosen to assume exclusive responsibility for property management.

The imposition of militarist authority in Egypt by the famous Kurdish commander Salah al-Din (the Crusaders' Saladin) in 1171, and the subsequent replacement of his Ayyubid dynasty by Mamluk slave-soldiers less than a century later, is widely known.[3] The Mamluk regime based in Cairo was more centralized than its predecessor and recruited its ruling class almost exclusively among adolescents imported from foreign regions as slaves, who were manumitted on completion of their training. During the first century of the regime's existence, most Mamluk novices (Julban) were purchased, at steep prices, from the Qipjak Steppes of Central Asia. The Turkish dialect of this region became the barracks language of the regime. From the late fourteenth century, Mamluks were collected from Circassia in the Caucasus, and its language was added to Qipjak as a lingua franca of the ruling elite.[4] Committed to preserving the alien distinctiveness of their class, the Mamluks also arranged for the transfer of women from their homelands, preferring them as concubinal and marriage partners. Yet the Mamluks did not construct a closed caste system that denied access to individuals from the Arab-speaking masses over whom they ruled. The contemporary biographical literature makes repeated reference to marriage ties that cut across ethnic lines, especially for subsequent generations. But the desire to retain ethnic separation remained a significant aspect of Mamluk identity throughout their dominion over Egypt and Syria. Certainly the majority of first-generation recruits, from whom virtually all future officers and autocrats emerged, consorted with women who had been born in their regions or were descended from Turkish or Circassian lineages.

Given this keen ethnic consciousness, women of Qipjak or Circassian origin were regarded as members of the ruling class by virtue of their "racial" background. Ann Lambton has noted the prominence of women who belonged to Central Asian military elites (Seljuks and Mongols) that dominated Iran throughout the Middle Ages. Although the Persian regimes were dynastic and based on heritable succession rather than slavery, the influence wielded by these women over politics and guardianship of property closely paralleled their contemporaries' leverage in Mamluk Egypt. Such mutual status may suggest that women in Muslim

Central Asia enjoyed a higher level of social equality and integration than those in the central Islamic lands.[5] In both Egypt and Iran, ethnic identity and membership in the ruling class contributed to the augmented position of these women compared with their civilian counterparts. The nature of marital preference itself certainly contributed to the prominence of Qipjak and Circassian women in Cairo, who shared with their male peers the distinction of foreign origin. The relative scarcity of such women and the financial requirements for their proper maintenance in the capital enhanced their position in a tradition that required men or their families to pay a dower to the bride.

Complementing this sense of ethnic parity between sexes, the political environment created by the Mamluk regime contributed decisively to the prestige of its female members. In the absence of any binding principle of hereditary succession or dynastic loyalty,[6] the Mamluks developed, on an ad hoc basis, a system of advancement and promotion that was highly egalitarian and rigorously merit-oriented, but exceptionally violent. Observers of Mamluk interfactional rivalries were uniformly dismayed at the endemic infighting that seemed ubiquitous in the Mamluk system.[7] Recent analysts of military slavery in the medieval Muslim world have become convinced that, for good or ill, such feuding was not at all an aberration but in fact had evolved as a basic, indeed fundamental, dimension of militarist politics. Mobility within ranks of slave-soldiers was invariably marked by intense rivalry and acrimonious competition. Although a special kind of camaraderie (*khushdashiya*) founded on barracks ties and cemented during arduous training sessions bound various factions together in fierce loyalty, no ambitious recruit bent on achievement allowed personal bonds to interfere with the ruthless attainment of his objectives. Accordingly, no tie of loyalty was absolute in this system. No personal bond overrode the seizing of opportunities when they arose or the forming of ad hoc and often precarious coalitions, even if they embraced members of hostile factions. Although this concept of mobility has convinced many historians of the inherent divisiveness of the Mamluk apparatus, it certainly weeded out incompetents. Few dull plodders ever made it to the sultanate in Cairo throughout this era.

But the system had its cost: a high rate of mortality among Mamluk men at every level, from raw trainee to senior officer who possessed his own troopers. The extreme risk to life and limb involved with advancement through the chaotic Mamluk hierarchy, aggravated by arrests, exiles, imprisonments, and executions, as well as casualty rates that were normative for a professional military class engaged in continuous warfare with foreign powers, compromised the actuarial chances of these men. In comparison, the life expectancy of their female counterparts was higher, even admitting the risk of death in childbirth.[8] Women enjoyed the status of membership in the ruling elite, but they shared few of its factional liabilities and none of the risks involved with military campaigns. Although women did participate in the rivalries that preoccupied their male relatives, they rarely faced the same level of retribution. We shall see that women were subjected to confiscation of assets, a phenomenon that became endemic during the later Mamluk period. But they seem largely to have been spared the recriminations that were meted out so savagely to men for losing in disputes between parties or competing coalitions. And since women did not take the field in battle, they were spared the ultimate consequence of a warrior's calling. Considering their lower mortality rate, women's role as stabilizers of familial and lineage groups seems less surprising.

In light of the insecurity and tension that so infused the political milieu, women served as guarantors of continuity in family structures that suffered repeated losses of male members. The prominence of women as custodians of estates stands as testimony to their security advantage over men, as will be seen below. But as living symbols of stability who might survive several generations of men cut down in their prime, women often presided over their houses as dowagers. They would command enormous respect even from rival groups who accorded no one else equivalent reverence. Such women often emerged as authority figures, especially during sudden crises or prolonged episodes of sedition. Indeed, at the inception of the Mamluk state, an ambitious woman attempted to establish herself as a co-ruler. Shajar al-Durr, a concubine of al-Malik al-Salih Ayyub (638–47/1240–49), upon her lord's death involved herself intimately with one of his grand amirs, Aibak. The two connived to found a new regime in Cairo, and the former concubine dared to proclaim herself "Sultana."[9] Most references in the narrative sources depict royal wives closely associated with husbands, or widows presiding over a harmonious succession.[10] But the widespread appointment of women as caretakers of estates and supervisors of trusts implies that this phenomenon extended far beyond the highest level of the Mamluk hierarchy.

Women attained esteem as symbols of longevity who provided the continuity necessary for the preservation of lineages over time as well as the integrity of estates. In civilian society, such a role was much less important since men did not participate directly in either factional disputes or battlefield activities. The actuarial ratios between men and women were more balanced, and women were therefore less vital as guarantors of familial cohesion. We should not assume that this lack of visibility automatically resulted in greater subordination of civilian women, for they do appear in the archival sources as trust supervisors. But the narrative sources contain fewer references to their political eminence.

Female members of the Mamluk elite, however, received a very special kind of respect, which accrued to them as a consequence of their actuarial gain and immunity to the violence that infused every facet of the male's universe. This respect was profound and apparently unique to the militarist governments that held sway over the central Islamic lands during the high and later Middle Ages. Although women of court circles often enjoyed great prestige in the Ottoman Empire, they belonged to a tradition of dynastic succession that posed no threat of extinction to the ruling house itself. The militarist regimes that the Ottomans absorbed usually eschewed dynastic principles, and therefore they faced special problems of continuity that women, through their own survival, could mitigate.

FISCAL DILEMMAS OF THE MAMLUK STATE

Women did not figure prominently in the custodianship of property and charitable trusts solely for the reasons discussed above. Their relative immunity from liabilities of male status also defrayed, at least in part, infringements by the regime on the integrity of estates. These depredations became acute during the last century of Mamluk rule in Egypt and Syria and contributed to a broad tendency toward hoarding assets in safe but conservative forms of investment. From the so-called Time of Troubles, which brought to an end the formative era of Sultan Baibars (658–76/1260–77) and Sultan Qala'un (678–89/1279–90),[11] the Mamluk regime was compelled to cope with either static or declining official revenues: land taxes, commercial tariffs, transit tolls, imposts charged to both domestic and foreign merchants, and so forth. The declines in part reflected the pilfering of revenues by the very cadres the system of land allotments (iqta') had been designed to support. But the productive capacity of Egypt's proverbial agriculture saw no increase after the Time of Troubles, and may actually have diminished.[12] Cairo's lucrative monopoly over the international trade between southern Asia and the Mediterranean in such exotic commodities as spices remained a vital aspect of the economy, but its level of profitability was tied to market forces increasingly beyond Cairo's control.[13]

Arrayed against these static sources of revenue were demands by an increasingly aggressive and unyielding military establishment, over which the autocrat himself often exercised only marginal disciplinary powers. All first-generation members of the Mamluk order, regardless of rank, were trained to view themselves as more than privileged. They considered their service of defense and protection of the Dar al-Islam as indispensable in a turbulent international environment. Both Mamluk officers and recruits, exploiting the tradition of competing factions, became adept at inflating their demands for salaries and for bonuses customarily paid as inducements to participate in a campaign. This was a highly sophisticated class of professional warriors, whose loyalty to patrons and regime was real but never isolated from scales of pay. Soldiering was, in the final analysis, a job—and one fraught with dangers. Loyalty was therefore always bought and commensurate to fiscal remuneration. In a flourishing polity, such attitudes could be profligately indulged, but the Mamluk Empire committed itself early on to preserving the status quo rather than to enlarging its frontiers or encouraging economic growth.[14]

Because the sultan had himself grown to maturity and developed his sense of competition within this system, he was rarely disposed to alter it. Indeed, even the most capable Mamluk autocrats found themselves constrained by the ironclad monopoly their troops held over the government. Keenly aware that the forces of insurrection and sedition that had placed so many of them on the throne could dislodge them from it, few autocrats sought to reform the political traditions of the military elite, or even to curb the grossest forms of exploitation inflicted by their subordinates on the population. No ruler between Qala'un and Qansuh al-Ghauri (906–22/1501–16) considered alternative sources of recruitment or training procedures that might create a less unruly military class.

In the second half of the ninth hijri/fifteenth century A.D., the effective "Pax Mamlukia," which had sheltered the eastern Mediterranean and southwest Asia for two hundred years, began to wane. Following the successful repulsion of the Mongols by Baibars at 'Ain Jalut in 659/1260 and the expulsion of the European Crusaders from the Levant by Qala'un, the Mamluk Empire cast a security blanket over the central Islamic lands. Preservation of the resulting equilibrium became a fundamental principle of Mamluk foreign policy, and the prime reason for the regime's prestige. But after 1450 this peace began to unravel, due to revolts by restive marcher vassals, threats from the Ottoman government to the north, now fully recovered from the disaster of Timur's invasion, sectarian imperialism by the newly established Safavid shahs in Iran, and aggression by Europeans seeking to break the Mamluk monopoly over the East-West trade. These developments, widely studied but still debated as to their relative significance, lie outside the scope of this chapter. Here we must note the problems these momentous changes posed for the Mamluk autocrat and his staff, already coping with static revenues and inflated demands on them.

Given the growing foreign menace to Cairo's vision of security, no Mamluk ruler dared to allow the combat readiness of his army to lapse, regardless of cost. The professional military class, fully aware of their sovereign's dependence, saw fit to pressure him for ever steeper increments to their pay scales. Almost without exception, every sultan who mobilized his troops for combat duty abroad found himself obliged to appease their demands. The narrative sources dwell at great length on the tensions between supreme commander and common soldier over money.[15] Several sultans threatened to abdicate rather than yield to the extravagant pressures of their army units, but none carried through. Ultimately, the autocrat would submit and promise to meet the requests of his troops rather than face insurrection at home or defeat abroad. But how was the regime to meet these demands?

The sultanate relied increasingly on ad hoc sources of revenue: troves of money amassed by military officers, regime bureaucrats, and wealthy merchants who had proven themselves adept at hoarding assets during periods of financial crisis. The autocrat, assisted by subordinates from both the military and civilian branches of government, proceeded to extract funds by force to meet its expenses. Confiscation of assets was hardly unique to the later Mamluk period, but what had occurred sporadically in earlier reigns now became routinized. Mulcting of fractious or overly ambitious amirs, crafty bureaucrats who had grown too rich, and merchants whose profits rendered them enticing targets provided the regime with the funds needed to stave off revolt by its troops. The figures reported in the biographical and narrative sources reveal enormous sums, acquired either from secreting iqta' rents or from acceptance of bribes, which the regime now expropriated on a systematic basis.[16] Indeed, a tacit partnership between the autocrat and sagacious officials, in which the former planted trusted clients in lucrative fiscal offices, may have matured during this period. The sultan allowed his staff to accumulate vast treasures through corrupt devices, ritually arrested them, seized their ill-gotten gains, and subsequently returned them to office.[17]

The sultan also stepped up his confiscation of private estates, in particular those acquired by dangerous military colleagues. Former rivals for the throne were particularly susceptible to this treatment, and the regime usually turned a deaf ear to the complaints of heirs who swore that they shared none of their parents' disloyalty and were being denied their rights under Islamic law.[18] The autocrat replied that such assets had been garnered by treasonous subordinates and thus appropriately reverted to the state. The sultanate also imposed extraordinary taxes on both luxury items and commodities traded in bulk. Quite often, such taxes were charged on a "futures" basis, with revenues collected in advance of the exchange or sale of the goods in question, before any profits had actually been made.[19] Stewards of landholders (mubashirun al-muqta'in) increasingly faced similar tactics and were compelled to pay taxes on crops that had not yet been harvested.[20] Finally, the sultanate impounded the yields of trust properties (waqfs) endowed to support charitable and scholastic activities. This type of action represented a truly desperate expedient and was rarely contemplated without at least pro forma consultation with eminent representatives of the ulama. Because members of the military elite invested heavily in waqfs, autocrats hesitated before tampering with this most sacrosanct of investments.[21] Nonetheless, the vast resources of land and property tied up in charitable trusts beckoned irresistibly to rulers plagued by unremitting demands from their troops.

The implications of these tactics for the long-term growth of the Egyptian economy have not been studied in any systematic way.[22] Historians have tended to castigate later Mamluk autocrats and their staffs for shortsighted obsession with expedients enabling them to survive immediate crises rather than engaging in prolonged speculation over their nation's future. Whether any government contemplating fiscal ruin could have afforded the luxury of reflection is open to question. But from the perspective of estate cohesion, these tactics posed a serious threat. All holders of substantial properties, both civilian and military, were extremely sensitive to such strategies.

WOMEN AND THE MANAGEMENT OF PROPERTY

The actuarial advantage of women who belonged to the Mamluk elite contributed more than any other factor to their prominence as custodians of estates built up by male relatives. Their greater life expectancy after marriage, due in part to their youth upon entering into betrothal, rendered women ideal choices as supervisors. Their relative security from the violence endemic to politics within the Mamluk system also enhanced their desirability, although we should not assume total immunity. Vast estates presided over by women who had inherited from fathers or husbands could be subject to confiscation. In Dhu al-Hijja of 874 (June 1470), Sultan Qaitbay demanded an "obligatory gift" of 150,000 dinars from the Lady Sada, daughter of the former Nazir al-Khass (supervisor of the special fund), Yusuf b. Katib Jakam, to help defray the expenses of an expedition against the Dhu al-Qadirid rebel, Shah Suwar, in southeastern Anatolia.[23] The lady demurred, "claiming that she had nothing to pay." But the sultan insisted that her father's legacy would enable her to meet this figure, and he placed all her assets under sequestration with no private transactions permitted. He subsequently arranged for the auctioning of enough property to yield up the required sum. "The Lady was then honored in a court ceremony, and allowed to resume her life as before." Qaitbay's respect for Sada should be compared with the rather more callous treatment men received when compelled to part with their wealth. Many were intimidated with the threat of torture, and several died before revealing where they had stashed secret troves. I have encountered no case of a woman undergoing physical duress to force her to reveal assets.[24]

The role of women as guarantors of familial continuity in Mamluk society counted for far more than maintenance of lineage. Women often contested in court challenges to their legal rights as caretakers of inherited assets, especially when the future of minor children was at stake. In Muharram of 875 (July 1470), the widow of the chief justice Sharaf al-Din al-Munawi brought suit against her husband's former agent, Zain al-Din al-Abutiji, who had expropriated lands in Anbaba, across the Nile from Cairo, designated for al-Munawi's children by a former wife.[25] Al-Abutiji contended that he, rather than their stepmother, had been appointed legal guardian of the children. The grand amir Inal al-Ashqar, who presided over the appeals case, acknowledged al-Abutiji's status as guardian, but ruled that he had acted negligently and had falsely claimed reconciliation with the second wife. He ordered al-Abutiji flogged on the buttocks and compelled him to make restitution.

Several months later (Dhu al-Qa'da/April–May 1471), the wife of an official in the service of Sharaf al-Din Ibn Gharib, Muqaddam al-Daula (custodian of the privy fund), appealed via the royal harem to the sultan on her husband's behalf.[26] She claimed that Ibn Gharib had falsely accused her husband of corruption for which he himself was responsible and had then exiled him to Upper Egypt (al-Sa'id). The wife used her influence in the harem because she belonged to "their faction" (jihati-hinna). Presumably heeding his own wife's pleas, the sultan recalled the official from exile and summoned him to the court for a confrontation with his employer's agent. Yet the sultan did not find Ibn Gharib at fault and honored the agent with a ceremonial robe. But the official was allowed to retire to private life in Cairo with no fine.

One of the most intricate cases reported in the chronicles involved a dispute between the daughter of Sultan al-Nasir Faraj (801–15/1399–1412), Khawand Shaqara, and the grand amir Khairbak Hadid al-Ashrafi over agrarian land in the Faiyum that the princess had inherited as a waqf supervisor. River flowage had eaten away this land, replacing it with several islands.[27] During the reign of al-Zahir Khushqadam, the wazir (prime minister) claimed that Shaqara had lost title to these islands because the original plot no longer existed. The princess appealed to Sultan Khushqadam, who recognized her transferred claim to the islands and confirmed the original waqf with a royal deed. Shaqara subsequently leased the islands to Amir Khairbak for a set term. Khairbak expended substantial sums on converting the islands to a profitable plantation, with a sugar press to harvest the cane. When Khawand Shaqara decided to rent out the property on her own, Khairbak claimed that it was now entirely occupied with his operation. He offered to pay her "appropriate rent" while insisting that he had greatly enhanced the value of the original island. Shaqara once again lodged an appeal before the sultan, this time al-Ashraf Qaitbay. She argued that Khairbak had usurped his profits from a trust property that he exploited solely for personal gain. Qaitbay found the matter too complicated for resolution at one hearing and convened all four chief justices to weigh the arguments. Even these august legal authorities could not handily resolve the case and they divided over whether Amir Khairbak had actually violated the proviso of the original waqf. The council ultimately ruled in favor of Khairbak's retaining his lease rights, since he had invested his personal funds alone rather than any return from the trust. The princess, now at an advanced age, was entitled only to the waqf yield itself based on the reconfirmation issued to her by Khushqadam. The amir had made no move to challenge her position as Nazira al-Waqf al-Sharif.

The limits to which a free-spirited woman with substantial assets might go to seek independence are revealed in the fascinating obituary of Sultan Tatar's (824/1421) daughter, penned by al-Sairafi.[28] This historian, who attended appeals sessions (majalis al-mazalim) at the royal court during Qaitbay's reign as a Hanafi na'ib (deputy judge), was something of a prude. His assessment of Khawand Fatima bt. al-Zahir Tatar, who died on 21 Safar 874/30 August 1469, is as entertaining as it is instructive. Having matured in the custody of Sultan Barsbay (825–41/1422–37), Fatima elected not to marry his ultimate successor, al-Zahir Jaqmaq (842–57/1438–52). Instead, she departed from the citadel with a trousseau of 100,000 dinars and took up private residence next to the house of the overseer of the Mansuri Hospital as a guest of his sister. Al-Sairafi claims that eunuchs (tawashiya) were soon attracted to her circle, as were "elderly people" ('aja'iz). Among her retinue was a certain Hana, a scribe who had grown up at the Azhar (Cairo's cathedral mosque) and "frequented eunuchs." Serving as Fatima's private secretary, he took on the airs of a nobleman, "this upstart who began as a peasant at the Azhar!" Fatima apparently fell into profligate ways under the influence of such persons. Having squandered her inheritance, she began to pawn her expensive apparel and jewelry, at "abysmally cheap prices." When all she originally possessed had been dissipated, Fatima took out loans and begged for charitable donations. A fortuitous marriage to the Qadi Sharaf al-Din al-Tata'i al-Ansari provided a respite from her troubles, but eventually her husband discarded her to avoid impoverishment and also to marry a divorced princess whose fortune was presumably intact. Wild with jealousy, Fatima appealed to Sultan Inal for justice, but al-Tata'i was found to be within his rights. Sultan Jaqmaq had granted Fatima an emergency loan of 5,000 dinars several years earlier, and he had placed the proceeds from the estate of a former Nazir al-Khass at her disposal to pay off her debts. "But in less than a year's time, her situation sank to its former sorry state." Her current grievance therefore went unheeded. Collectors pounded at her door and auctioneers demanded the right to inventory her possessions.

Yet Fatima seems to have pursued her social interests with remarkable alacrity, in spite of her desperate financial condition. Al-Sairafi claims that she gained influence with women of Inal's harem and proceeded to "serve them in important matters." She became notorious for her "excessive elegance (*labaqa*) in food and drink" and entered into subsequent liaisons, one of which resulted in another abortive marriage. According to al-Sairafi, Fatima set a bad example to the public for acts of vileness "no one else dared to commit. . . . Neither the merchants nor the commons could put an end to her depravity." Upon her death, Sultan Qaitbay provided a shroud for her burial and 40 dinars to defray funeral expenses. Although he refused to attend her prayer services, women "of the ignorant masses" did so, slapping their cheeks, rending their breasts, and keening the ritual wail for the deceased. Following her interment, Fatima's creditors petitioned the sultan for redress. Due to the gravity of their claims, Qaitbay reluctantly agreed to grant them justice by expropriating her father's waqfs.

This extraordinary person was remarkable not only for her arrogance, but also for her indifference to societal stricture. Throughout his reign, Qaitbay made a great public show of encouraging moral probity. He rarely plundered trust properties, but he believed that the heinousness of Fatima's offense had negated the sanctity of her father's endowment. He therefore allowed her creditors to recover some of their losses from its proceeds. Fatima's behavior was hardly typical, and I have encountered no biography of a woman from any rank that remotely compares with hers. Nonetheless, her example suggests what elite women could get away with in Mamluk society, regardless of sanctions applied to reform them. The negative tone of al-Sairafi's remarks also suggests that the establishment regarded her profligacy as undignified. In the final analysis, Fatima was judged unworthy as a representative of her class because of her flagrant disregard for the integrity of assets she inherited.

The notorious in society always attract attention, but few of her contemporaries imitated the antics of Fatima bt. Tatar. Indeed, al-Sairafi provided obituaries of several women who were models of decorum, shrewd managers of estates, and munificent patrons of charity. Notable among these was the Lady Amina bt. Isma'il, known as Bint al-Khazin (daughter of the treasurer).[29] After her father's death, the Shafi'i chief justice had demanded rights of custody over his trusts, but the sultan decided in the daughter's favor, claiming: "I shall act for them according to legal principle, and shield them against usurpers." Amina manipulated the properties and trusts she received from her father so prudently that she left "vast assets" (*amwalan jammatan*) at her death.

Equally respected was the princess Mughul, daughter of the famous judge and confidential secretary Nasir al-Din Ibn al-Barizi and wife of Sultan Jaqmaq.[30] Previously married to another eminent *qadi* (judge), Mughul was a sterling example of a civilian who crossed caste lines to reach the pinnacle of Mamluk society. Upon Jaqmaq's demise, Mughul resided in the home of her daughter's husband, the famous Atabak (supreme field commander) Azbak. Azbak so venerated his mother-in-law (who presumably received a legacy from Jaqmaq), that when his wife died he declared Mughul guardian of his son, mistress of his house, and manager of his affairs—"even the slave girls who were his concubines." He appointed her nazira over the waqfs of her father, brother, and former husband and personally witnessed the legal confirmation. Al-Sairafi extolled Mughul's beneficence, describing the *madrasa* (legal academy) that she founded and her support of the poor and indigent in Jerusalem. Unlike Fatima bt. Tatar's final rites, Khawand Mughul's funeral was attended by the sultan and most of the royal court. Qaitbay personally led her prayer service. She was buried in the courtyard of the Shrine of Imam al-Shafi'i, fitting testimony to the respect accorded her.

The endowment deeds surviving from the Mamluk period include many examples of less-eminent women who endowed charitable trusts on their own or managed the estates left them by their fathers or husbands. Of roughly 1,000 deeds examined by M. M. Amin,[31] 283 are listed under a woman's name and the great majority belong to the second category. They reveal specific details about estate preservations and lineage continuity lacking in the narrative sources. One of the most illustrative examples is the deed of al-Masuna (virtuous) Tatarkhan, daughter of the Silahdar (royal arms bearer) Tashtamur al-Husami, dated Rajab of 797/April-May 1395.[32] This deed spells out in precise language the discretionary powers granted to the amir's daughter over his estate, which is then itemized. Her patrimony was large: several hundred faddans (1 F. = 4,200.8m^2) of land in Sharqiyya Province of the Delta, six town houses, numerous shops (*hawanit*), and other rental properties in Cairo. The writ identifies Tatarkhan as sole supervisor of the estate and guardian of the family's interests to her own death. Tatarkhan's legal powers were representative of the status enjoyed by women of her class, virtually all of whom exercised genuine authority over property accumulated by male relatives. Rather than expecting to find the kind of independent disposition of assets as defined by the norms of modern Western societies, we should seek the autonomy of these women in the context of their partnership with spouses, immediate families, and extended lineages. Nowhere is this sort of relationship more clearly personified than the career of Khawand Fatima, wife of Sultan Qaitbay.

Fatima bt. 'Ala' al-Din 'Ali b. Khalil b. Khassbak belonged to an august *walid nas* (scion of Mamluk) house of Cairo. She descended from Saif al-Din Khassbak al-Nasiri (d. 734/1334),[33] a prominent amir in Egypt and Syria during the reign of al-Nasir Muhammad. Her father was described by 'Abd al-Basit as an iqta' holder who was honorable, just, and learned.[34] Fatima's personal life remains elusive since biographical details about her are sparse. Ibn Iyas noted that she was more than sixty years of age at her death on 22 Dhu al-Hijja 909 (6 June 1504).[35] Since her husband, Qaitbay, was in his eighty-third year when he died in 901, we may assume that Fatima was some three decades his junior. None of Qaitbay's lengthy biographies, which praise his piety and extol his generosity but provide only offices prior to his enthronement, reveals the date of his marriage to Fatima.[36] Nonetheless, adhering to his predecessors' preference, Qaitbay took no other legal wife throughout his lifetime.[37]

We can surmise what Fatima's background was like from the pattern of her own endowments, the careers of her contemporaries, and the great esteem she received from husband, peers, and the public at large. From the network of agents and judges through whom Fatima established her personal estate, we may assume that the princess was familiar with property management long before her betrothal. Fatima appears in several deeds as supervisor for her two siblings, al-Nasir Muhammad and al-Masuna 'A'isha.[38] She apparently served as her father's executor, even though there was a surviving son. Fatima thus brought a substantial fortune to her marriage. For his part, Qaitbay had assiduously managed his own sizable assets during his distinguished career as an amir.[39] Accordingly, upon his enthronement in 872/1468, the two already were rich and well versed in the techniques of estate preservation. But fate was not kind to this couple who demonstrated such farsighted conduct of their affairs. Their marriage produced only two children, both of whom succumbed to the plague in childhood.[40] Qaitbay's heir, al-Nasir Muhammad, was the issue of a concubine, Aslbay, and born late in his reign.[41] Yet these personal tragedies never blighted his relationship with Fatima, which remained a close personal bond.

Fatima appears in the chronicles on only three occasions: when she ascended the citadel once her husband felt secure enough to transfer his household from his former residence to the palace;[42] when she participated in the pilgrimage of 879/1475, without her husband (who went four years later);[43] and when she died (see note 35). Fatima received a lavish reception upon her return from the Hijaz. She was accompanied to the citadel by the four chief justices, who walked beside her palanquin. Cantors bearing tambourines heralded her progression. As she ascended to the citadel from Rumaila Square, the parasol and the bird, emblems of royalty reserved for the supreme autocrat, were held over her head. Gold and silver pieces were strewn about her, and when she entered the palace, gifts commemorating her safe return were presented by rejoicing courtiers.

Fatima's obituary notice emphasizes her great fortune and immense estate (*taraka hafila*). Ibn Iyas states that she presided as mistress over the court for thirty years and possessed her own quarters. But he also notes that, following her husband's decease, she was subjected to various indignities because of her wealth. The Julban recruits dared to invade her dwelling by the Aq Sunqur Bridge to demand a bonus. They heaped insults on her and threatened assault if she did not accede. When Qaitbay's heir, al-Nasir Muhammad, learned of their brazenness, he forbade any Mamluk to approach her residence on pain of death. The Julban believed that Fatima had participated in a conspiracy to murder the grand amir Qansuh Khamsmi'a, whom she married, following his enthronement, to defend her estate. Fatima's involvement was never proved, but she remained vulnerable. She therefore sought security through yet another marriage—to al-'Adil Tumanbay—which lasted only two months. Fatima's health declined rapidly thereafter, and she died in Bulaq of an ulcer.

Some thirty-nine deeds granted by Fatima alone have been preserved. We should recall that this collection of documents may represent only a remnant of Fatima's total endowment program. Nonetheless, the sample still extant does suggest an investment strategy. The longest writ, Fatima's own primary waqf, drawn up well into her career, repeats many properties listed in individual bills of sale (*buyu'*), which provide both shares and prices.[44] Indeed, most of the remaining documents identify Fatima's purchases.[45] The earliest dates from 21 Rabi' I 878/16 August 1473, the last from 27 Rajab 909/15 January 1504, just months before her death. She spent a total of 16,500 dinars and 10,000 dirhams (silver coins) during this thirty-year period. According to the surviving deeds, she was most actively engaged in acquisition of real estate between 894 and 896 (1488–91), which period also witnessed the first signs of her husband's declining vigor. Fatima may well have been concerned about her security after Qaitbay broke his leg during a polo match three years earlier, and began to plan for future exigencies. Two-thirds of the properties she bought were commercial or rental structures in Cairo or its environs, with notable clusterings in the Aq Sunqur (where she made her private home outside the citadel), Bab Sha'riyya, and Bulaq districts (total purchase value 9,900 dinars); one-third were agricultural lands in Gharbiyya (Delta), Ashmunain (Upper Egypt), and al-Matariyya (north of Cairo) (total purchase value 6,400 dinars). All of this property was clearly differentiated from that of her husband. Fatima, however, did buy shares in real estate partially owned by powerful amirs of her husband's faction who were his trusted colleagues, perhaps in an effort to hedge against the threat of confiscation were he to die suddenly. Upon her own demise, of course, Sultan al-Ghauri assumed title to all her property. The transfer was completed in one day: 24 Safar 910/6 August 1504, terminating one of the largest Mamluk fortunes of the ninth/fifteenth century.[46]

Yet Fatima managed to maintain her control over this estate throughout her lifetime—no mean feat. Al-Ghauri acquired a notoriety unparalleled even by members of his caste as a confiscator of charitable trusts, but even he waited until Fatima's death before seizing her assets. And he could claim with justice that no legal heirs survived her. Whether Fatima secretly agreed to will all her property to al-Ghauri if he respected her position until her death is not clear, but stands as a reasonable hypothesis. Al-Ghauri displayed elaborate disinterest throughout his turbulent reign for the feelings of those he abused. His respect for Fatima's rights during her life suggests that he had been assured some profit. In any case, from the profile of Fatima's investments, we detect a skilled partner who contributed to her husband's tactics for enlarging a fiscal preserve and an adept politician who controlled a vast estate after his demise. Fatima is a particularly salient example of a woman familiar with the total spectrum of her male relatives' finances.

What does this kind of familiarity suggest about women's function and influence over policy formation in the Mamluk state? We must distinguish between evidence clearly provided by the narrative and archival sources, and speculation over its possible implications. We know the following. First, the literature repeatedly refers to women autonomously managing property acquired from male relatives. They possessed the power to initiate litigation in defense of their rights, thereby sheltering their assets. Second, women were regarded as desirable custodians of estates because of their actuarial gain over men, their junior age at marriage, and their lesser susceptibility to the violence and feuding that sapped men's energies. As a consequence of these advantages, women were esteemed as guarantors of familial stability and lineage continuity. A woman who outlived one or more generations of her male kin often became a dowager, a revered symbol of her house and the head of her family. These readily verifiable facts go far to explain the augmented status of elite women in Mamluk society.

We may surmise from this evidence that some of these women served as effective colleague-consorts in the administration and preservation of their male relatives' estates. This sort of collusion in activities considered vital to ensuring the social rank and economic dominance of their class would elucidate their visibility in both the narrative literature and the documentary sources. Moreover, it is quite likely that these women were intimately involved in the unofficial or clandestine economy that provided the ruling elite with much of its funding. Qaitbay was a pioneer in attempts to circumvent his regime's dependency on traditional taxes by creating a private fiscal preserve through artful manipulation of trust properties. Can we assume that his wife's activities as a waqf purchaser, unparalleled in scale during the later medieval period, had some bearing on this strategy? Given the dearth of concrete information, we cannot be sure of Fatima's hidden motives. But we can place our current knowledge in a more intriguing setting by raising such hypotheses. When Ibn Iyas observed that Khawand Zainab administered state affairs on behalf of her husband, he may have inferred more than he would openly describe. Did he assume that his readers would know enough to appreciate the significance of his remarks? Recapturing the gist of such assumptions poses a challenge to our generation of historians, who seek to comprehend the behavior and aspirations of vibrant actors of both sexes in premodern Muslim societies.

Notes

1. Ibn Iyas, *Bada'i' al-zuhur fi waqa'i' al-duhur*, ed. Muhammad Mustafa (Cairo: Bibliotheca Islamica, 1963), 3:156, l. 19.

2. An entire Sura (chapter) of the Quran, no. 4, deals with women's rights and obligations as believers, wives, wage earners, heirs, and parents. Several of its verses, in particular no. 38 (as counted by A. J. Arberry, *The Koran Interpreted* [New York: Macmillan, 1955]), have aroused such controversy that they cannot be evaluated in isolation from the social context of the Prophet's own age. See Nabia Abbott, "Women and the State on the Eve of Islam," *American Journal of Semitic Languages and Literatures* 58 (1941): 259–84; Abbott, "Women and the State in Early Islam," *Journal of Near Eastern Studies* 1 (1942): 106–26; and Jane I. Smith and Yvonne Y. Haddad, "Women in the Afterlife: The Islamic View as Seen from Qur'an and Tradition," *Journal of the American Academy of Religion* 43 (1975): 39–50. For views of prominent political theorists of the Middle Ages on the status of women, see Nasir al-Din Tusi, *Ethics*, trans. G. M. Wickens (London: George Allen and Unwin, 1964), 161–77; and Nizam al-Mulk, *The Book of Government*, trans. Hubert Darke (London: Routledge, 1978), 179–86.

3. On general background to this period, see David Ayalon, "Aspects of the Mamluk Phenomenon," *Der Islam* 53 (1976): 196–225; Ayalon, "Ayyubids, Kurds and Turks," *Der Islam* 54 (1977): 1–32; Andrew Ehrenkreutz, *Saladin* (Albany: State University of New York Press, 1972); P. M. Holt, *The Age of the Crusades: The Near East from the Eleventh Century to 1517* (London: Longman, 1986); R. Stephen Humphreys, *From Saladin to the Mongols: The Ayyubids of Damascus, 1193–1260* (Albany: State University of New York Press, 1977); Robert Irwin, *The Middle East*

in the Middle Ages: The Early Mamluk Sultanate, 1250–1382 (Carbondale: University of Southern Illinois Press, 1986); Malcolm Cameron Lyons and D. E. P. Jackson, *Saladin: The Politics of the Holy War* (Cambridge: Cambridge University Press, 1982); and Gaston Wiet, *L'Egypte arabe*, vol. 4 of Gabriel Hanotaux, ed., *Histoire de la nation égyptienne* (Paris: Société de l'Histoire Nationale, 1937).

4. See the following by David Ayalon: "The Circassians in the Mamluk Kingdom," *Journal of the Royal Asiatic Society* 69 (1949): 135–47; "Names, Titles and Nisbas of the Mamluks," *Israel Oriental Studies* 5 (1975): 189–232; "Le régiment bahriya dans l'armée mamelouke," *Revue des études islamiques* (1951): 133–41; and "The European-Asiatic Steppe: A Major Reservoir of Power for the Islamic World," *Acts of the Twenty-fifth Congress of Orientalists* (Moscow, 1960), 2:47–52.

5. Ann K. S. Lambton, "The Constitution of Society," pt. 2, "Women of the Ruling House," chap. 8 in *Continuity and Change in Medieval Persia*, Bibliotheca Persica (Albany: State University of New York Press, 1988), 258–96. See also Shirin Bayani, *Zan-i irani dar 'asr-i Mughul* (Iranian women during the Mongol period) (Tehran: Tehran University Press, 1352/1973); and Karl Jahn, "Timur und die Frauen," *Anzeiger der Österreichischen Akademie der Wissenschaften, Philosophisch Historische Klasse* 3, no. 24 (1974): 515–29.

6. In general, the Mamluk elite rejected the principle of a ruling dynasty. The requirement that senior officers and the sultan himself had to advance from the ranks of first-generation imported slaves dated from the origins of the regime, during the turbulent decades following the death of al-Malik al-Salih in 1249. See Irwin, *Middle East*, 1–36; Ira M. Lapidus, *Muslim Cities in the Later Middle Ages* (Cambridge: Harvard University Press, 1967), 1–8; and Carl Petry, *The Civilian Elite of Cairo in the Later Middle Ages* (Princeton: Princeton University Press, 1981), 19–25. The descendants of Sultan Qala'un did constitute a dynasty of sorts, since they occupied the throne for much of the eighth/fourteenth century. But their right of inheritance was never absolute, nor did it go unchallenged.

7. Every generation of chroniclers produced critics of Mamluk rivalry and violence. During the later period, 'Abd al-Basit b. Khalil, Ibn Iyas, and al-Sairafi al-Jauhari were representative of the concern voiced by literate civilians over the endemic violence of Mamluk politics. See 'Abd al-Basit, *al-Raud al-basim fi hawadith al-'umr wa'l-tarajim*, MS, Arabo 728–29, fol. 251, l. 23, Vatican Library; Ibn Iyas, *Bada'i'* 3:45, l. 9, on the tyranny of Amir Inal al-Ashqar, mentioned below, 3:72, l. 15, on violent dispute between the Atabak and an officer over results of polo match; al-Sairafi, *Inba' al-hasr bi-abna' al-'asr*, ed. Hasan Habashi (Cairo: Dar al-Fikr al-'Arabi, 1970), 193, l. 1, on a Mamluk soldier shooting a soldier from rival unit while drunk, 232, l. 17, on amirs quarreling over flaying of a bedouin. Robert Irwin offers a brief but perceptive analysis of Mamluk violence in *Middle East*, 86–102.

8. The contemporary sources do not provide any references to mortality related to childbirth, so no statistics can be drawn. Since chronicles do emphasize the choice of females as custodians of property because of their longevity, we may assume that the actuarial gain of women outweighed this risk, at least to some degree.

9. Al-Maqrizi, *Kitab al-suluk li-ma'rifa duwal al-muluk*, ed. Mustafa Ziyada (Cairo: Committee on Authorship, Translation, and Publication, 1936), 1:324–44,

361-68; Humphreys, *From Saladin to the Mongols*, 303–4; G. Schregle, *Die Sultanin von Ägypten* (Wiesbaden: F. Steiner, 1961).

10. For examples of women active in Mamluk politics, see Carl Petry, "A Paradox of Patronage during the Later Mamluk Period," *Muslim World* 73, nos. 3–4 (1983), esp. nn. 39, 43. An interesting case involved Aslbay, a concubine of Sultan Qaitbay and the mother of his heir. Sultan al-Ghauri refused to allow her to return from the pilgrimage to Mecca due to her alleged conspiracy with Qaitbay's loyal retainers. See Ibn Iyas, *Bada'i'* 4:131, l. 11, 159, l. 15.

11. Irwin, *Middle East*, 85–102, 125–49; Lapidus, *Muslim Cities*, 25–38.

12. On reversion of arable land to pasturage or waste, see Jean-Claude Garcin, *Un centre de la haute Egypte médiévale: Qus* (Cairo: Institut Français d'Archéologie Orientale, 1976), 499–506, and Garcin, "La méditerranéisation de l'empire mamlouk sous les sultans bahrides," *Rivista degli studi orientali* 48 (1974): 109–16.

13. Eliyahu Ashtor, *Levant Trade in the Later Middle Ages* (Princeton: Princeton University Press, 1983), 200–216, 433–50; Jean-Claude Garcin, "The Mamluk Military System and the Blocking of Medieval Muslim Society," in *Europe and the Rise of Capitalism*, ed. Jean Baechler (Oxford: Oxford University Press, 1988), 113–35; Subhi Labib, *Handelsgeschichte Ägyptens im Spätmittelalter (1171–1571)* (Wiesbaden: F. Steiner, 1965), 402–8.

14. Little has been written on the ideological orientation of the Mamluk regime. But its policies, first articulated during the reign of al-Zahir Baibars, clearly indicated a commitment to preservation of the status quo rather than expansionism. See David Ayalon, "Preliminary Remarks on the Mamluk Military Institution in Islam," in *War, Technology and Society in the Middle East*, ed. V. J. Parry (Oxford: Oxford University Press, 1975), 44–58; P. M. Holt, "Some Observations on Shafi' b. 'Ali's Biography of Baybars," *Journal of Semitic Studies* 29 (1984): 123-30; Irwin, *Middle East*, 37–58; Abd al-Aziz Khowaiter, *Baibars the First: His Endeavors and Achievements* (London: Green Mountain Press, 1978); and Peter Thorau, *Sultan Baibars I. von Ägypten* (Wiesbaden: Ludwig Reichert, 1987), 143–60, 169–86.

15. Ibn Iyas, *Bada'i'* 3:5, l. 12 (sultan refuses to pay accession gift), 27, l. 3 (sultan compelled to grant 400,000-dinar bonus for expedition), 3:236, l. 10 (sultan forced to pay special bonus to quell revolt), 3:251, l. 13 (sultan distributes 1 million dinars in bonuses alone for Ottoman expedition), 3:261, l. 16 (sultan threatens to abdicate due to impending bankruptcy); 'Abd al-Basit, *Raud*, fol. 203-b, l. 22; al-Sairafi, *Inba'*, 16, l. 16, 24, l. 5 (sultan omits stipend to *aulad al-nass* (descendants of Mamluk) due to depletion of treasury), 35, l. 13, 40, l. 11 (sultan reduces stipends to Sultani Mamluks).

16. Petry, *Civilian Elite*, 202–21.

17. Ibid., 312–25; Ibn Iyas claimed that Sultan al-Ghauri so abused his civil officials that he upset this tacit partnership. *Bada'i'* 5:91, l. 15.

18. See, for example, 'Abd al-Basit, *Raud*, fol. 174-b, l. 17 (Qaitbay's confiscation of the former grand dawadar's estate at the outset of his reign); al-Sairafi, *Inba'*, 56, l. 12; Ibn Iyas, *Bada'i'* 3:39, l. 13 (Qaitbay arrests Zain al-Din the Ustadar and demands 100,000 dinars; latter claims to own only house and *waqf*), 4:12, l. 6 (upon his accession al-Ghauri imprisons the treasurer Timurbay), 4:405, l. 3 (upon the Amir Khairbak al-Khazindar's death, huge hidden estate discovered), 4:428, l.

24, 476, l. 1 (al-Ghauri tortures Ustadar to compel revelation of assets); 5:32, l. 8 (al-Ghauri seizes property of daughter of inspector (*kashif*) of Gharbiyya Province), 5:90, l. 1 (author castigates al-Ghauri for confiscating inheritances).

19. Al-Sairafi, *Inba'*, 38, l. 1 (on unfair taxes charged by *wazirs*, in contrast with past); Ibn Iyas, *Bada'i'* 3:260, l. 16 (futures tax on merchants to raise bonus money); 3:262, l. 19, (masses revolt against qadi who recommended futures tax), 3:278, l. 5 (sultan imposes huge ad hoc tax to defray cost of Ottoman expedition), 3:315, l. 12 (futures tax on grain), 3:302, l. 10 (author criticizes sultan for charging five-months futures tax), 4:20, l. 7 (sultan's agents demand seven-months futures tax).

20. Ibn Iyas, *Bada'i'* 3:253, l. 13 (sultan places tax of one-fifth yield on iqta' holders), 3:269, l. 8 (fifth tax on iqta' holders in Sharqiyya to fund Ottoman expedition), 4:24, l. 10 (iqta' holders forced to pay double *kharaj*), 4:262, l. 12 (prefects of Gharbiyya and Sharqiyya charge futures yield tax), 4:291, l. 9 (sultan forces iqta' holders to pay for dyke and canal repairs).

21. 'Abd al-Basit, *Raud*, fol. 183, l. 2; al-Sairafi, *Inba'*, 34, l. 14 (sultan contemplates collecting portion of waqf yields to pay bonuses); Ibn Iyas, *Bada'i'* 3:13, l. 21 (sultan convenes council of qadis to debate tapping waqf yields to raise expedition money), 3:192, l. 9 (sultan appoints extortionist supervisor of trusts (nazir al-auqaf), 3:331, l. 1 (author denounces Qaitbay for allowing his dawadar, Yashbak, to alienate waqfs), 4:14, l. 13 (sultan convenes qadis to discuss waqf confiscation), 4:260, l. 5 (sultan confiscates Shafi'i waqfs), 5:91, l. 1 (author implies that God has allowed Ottoman conquest as revenge for al-Ghauri's tampering with trusts).

22. Muhammad Amin has explored the consequences of waqf manipulation. See his *al-Auqaf wa'l-hayat al-ijtima'iyya fi Misr* (Cairo: Dar al-Nahda al-'Arabiyya, 1980), 361-72. Lapidus discusses urban decline brought on by insecurity of assets (*Muslim Cities*, 27–38). I have touched on the subject in a general way. *Civilian Elite*, 19–33, 246–54.

23. Al-Sairafi, *Inba'*, 429, l. 1 (who refers to Sada as his mother); Ibn Iyas, *Bada'i'* 3:46, l. 17.

24. Indeed, the only case of a Mamluk woman suffering torture that I have discovered was Khawand Jankaldi, wife of Sultan al-Zahir Qansuh (a predecessor of al-Ghauri), who was interrogated about the hiding place of her husband. Ibn Iyas, *Bada'i'* 4:205, l. 19.

25. Al-Sairafi, *Inba'*, 19, l. 1.

26. Ibid., 286, l. 9.

27. Ibid., 471, l. 9 (18 Muharram 877/26 June 1472).

28. Ibid., 131, l. 14.

29. Ibid., 225, l. 14 (d. 16 Jumada I 875/25 Dec. 1466).

30. Ibid., 426, l. 6; Ibn Iyas, *Bada'i'* 3:70, l. 13 (d. 28 Shawwal 876/8 Apr. 1472).

31. Muhammad M. Amin, *Catalogue des documents d'archives du Caire de 239/853 à 922/1516* (Cairo: Institut Français d'Archéologie Orientale, 1981).

32. Daftarkhana, hujjat 913 jadid (Amin #339), Ministry of Waqfs, Cairo.

33. Ibn Taghri-Birdi, *al-Manhal al-safi wa'l-mustaufi ba'd al-wafi*, Ms (Cairo: Dar al-Kutub, Ta'rikh 1113); Gaston Wiet, "Les biographies du Manhal Safi," *Mémoires de l'institut d'Egypte* 19, no. 944 (1932): 139.

34. 'Abd al-Basit, *Raud*, fol. 181, l. 29. See also Ibn Iyas, *Bada'i'* 3:302, l. 14.

35. Ibn Iyas, *Bada'i'* 4:64, l. 6.

36. See al-Sakhawi, *al-Dau' al-lami' fi a'yan al-qarn al-tasi'* (Beirut: Dar al-Maktaba al-Haya, 1934), 4, p. 201, no. 697, for the lengthiest and most adulatory biography.

37. Few Mamluk sultans elevated more than one connubial partner to the status of legal wife, even though Islamic law entitled them to four. Most took concubines simultaneously, however, and progeny from the latter enjoyed equal inheritance rights.

38. Fatima's two siblings are referred to in the context of her "donation" (*hiba*) to Sultan al-Ghauri. Fatima made this donation of property in the role of caretaker of her inheritance and that of "her siblings (*ikhwaha*) by her father: The Honorable (Janab) al-Nasir Muhammad and the Lady the Virtuous (Masuna) 'A'isha." See Daftarkhana, hujjat 104 jadid (Amin #450), Ministry of Waqfs.

39. The earliest surviving deed drawn up for Qaitbay is dated 29 Dhu al-Qa'da 855/23 Dec. 1451, seventeen years before his enthronement (Mahkama Shar'iyya: Mahfaza 18, hujjat 111, National Archives, Cairo [Amin #116]). He is referred to as al-Saifi Qaitbay b. 'Abd Allah al-Mahmudi. As amir he purchased 26.7 percent of a plot of land in Nahiyat Salmun, Gharbiyya Province, for 1,100 dinars. Since this property does not appear in later waqf documents designating its yield for support of a foundation, the purchase presumably was reserved for Qaitbay's own estate.

40. Al-Sairafi, *Inba'*, 60, l. 1; Ibn Iyas, *Bada'i'* 3:30, l. 12.

41. The son was born in Shawwal 887/November 1483, to "the Sultan's favorite, Aslbay al-Jarkasiyya" (Ibn Iyas, *Bada'i'* 3:197, l. 4). Sultan al-Ghauri later confiscated all of Aslbay's estate: ibid., 4:20, l. 12.

42. 'Abd al-Basit, *Raud*, fol. 181, l. 29; Ibn Iyas, *Bada'i'* 3:12, l. 4 (on 4 Dhu al-Qa'da 872/26 May 1468).

43. Ibn Iyas, *Bada'i'* 3:106, l. 18.

44. Daftarkhana, hujjat 775 jadid (Amin #506), Ministry of Waqfs.

45. When Sultan al-Ghauri assumed ownership of Fatima's estate, he took over most of the surviving deeds. They are all in Daftarkhana, the "new" (jadid) collection, Ministry of Waqfs.

711 (Amin #376), purchase, 12 Rabi' II 894/15 Mar. 1489

205 (Amin #421), transfer, 24 Shawwal 904/3 June 1499

765 (Amin #427), purchase, 2 Jumada II 903/26 Jan. 1498

443 (Amin #430), purchase, 22 Dhu al-Hijja 895/6 Nov. 1490

428 (Amin #435), purchase, 23 Sha'ban 894/22 July 1489

209 (Amin #438), transfer, 22 Dhu al-Hijja 905/19 July 1500

490 (Amin #439), purchase, 22 Dhu al-Hijja 895/6 Nov. 1490

410 (Amin #442), purchase, 17 Rabi' I 896/28 Jan. 1491

104 (Amin #450), transfer, 19 Dhu al-Hijja 890/27 Dec. 1485

707 (Amin #469), waqf, 21 Rabi' I 878/16 Aug. 1473. This deed was not taken over by al-Ghauri.

194 (Amin #481), purchase, 11 Muharram 890/28 Jan. 1485

579 (Amin #502), rent, 2 Jumada I 900/29 Jan. 1495

471 (Amin #504), repossession, 3 Dhu al-Hijja 888/2 Jan. 1484

77-a (Amin #510), purchase, 26 Jumada II 903/19 Feb. 1498

447 (Amin #518), purchase, 19 Dhu al-Hijja 890/27 Dec. 1485
427 (Amin #519), purchase, 6 Dhu al-Qa'da 894/1 Oct. 1489
433 (Amin #528), purchase, 11 Dhu al-Qa'da 891/8 Nov. 1486
448 (Amin #543), purchase, 5 Rabi' I 894/6 Feb. 1489
492 (Amin #544), purchase, 12 Rabi' II 894/15 Mar. 1489
474 (Amin #545), purchase, 12 Rabi' II 894/15 Mar. 1489
472 (Amin #546), purchase, 23 Dhu al-Hijja 894/18 Nov. 1489
455 (Amin #548), purchase, 23 Dhu al-Hijja 894/18 Nov. 1489
438 (Amin #553), purchase, 17 Rabi' I 896/28 Jan. 1491
50 (Amin #555), transfer, 6 Dhu al-Qa'da 904/15 June 1499
178 (Amin #556), purchase, 15 Shawwal 896/24 Aug. 1491
59 (Amin #565), purchase, 6 Shawwal 899/10 July 1494
469 (Amin #566), purchase, 6 Jumada I 900/2 Feb. 1495
109 (Amin #567), transfer, 27 Rajab 909/15 Jan. 1504
435 (Amin #576), purchase, 15 Dhu al-Qa'da 901/26 July 1496
409 (Amin #577), purchase, 15 Dhu al-Qa'da 901/26 July 1496
212 (Amin #583), transfer, 16 Safar 903/14 Oct. 1497
77-b (Amin #592), purchase, 6 Dhu al-Qa'da 904/15 June 1498
453 (Amin #594), purchase, 13 Rabi' II 905/17 Nov. 1499
123 (Amin #595), purchase, 14 Rabi' II 905/18 Nov. 1499
465 (Amin #608), purchase, 20 Jumada II 906/11 Jan. 1501
466 (Amin #622), purchase, 10 Ramadan 907/19 Mar. 1502
677 (Amin #660), purchase, 27 Rajab 909/15 Jan. 1504

46. The assumptions are designated as *intiqal* (transfer) or *hiba* (gift). They name al-Ghauri as executor of Fatima's estate and place all properties within the sultan's waqf supporting his *khanqah* (mystic hospice) and *madrasa* (known as the Ghuriya today). The presiding judge was Sari al-Din 'Abd al-Barr b. al-Shihna al-Hanafi, who was deeply involved in the sultan's expropriations until his fall from grace in 919/1513. The scribes (*muwaqqi'un*) were 'Abd al-Karim b. 'Ali al-Majuli and Musa b. 'Abd al-Ghani al-Maliki.

8

Women and Islamic Education

in the Mamluk Period

JONATHAN P. BERKEY

> How splendid were the women of the *ansar* [the Medinese
> "helpers" of the Prophet]—shame did not prevent them from
> becoming learned in the faith.—'A'isha, wife of the Prophet.

Islamic legal and religious education was in origin and remained throughout the Middle Ages a fundamentally informal system. From the primary level to the final stages of
instruction and the transmission of knowledge, one's education depended more on a personal relationship with a teacher or teachers than it did on an attachment to any institution.
The community of scholars whose standards and principles
arbitrated all questions of intellectual accomplishment
looked not to an attestation that one had studied in any
particular school, but rather to the *ijaza*, the certification by a
teacher that a particular student was qualified to teach a particular subject, or to transmit a specific book or collection of
traditions. The bonds between teacher and student may
have been informal, but they could also prove extremely
close, and not infrequently grew out of actual ties of kinship.
In such a system, as we shall see, women could play a significant role.

To be sure, the rise of the institution known as the *madrasa*
resulted, to a certain degree, in the "formalization" of the
educational process. Before the eleventh century, mosques
provided the principal venue for the teaching circles (*halqa*,
majlis) in which all Islamic higher education took place. Prospective students made private arrangements with the
shaikhs (masters, teachers) who taught at such sessions, the
teachers drawing an income from fees paid to them by their
students, or from the occasional largesse of the caliph or

Portions of this chapter appear in somewhat different form in *The
Transmission of Knowledge in Medieval Cairo: A Social History of Islamic
Education* (Princeton University Press, 1992).

some other wealthy individual. The establishment of the Nizamiyya madrasa in Baghdad in A.H. 459/A.D. 1067, however, significantly altered the equation. Closely associated with the Sunni revival of the twelfth century, the madrasa spread rapidly through Syria and later, Egypt, under the patronage of Zangid and Ayyubid sultans. For the first time, the Islamic world produced an institution, distinct from mosques and other religious establishments, devoted specifically to the inculcation of the Islamic religious sciences and, in particular, of *fiqh*, the science of Islamic jurisprudence.[1]

The task of identifying with precision the distinctions between the madrasa and other institutions of Islamic learning raises difficulties of its own, problems that cannot be dealt with here. For our present purposes it suffices to note that madrasas systematically provided, first, endowed teaching posts with guaranteed stipends for those professors who held them, and second, stipends and often living accommodations for students. Even after the collapse of the Shi'i governments and the withdrawal from Palestine of the Latin Crusaders—the twin threats that had motivated the Zangid and Ayyubid princes to construct and endow institutions to train a class of legal and religious officials—madrasas continued to be built. In the city of Cairo, capital of the Mamluk regime from its inception in the year 648/1250 to its demise at the hands of the Ottoman sultan Selim in 922/1517, madrasas emerged as the leading institutions of Islamic education, their endowed professorships and student scholarships supporting a corps of trained legal scholars and officials.

Many women of the Mamluk period were associated with madrasas as benefactors, supplying the endowments necessary to establish and maintain the schools. A minimum of five such schools, founded by women, existed at some time in Mamluk Cairo: one established by the wife of a powerful Ayyubid amir at least half a century before the fall of that dynasty; one established in the seventh/thirteenth century by the daughter of an Ayyubid prince, who herself was learned in hadith (the Prophetic traditions); one endowed by a daughter of the Mamluk sultan al-Nasir Muhammad, which included a tomb for her own burial; another, and perhaps the most famous, established by Barakat, the mother of Sultan al-Ashraf Sha'ban, in 771/1469–70; and one built by Fatima, the daughter of Qanibay al-'Umari al-Nasiri and wife of Taghri Birdi al-Mu'adhdhi, in the late ninth/fifteenth century.[2] At least one more was established within a decade of the Ottoman conquest.[3] According to a sixteenth-century history of Damascene madrasas, the Syrian capital boasted even more.[4] Other women shared in the abiding interest felt by their families for schools established by an ancestor, for example, by bestowing endowments on them at a future date. Quite a few—

daughters and wives of Mamluk as well as scholarly families—were buried in tombs attached to madrasas founded by a husband, father, or grandfather.

A woman could also be vested with a supervisory role in the administration of a madrasa. Deeds of endowment (*waqfiyyas*) establishing madrasas normally left ultimate financial and administrative control (*nazar*) of the institutions and their endowments in the hands of the founders and, after them, their children and descendants—usually specified as "the most rightly guided" (*al-arshad*) of the descendants—their trusted retainers, powerful amirs, judges, or some combination thereof. How often such stipulations resulted in a woman's assuming the controllership of Cairene madrasas is not clear, although one researcher who knows the documentary sources well has concluded that the practice was common.[5] Several waqfiyyas stipulated specifically that the female as well as the male descendants of the founder were to be eligible to serve as controller of endowments supporting madrasas.[6] Nonetheless, it lay within the founders' discretionary powers to exclude their daughters and female descendants from the nazar, and sultans al-Zahir Barquq and al-Mu'ayyad Shaikh, among others, chose to make such a stipulation in establishing their madrasas.[7]

Thus the wives and daughters of the Mamluks and of the academic elite were hardly strangers to the world of institutionalized education, and they participated actively in the creation and administration of the endowments on which that world relied. As benefactors, several women invested substantial sums in the establishment of institutions of learning, like their male counterparts appropriating to themselves the *baraka* (blessing) thought to be gained from supporting the pious activities of the schools. As administrators, they found themselves, at least in theory (for substitutes could be appointed), actively managing a school's assets and appointing its professors and other functionaries.

Women, however, played virtually no role, as either professor or student, in the systematic legal education offered in the madrasas. To the best of my knowledge, the chronicles and biographical dictionaries of the Mamluk period yield not a single instance of the appointment of a woman to a post in a madrasa, or to an endowed post in any educational institution.[8] This is hardly surprising, and the explanation is not difficult to discover. Quite simply, women were excluded from active participation in those occupations—litigation, judging, administration—for which the systematic legal curriculum of the madrasa was designed to produce qualified candidates.

Yet immediately an anomaly confronts us. As the sources attest, many medieval women were, in some sense, educated. Of the 1,075 women listed in al-Sakhawi's *al-Dau' al-lami' li-ahl al-qarn al-tasi'*, a biographical dictionary of the leading figures of the ninth/fifteenth century, 411 can definitely be said to have received some degree of education: to have memorized the Quran, or studied with a particular scholar, or received an ijaza. The biographies of the other women are not detailed enough to allow definitive judgments as to the extent of their intellectual training, but given al-Sakhawi's interests, it seems probable that they, too, were educated: the eleven volumes devoted to men consist largely of details of the lives and careers of the educated elite. But if women were excluded from the madrasa, what did they study, where, with whom, and why?

The answer lies in the persistent informality of Islamic education. The remarkable growth in the number of madrasas notwithstanding, the institution never established a monopoly on the inculcation of the Islamic sciences. Endowment deeds for madrasas often made precise stipulations as to which classes were to be held when and in which parts of the building, and who was to attend, but we should not be led to believe that lessons occurred only at those times and places. On the contrary, many scholars continued to teach in less formal settings: in public teaching circles in mosques and in private homes. In such venues, women might be found alongside men, receiving instruction or attending the recitation of hadith. Hence, as we shall see, the moral outrage of the fourteenth-century puritan Ibn al-Hajj at the popular practice of women coming together with men in mosques to hear a recitation of books (*sama' al-kutub*) by a shaikh or an *imam* (literally, a prayer leader).

The transmission of knowledge in the later Middle Ages continued to depend far more on the personal relationship between teacher and student than it did on any institutional framework. Most educations began with the closest relationship of all, that of kinship. When listing those with whom a particular individual studied, al-Sakhawi and other biographers often began with the subject's father, grandfather, or uncle, and only then moved on to others. For women, this was particularly true. Zainab al-Tukhiyya (d. 894/1388), for example, the daughter of 'Ali ibn Muhammad al-Diruti al-Mahalli, received from family members a basic but substantial education typical of that given many girls. When she was a child in Mahalla, her father made her memorize the Quran and taught her to write, but he also instructed her in a number of books that formed core elements in the advanced education of any late medieval Muslim of the Shafi'i *madhhab* (school of law). Zainab studied several fundamental works of Shafi'i jurisprudence, including Najm al-Din 'Abd al-Ghaffar al-Qazwini's work *al-Hawi al-saghir fi al-furu'* and the *mukhtasar* (abridgment) of Abu Shajja' Ahmad al-Isfahani, as well as a treatise in verse on Arabic grammar entitled *al-Mulha*, written by Abu Muhammad Qasim al-Hariri.[9]

But husbands, no less than fathers, grandfathers, and uncles, assumed a responsibility for the education of their wives. Thus, after her marriage, Zainab al-Tukhiyya's husband undertook to continue her education, guiding her through the two principal collections of hadith, the *Sahih* of al-Bukhari and that of Muslim ibn al-Hajjaj.[10] The jurist Qadi Khan recognized few situations in which women were permitted to leave their homes without their husbands' permission, but among them was that of a woman who wanted to attend a lesson (*majlis al-'ilm*) *and* whose husband was not a *faqih*—that is, was not himself qualified to instruct her. Clearly, the jurist understood that the primary responsibility for a woman's education lay with her husband.[11]

Families of the scholarly elite took special care to educate their female offspring. The biographical dictionaries frequently comment that boys who were to become famous scholars began their education, or received ijazas permitting them to transmit a certain book or collection of traditions, at extraordinarily young ages; girls, too, shared in this distinction. Another Zainab (d. 865/1461), daughter of 'Abd al-Rahim ibn al-Hasan al-'Iraqi al-Qahiri, began her education by accompanying her brother to classes at the start of her fifth year. Her older contemporary Zainab bint 'Abd Allah ibn Ahmad, known as Bint al-'Aryani (d. 856/1452), was similarly brought before a scholar for the first time at the age of two.[12]

The long-term intellectual benefits of these early contacts between scholars and pupils aside, such exposure held value chiefly as a first step in a process of including young students in the academic world. The full significance of their attendance will become apparent soon. For the moment, however, it is important to recognize that girls as well as boys were consciously drawn into the process and that, at such ages, the initiative for educating them lay with their families, that is to say, with fathers or possibly older brothers. In the *al-Majma' al-mu'assas bi'l-mu'jam al-mufahras,* an account of his education and a list of his teachers covering more than four hundred manuscript pages, Ibn Hajar al-'Asqalani carefully indicated those shaikhs from whom he had secured ijazas for his daughters.[13] That the scholarly Bulqini family produced many learned women whose biographies are found in al-Sakhawi's collection should therefore come as no surprise. Indeed, so accepted was the education of women among families of learning that al-Sakhawi commented of one woman, although he had no direct knowledge of her education, "I do not doubt that she had obtained ijazas, as her family was well-known [for its learning]."[14]

At one level, the care with which scholarly families (the ulama) educated their daughters reflected a concern for their spiritual well-being. Islamic education, after all, aims not only at producing a cadre of judges and scribes to regulate social intercourse, but also at inculcating the principles and practices that shape the character and behavior of a good Muslim—in other words, at the individual soul, which concerned men and women equally. Obviously, not everyone possessed the means to become an 'alim, a fully trained scholar, but all Muslims were expected to obtain the degree of knowledge requisite for their station in life, according to an important treatise on knowledge and learning that circulated widely during the Mamluk period. Everyone, for example, was required to know enough of the law to fulfill his or her duties to pray, fast, pay zakat (the obligatory alms tax), and perform the pilgrimage, duties incumbent on women as well as men. But 'ilm (religious and legal learning) involved more than the minimum knowledge needed to fulfill one's religious obligations. The same text noted that "[knowledge has an important bearing] on all other qualities [of human character] such as generosity and avarice, cowardice and courage, arrogance and humility, chastity [and debauchery], prodigality and parsimony, and so on. For arrogance, avarice, cowardice, and prodigality are illicit. Only through knowledge of them and their opposites is protection against them possible. Thus learning is prescribed for all of us."[15]

For all of us—including women. Although women did not function in society as lawyers and judges, scribes and administrators, they had no less need of 'ilm at the personal level than men did, a point that apparently did not escape the ulama. Islamic lawyers busied themselves with prescribing rules for the regulation of women's personal and social affairs and for their ritual and hygenic behavior—one need consider only the extensive chapters in the law books on menstruation and other matters of ritual purity of special interest to women. Those precepts and regulations then had to be transmitted to those they most concerned.

The only question was how this knowledge was to be transmitted to women and young girls. The matter was a delicate one, for somehow it had to be accomplished without threatening the gender boundaries that cut across the medieval Islamic world, which the ulama, with their greater familiarity with the precepts of the law, perhaps took more seriously than others did. Though many women participated actively in other religious, economic, and literary pursuits, including the transmission of knowledge, there was a certain reluctance to encourage the education of women, which although often overcome nonetheless doggedly shadowed their intellectual pursuits.[16] One reason women were excluded from education in madrasas was the intrinsic threat to sexual boundaries and taboos their presence was believed to represent in an institution housing any number of young male Muslims. Madrasas were not monasteries—many people lived inside them, including married scholars with their families (as witnessed by the not infrequent reports in the chronicles that a particular individual had been born in one madrasa or another). Many felt, however, that a stricter separation of men and women would prove more conducive to education. Women, wrote the fourteenth-century scholar Badr al-Din Ibn Jama'a in a treatise on the manners and methods of education, should not live in the madrasa, or nearby where men and boys from the madrasa would pass by their doors, or even in buildings with windows overlooking the courtyards of the schools.[17]

As we have already noted, however, Islamic education was by no means confined to the madrasa, and in the less formal venues in which it thrived—private teaching circles in mosques and homes—women could be found studying alongside men. There is no question that this occurred; how frequently and how well it was accepted are more problematic. Consider the complaint of Ibn al-Hajj, who wrote a lengthy treatise describing practices of which he did not approve:

> [Consider] what some women do when people [that is, men] gather with a shaikh to hear [the recitation of] books. At that point women come, too, to hear the readings; the men sit in one place, the women facing them. It even happens at such times that some of the women are carried away by the situation; one will stand up, and sit down, and shout in a loud voice. [Moreover,] private parts of her body will appear; in her house, their exposure would be forbidden—how can it be allowed in a mosque, in the presence of men?[18]

"Private parts of her body"—the term Ibn al-Hajj used was 'aurat, literally, "that which it is indecent to reveal." In the case of women, that might include everything except the face and hands. Clearly what concerned Ibn al-Hajj was not explicit exhibitionism, but the threat to established sexual boundaries represented by the mixing of men and women in these informal lessons.

Under these circumstances, alternative arrangements were generally made for the education of women. Women could be educated and sexual boundaries preserved by providing for instruction from family members: fathers, brothers, or husbands. Even so, many women studied with and received ijazas from scholars outside the immediate family circle, and often the scholars with whom they studied were themselves women. I do not mean to suggest that education took place exclusively in groups segregated by sex. On the contrary, many whose biographies were recorded in such compilations as al-Sakhawi's dictionary of fifteenth-century luminaries, males as well as females, were instructed by and received ijazas from learned women, a point to which we shall return. But a thorough perusal of the Kitab al-nisa', the volume of al-Sakhawi's work that is devoted to women, leaves the impression that girls, more than boys, received their instruction from other women. Some educated women shouldered the specific responsibility for "teaching women the Quran and instructing them in 'ilm and righteous deeds."[19] Al-Sakhawi offers an insight into a world in which learned women transmitted to other women the precepts of the law—that is to say, 'ilm—of special concern to them. A certain Khadija, daughter of 'Ali ibn 'Umar al-Ansari who died in 873/1469, "informed [other] women concerning the chapters [from the law books] on menstruation and like matters."[20] Women may not have explicitly formulated the law, even concerning specifically feminine matters, but they did play an active role in transmitting its principles and regulations to one another.

It was not necessary to establish a completely separate structure for this purpose. As we have seen, even in Mamluk Cairo structure was a secondary element in the organization of education and the transmission of knowledge. Historians of the period occasionally refer to girls whose fathers or brothers brought them to classes or lectures at a madrasa.[21] Nonetheless, the need to preserve sexual boundaries did encourage a focus on particular institutions and locations for the education of women. The forum might well be—a point worthy of special note—a private home, such as that of one learned woman of the fifteenth century whose family seems to have committed itself especially to the religious edification of women, for "her house was a gathering place for divorced and widowed women, devoted to the instruction of young girls."[22]

By extension, a secondary objective of the education of women involved the regulation of what might be called "female space." Consider, for example, the institution known as the *ribat* al-Baghdadiyya, established in 684/1286 by a daughter of the Mamluk sultan Baibars. Little is known of this hospice and others like it, although apparently at least five were established in Cairo over the course of the Mamluk period, in addition to a large number in the necropolis outside the city.[23] They seem to have served principally as places of residence for elderly, divorced, and widowed women who had no place of abode, until their death or remarriage.

In addition to providing women with shelter, however, at least some of these institutions were expected to satisfy the intellectual and spiritual needs of those without family members capable of providing them with a suitable education. This was particularly true of the ribat al-Baghdadiyya, where the shaikha who administered the institution routinely preached to the female residents and instructed them in fiqh, the science of Islamic jurisprudence, "until such time as they should remarry or return to their husbands."[24] Here, then, the instruction of women actually played a role in protecting and reaffirming sexual boundaries that the independent status of a divorced or widowed woman might threaten.

At first glance, education seems to have represented a world in which gender barriers, if not actually dissolved, were at least permeable. Al-Sakhawi himself, in his biographical dictionary, specifically refers to having studied with or received ijazas from sixty-eight women; this figure does not include those of an earlier generation whom his own teacher, Ibn Hajar al-'Asqalani, numbered among his instructors. Even in these settings, however, actual contact between men and women might be limited, since the standards of the time made it possible to receive an ijaza from a scholar without actually studying or reciting a work in his or her presence.[25] Here again, the family connection was crucial. Two sisters, for example, received ijazas by virtue of their association with their scholarly brothers.[26] In an ijaza issued by al-Sakhawi himself, the scholar authorized Abu Bakr ibn al-Hishi and his three sons, who had "heard" him recite his collection of traditions known as the *Kitab al-buldaniyyat*, to transmit the work; the same ijaza was issued to Ibn al-Hishi's younger daughter 'A'isha, although there is no evidence that she was actually present at the recitations.[27] Yet in other contexts men and women, boys and girls, did study and hear lessons together—a certain Asiyya al-Dimashqiyya (d. early tenth/sixteenth century), for example, heard lessons given by her grandmother in the presence of her brothers and al-Sakhawi.[28] Ibn al-Hajj's complaint that men and women were congregating in mosques to hear the recitation of a book, while suggesting that a certain section of the population frowned on the practice, nonetheless confirms that it was not uncommon.

In no field was this more true than in the transmission of hadith, the Prophetic traditions that form an important basis of Islamic law.[29] Well-known *muhaddithun* (those who had memorized and taught traditions) routinely compiled lists of those on whose authority they recited hadith; in them, most important male scholars included significant numbers of women. In his list of 172 names, Taj al-Din 'Abd al-Wahhab al-Subki (d. 771/1370) included 19 women.[30] Ibn Hajar al-'Asqalani provided the names of 53 women with whom, in one way or another, he studied traditions.[31] No less a scholar than Jalal al-Din al-Suyuti (d. 911/1505) relied heavily on women as his sources for hadith: of the 130 shaikhs of exceptional reliability on whose authority he recited traditions, 33—more than a quarter of the total—were women.[32]

'A'isha, the daughter of Muhammad ibn 'Abd al-Hadi, achieved a position in the transmission of hadith unequaled by many men, and her life provides a model for female transmitters. Born in Damascus in the early eighth/fourteenth century,[33] in her fourth year she was brought before Abu al-'Abbas Ahmad al-Hajjar, a prominent muhaddith who died in 730/1329, from whom she heard two small but popular collections of hadith.[34] She later studied Muslim ibn al-Hajjaj's important compendium of traditions, the *Sahih*, with Sharaf al-Din 'Abd Allah ibn al-Hasan[35] and others, and Ibn Hisham's *sira* (biography) of the Prophet. During her lifetime she collected ijazas from scholars in Aleppo, Hama, Nablus, and Hebron, and she herself became one whom the *rahhala*— those scholars and others who traveled the Islamic world in search of hadith—eagerly sought out. Her fame spread; as important a scholar as Ibn Hajar was proud to list her among his principal teachers.[36] The seventeenth-century historian Ibn al-'Imad gave her the epithet "*muhadditha* of Damascus" and remarked that she was "the most supported [that is, in the reliability of her transmission] of the people of her time."

The very nature of the culture of hadith transmission ensured that women, no less than men, could become prized teachers. Clearly it was imperative that one study hadith with a shaikh of wide knowledge and blameless reputation, not only to increase the number of traditions one knew and could transmit, but also to draw on a shaikh's authority and so enhance one's own reputation as a muhaddith. But the selection of a teacher of hadith involved another criterion as well: reducing the number of transmitters in a given chain of authority (*isnad*). In other words, a man or woman might become a prized teacher of hadith because he or she could claim to have studied directly with an especially revered transmitter of traditions. An inevitable consequence was that young pupils preferred older teachers, for these privileged students, as they aged, might become the sole surviving muhaddith in a particular city or region to recite traditions on the direct authority of a prominent shaikh.

At this level women could compete directly with men, and in fact a number of women distinguished themselves as the sole surviving transmitter of traditions from prominent teachers. The muhadditha 'A'isha bint 'Abd al-Hadi, for example, well deserved the great respect in which she was held, for she "aged until she stood alone [as a transmitter] from the majority of her shaikhs."[37] It is here that the early education of girls (and boys) played a critical role, by allowing women to establish independent reputations as valuable links in the chains of authority on which Muslim learning rested. 'A'isha was four when she heard the *Sahih* of al-Bukhari from the famous traditionist al-Hajjar, then more than a hundred years old. In 'A'isha's old age, as her student Ibn Hajar al-'Asqalani announced proudly in his account of his education, "no one other than ['A'isha] remained on the earth who transmitted from al-Hajjar."[38]

'A'isha bint 'Abd al-Hadi was by no means unique in this respect. Other women achieved distinction as prominent transmitters of hadith, among them Khadija bint Ibrahim b. Ishaq al-Dimashqiyya, who when she died at the age of almost ninety in 803/1400–1401, was the last to transmit hadith on the authority of al-Qasim Ibn 'Asakir, a prominent Syrian traditionist who died in 723/1323, "bi'l-sama'" (that is, having heard Ibn 'Asakir himself read traditions).[39] Both Maryam bint Ahmad ibn Ibrahim (d. 805/1402–3) and Fatima bint Khalil ibn Ahmad (d. 838/1434) ended their lives as the sole authorities for the direct transmission of traditions from a number of their shaikhs. Both, moreover, achieved the further distinction of having *mashyakhas* (lists of those on whose authority they transmitted hadith) composed for them—in the case of Fatima, by Ibn Hajar al-'Asqalani himself—a further indication that women studied traditions not only as pious adherents, but also as active participants in the transmission of this important field of Muslim intellectual endeavor.[40]

That women frequently excelled in the transmission of hadith, however, should not disguise from us the fundamental difference between the character of the education they received and that accorded men. The most practical consequence of this difference—namely, the absence of women in endowed positions in madrasas—we have already noted. The gender barrier affected the core of the relationship between teacher and student as it was known in medieval Islam. Instruction, it may be argued, necessarily implies a power relationship between instructor and student. Certainly Islamic pedagogical literature abounds with metaphors and normative guidelines that reinforced the subservient role of the instructed. A student should respect and obey his shaikh in all matters, commented an important fourteenth-century writer, "as the patient [obeys] the skillful doctor."[41] Another jurist preferred the metaphor of father and child: "Every student and teacher should show respect for the other, especially the former [that is, the student especially should be respectful], because his teacher is like the father or even greater, since his father brought him into the world of perdition, while his teacher leads him to the world of eternal life."[42] Inside the madrasa, or in situations of special intimacy between instructor and instructed, a teacher's control over his pupils extended to a close supervision of their behavior and morals, as well as their educational progress.[43] Consequently, a careful reader of the biographies of women in al-Sakhawi's *al-Dau' al-lami'* and in other biographical dictionaries will note the dearth of such terms as *suhba* and *mulazama*, terms that describe the intimate personal and intellectual relationships between gifted students and particular prominent teachers, and terms that occur with such frequency in the biographies of men.[44]

Moreover, the biographical dictionaries reveal a paucity of women said to have excelled in jurisprudence, or in *usul* (the bases of jurisprudence), or in *kalam* (theology), or in any subjects in which male scholars were often said to have been proficient. This is not to say that such areas of study were entirely off limits to women. Girls could receive instruction in the fundamentals of fiqh, as did Zainab al-Tukhiyya. Many popular introductory texts formed part of the curriculum of the education of females, such as Ibn Malik's versified introduction to Arabic grammar, *Ulfiyya;* al-Qasim al-Shatibi's popular poem on the Quran; and Sharaf al-Din al-Busiri's *qasida* (poem) in praise of the Prophet. But beyond the elementary stages, a woman's education focused almost exclusively on hadith, and in that field lay her surest path to prominence.

The study of hadith, of course, formed a core element in the education of any medieval Muslim, including those such as merchant-scholars, who though not full-time academics, nonetheless devoted great time and energy to the pursuit of 'ilm. Moreover, the hadith themselves played a formative role in the shaping of Islamic thought and society. The Prophetic traditions not only constituted one of the bases—in many ways the most important basis—of Islamic law, but their public recital on feast days, during the months of Rajab, Sha'ban, and Ramadan, and on other special occasions was also a central feature of popular Muslim religious celebration.

But the culture of hadith transmission differed sharply from the nature of the inculcation of fiqh, that is, it differed from the systematic legal education offered in the madrasas. In the first place, most women (and men, for that matter) became prominent transmitters of hadith only at a relatively advanced age, when their chains of authority were comparatively shorter; to a system protective of its gender boundaries, an elderly woman transmitting a text or a body of traditions posed a less serious threat than one younger.[45] Moreover, the most important quality of the muhaddithun was memory, the ability to remember and transmit accurately traditions that they themselves had studied, as well as the chains of authorities on which their transmission rested. Such stress was laid on memory that medieval writers sometimes complained of traditionists who merely memorized and recited hadith, without understanding them.[46] Memorization, of course, played a critical instructional role in other fields as well, but the study of fiqh and related subjects revolved around *munazara*, the disciplined disputation of fine points of the law and the resolution of controversial questions.[47] That women played a critical role in the transmission of hadith, and virtually none in higher legal training, may reflect this pedagogical difference. Women were systematically excluded from holding judicial positions that would require them to resolve disputes among men or formal instructional positions that carried a personal, institutional, or metaphorical authority over young men. A similar subconscious concern may have lurked behind their apparent exclusion from the study of such subjects as fiqh, where a woman's assertion of analytical and forensic skills could place her—intellectually, at least—in a position of authority over men. In the transmission of hadith, of course, disputes might also arise, over the accuracy of a transmitter's memory, for example, but such disputes could be resolved by reference to a text.

Such limitations, however, should not disguise the prominent role that women did play in the transmission of a critical field of traditional Muslim learning. The extent of their contribution is difficult to measure, obscured as it is by the indifference or embarrassment of sources written exclusively by men, and by the private venue in which most of their teaching took place. But the fact remains that prominent hadith scholars of the stature of Ibn Hajar and al-Suyuti openly relied on many women for secure and persuasive chains of authority. Their reliance suggests that active participation in the transmission of Muslim knowledge in the Middle Ages was by no means an exclusively male preserve.

Notes

1. See George Makdisi, *The Rise of Colleges: Institutions of Learning in Islam and the West* (Edinburgh: Edinburgh University Press, 1981).

2. For information on these madrasas—known as al-'Ashuriyya, al-Zutubiyya, al-Hijaziyya, the madrasa of Umm al-Sultan, and the madrasa of Umm Khawand—see Taqi al-Din Ahmad al-Maqrizi, *al-Mawa'iz wa'l-i'tibar bi-dhikr al-khitat wa'l-athar,* 2 vols. (Bulaq: Dar al-Taba'a al-Misriyya, 1853; reprint, Beirut: Dar al-Sadir, [1970?]), 2:368, 382, 399–400; and Shams al-Din Muhammad al-Sakhawi, *al-Dau' al-lami' li-ahl al-qarn al-tasi',* 12 vols. (Cairo: Maktabat al-Qudsi, A.H. 1353; reprint, Beirut: Dar Maktabat al-Hayat, 1982), 12:98.

3. By Khadija bint al-Dhirham wa Nisf; see Muhammad ibn Ahmad Ibn Iyas, *Bada'i' al-zuhur fi waqa'i' al-duhur,* ed. Paul Kahle and Muhammad Mustafa, 5 vols. (reprint, Cairo: Al-Hai'a al-Misriyya al-'Amma li'l-Kitab, 1982–84), 5:336.

4. 'Abd al-Qadir al-Nu'aimi, *al-Daris fi ta'rikh al-madaris* (Damascus: Al-Majma' al-'Ilmi al-'Arabi, 1948–51).

5. Carl Petry, "A Paradox of Patronage," *Muslim World* 73 (1983): 199; on 200–201 Petry lists a number of women who served various endowments as *nazirat* (controllers).

6. See, for example, the following waqfiyyas (all deeds cited are found in one of two Cairene archives: Dar al-Watha'iq al-Qaumiyya and Wizarat al-Auqaf): Mughultay al-Jamali, Wizarat al-Auqaf o.s. no. 1666; Zain al-din Sidqa, Dar al-Watha'iq no. 59; Sudun min Zada, Dar al-Watha'iq no. 58; and Jamal al-Din al-Ustadar, Dar al-Watha'iq no. 106.

7. Waqfiyyat Sultan Barquq, Dar al-Watha'iq no. 51; Waqfiyyat Sultan al-Mu'ayyad Shaikh, Wizarat al-Auqaf o.s. no. 938.

8. There is one possible exception. In A.H. 891 a certain Qilij al-Rumi al-Adhami died, and his wife was appointed—the world used is *qurrirat*—to his position as "shaikh" of the Sultan Qaitbay's *zawiya.* The significance of this event is not

at all clear, although the chronicler does record his surprise at the occasion. Ibn Iyas, *Bada'i'* 3:233.

9. Al-Sakhawi, of course, refers to these works only in a shorthand form—for example, as al-Hawi or al-Mulha. Their identification is based on other references in al-Sakhawi's biographical dictionary and those in Hajji Khalifa's seventeenth-century encyclopedia of Muslim learning, *Kashf al-zunun 'an asami al-kutub wa'l-funun* (Istanbul: Maarif Matbaasi, 1941).

10. Al-Sakhawi, *al-Dau'* 12:45.

11. Fakhr al-Din Qadi Khan, *Fatawa* (Cairo: Matba'at al-Shaikh Muhammad Shahin, 1865), 1:374.

12. Al-Sakhawi, *al-Dau'* 12:41–42.

13. Ibn Hajar al-'Asqalani, *al-Majma' al-mu'assas bi'l-mu'jam al-mufahras*, Dar al-Kutub al-Misriyya, "Mustalah al-Hadith" MS. 75 [= Ma'had Ihya' al-Makhtutat al-'Arabiyya, "Tarikh" MS. 780].

14. Al-Sakhawi, *al-Dau'* 12:6.

15. Burhan al-Din al-Zarnuji, *Ta'lim al-muta'allim, tariq al-ta'allum* (Cairo: Dar al-Nahda al-'Arabiyya, 1977), 9, 11; see the translation by G. E. von Grunebaum and Theodora M. Abel, *The Instruction of the Student: The Method of Learning* (New York: King's Crown Press, 1947), 21, 22.

16. A detailed summary of some of the occupations in which women were active can be found in Ahmad 'Abd ar-Raziq, *La femme au temps des mamlouks en Egypte* (Cairo: Institut Français d'Archéologie Orientale, 1973).

17. Badr al-Din Ibn Jama'a, *Tadhkirat al-sami' wa'l-mutakallim fi adab al-'alim wa'l-muta'allim* (Hyderabad: Da'irat al-Ma'arif al-'Uthmaniyya, A.H. 1353), 87.

18. Ibn al-Hajj, *Madkhal al-shar' al-sharif* (Cairo: Al-Matba'a al-Misriyya, 1929; reprint, Beirut: Dar al-Hadith, 1981), 2:219.

19. Ibn Hajar al-'Asqalani, *al-Durar al-kamina fi a'yan al-ma'ia al-thamina* (Cairo: Dar al-Kutub al-Haditha, 1966), 1:383.

20. Al-Sakhawi, *al-Dau'* 12:29.

21. See, for example, al-Sakhawi, *al-Dau'* 12:29.

22. Ibid., 12:148. More than one male scholar, too, made his home a "gathering spot" for "widows and the like." Ibid., 1:207, 2:111–13.

23. 'Abd ar-Raziq, *La femme au temps des mamlouks*, 72–74, discusses the scattered references in the sources. Fragmentary evidence points to at least five such institutions in Cairo; see al-Sakhawi, *al-Dau'* 12:26, 45; Ibn Iyas, *Bada'i'* 2:59; and al-Maqrizi, *Khitat* 2:397. On those in the Qarafa, see ibid., 2:454.

24. Al-Maqrizi, *Khitat* 2:427–28.

25. Ignaz Goldziher, *Muslim Studies,* trans. C. R. Barber and S. M. Stern (London: George Allen and Unwin, 1971), 2:176–78.

26. Al-Sakhawi, *al-Dau'* 12:120.

27. A. J. Arberry, *Sakhawiana* (London: Emery Walker, 1951), 4–5. Arberry suggests that 'A'isha may have "sometimes" attended the lessons with her father, but that hardly follows from the evidence of the ijaza itself. That the license was issued in her name does not guarantee that she was present.

28. Al-Sakhawi, *al-Dau'* 12:3.

29. One of the first Western historians to recognize the opportunities pre-

sented to women by the transmission of hadith was Ignaz Goldziher; see his *Muslim Studies* 2:366–68.

30. Taj al-Din 'Abd al-Wahhab al-Subki, *Mu'jam shuyukh al-Subki*, Dar al-Kutub al-Misriyya, Ahmad Timur Pasha Collection, "Tarikh" MS. no. 1446 [= Ma'had Ihya' al-Makhtutat al-'Arabiyya, "Tarikh" MS. 490].

31. Ibn Hajar, *al-Majma' al-mu'assas.*

32. Jalal al-Din al-Suyuti, *al-Tahadduth bi-ni'mat Allah*, ed. Elizabeth M. Sartain (Cambridge: Cambridge University Press, 1975), 43–70.

33. The information for her life is drawn from the accounts of these three biographers: Ibn Hajar al-'Asqalani, *Inba' al-ghumr bi-abna' al-'umr* (Hyderabad: Jam'iyyat Da'irat al-Ma'arif al-'Uthmaniyya, 1967; reprint, Beirut: Dar al-Kutub al-'Ilmiyya, 1986), 7:132–33; al-Sakhawi, *al-Dau'* 12:81; 'Abd al-Hayy Ibn al-'Imad, *Shadharat al-dhahab fi akhbar man dhahab* (Cairo: Maktabat al-Qudsi, 1931; reprint, Beirut: Dar al-Masira, 1979), 7:120–21.

34. For al-Hajjar's biography, see Ibn Hajar, *al-Durar* 1:152–53.

35. Probably Sharaf al-Din 'Abd Allah ibn al-Hasan (not al-Husain) ibn 'Abd Allah al-Maqdisi al-Hanbali (d. 732/1332), who, significantly, seems to have been a colleague of 'A'isha's father, Muhammad. Ibid., 2:361–62.

36. Ibn Hajar, *al-Majma' al-mu'assas*, 240–43.

37. Al-Sakhawi, *al-Dau'* 12:81.

38. Ibn Hajar, *al-Majma' al-mu'assas*, 240.

39. Ibid., 104ff.; al-Sakhawi, *al-Dau'* 12:24.

40. On Maryam, see Ibn Hajar, *al-Majma' al-mu'assas*, 322–27, and al-Sakhawi, *al-Dau'* 12:124; on Fatima, see ibid., 12:91, and on Fatima's mashyakha, see Jacqueline Sublet, "Les maîtres et les études de deux traditionnistes de l'époque mamelouke," *Bulletin d'études orientales* 20 (1967): 9–99.

41. Ibn Jama'a, *Tadhkirat al-sami'*, 87.

42. Zakariyya Abu Yahya al-Ansari, *al-Lu'lu' al-nazim fi raum al-ta'allum wa'l-ta'lim* (Cairo: Idarat al-Taba'a al-Muniriyya, A.H. 1319), 6–7; Abu Zakariyya Muhiy al-Din al-Nawawi, *al-Majmu'* (Cairo: Idarat al-Taba'a al-Muniriyya, n.d.), 1:31.

43. Ibn Jama'a, *Tadhkirat al-sami'*, 60–61; cf. the opinion of Taqi al-Din 'Ali al-Subki, *Fatawa al-Subki* (Cairo: Maktabat al-Qudsi, 1936–37; reprint, Beirut: Dar al-Ma'rifa, n.d.), 2:126–27.

44. On the significance for Muslim education of the concept of *suhba* (companionship) and its related verbs, see George Makdisi, "Suhba et riyasa dans l'enseignement médiéval," in *Recherches d'Islamologie: Recueil d'articles offerts à Georges C. Anawati et Louis Gardet par leurs collègues et leurs amis* (Louvain: Peeters, 1977), 207–11; and Makdisi, *Rise of Colleges*, 128–29.

45. Elizabeth Sartain makes this point in her outstanding study *Jalal al-Din al-Suyuti*, vol. 1, *Biography and Background* (Cambridge: Cambridge University Press, 1975), 127.

46. On this point and on instruction in hadith generally, see Makdisi, *Rise of Colleges*, 210–13.

47. Ibid., 109–11.

Modern

Turkey

and

Iran

Ottoman Women, Households, and Textile Manufacturing, 1800–1914

DONALD QUATAERT

In spite of their central place in Ottoman social and economic life, we know little about nineteenth-century Ottoman manufacturing women, the households in which they lived and worked, their economic activities, and changes in these pursuits over time. Women and their households mediated the process of growing Ottoman participation in the world economy, and changes in household processes of production and the household division of labor should be understood as adaptations to changing market opportunities, both domestic and international. Thus, I believe, there are relations between changes in Ottoman household economies and the regional and world economies of the nineteenth century. But to view the evolution of nineteenth-century Ottoman household economies as merely a story of transformation from subsistence to market production would be too simplistic. Many Ottoman households already were committed to manufacturing for the market, at varying levels, well before 1800. As a famous example, in the town of Ambelakia in Ottoman Thessaly, the manufacture of red yarn was a family business in the eighteenth century. "Every arm, even those of the children, is employed in the factories; whilst the men dye the cotton, the women prepare and spin it."[1]

Vigorous and vibrant putting-out systems interlaced the Ottoman Empire, exchanging raw materials and semi-processed goods among its European, Anatolian, and Arab provinces. Women and men in north Anatolian towns such as Zile and Merzifon, for example, received raw cotton from the Mediterranean south and spun it into thread. Some of the newly made thread was exported to the Ottoman Crimea, and local weavers used some to make a coarse calico for regional use and for export.[2] Other Ottoman households were subsistence producers as of 1800 and, in declining numbers, remained so throughout the period. Also, as I will show, the nature of Ottoman household economies varied by region, as did changes in those economies.

A focus on households and women's work is a key to properly understanding the history of Ottoman manufacturing in the nineteenth century. It is widely held that Ottoman manufacture "declined" in the age of the European Industrial Revolution. But what is meant by decline? Perhaps there was no decrease in gross Ottoman industrial output between 1800 and 1900. After all, the domestic Ottoman market as well as the export market for select Ottoman manufactures was much larger at the beginning of the twentieth century than before (see below).[3] The oft-cited Ottoman industrial decline may in fact reflect a decrease in the output generated by organized guild *male* labor. It thus is critical to examine the household division of labor by gender. Manufacturing output by urban guilds, which were male dominated, did fall off sharply in many areas. But, as I will demonstrate, manufacturing production by females working at home did not merely continue but sharply expanded in some regions and textile handicraft sectors. In addition, factory labor increased, particularly after 1880, and the majority of the textile workers were girls and women.

Rural households accounted for at least 80 percent of the Ottoman population and usually consisted of the nuclear family, that is, a husband and wife (usually one) and their children. Rural households in the Black Sea coastal areas of Anatolia averaged 6.5 persons and as few as 5.3 persons elsewhere, figures that place Anatolia just above the average for preindustrial Europe. Multiple-family households in rural Anatolia did not account for more than 30 percent of the total, whereas simple, or nuclear, households made up 50 to 60 percent.[4] In the capital city of Istanbul, similarly, very good data reveal that the extended family made up only 16 percent of all households counted. Upper-class Istanbul households averaged 5.7 persons, and those further down the social ladder averaged 4.5 persons. Polygyny was rare in the capital, involving only 2 percent of all married Muslim men. In the Arab town of Nablus, the polygyny rate was higher, 16 percent of the men enumerated.[5] It must be stressed that in both urban and rural households, the males often were absent, engaged in wage-earning labor at sites some distance from their homes. Migratory labor, involving work in other rural areas as well as in both remote and nearby urban centers, was a normal condition of existence for Ottoman families. Finally, a considerable amount of time in the average Ottoman rural household was devoted to manufacturing activities, sometimes for family use and at other times for sale. That manufacturing was an everyday part of Ottoman rural (and urban) life has been overlooked almost completely in the literature on both Ottoman manufacturing and Ottoman agriculture. Scholars of manufacturing

have focused on urban male guilds, whereas researchers of the countryside usually have considered only crop growing and animal husban-
dry. Rural households were not simply agricultural producers. Instead,
they were engaged in a mix of economic activities, for example, crop
growing, mining, manufacturing, and fishing, the composition of which
changed according to region, season, and opportunity. If crop prospects
were poor, then the family would devote increased attention to manufacturing for sale to earn cash for purchasing foodstuffs.

Information on the nineteenth-century Bursa silk industry offers
powerful hints but frustratingly little concrete data concerning the impact
of female labor on changes in the gender division of household labor. For
centuries, the town of Bursa and its environs had been renowned for rich
brocades and fabrics. The gender division of labor in the industry varied
according to its rural or urban location. Village families, both male and
female members, provided the raw silk, unraveled in a single length from
the cocoon. In the town itself, however, silk spinning may have been an
exclusively female occupation as the century opened, as it was in the city
of Damascus, located in a Syrian province of the Ottoman Empire. At
Bursa, as in Damascus, male weavers, organized into guilds, wove almost all the silk cloth produced, although a few female workers were
engaged as well. The involvement of the guildsmen weavers in the Bursa
silk industry fell as silk cloth production plummeted after 1830. For several decades, redundant male weavers may have found work in the expanding industry of raw silk, which at that time was spun largely by
hand. In 1812, total production of raw silk at Bursa, all of it manually
reeled by both men and women, averaged 150,000 pounds.[6] Subsequently, thanks to rising foreign demand and new technology, output
soared. The new technology came in the form of steam-powered machinery, housed in factories, that spun the raw silk from cocoons. In 1850
such spinning mills produced 10 percent of total raw silk. By 1860, when
Bursa raw silk output equaled 1.5 million pounds, 98 percent of it was
reeled in a factory setting—in nearly fifty mills that employed at least
4,200 persons.

In the Bursa factories, the labor force was entirely female, both girls
and women, except for male superintendents and mechanics tending the
engines. The same gender distribution simultaneously came to prevail in
the silk-spinning mills being established in the Lebanon region, similarly
founded to meet mounting European demand. In the first days of these
mills, entrepreneurs at Bursa and in the Lebanon struggled with a labor
source reluctant to enter a factory, and in both regions they employed a
variety of methods, sometimes remarkably similar, to overcome impediments to labor recruitment. Both sets of entrepreneurs brought in women

from France and Switzerland, experienced in silk reeling, to instruct in the new technology and to demonstrate by example that women could work safely in such factories.[7] These entrepreneurs also found allies in religion, both Christianity and Islam. Around the 1860s, the Roman Catholic pope issued a decree permitting Bursa-area girls of Armenian background to work in the mills, and in Lebanon local ulama as well as the Christian clergy played key roles in persuading local girls to work under foreign women supervisors in foreign-owned silk-reeling mills.[8] Appealing to the workers' more worldly needs, Bursa factory owners also offered high wages; a reeler in the mid-1850s earned five times as much as she needed for her daily bread. But wages quickly dropped. Labor supplies were augmented as urban Turks from Bursa and village girls from surrounding areas became available; silk reelers soon were among the most poorly paid factory workers in Ottoman manufacturing. The "lowest daily wages were paid in the silk (and tobacco) factories in which mainly women worked."[9] Married Turkish women in the city provided at least some of the labor. According to one European observer in the late 1860s, this wage labor enhanced the women's status in the eyes of their husbands since it increased family income. And, he approvingly noted, since the women dutifully returned to the women's quarters on coming home from work, wage labor had brought only advantages to the Ottoman Turkish family at Bursa.[10] Bursa entrepreneurs also turned to labor supplies outside the city. They recruited "very" young girls from surrounding rural areas and housed them in dormitories built adjacent to the mills. These village girls, who began as apprentices as early as ten years of age, arrived in caravans for the labor-intensive reeling season. When the season ended, the girls and young women, who won a certain local fame for their purchases of fashionable clothing, as did the Lebanon reelers, returned home with "practically all" of their wages. Once married, they generally quit the factory and usually did not return unless widowed.[11] But beyond their clothing purchases, we know little about how the wages were used—whether the girls retained the money and brought it into their marriages or turned it over to their parents. A tidbit of information from the 1850s implies that the young women helped to support their families, but we cannot generalize from that. There are other uncertainties. It is not totally clear if there was a net increase in the use of female labor in the silk industry or simply a continuation, in mechanized form, of established patterns and levels. Nor is it known if this work represented the entry for most families into wage labor or their shift from one wage-earning activity to another. The rise of mechanized silk reeling does coincide exactly with the sharp decline in cotton spinning in the Bursa area during the pre-1850 period; the availability of (temporarily) high-paying jobs in silk reeling might well have accelerated the decline of local cotton spinning.

The overwhelming predominance of female labor in the Ottoman silk-spinning industry can be explained by several factors. The Ottoman economy generally was labor scarce, and employing women solved the serious problem for factory owners of finding cheap labor. Also, the mills did not provide a reliable source of full-time income for their workers. After the great burst of factory building, the industry suffered from over-capacity and spinning factories were consistently underutilized. In the 1850s, the 1870s, the 1890s, and the early twentieth century, we are told, they typically operated not more than two hundred days per year. The mills thus offered a kind of part-time labor that corresponded well with Ottoman society's view of female labor as supplemental. Such an activity also fit nicely with the time demands that raising silkworms placed on Ot-toman families. Given the prevailing labor scarcities around Bursa, for example, it is hardly coincidental that cocoon raisers devised a method for feeding the silkworms that reduced the labor input by 70 percent, compared with methods in France and Italy. Part-time factory work also was compatible with the demands of agricultural and domestic tasks on the workers. Mechanized silk reeling, as it evolved in the Ottoman lands, interfered minimally with the preexisting division of labor within the household, whether rural or urban. For the factory owner, the arrange-ment had only one long-term disadvantage. Throughout the entire pe-riod, most factories operated well below capacity, although they often could have spun profitably the year round.[12]

Girls and women played an essential role in three arenas of textile production. They made yarn and cloth at home for immediate use by household members, they produced at home for the market, and they labored in workshops, away from the home setting.[13] Until the second quarter of the nineteenth century, a large proportion of female labor in textile production had been involved with spinning, with either the wheel or the distaff. But the import of European-manufactured factory-spun cotton yarn then rose incredibly, dramatically affecting the eco-nomic and social status of Ottoman women. Annual Ottoman imports of cotton yarn, a mere 150 tons in the early 1820s, rose to some 7,750 tons in the 1870s. The impact of this increase must have varied considerably, depending on whether the women had been spinning primarily for the marketplace or for domestic use. For most commercially oriented female spinners, the foreign yarn meant, in the long run, the loss of their spin-ning jobs and, in the short term, sharply declining wages as they ac-cepted lower wages to compete with the cheap and strong imported product. To the extent that commercial cotton spinning was a preserve of women, the use of imported thread contributed to the displacement of these females from the work place. And if the unemployed women did not find wage employ in the weaving of cloth from the imported yarn, the work force might have become more gender homogeneous over time, that is, more exclusively male. This last assumption, however, is questionable. One of the major trends in nineteenth-century Ottoman manufacturing was the shift from guild to nonguild labor, quite probably accompanied by a rise in the importance of female labor in the overall production of cotton cloth and other textiles. If the rising imports of yarn had a negative or mixed impact on commercial yarn spinners, the effect on women spinning for home use was much more certain and definitely more positive. The hand spinning of yarn required to provide the average Ottoman family's clothing needs consumed a vast amount of time, an estimated one-twelfth of the woman's total labor output.[14] This household division of labor began to change in the second quarter of the nineteenth century when imports of machine-made European yarn began flooding into the Ottoman Empire. Purchase of imported yarn must have been attractive to hand spinners, who thus were relieved of a time-consuming and quite unremunerative task. Between 1820 and 1870 yarn imports freed an estimated 160,000 Ottoman women (calculated on the basis of full-time job equivalents) from the onerous and unprofitable task of spinning cotton.[15] The release of these women dramatically affected their households' distribution of labor through a combination of increased leisure time, increased cloth production for family consumption, and increased market production of agricultural commodities and cloth to pay for the purchased yarn.

In spite of the advantages, however, poverty kept many Ottoman women spinning cotton yarn at home both for domestic consumption and for sale. Since many families did not assign monetary value to the time spent spinning, the homespun yarn could undersell the European product. Though not necessarily yarn of comparable quality, it was usable for making lower-grade clothes. As the price of imported yarn and textiles fell steadily over the course of the century, so did the remuneration of spinners producing for the market. In the winter of 1857, "all" the Kurdish women in the districts surrounding Diyarbakir occupied themselves by spinning for men in the town who wove *bez* cloth. These women were too poor to buy the raw cotton for spinning, much less imported yarn. Instead the women gathered and picked cotton and in return retained a small percentage of it. A woman would spin six pounds of cotton into yarn and then exchange it in town for nine pounds of raw cotton. She kept at this cycle until she had enough twist, "which the husband converts into cloth, using for his family what is necessary and selling the rest."[16] Hand spinning persisted through at least the 1860s around

Erzurum, and in the Sivas region it was commonplace during the late 1880s. "What goods are manufactured such as carpets, rough woollen cloth, yarn, leather, is done by the people (mostly the women) at their homes. . . . Great quantities of yarn are used. It is now all made by the people (mostly the women) at home on the rudest kind of spinning wheels."[17]

In the early twentieth century, at the great cloth-manufacturing center of Aleppo, women working at home annually spun an estimated 100,000 kilograms of cotton yarn used for making the coarser cloths.[18] At nearby Maras, spinning yarn did "not constitute a profession properly speaking." Nonetheless, women "in all the poor homes—that is, among nearly all families . . . during their spare moments" annually spun 90–100,000 kilograms of cotton yarn.[19]

Ottoman girls and women dominated the cotton and wool yarn spinning work force in the steam-powered mills that emerged late in the nineteenth century. These were concentrated in Salonika and inland Macedonia as well as in Izmir, Adana, and Istanbul. Young girls formed the bulk of the labor force and, in common with their European and American (and Bursa) sisters, did not remain long enough to acquire skills, much to the irritation of the owners.[20] Jewish girls in the Salonika mills, for example, worked until they married, as early as age fifteen, or until they had accumulated the necessary dowry.[21] One mill, in the Yedikule district of Istanbul, employed some 300 women and children to make 500,000 packets of yarn per year. In the Adana region of southeast Anatolia, one mill with 2,700 spindles employed 300 women and children, who annually produced 1 million kilograms of yarn. A nearby mill employed 550 persons, usually children and women, who worked twelve hours a day.[22] Around 1880 one of the mills in the European provinces of Salonika employed altogether 250 young women and 50 males. In the city of Salonika in the 1890s, mills employed 480 girls, twelve to eighteen years of age, and 160 men and boys. The men received two or three times the boys' wages, whereas girls' starting pay was half that of the boys. Approximately 75 percent of the 1,500 workers in the Macedonian spinning mills were females, usually girls, some as young as six years of age. In the 1890s they worked fifteen hours a day in summer and ten in winter, with a thirty-five-minute break for dinner but none at all for breakfast. Women working in inland mills, for example at Karaferia and Niausta, were in a worse position than their Salonika counterparts. In early-twentieth-century Salonika, the combination of a booming tobacco-processing industry that competed for relatively scarce labor and an active workers' movement escalated wages in the cotton mills. (Women also dominated the work force of the tobacco-processing factories.) But the inland mill workers had few wage-earning options.[23]

The weaving of cloth by women also remained commonplace through-out the period, long after indigenous cloth manufacture supposedly had disappeared from the Ottoman lands. Around Bursa in the 1860s, "the peasantry find an economy in the women weaving at home stout articles for common wear."[24] At Trabzon, similarly, the "countrywomen" both worked in agriculture and spun woolen cloth for family members' outer garments.[25] At about this time, nearly 12,000 hand looms in the east Anatolian provinces of Diyarbakir and Erzurum employed that many men in addition to 6,000 youths under sixteen years of age. Two-thirds of these looms were used to weave cotton cloth and were located in the countryside, not in the towns. These rural weavers obtained the twist from women villagers, who in exchange received an equal weight in cloth.[26] We do not presently know the rural weaver's contribution to total family income, but only that other members of the family engaged in agriculture. In the towns of the region—Bitlis, Diyarbakir, Mardin, and Harput—the male weavers provided most of the family's cash and the wife earned about one-seventh of the total.[27]

At the end of the century, "almost every family" in Asia Minor still owned a hand loom. "They can make their own cloths while vast num-bers would be unable to earn the money with which to purchase foreign cloth."[28] This tenacious retention of looms well into the era of massive Ottoman imports of European cloth hints at the Ottoman household's flexible responses to changing market opportunities. In years of strong demand for agricultural products, the looms might be neglected, but in times of famine or weak demand for agricultural goods, cloth again might be made for the family or the market. Women in the province of Sivas in the 1890s used both locally spun and British yarn to weave a coarse cloth for men's trousers and other garments. These female weavers worked on as many as 10,000 looms in the province. In the district (*kaza*) of Davas in Aydin Province, about 185 looms were employed in weaving various cotton and linen textiles for sale, and girls and women operated a full three-quarters of them.[29] In the province as a whole, some 10,000 hand looms wove striped cloth (*alaca*) for home consumption and for sale.[30] These households simultaneously engaged in agriculture and manufac-turing oriented toward the marketplace. Weaving output fluctuated with the harvest, another example of household labor ebbing and flowing with income opportunities and requirements, from agriculture to manufactur-ing and back again. During the 1870s rural artisans who manufactured goods for sale to their neighbors earned two-thirds of their income from agricultural sources and one-third from handicraft activities.[31]

As these examples demonstrate, female participation in the wage-earning manufacturing labor force was predicated on very low wages.

Late in the nineteenth century, imported yarn created thousands of new jobs for women in the Istanbul area. Working at home in their newly found employment, these women used foreign yarn to crochet lace for export, earning piecework wages that were extremely low by Ottoman standards of the time, approximately 1.5 piasters per day. Similarly cheap female labor, earning no more than 1.5 piasters per day, permitted Ottoman hand-printed textiles to remain competitive with the mechanical imprints of European factories.[32] The significance of such wages can be illustrated if we assume that a family of six persons purchased all its bread needs. Around 1900 such a family would have required 35 to 40 piasters per week merely for its minimum bread requirements, exclusive of the monies needed for other foodstuffs, for housing, and for clothing. A lacemaker or a hand printer earned on the average 20 percent of the sum needed to keep the family just in bread. Put another way, each woman's wages provided the bread she needed to survive plus a fraction of the bread needed by one other member of her family.

As an example outside of textiles, shoemaking in Istanbul demonstrates, together with Bursa silk reeling, that low wages were not confined to home industries and provides another indirect glimpse into the household division of labor. At the end of the century as many as fifty men and women labored together in shoemaking workshops. Male operators of sewing machines made half-shoes and earned up to 1.25 piasters per day. With an average urban family of five, if he worked seven days a week he could earn 25 percent of his family's weekly bread. The sewing machine operator's wife, if employed in the shop, would finish buttonholes or sew on buttons. But she earned, again assuming a seven-day work week, only 10 to 15 percent of the sum needed to buy the family's total bread. Labor from the children, which was quite common in nineteenth-century Ottoman manufacturing, clearly was necessary to meet the minimum subsistence requirements of the family.[33]

Women also were actively involved in the famed mohair industry of Ankara, a participation that dated back to the mid-eighteenth century, when they spun the lower-quality grades, and probably earlier. In the 1830s and 1840s, the mohair-weaving guild, struggling to meet European competition, implemented what was hailed as an innovation in the industry. Previously the guild sheikh had bought raw mohair at fixed prices and given it to the spinners (both female and male). But now the guild made contracts with "poor women" who bought mohair in the local markets, spun it, and then sold it to the guild for whatever price they could command. As the guild sought to compete with the "cheap price" of the European producers, the women supplemented rather than replaced the earlier method of obtaining yarn.[34] A free female labor force thus coexisted with the male spinning guild, a pattern also encountered in the Bursa silk industry, as well as in furniture and shoemaking in Istanbul and textile production at Aleppo. Similarly, in the area of the southern Balkan mountains, male braidmakers belonged to the guild (*gaitanci esnafi*), but the women who spun the wool yarn for them did not.[35]

The carpetmaking industry offers a good example of how the gender distribution of labor in a particular industry varied regionally. This variation indicates the absence of a uniform Middle Eastern or Islamic value system regarding the participation of women in the work force. In the Middle East generally the carpet industry boomed in the late nineteenth century. In western and central Anatolia, for example, soaring output after 1850 employed perhaps 60,000 persons by World War I, most of them girls and women. In certain areas of Anatolia, women historically had been engaged in all phases of carpetmaking—that is, in the spinning and dyeing of the wool and the knotting of the rugs. From Sivas in 1888 we have this description. "The dy[e]ing, spinning, weaving etc are all conducted unitedly, the women of each family engaged in the business doing all the work from the spinning of the yarn by hand, dyeing it with vegetable dyes, to the weaving and completion of the carpet."[36] In this case a single (female) individual carried out all the steps involved in making a rug. But elsewhere divisions of labor were common and apparently were proportionate to an area's involvement in commercial carpet production. In the late nineteenth century, for example, men at the great production center of Usak washed and bleached the wool and women spun it into yarn. This division of labor changed in the final three decades of the nineteenth century as the production of rugs tripled but the number of carpet looms only doubled. To accomplish this feat, Usak rugmaking families rearranged their lives so that the women could spend more time at the looms: for a brief period in the late 1890s, Usak men took over the task of spinning the wool yarn. Steam-powered spinning factories then were built in the town. Similarly, in one area of modern Iran, as women's commercial rug knotting became more valuable, men assumed such traditionally female tasks as carrying water. (In this case, there was no accompanying ideological shift in gender roles.)[37] At Usak, the division of labor changed in other ways as well: the early-nineteenth-century practice of women dyeing the yarn had given way to male dyeing by the 1880s. But at the important export center of nearby Kula, different divisions of labor prevailed. There women continued to dye the yarn until the century's end. Again, by way of contrast, men as well as women knotted commercial carpets at Gördes and Kula. In Qajar Iran during the same era tribal males usually did not work in carpet knotting but the women did.

In some areas of Iran at this time, however, men played an active role in the industry. At Meshed and other major urban centers, males regularly worked as rug knotters; in cities such as Tabriz they worked together with women on the same looms. But in other Iranian cities, such as Kerman, only women knotted.[38]

These examples demonstrate the absence of clear-cut patterns of gender division of labor in nineteenth-century Middle Eastern manufacturing, at least in rugmaking. Ottoman (and Qajar) men and women readily interchanged productive roles to maintain family livelihoods. The presence of male and female rug knotters at Kula and Gördes and in several cities of Qajar Iran reflects a gender sharing of Middle Eastern jobs that popular stereotypes hold to be the monopoly of women. These Anatolian and Iranian examples also show that the division was not characterized by male domination of those activities that were heavily committed to market production; in all the highly commercialized production centers, both males and females knotted rugs. The presence of male and female workers in the shoemaking shops of Istanbul, for its part, seems to suggest an easier set of gender relations than stereotypes would permit. In these situations the rigid barriers that are presumed to have existed between the sexes and in the gender division of labor simply were not present. That is, our assumptions about such divisions are incorrect, at least some of the time.

But the patterns of gender sharing in carpetmaking tasks at Usak and other long-established commercially oriented production centers were not universal in the industry. As Western demand for carpets mounted, Izmir and Istanbul merchants established new workshops in many regions. Similarly, a European merchant founded a new knotting center in 1912 in the Iranian town of Hamadan. Only girls and women knotted at these workshops, where unlike in the traditional centers they worked away from the home.[39] Thus in the late nineteenth century tens of thousands of girls and women were employed outside the home for the first time. Again, we have no data on consequent changes in the status of the female workers within the family or on the distribution of domestic and agricultural tasks within the household.

We do not know the causes of this exclusion of male knotters from the workshops founded in late-nineteenth-century Anatolia (and at Hamadan). Whether it resulted from the decisions of the families or of the West European merchants who organized the workshops is uncertain. The contemporary rugmaking industry of the late twentieth century is significant in this context. One of the largest firms presently organizing the hand knotting of rugs in the Middle and Far East employs female knotters at one location, males at another, and females at yet a third. To this company, gender is irrelevant; clearly, the firm has adjusted to prevailing local practices that make both groups available for knotting rugs.

The nineteenth-century growth in the three most important export industries—silk reeling, lacemaking, and carpetmaking—was fueled by European demand and, it seems important to repeat, sustained by a work force that was overwhelmingly female and poorly paid.

In the textile industries generally, men previously had formed the vast majority of the urban guild weavers. As European competition mounted, these men continued to weave, but for declining wages, contributing relatively less to overall family income through their manufacturing tasks. In many of the industries that were either newly born, or expanding, or successfully adapting to changing conditions, female labor was dominant. This was true of the hand-spun yarn produced in the home and the machine-made yarn produced in factories, of carpet, lace, and raw silk production, and of linen and silk weaving in some areas. The importation of foreign yarn, for its part, relieved many women of spinning tasks and freed them to use this newly available time in more lucrative forms of manufacturing activity. But men as well as women wove, both for the market and for subsistence needs.

The situations examined here seem to support several conclusions concerning Ottoman women, households, and manufacturing. First, as should be obvious by now, women played an integral role in the textile-manufacturing life of the Ottoman Empire, both in the home and in the workshop. Many worked outside the home—Muslim, Christian, and Jewish Ottoman women and girls alike. Certainly this changes our view of day-to-day life in the Ottoman Empire. But does it not also speak to the issue of industrialization itself? Most of the activities recorded here took place not in mechanized factories but rather in small workshops and in households. By tracing women's work back into their homes, we have discovered a universe of manufacturing activity that simply is lost when the focus is on the factory. At the same time, by seeing the (apparently) rising incidence of women's work outside the home, we begin to understand more clearly the magnitude of the nineteenth-century changes. That female labor occupied the very bottom of the wage scale, receiving fractions of their male counterparts' pay, hardly was coincidental. From the poor wages they received we must conclude that women's work was considered supplementary and nonprofessional. But this work was absolutely essential to the survival of the Ottoman textile industries in the nineteenth century, when costs and prices fell steadily. Western market demands may have enhanced the economic importance of the female members of Ottoman households engaged in manufacturing. Finally, many nineteenth-century Ottoman households demonstrated considerable flexibility in the gender division of labor.

In several respects, the conclusions of this chapter have been corroborated by ethnographic research in the modern-day Middle East. A number of recent studies unambiguously demonstrate the vital importance of female labor in the economic survival of the contemporary Turkish village household and so make important links with the Ottoman past. Several of these studies, however, did not find the gender sharing of jobs that seems to have been common in the nineteenth century. Research focusing on villages in the Konya region of central Anatolia, for example, reveals no such sharing today. In general, this group of scholars argues that tasks are rigidly defined as male or female. Further, they observe that when women assume new manufacturing responsibilities, men not only allow them to work harder and longer than before but also refuse to assume any additional tasks at home. Nor do these researchers find any enhanced power or status within the household resulting from the increased wage work of modern Turkish women.[40] These conclusions, however, are flatly contradicted by another researcher working on carpetmakers near Ayvalik, in western Anatolia. These workers became involved in carpet production quite recently, as part of a Turkish university's effort to restore the use of natural dyestuffs in the industry. The women and men freely interchange carpetmaking and household-maintenance tasks.[41] Thus places that are physically near to one another differ fundamentally in the gender division of labor. The difference simply may be a matter of variation by location, a phenomenon encountered often enough in the research presented here. Or perhaps ideology is shaping what researchers observe in the contemporary work sites and households. That is, the respective researchers find the gender sharing or gender division of work tasks that they are looking for.

The role of the historical past in transforming the status of contemporary manufacturing women remains uncertain. Is there more or less gender sharing of manufacturing tasks in the Middle East of the 1980s than during the preceding century? The question posed is difficult to address using the historical sources. What was the impact of rising nineteenth-century manufacturing for the marketplace on the status of wage-earning Middle Eastern women and on their family relationships? Did it spark a social reaction whereby men perversely imposed tighter social controls over women whose economic importance was being enhanced? We should expect to see considerable change in the role and status of these manufacturing women over time. After all, during the 1980s the popular classes veiled and secluded women much more than formerly. But whether such trends produced a stricter gender division of labor has not been determined.

Notes

1. David Urquhart, *Turkey and Its Resources* (London: Saunders and Otley, 1833), 47–51, 24.

2. Halil Inalcik, "Osmanli pamuklu pazari, Hindistan ve Ingiltere: Pazar rekabetinde emek maliyetinin rölü," *Middle East Technical University, Studies in Development 1979–80*, special issue, 1–65; Public Record Office (London), Foreign Office (hereafter FO) 78, various reports by Brant at Trabzon in the 1830s.

3. Over the period, the population increased at an annual rate of 0.8 percent; the territorial base of the state, however, steadily shrank. Charles Issawi, ed., *The Economic History of Turkey, 1800–1914* (Chicago: University of Chicago Press, 1980), 11.

4. Justin McCarthy, "Age, Family and Migration in the Black Sea Provinces of the Ottoman Empire," *International Journal of Middle East Studies* 10 (1979): 309–23; McCarthy, *Muslim and Minorities: The Population of Anatolia and the End of the Empire* (New York: New York University Press, 1983), 110–11; FO, *Further Reports from Her Majesty's Diplomatic and Consular Agents Abroad Respecting the Condition of the Industrial Classes and Purchasing Power of Money in Foreign Countries* (London: Harrison and Sons, 1871).

5. Alan Duben, "Turkish Families and Households in Historical Perspective," *Journal of Family History* 10 (Spring 1985): 75–97; Duben, "Muslim Households in Late Ottoman Istanbul" (unpublished paper, 1986); Judith E. Tucker, "Marriage and Family in Nablus, 1720–1856: Toward a History of Arab Marriage," *Journal of Family History* 13, no. 2 (1988): 165–79; Tucker in this volume.

6. Halil Inalcik, "Bursa," *Encyclopaedia of Islam*, 2d ed. (Leiden: E. J. Brill, 1960), 1:1333–36; Hatt-i hümayun #16757, 1225/1810, Başbakanlik Arşivi (hereafter BBA).

7. Consular Reports of the United States, Department of State, National Archives, Washington, D.C. (hereafter CRUS), reel T194 R.#2, Schwaabe at Brousse 1 Oct. 1847; Régis Delbeuf, *Une excursion à Brousse et à Nicée* (Istanbul, 1906), 140 n. 1, 142, 166–69; author's interview with Rana Akdiş Akay at Bursa, June 1986; cf. wages and prices cited in Issawi, ed., *Economic History*, 44–45, and FO 78/905, Sandison at Bursa, 6 Aug. 1852. For a fuller account, see Donald Quataert, "The Silk Industry of Bursa, 1880–1914," *Collection Turcica III: Contribution à l'histoire économique et sociale de l'Empire Ottoman* (Paris: Peeters, 1983), 481–503.

8. Akay 1986 interview; Edward C. Clark, "The Emergence of Textile Manufacturing Entrepreneurs in Turkey, 1804–1968" (Ph.D. diss., Princeton University, 1969), 34; Roger Owen, "The Silk-Reeling Industry of Mount Lebanon, 1840–1914," in *The Ottoman Empire and the World Economy*, ed. Huri Islamoğlu-Iran (Cambridge: Cambridge University Press, 1987), 276–77.

9. Quotation is from A. Gündüz Ökçün, trans., *Osmanli sanayii. 1913, 1915 yillari sanayi istatistiki* (Ankara: Ankara Universitesi Sosyal Bilimlez Fakulultesi Yayinlari, 1970), 22; also see CRUS, reel T194 R. #2, Schwaabe at Bursa, 1 Oct. 1847.

10. Alexander Treshorn von Warsberg, *Ein Sommer im Orient* (Wien: C. Gerold's Sohn, 1869), 146.

11. See sources cited in n. 5, above.

12. See sources in n. 5, above. Also see Hüdavendigâr Vilayeti Salnamesi

(hereafter vs) 1324/1906, 278; CRUS, reel T194; FO 195/299, Sandison at Bursa, 24 May 1851, 195/393, Sandison at Bursa, 13 Aug. 1855. To reduce labor costs, much of the industry moved out of the city altogether; at the turn of the century, 75 percent of the mills' productive capacity was situated in towns and villages outside of Bursa. *La revue commerciale du Levant: Bulletin de la chambre de commerce française de Constantinople*, 30 Nov. 1909.

13. The documents consulted for this study often were unhelpful or misleading on the gender identity of the work force. English- and Turkish-language sources usually refer to *worker* or *isci* without elaboration, only occasionally noting the person's gender. French- and German-language sources designate workers generally as *ouvrier* or *arbeiter* and sometimes use these masculine forms to refer to workers who, I knew from other sources, were female.

14. Urquhart, *Turkey*, 149–50.

15. Sevket Pamuk, "The Decline and Resistance of Ottoman Cotton Textiles, 1820–1913," *Explorations in Economic History* 23 (1986): 205–25.

16. FO 195/459, Holmes at Diyarbakir, 14 Apr. 1857.

17. CRUS, 26 May 1887.

18. Germany, Reichsamt des Innern, *Berichte über Handel und Industrie* (Berlin: Carl Hermanns), I, Heft 9, 10 Aug. 1907.

19. *La revue*, 31 mar. 1904, Lettre de marache, 30 Mar. 1904.

20. Great Britain, Parliamentary Papers, Accounts and Papers (hereafter A&P), 1899, 103, 6241, Sarell on Constantinople, 1893–97.

21. A&P, 1893–94, 5581, Salonica for 1891–92 (Blunt, 30 Sept. 1893).

22. Austria-Hungary, *Berichte der K. u. K. Österr.-Ung. Konsularämter über das Jahr 1901* (Vienna: Handelsmuseum) (hereafter KK), 1901, vol. 19, p. 1, and for 1902 and 1903; Ministère du Commerce, *Rapports commerciaux des agents diplomatiques et consulaires de France* (Paris, 1883–1914) (hereafter RCC), no. 109 (Mersin for 1892); *Berichte*, I, Heft 9, 20 Aug. 1907.

23. RCC, no. 76, reel 33, Salonique for 1900, reel 35, Salonique for 1902; *Bulletin du Comité de l'Asie française*, Salonique, 25 juillet 1883. See also A&P, 1893–94, 97, 5581, Salonica for 1891–92 (Blunt, 30 Sept. 1893), 1908, 7253, 17, Salonica for 1907, 7472, 103, Salonica for 1910; *Berichte*, XIX, Heft 6, 18 Apr. 1913; and KK, 1905, vol. 2, p. 6, Salonich.

24. FO 195/774, Sandison at Bursa, 28 May 1864.

25. A&P, 1878–79, Biliotti at Trabzon for 1877–78.

26. FO, *Further Reports*, 797.

27. Ibid., 795.

28. CRUS, reel T681, Jewett at Sivas, 30 June 1893.

29. vs (Aydin) 1307/1891.

30. *Berichte*, Bd. VII, Heft 4, 19 Juli 1904, 300; CRUS, reel T681, Jewett at Sivas, 26 May 1893.

31. FO *Further Reports*, 743.

32. *Berichte*, Bd. VII, Heft 4, 19 Juli 1904, 274, 301, 306–8. See also A&P, 1878–79, Biliotti at Trabzon for 1877–78.

33. This assumes a per capita consumption of 1.8 lbs./0.83 kgs per day at an average price of 1.0 kurus/okke of bread. Donald Quataert, "Limited Revolution:

The Impact of the Anatolian Railway on Turkish Transport and the Provisioning of Istanbul, 1890–1908," *Business History Review* 51, no. 2 (1977): 139–60. *Berichte*, Bd. VII, Heft 4, 19 Juli 1904, 306–8. See, for example, vs (Adana) 1318/1902, s. 188.

34. Cevdet Iktisat #52, 6 Za 1241/July 1826, #31, 3 B 1244/January 1829, #694, 6 Za 1244/June 1829, bba; Mesail-i mühimme Ankara eyaletine dair #2073, 1261/1845, bba.

35. Nikolai Todorov, *The Balkan City, 1500–1900* (Seattle: University of Washington Press, 1983), 228; Salaheddin Bey, *La Turquie à l'exposition universelle 1867* (Paris: Hachette et Cie, 1867), 129; Michael R. Palairet, "The Decline of the Old Balkan Woolen Industries, c. 1870–1914," *Vierteljährschrift für Sozial und Wirtschaftsgeschichte* 70 (1983): 331–62.

36. crus, reel T681, Jewett at Sivas, 22 July 1888.

37. Nikki Keddie to author, 4 Oct. 1988.

38. *Uşak il yıllığı* (Istanbul, 1968), 269; A. Cecil Edwards, *The Persian Carpet: A Survey of the Carpet-Making Industry of Persia* (London: G. Duckworth, 1953), 28, 59–60, 201. Further east, in the mid-twentieth century, Indian men also were commonly employed as knotters of commercially made rugs.

39. For a fuller account of the carpet industry, see Donald Quataert, "Machine Breaking and the Changing Carpet Industry of Western Anatolia, 1860–1908," *Journal of Social History* 11 (Spring 1986): 473–89, and sources therein; and Edwards, *Persian Carpet*, 90–91.

40. Günseli Berik, "From 'Enemy of the Spoon' to Factory: Women's Labor in the Carpet Weaving Industry in Rural Turkey" (paper presented at the annual meeting of the Middle East Studies Association, New Orleans, La., 22–26 Nov. 1985); Berik, "Invisible Carpet Weavers: Women's Income Contribution in Rural Turkey," Nilufer Isvan-Hayat, "Rural Household Production and the Sexual Division of Labor: A Research Framework," and E. Miné Çinar, "Disguised Employment—The Case of Female Family Labor in Agriculture and Small Scale Manufacturing in Developing Countries; the Case of Turkey" (papers presented at the annual meeting of the Middle East Studies Association, Boston, 20–23 Nov. 1986).

41. Josephine Powell, "The Role of Women" (paper presented at a symposium on village life and village rugs in modern Turkey, Georgetown University, Washington, D.C., 1987. Similarly, there is considerably disagreement among European historians concerning gender roles in rural manufacturing. See the works by Gay Gullikson, Hans Medick, and Jean Quataert.

10 The Impact of Legal and Educational Reforms on Turkish Women

NERMIN ABADAN-UNAT

Turkish society has undergone drastic changes in the past sixty years, but how this has affected the status of women is much debated. Staunch supporters of Ataturk's reforms, while deploring the fundamentalist movements of recent years, point to the education and training of large numbers of professional women as a unique accomplishment. Those who oppose the trend toward Westernization in general, and its endorsement of secularism and the emancipation of women in particular, are more sharply critical. They welcome the recent emergence of astonishingly large numbers of young zealous Islamic women. For the fundamentalists, Ataturk's reforms served only to produce a decadent Western way of life and to destroy the moral basis cherished during centuries of Ottoman rule. The truth lies somewhere in between and is far too complex to be encapsulated in a single argument.

It is true that Ataturk and his supporters based their system of women's reforms on the twin pillars of law and education, thus serving a predominantly urban female elite. Socioeconomic indicators have proved that the majority of Turkish women still endorse traditional values and mores, reflecting the attitudes of a conservative rural community. One is forced to agree with Binnaz Toprak that Turkish women have been emancipated but not yet liberated.[1] An evaluation of this unique process requires a brief examination of the status of women in Ottoman society and of Ataturk's reforms.

Until the end of the nineteenth century the social division of labor according to sex was based on a rigid interpretation of the Muslim ethic. The first slow steps toward the education of women began in 1863 with the foundation of a college for the training of women teachers in Istanbul, followed by the opening of primary schools for girls.[2] The return to constitutional monarchy in 1908 brought into positions of power men whose political and social creed laid strong emphasis on

women's education. During this period women started to organize themselves. An impetus for genuine reform came with World War I, which
created jobs for women in ammunition and food factories.

In a parallel movement, banks, postal services, central and municipal
administration, and hospitals began to open their doors to women. But
though the changes were accelerated by the demands of the war machine, they did not meet with universal approval. Official policies prescribed permitted skirt lengths and a special imperial decree was needed
before the veil could be discarded during office hours.

In 1919 the collapse of the Ottoman Empire, the occupation of Istanbul
by British soldiers, and the landing of Greek soldiers in Izmir aroused a
storm of outrage and protest throughout all strata of the population.
Turkish women also were provoked into political activism. They participated in open-air meetings and were addressed for the first time by such
well-known women writers and educators as Halide Edib and Nakiye
Elgun.

Even during the War of Independence, on his various visits to the
countryside Ataturk continued to voice his support for egalitarian measures with regard to women. Addressing the Turkish Grand National
Assembly, Ataturk publicly acknowledged the heroic deeds of Anatolian
women in his speech of 3 February 1923. He formally promised that
"Turkish women shall be free, enjoy education and occupy a position
equal to that of men, as they are entitled to it."[3] In this way he prepared
public opinion for radical changes.

ATATURK'S REFORMS CONCERNING WOMEN

Following the foundation of the Turkish Republic in October 1923,
Ataturk was disappointed by the slow and conservative approach of the
Turkish Parliament when considering issues pertaining to the legal status
of women. Asked to amend and codify a family law proposal first drafted
in 1917, the commission in charge approved of marriage at age nine for
girls and age ten for boys and opted to retain polygyny. Furthermore, the
commission gave women the right to divorce only exceptionally but upheld a man's right to repudiate his wife. Ataturk and his supporters, who
were determined to adopt Western standards, vehemently disapproved
of this bill.

Ataturk increasingly became convinced that the only way to modern-
ize Turkish society was to eliminate the power of religious rules and laws,
customs and arrangements. His ambition was to achieve no less than a
national revolution based on secular and positivist thought. In emancipating Turkish women he wanted to lay the foundation for a more

egalitarian and harmonious family life. In March 1923 he announced his ultimate goal: "Our enemies claim that Turkey cannot be considered a civilized nation because she consists of two separate parts: men and women. Can we shut our eyes to one portion of a group, while advancing the other and still bring progress to the whole group? The road of progress must be trodden by both sexes together marching arm in arm."[4] Anxious to present a modern face to the world, Ataturk began to encourage significant initiatives to eliminate the obvious inequalities in public life. In his determination to fight the conservative forces gathered around the Ministry of Shari'a, Ataturk managed to impose legislation that had a definitive effect on the orientation of public policies. On 3 March 1924 two new laws were passed. The first abolished the caliphate, and the second unified instruction by eliminating all religious educational institutions. The law for unification of instruction in effect assured both sexes of their right to education, thus opening the door to coeducation.

Ataturk had no intention of waiting for long-term evolutionary processes to take their course, and he turned to codification as an accelerator of social change. On 17 February 1926 a slightly modified version of the Swiss civil code was adopted. For Ataturk and his supporters, granting equality to men and women was the fulfillment of an earlier promise. It symbolized Turkish determination "to reach a level of contemporary civilization." Arguments put forward in favor of the new law reflected, among others, the belief that "monogamy and the right to divorce are principles required for a civilized world." One might conclude that the major rights conferred on Turkish women were a product of the unrelenting efforts of a small revolutionary elite rather than of large-scale demands by Turkey's female population.

This observation might also apply to the granting of political rights. Although the Turkish Women's League presented publicly articulated demands in 1928, again it was the personal intervention of Ataturk and his close supporters that led to the 1931 constitutional amendment granting Turkish women the right to participate in municipal elections. Three years later, on 5 December 1934, Turkish women were given the right to vote and to be elected at general elections—some fourteen years earlier than those rights were granted to women in France, Italy, and Belgium. In 1935 eighteen women deputies entered the Turkish Grand National Assembly.

EXPLAINING THE REFORMS

How can the lasting success of these reforms be explained? The following factors may provide a partial explanation.

Absence of colonial rule. Neither the part of the Ottoman Empire that became Turkey nor the Turkish Republic had ever experienced foreign rule. The dilemma of emancipating women in an Islamic society therefore did not present itself in quite the same way that it would have in a former colony.

The long past of modernization in the Ottoman Empire. Westernization or Europeanization began as early as 1793, initiated from within the society. It was conceived and engineered by a group of indigenous Ottoman elite consisting of sultans and high-ranking bureaucrats. It manifested itself in a concrete way with changes in the military sector, leading to the concept of "defensive modernization."[5] Islamic and Western institutions existed side by side, especially in the fields of education and law.[6]

The issue of women in public discourse. The three major ideologies that preoccupied the minds of Ottoman intellectuals in the second half of the nineteenth century all gave considerable place to the status of women. Those in favor of a radical Westernization of Ottoman society advocated the adoption of a European civil code, the abolition of polygyny, and the outlawing of repudiation. Supporters of Turkish nationalism, although critical of European education, deplored polygyny, repudiation, and the veil. Even Islamic traditionalists, who advocated segregation, were ready to concede women the right to dispose of their own property and to attend primary and secondary schools. This long period of gestation later enabled relatively large-scale implementation of reforms.[7]

The strongest public advocates of the importance of educating women and raising their status were men—men with political ambitions. During the 1890s and early 1900s the problem of women in Turkey became an ideological controversy incorporating questions of Ottoman, and later Turkish national identity. The single most important factor in the transformation of the issue was to be found in nationalist state ideology.

Women's contribution. After constitutional monarchy was restored in 1908, a significant number of Ottoman women writers established a rich array of women's magazines, further developing the discussion in favor of equal rights.[8] They contributed to a growing dynamism in urban public opinion, presenting a significant body of argument in favor of radical change in the status of women and enhancement of their educational opportunities.

The collapse of the empire and the discrediting of the sultan-caliph. Islamic values and the traditional social order, which until the end of World War I were defended by an omnipotent ruler. were irreparably shaken when the sultan was discredited. Following the defeat of the empire, Mustafa Kemal, the victorious general of the Ottoman army, later given the surname Ataturk—Father of Turks—started a war of independence in Anatolia against all invaders and occupying forces. The struggle for independence was rejected by the sultan, who condemned Mustafa Kemal to death in absentia. The rift between the sultan, who collaborated with the Allies, and the nationalist forces came to an end when the former fled from the country on a British warship. The disintegration of a six-century-old dynasty, followed by the abolition of the caliphate in 1924, greatly facilitated the adoption of secularism as one of the fundamentals of the new republic. At the same time it deprived the traditionalists of a powerful protector.[9]

Ataturk's personality. There can be no doubt that the charismatic personality of Ataturk was a major contributor to the uncontested acceptance of all major reforms in favor of women. In spite of his military background, once Ataturk gained legitimacy he based his power on legal norms. With regard to such delicate issues as the discouragement of the wearing of the veil he eschewed special laws in favors of persuasion through public addresses. (He did not, as is widely believed in the West, outlaw veiling.) His sincere belief in secular and scientific thought, and his commitment to the supremacy of Western civilization, enabled him to infuse new hope into a defeated and impoverished nation.

RECENT DISCUSSION

Since the end of World War II, there have been many discussions as to what the strategic goals of these reforms were. First-generation republican women looked on these reforms as a major component in the making of a democratic civic society. More recently Sirin Tekeli has argued that the singling out of women as the group most visibly oppressed by religion was absolutely central to Ataturk's attacks on the theological state, culminating in the abolition of the caliphate. Furthermore, Tekeli argues, Ataturk was equally desirous to dissociate his single-party regime from the European dictatorships of the time (Hitler's Germany and Mussolini's Italy).[10] In contrast to the Kinder-Küche-Kirche ideology of these fascist states, Turkey presented itself as a country that granted political rights to its women, thereby symbolically claiming a rightful place among Western democratic nations.

As Deniz Kandiyoti rightly points out, the Turkish case proves that the state can be a powerful instigator of change through its policies. These may meet various forms of resistance or, on the contrary, be facilitated by new political alliances in the socioeconomic sphere. Turkey illustrates both the potential, and the limitations, of reforms instigated by a political vanguard in the absence of a significant women's movement.[11] The process of secularization, which diminished the impact of Islamic values, undoubtedly left its mark right up to the 1950s, particularly on the rapidly increasing urban population.

It would be a mistake, however, to think that state authority and elitist legislation have been able to transform all strata of society. On the contrary, progressive legislation has led to sharp polarizations between traditionally oriented predominantly rural values, and the progressive values adopted in urban areas. Yet even here a rigid dichotomy is not applicable; levels of development are the decisive factor.[12]

The wish to hold on to, or return to, the past manifests itself in the rejection of civil marriage (the only legally recognized form) in favor of a religious ceremony with its potential for polygyny, repudiation, and illegitimacy; the demand for a brideprice in the marriage agreement; a decline in the number of females attending school beyond compulsory primary education; and an emphasis on women's fertility and reproductive role. By and large, the Kemalist reforms concerning the emancipation of women have penetrated the countryside only unevenly.

REFORMS AND REALITY

The balance sheet of the past sixty years clearly indicates that revolutionary efforts through law have resulted in only partial changes. Republican reforms have been unable to remove vast national disparities. The clear discrepancies between town and country, class and region, persist. Bound by the traditional patterns of society, women have been slow to change their attitudes toward the selection of spouses, marriage, and inheritance. A policy of openness in the field of education has created a sizable women's elite, particularly visible in academia, the liberal professions, art, and literature. Yet Turkish women, particularly those living in undeveloped rural areas, are still afflicted by a multitude of problems. And it is these problems that force us to reconsider the merits and efficacy of past policies. They also lead us to ask a series of important questions: To what extent can revolutions of legal systems change the traditional way of life of the majority of women in a given country? Which major economic, social, and political factors are directly or indirectly responsible for accelerating or retarding this process? Does a significant participation of women in the organized labor force during such crisis periods as war encourage a social movement in favor of equality for women? And if so, once the extraordinary conditions pass, will the old patterns return? Does religion, ideologically or in terms of values, maintain its decisive hold on the amount and degree of women's social and political participation? Is a high degree of electoral mobilization and participation sufficient to eliminate women's marginal position in politics?

Sociological, anthropological, and sociopsychological theories, such as those of William J. Goode and E. Bott, all seem to indicate that shifts in the role of sexes, or changes in the economic status of women, depend directly on changes in the economic system. A different interpretation, centered on social crisis, furnishes an additional dimension. According to this approach, defended by Elise Boulding, rapid modernization and such crises as wars often seem to elevate women into "male" positions, at least temporarily.[13] In Turkey structural factors predominated, such as the systematic efforts to reform education as part of a comprehensive Western-oriented modernization program and the introduction of technologies leading to growth in the industrial and service sectors, and were abetted by such crises as the War of Independence in 1919–23.

EDUCATION: SUCCESS OR FAILURE?

The founders of modern Turkey viewed education as the most powerful peaceful means to transform individuals from passive subjects to active citizens. A brief assessment of the results of public education reveals that in spite of free and compulsory education, girls have been neglected in terms of schooling, especially in rural areas. In 1984 the literacy rate stood at 62.5 percent for women, as opposed to 86.5 percent for men. There is an important relation between labor-force participation and education. A nationwide survey carried out by Hacettepe University in 1975 showed that 9 percent of uneducated women in urban centers were employed, compared with 28 percent of those who graduated from secondary or higher level schools, whereas in rural areas employment levels decreased as educational attainment increased. The survey emphasized cash earnings, so in rural areas the majority of women were classified as unpaid family members. Thus only wage-earning agricultural laborers and such government workers as primary school teachers, nurses, and midwives fit the employed category. There is also an inverse relation between the degree of education and agricultural production: 92 percent of the uneducated female labor force participate in agricultural production, 84 percent of the primary school graduates, and 5 percent of the secondary school or higher-level graduates.[14] School attendance is undercut by a high rate of absenteeism among those who drop out to participate in agricultural tasks.

In terms of primary school attendance Turkish figures for both sexes are low compared with other EEC countries: 82 percent compared with 92 percent. But the real discrepancy becomes visible at higher levels. Whereas the percentage of girls in secondary education in industrial countries varies between 49 and 51, in Turkey it reaches only 35. Similarly, whereas the percentage of girls in vocational schools in industrial countries ranges between 45 and 62, in Turkey it attains a mere 28.[15] Turkey's higher education, however, shows a steady growth and an average of 32.4 percent, compared with industrialized countries, which range between 33 and 51 percent. Given that the percentage of Turkish female students in

Table 10.1: Male and Female University Students in Absolute Numbers, 1927–83

| | Students | | | Percentage of |
Years	Men	Women	Total	Women Students
1927–28	3,477	441	3,918	11.2
1937–38	7,820	1,564	9,384	16.6
1947–48	20,153	4,541	24,694	18.4
1957–58	35,415	6,545	42,060	15.8
1967–68	100,180	23,503	123,683	19.0
1977–78	247,145	79,538	345,476	23.0
1982–83	197,962	83,577	281,539	29.7

Source: Eser Danyal Köker, "Education, Politics and Women in Turkey" (Ph.D. diss., Ankara University, 1988; in Turkish), tables 13, 19, 32.

Turkey's twenty-seven universities reached an average of 32.4 in 1985–86, their number has grown thirteenfold in the space of thirty years (see table 10.1).

It is a puzzling picture: an unrealized mass education program and at the same time a constantly growing number of female university students.[16] There is no doubt that in this respect Turkey holds the lead among Middle Eastern countries. The relatively high percentage of women in the civil service is further evidence of the growing presence of qualified female personnel in public life (see table 10.2).

When measuring the educational attainment of these women officials, the first fact to be noted is that the levels they reach are, on average, higher than those of their male counterparts. In addition, the most qualified female labor seems to be concentrated in the service sector—be it private enterprise or government service.

With regard to professional women, a trend familiar to studies of Third World countries also seems to be the rule in Turkey. It can be characterized as follows: (1) the percentage of women professionals is higher than in capitalist countries; (2) professional women are mainly concentrated in metropolitan and urban centers; (3) since they seek security and facilities related to their work rather than quick promotional opportunities, they prefer government employment.[17]

Turkish women who do not go into public administration are increasingly pursuing academic careers. This is the case not only in such traditionally women-oriented disciplines as humanities, social sciences, and social services, but also in the male-dominated preserves of medi-

Table 10.2: Distribution of Female Civil Servants, 1938–82

Year	Total Civil Servants	Female Civil Servants	
		N	%
1938	134,779	12,716	9.5
1946	159,166	30,046	13.5
1963	443,869	72,702	16.0
1970	655,737	123,812	19.0
1978	1,038,777	277,622	27.0
1982	1,294,418	318,470	25.0

Sources: For 1938, 1946, 1963, and 1970, Mesut Gülmez, "Numerical Evolution of Turkish Civil Servants," *Public Administration Review* 6, no. 3 (in Turkish): 27–47; for 1978 and 1982, *State Personnel Organization Survey, 1978* (Office of the Prime Minister, 1979); and *State Personnel Organization Survey, 1982* (Office of the Prime Minister, 1983).

cine, law, engineering, and science. A retrospective on Turkish academic women reveals a rather astonishing steady rise in numbers, running parallel to that of female university students (see table 10.3).

At the time of the basic reorganization of Turkish universities in 1932, there was only one female faculty member. Fifty years later Turkey's twenty-seven universities were employing roughly six thousand women academics. The distribution according to disciplines shows some equally interesting features. In medicine, women have occupied important positions since the late 1940s; in 1946–47 the existing medical faculties contained 199 men and 53 women, 21 percent of the total. This proportion has stayed fairly constant, being 27 percent in 1980–81.[18] Women academics increasingly have been elected or appointed to important decision-making positions.[19]

The question of why so many of Turkey's professional elite are female has been treated most extensively by a well-known Turkish sociologist, Ayşe Öncü.[20] Having established that one in every five practicing lawyers and one in every six practicing doctors in Turkey is female, Öncü attempts to determine whether this trend is relatively new, growing, and particular to Turkey. Öncü argues that although women enjoy wider work opportunities in the professional labor market in Turkey than women do in most industrialized societies in the West, Turkey is not unique in this respect. A number of developing countries that have become rapidly integrated into the world market in recent years—Mexico, Argentina, Costa Rica, and India, for example—provide women with more options in the professional labor market than do most of their Western industrialized counter-

Table 10.3: Distribution of Turkish Female Faculty Staff, 1932–82

| Years | Number of Academicians | | Total | Percentage of Female Academicians |
	Men	Women		
1932–33	501	1	502	0.1
1942–43	927	196	1,123	17.4
1952–53	1,692	308	2,000	15.4
1962–63	3,432	1,029	4,461	23.1
1972–73	8,399	2,699	11,098	24.3
1982–83	15,975	5,839	21,814	26.8

Source: Köker, "Education, Politics and Women in Turkey," tables 15, 27, 41.

parts.[21] The main reasons seem to be the new growth in the economic realm, demographic losses due to emigration of the high-skilled labor force, and the like, which make openings for a woman easier to find than in the West, where the supply outruns the demand. In many developing countries law, medicine, and dentistry constitute a cluster of occupations that appear to women as alternatives.[22]

The classical argument to explain this trend is based on class inequalities. Rapid rural migration to the cities and a scarcity of factory employment result in a large pool of unskilled female labor in large urban areas, which upper-class women are able to exploit. For these women are then able to fulfill both a professional and a marital role because domestic labor is available and although most families are nuclear, the extended family network can be relied on for child rearing. Although Öncü accepts the irrefutable validity of these arguments, she posits another relevant factor. Whereas Western industrial societies subject the most skilled, prestigious, and highest-income professions to a tight self-regulating system, Third World countries are unable to maintain such self-perpetuating and elite recruitment patterns. When they open their doors the first to enter are women from professional and white-collar backgrounds, because they have or can easily obtain the requisite education. As Öncü emphasizes, "the admission of women serves to maintain closure by keeping it a family affair."[23] The elite background of professional women thus is significant from two points of view: (1) the ready availability of lower-class women as domestics in private homes "emancipates" the upper-class women to pursue professional careers; and (2) state policies that deliberately aim at the rapid expansion of the professional cadres actively encourage women to enter prestigious professions.

SECULARISM VERSUS FUNDAMENTALISM

Has there been a noticeable change in this interpretation? One might say yes. With the increase in female university students from rural and low-income urban families the clash between liberal and conservative values has become increasingly evident. This trend has been reinforced by the return to compulsory religious education in primary and secondary schools. Some women students seem to be facing serious dilemmas concerning Muslim identity and secularism.[24] One indication of this clash is the continuing struggle by women students determined to wear head scarves in classes, exams, and graduation ceremonies against the official university policy, which was recently reaffirmed by a constitutional court decision. The university administrators and the Higher Education Council based their arguments on the assumption that certain types of clothing—head scarves and ankle-length, shapeless, drab-colored coats—constitute a response to demands formulated by fundamentalist religious or political leaders and as such are political symbols. In recent years political parties have been openly championing the cause of a return to the shari'a and the adoption of "Islamic dress." These political views are in opposition to the Dress Regulation, introduced after the military intervention of 1980, which prohibits all male government employees from wearing beards, moustaches, and baggy trousers, and females from wearing head scarves and veils.[25]

Meanwhile, the issue has become a steady source of conflict between fundamentalist students and university administrators. During the legislative session of 1988 the government party passed a law granting to female students the right to cover their heads. This law was first vetoed by the president, and after it was readopted by Parliament, the president sent the law to the constitutional court. The decision of the constitutional court reaffirmed the contention that special privileges with regard to dress violate the principle of equality before the law. Right-wing political parties openly sustain the claims of these students, whereas left-wing parties also support the claims, but on the basis of freedom of conscience and democratic liberties.

Social scientists such as Şerif Mardin and Çiğdem Kâğitçibaşi have interpreted the religious revival in Turkey and its impact on the student body as the result of attempts to deal with the increasing stress of living in a society in the throes of rapid social change. In addition to such sociological interpretations, one must also attach importance to the ideological polarization into which Turkish post-1980 democracy has been forced. The military and civilian governments have supported a growth in religion in order to combat extreme leftist movements. During the past five years the General Directorate of Religious Affairs has been opening 1,500 mosques and prayer rooms a year, with more than 633,000 students attending official Quran courses.[26] These activities are complementary to article 24 of the new constitution of 1982, which introduced compulsory instruction in religious culture and moral education in primary and secondary schools.

The increasing importance that such Islamic sects and Sufi orders as the Nakşibendis, the Süleymanlis, and the Nurcus have been gaining both inside Turkey and among Turkish workers in various European industrial countries can be detected in the economic and social life of Turkish society. Banks with capital from Saudi Arabia and the Emirates are distributing "profit dividends" instead of interest. Foundations of a religious character are establishing secondary schools and even attempting to found private universities. These efforts to create a favorable climate for an Islamic republic are also supported by associations of Turkish workers living abroad. Within this conflict the issue of women is playing a decisive role.

LEGAL REFORMS

As stated earlier, Ataturk used legal reforms as a revolutionary tool to eliminate the traditional Islamic norms and jurisprudence. In this sense one could label his actions as the implementation of a kind of state feminism. More than sixty years have passed since the adoption of the Swiss civil code in 1926. Of course, legal reforms cannot change attitudes, customs, and institutions overnight. Their real importance emerges only when socioeconomic structural changes have exercised a lasting effect on both sexes. In regions with a predominantly agrarian character, where large landownership remains the privilege of a highly influential group of local notables, marriages, divorces, and matters of inheritance are carried out in the traditional way. Thus one may speak of legal dualism. Proof of this is most evident in the situation of children born from de facto unions (Islamic marriages), who were deprived of their civic identity. This crucial problem was solved in two ways: (1) by a series of amnesty laws recognizing the paternity of such children, a total of 7,724,419 up until 1950; and (2) after 1960 by introducing a simplified procedure for recognizing paternity.[27]

How egalitarian is the Turkish civil code? Like the Swiss civil code it reflects traditional European values. There is no absolute equality between husbands and wives. The husband is the head of the family (art. 154), and the right to choose a domicile belongs to him (art. 152 II). Should the wife wish to assume a profession or work outside the household, she must obtain the consent of her husband, which might be tacit approval (art. 159). This clause, which in recent years was constantly criticized by the press and feminist groups, has been revoked by the decision of the constitutional court in March 1990. The wife, however, may freely dispose of her material goods. The rule in marriage, unlike, for instance, that of the Napoleonic Code, is separation of property and goods.[28]

Among the demands proclaimed by twenty-seven Turkish women's associations in 1975, on the occasion of the International Women's Year, were the following legal requirements:

1. Husband and wife should be entitled to represent the marital union.

2. The wife should not be obliged to adopt the husband's family name.

3. The prerogative of a husband to forbid his wife the practice of a profession or employment should be abolished.

4. Legal, educational and administrative measures to abolish the "bride price" [başlik] should be implemented.

5. The prohibition of a religious ceremony before a civil marriage has been registered should be reinforced.

6. In order to equalize tax obligations, individual tax declarations for husband and wife should be required.

7. Women civil servants and workers should be able to take one paid year's leave of absence after childbirth.

8. Rural women should be able to benefit from social security rights.

9. The exploitation of apparently "adopted" female children, employed in domestic service should be prevented by legal provision.[29]

In May 1989 the first women's convention in Turkey assembled in Istanbul, attracting women of various feminist and feminist-socialist organizations. The women's platform contained the following new demands: the elimination of sexism in all school books; a close follow-up of discriminatory programs in the media; the lifting of legal prohibition on the establishment of women's branches within the existing political parties; the adoption of a quota system to increase women's representation in politics; the abolition of legalized prostitution; and the revision of the penal code in order to prevent violence within the family.[30]

The right of abortion up until the tenth week of pregnancy has been granted (27 May 1983; law no. 2827); in the case of married couples the consent of the husband is required. Abortions and family-planning services are provided in most government hospitals; though underutilized in less-developed rural areas, they are in strong demand in large cities. The right to abortion, as with previous legal innovations, was granted not as a result of the struggles of mobilized women voters or nongovernmental agencies, but because the government is eager to promote large-scale voluntary population control.

In the area of political rights, representation in Parliament since 1934 has shown a downward trend. During the legislative period of 1935–39 eighteen women were elected to Parliament (4.5 percent), but after the transition to a multiparty system in 1946 the figure declined; only nine (1.2 percent) were elected in 1977–80. At the last general election, in 1987, just six women (1.3 percent) entered the national assembly. More women than previously, however, have assumed leading decision-making positions.

Yet it cannot be denied that public involvement is restricted for women by the patriarchal nature of society. As has been shown by the young political scientist Yesim Arat, until the 1980s women parliamentarians in Turkey were drawn into politics by men. The very legitimacy of male power, which usually ties down the household, ironically promotes the initiation of women into politics. The asymmetry of power between men and women apparently was used in an instrumental sense to promote women. The sixty-nine women deputies who served from 1935 to 1980 were predominantly back-benchers. The constitution of 1982 prohibits the setting up of youth and women's sections within political parties, further reducing the chances to develop a healthy democratic system.

The climate of opinion concerning women's issues nevertheless has changed drastically since 1983 and the return to a multiparty system. The major opposition party, the Social Democratic Populist party, endorsed the principle of realizing within ten years an intra-party female representation of 25 percent. Various feminist organizations have mounted protests against juridical discrimination in court decisions, wife battering, violations of the freedom of expression and of conscience, and the like.

But the most militant women's movement of the day is Islamic. Though it has no declared leader, its mouthpiece, a monthly magazine called *Kadin ve Aile* (Women and family), reflects the outlook of the Naksibendi order in Turkey on women's issues. The movement is ideologically supported by the fundamentalist wing of the government party, ANAP. The female students who have staged sit-ins, hunger strikes, and boycotts of examinations are closely linked to the conservative political parties.

The legal and educational reforms undertaken sixty years ago opened the doors of coeducation to Turkish women, by offering them free schooling from primary level to university graduation. The value judgments that had upheld a sex-segregated social order were discredited by a strong emphasis on secularism. Until the transition to a multiparty system, public policies fostered the development of active, career-minded, creative women, presenting these pioneers as role models for the new generation. Today, a fast-growing competitive economy and the impact of the mass media, particularly television, have led to the projection of different role models. The ideal woman is presented as a loving partner and a devoted mother.

The equality of the sexes in the eyes of the law has permitted the overall application of the principle "equal pay for equal work." The major beneficiaries of this process have been the qualified urban female genera- tions of medium-sized and large cities. The restrictions of the constitu- tion of 1982 concerning trade union affiliation have been a major hand- icap for the application of this principle to the growing number of industrial workers.

Because transforming the status of Turkish women was regarded as an inherent element of the Kemalist state ideology, women in relevant exec- utive positions did not assume any responsibility for tackling specific women's issues. The rapid changes in Turkish society have led to grow- ing uncertainty about sexual mores. By adhering to conventional stan- dards in their private lives, career women try to protect their authority in public.

The large numbers of professional and academic women in Turkey are no doubt the result of close economic and ideological ties between upper- class and upper-middle-class groups and the West.[31] As Nikki Keddie rightly pointed out in 1979, working urban, rural, and tribal groups in modernizing Middle Eastern countries are losing their productive role and status, whereas the top urban groups, which include women, are gaining.[32] The close cooperation between the Turkish male elite and Western businessmen and politicians has had a spill-over effect on the status of women. Such men, moving largely in Westernized circles, are encouraging women's demands for modern education, unveiling, and the chance to lead professional lives. The extremely skewed income dis- tribution of nearly all Middle Eastern countries heightens the sense of two distinct cultures.

The crucial problem Turkey faces today is both structural and cultural. The major reforms undertaken by Ataturk rested on the assumption that Islam and feminism are basically incompatible, which has resulted in massive public debates about the meaning and basis of secularism. All the historical data clearly indicate that the entrance of Turkish women into the political struggle at the birth of the republic served as an ideologi- cal lever. With the transition to multiparty democracy, the debates on women's societal function began to express a tension between Western- ization, Islam, and socialism. That Kemalist republicanism (with its cul- tural Westernism) is no longer the sole ideology has to be reckoned with. The 1970s, even more than the 1980s, witnessed a resurgence of polemical writings on women, involving Marxist and Islamist currents. New protagonists of women's issues are becoming more self-consciously politicized and better organized.

Conservative political parties, such as the National Salvation party (at present dissolved) and its successor, the Welfare party, have succeeded in creating a new female elite, which is attempting to legitimize traditional sex roles. The Islamic framework concerning sexual differences is operative both at elite and at mass levels. At the mass level, the modernists, while strongly defending equality in public life, do not reject the Islamic moral code concerning the predominance of male authority in private life.

The educational and legal reforms of the Turkish Republic have, over the decades, produced three generations of articulate, highly qualified professional women. Whether the achievements of this elite can inspire the young generations of today; whether today's young women have a commitment to democratic values that will lead them to ignore the built-in constraints of the Islamic ethic; and whether women's movements and feminist currents will be able to produce independent voices for greater individual freedom and democratization are open questions.

Whether a serious backlash could occur in Turkish society depends on a great many factors, all centered on the discussion of secularization and democracy. Until an increased awareness and consciousness lead Turkish women to defend an enlarged catalog of social and political rights, women's issues will remain a sensitive item in the arena of political confrontation, and thus an acid test by which to assess the characteristics of the state.

Notes

1. Binnaz S. Toprak, "Religion and Turkish Women," in *Women in Turkish Society*, ed. Nermin Abadan-Unat (Leiden: E. J. Brill, 1981), 281–92.

2. Tezer Taşkiran, *Cumhuriyetin 50 ci yilinda Türk kadin haklari* (Turkish women's rights at the 50th anniversary of the republic) (Ankara: Basbakanlik Kültür Müstesarligi, 1973), 27–28.

3. Afet Inan, *Tarih boyunca Türk kadinin hak ve görevleri* (Rights and obligations of Turkish women in history), 3d ed. rev. (Istanbul: Milli Egitim Basimevi, 1975), 97.

4. *Atatürk'ün söylev ve demeçleri* (Speeches and statements of Ataturk), 2d ed. (Ankara: Türk Tarih Kurumu, 1961), 2:150.

5. Dankwart A. Rustow, "The Military: Turkey," in *Political Modernization in Japan and Turkey*, ed. Robert E. Ward and Dankwart A. Rustow (Princeton: Princeton University Press, 1964), 353.

6. Roderic H. Davison, *Turkey: A Short History* (Walkington: Eothen Press, 1968), 82–83.

7. Pervin Esenkova, "La femme turque contemporaine: Education et rôle social," *Bulletin International d'Etudes Arabes* (Tunis) (Spring 1951): 280–96.

8. Tezer Taskiran, *Women in Turkey* (Istanbul: Redhouse, 1976), 45.

9. Lord Kinross, *Ataturk: A Biography of Mustafa Kemal* (New York: William Morrow, 1965), 439.

10. Sirin Tekeli, "Women in Turkish Politics," in *Women in Turkish Society,* ed. Abadan-Unat, 293–310.

11. Deniz A. Kandiyoti, "Emancipated but Unliberated? Reflections on the Turkish Case," *Feminist Studies* 13 (1987): 317–38.

12. Nermin Abadan-Unat, *Women in the Developing World: Evidence from Turkey* (Denver: University of Denver Graduate School of International Studies, 1986), 46.

13. William J. Goode, *World Revolution and Family Patterns* (New York: Free Press, 1963); E. Bott, *Family and Social Network* (New York: Free Press, 1954); Elise Boulding, *The Underside of History: A View of Women through Time* (Boulder, Colo.: Westview, 1976), 733.

14. Ferhunde Özbay, "Women's Education in Rural Turkey," in *Sex Roles, Family and Community in Turkey,* ed. Çiğdem Kâğitçibaşi (Bloomington: Indiana University Press, 1982), 135.

15. TUSIAD, *Indicators of Turkey's Modernization: Industrialization* (Istanbul: Association of Turkish Industrialists and Businessmen, 1988), 27, table 3.6.

16. Eser Danyal Köker, "Türkiye'de kadin, eğitim ve siyaset" (Education, politics and women in Turkey) (Ph.D. diss., Ankara University, 1988), 205; Köker notes that the twenty governments that took office between 1960 and 1980 allocated little to women's issues. None of the programs made any reference to an equalization between the sexes in terms of educational performance.

17. Nermin Abadan-Unat, "Women in Government as Policy-Makers and Bureaucrats: The Turkish Case," in *Women, Power and Political Systems,* ed. Margherita Rendel (London: Croom Helm, 1981), 101.

18. Köker, "Türkiye'de kadin, eğitim ve siyaset," 188.

19. During the academic year 1988–89, at Ankara University the deans of the schools of law, humanities, science, theology, and journalism as well as of the graduate school were women.

20. Ayşe Öncü, "Turkish Women in the Professions: Why So Many?" in *Women in Turkish Society,* ed. Abadan-Unat, 185.

21. C. Safilios-Rothschild, "A Cross-Cultural Examination of Women's Marital, Educational and Occupational Options," in *Women and Achievement,* ed. M. T. S. Mednick et al. (New York: John Wiley and Sons, 1971), 322; in 1980–81 Turkish universities had sixteen medical, six dentistry, and four pharmacy schools. The distribution of female students was as follows: 25 percent in medical, 33.3 percent in dentistry, and 55.7 percent in pharmacy schools. Köker, "Türkiye'de kadin, eğitim ve siyaset," 269, table 34.

22. Rudolp C. Blitz, "An International Comparison of Women's Participation in the Professions," *Journal of Developing Areas* 9 (July 1975): 505.

23. Öncü, "Why So Many?" 189, 193.

24. It should be pointed out that in Turkish *secularism* is not equivalent to the

American term, which generally refers to the separation of church and state. Rather it is a concept based on the European notion of laicism, according to which religious practice and institutions are regulated and administered by the state.

25. Emilie A. Olson, "Muslim Identity, Secularism in Contemporary Turkey: The Headscarf Dispute," *Anthropological Quarterly* 58, no. 4 (1985): 161–78. Assistant Professor Koru of Ege University (in Izmir), a chemical engineer, refused to remove her head scarf, consequently resigned, and went to court, claiming that her constitutional rights had been abridged; see *Milliyet*, 27 July 1985.

26. The number of personnel employed in the General Directorate of Religious Affairs has increased by 58 percent during the past five years: in 1983 the number of civil servants in the directorate was 53,582; in 1988 it was 84,712. Parallel to this increase, the number of persons participating in the pilgrimage to Mecca has also significantly increased; from 30,450 in 1984, this figure climbed to 285,724 in 1988. Pilgrimage to Mecca also is organized by the General Directorate of Religious Affairs. *Cumhuriyet*, 23 Jan. 1989, 8.

27. Nermin Abadan, *Social Change and Turkish Women* (Ankara: Faculty of Political Science Publication SBF 171-153, 1963), 23.

28. The French and German civil codes were rejected by the Turks because they imposed too subjugated a role on the woman within marriage. Since then both these codes have been substantially revised. The major reason for preferring the Swiss civil code, however, was that the code had satisfied various linguistic communities with different cultural backgrounds and therefore might be compatible even in a totally different society. See Mary Zwahlen, *Le divorce en Turquie: Contribution à l'étude de la reception du Code civil Suisse* (Lausanne: Université de Lausanne, Faculté de Droit, 1981), 68–69; and Sabine Dirks, *La famille musulmane* (Paris: Mouton, 1969), 34–40.

29. Nermin Abadan-Unat, "Turkish Women and Social Change," in *Women in Turkish Society,* ed. Abadan-Unat, 14–15.

30. Sidika Rezzan Alp, "I. kadin kurultayi" (First women's convention), *Mülkiyeliler Birliği Dergisi,* no. 108 (June 1989): 28–30.

31. For the impact and trends of Turkish feminism, see the comprehensive article by Nükhet Sirman, "Feminism in Turkey: A Short History," *New Perspectives on Turkey* 3 (1989): 1–34. For the scope and targets of governmental policies, see Günseli Berik, "State Policy in the 1980s and the Future of Women's Rights in Turkey," *New Perspectives on Turkey* 4 (1990): 59–81.

32. Nikki R. Keddie, "Problems in the Study of Middle Eastern Women," *International Journal of Middle East Studies* 10 (1979): 225–40.

The Dynamics of Women's Spheres of Action in Rural Iran

ERIKA FRIEDL

Shifts in gender roles in Iran over the past few decades have been attributed to the Pahlavi regime, to Western influences tied to modernization and economic development, and later, to the functionaries of the Islamic Republic. These shifts include such contradictory phenomena as the unveiling of women and the Islamic dress code; birth control and glorified motherhood; women dependent on male wage earners and female guerrilla fighters; monogamy and polygyny; limited access to resources for women in an officially egalitarian society; and so on. The logic behind these developments has been sought in the dialectic of the public-private dichotomy, the rules of patriarchal politics, the processes of disenfranchisement in capitalist economies, and in the ideologies of liberation put into action. No matter what the frame chosen, actual gender roles are hard to delineate and the theoretical concept of gender role remains elusive: it is an imprecise tool for analyzing social processes that seem to proceed in different directions simultaneously.

This difficulty in applying the role concept to sociohistorical processes holds true even for rural communities, which presumably offer relatively few roles and retain gender-role patterns longer than complex, fast-changing urban centers. Working up data on gender issues gathered over the past twenty years in a tribal rural area of southwestern Iran, I thus found the term *gender role* not equal to the data's complexities, even for this one village.

In this village as elsewhere, for example, a woman's economic role is said to be essentially domestic, whereas men work in the fields. Yet while women indeed do not work in

An earlier version of this chapter was read at the Seventh Berkshire Conference on the History of Women, Wellesley College, Wellesley, Mass., 19–21 June 1987.

wheat fields (except at the tail end of harvesting), they are seen working in other fields and in vineyards. A woman's role allows her to bring home firewood on her back, but not on a donkey. As a mother, a woman is responsible for the welfare of her children, yet her sons from about the age of nine have the authority to order and control her.

Under close scrutiny, actual gender performances are so highly contextualized, variable, and overlapping, even in this small, relatively homogenous community, that normative rules can be isolated only with so many exceptions that the "norm" is rendered heuristically dubious. Likewise, and for the same reasons, the popular concept of public versus private proved to be of limited use in the context of tracing shifts in male-female performances historically, or in making sense of the great diversity operative in gender definitions today. On first sight, for example, what women do and where they do it in the village seems confusing; locally, women are said to "belong in the house," yet one sees many women out on apparently legitimate errands, often all day and far from home. A respectable woman will argue that she cannot walk even a few steps down the lane to visit a relative without being wrapped in a long veil, yet the same woman can be seen working at the public water channel, not only sans cumbersome veil but with her shirt sleeves rolled up to her elbows; a girl is taken out of school after the third grade because it is not right for her to be among strangers, but the next day she is working in an outpost camp in the mountains, in full view of women, men, relatives, and strangers alike.

Such seeming inconsistencies have given rise to contradictory generalizations about rural tribal women in Iran, depending on which side one wishes to emphasize: women appear either as downtrodden beings without much of a face or a voice,[1] or (and just as legitimately) as powerful personages to be reckoned with in the domestic and political sphere.[2] The terms *public* and *private* are used to argue both positions.[3] One can say, for example, that the woman washing clothes at the water channel is out in the open, but that the public space is transformed symbolically into a private one by virtue of her domestic activity—an elegant sleight of hand. If indeed this were the case, the woman also would have to behave as she would in a private setting, however temporarily. In fact, however, her face and her body attitude send distinct off-limits signals to any man or stranger, that is, she shows that she very much feels herself to be in public, and that furthermore her appearance, her activity, and her contacts during this time are open to public scrutiny—in this sense she becomes an entirely public being and is seen as such by others. A simple public-private dichotomy thus does not help much to sort out what is going on in the dynamic, action-created reality of village life.

To escape this semantic impasse, I decided to return to the basic vantage point of observation of gender performance. The sexual division of labor, that is, the relation between gender and economic activities, including their social ramifications and the manipulation of ideological superstructures, can be observed, questioned, challenged, and elicited for the living-memory past through interviews, life histories, and various data on demographic and economic processes. While keeping my attention firmly focused on gender behavior in an economic context, I thus analyzed gender-related developments in the village over the previous three generations, eventually arriving at a model useful for understanding present muddled conditions in terms of an interplay of economic systems that evolved at different developmental stages. Each of these stages I see as a productive system, a "sphere of action," that is, the physical, social, and psychological space in which men and women move. These spaces form closed spheres in which action and meaning are coherently connected in a logic, a world view of their own.

Four such productive systems operate in the village: (1) the hunting-gathering system; (2) the pastoral system; (3) the agricultural system; and (4) a system created by pre-revolutionary economic development and post-revolutionary conditions. These last two developments produced similar parameters for actions and therefore are dealt with as one system. Each of the systems has its own dynamic in the gender discourse, its own logic and historical connectors. The first three were fully operative simultaneously in the village until about 1970, when the intensive proletarianization of the Iranian countryside promoted the fourth sphere to dominance. To a much lesser degree than before, however, the other three systems are still operative.

For individual villagers in the action grid of daily life, these systems overlap or alternate, depending on the task at hand, creating inconsistencies and fuzzy borders that confuse actors and observers alike. Most important, however, they provide points of leverage for political manipulations, especially those informed by androcentric goals. This point deserves emphasis, as it is of key importance to the success of the ongoing patriarchalization of Iran.[4] Contrary to some popular romantic notions, the seeming relative freedom of rural women (signified by casual veiling, outdoor work, and spatial mobility) is not securely grounded anywhere in ideology or in practice, but is a function of circumstantial, largely economic, necessity. It is a brittle freedom.

The fragility of women's position in their society—rural, pre-proletarian, so-called traditional as it is (or was a few years ago)—of their sources of power and sense of self (vis-à-vis men), is directly correlated to certain factors of what I call the patriarchal feature set. These include an androcentric world view with ideological and philosophical tenets that provide little stimulus for women's identity formation; the authoritarian structure of social life; a hierarchy of gender-indexed space, things, and activities; and a paucity of rituals for women. In situations where shifting boundaries of the various action spheres creates liminal areas, marked by contradiction and conflict of rules, little effort is needed by anyone in a position of authority to unhinge the delicate systems and open up the whole complex for disenfranchisement, restriction, suppression, or other processes of patriarchalization. This process does not even depend much on law enforcement or political decisions aimed explicitly at the subordination of women, but works on a much deeper, more subtle level of cultural articulation. Indeed, it can be argued that the Islamic Republic is given entirely too much credit (or blame) for the recent shifts in gender performance and spheres of actions for men and women in Iran. Rural Iran was well prepared for this shift before 1979, after two decades of so-called modernization, economic development, and Western-type education had shifted the boundaries of the traditional spheres in the village to such an extent that women could be pushed to the fringes of their world without much resistance.[5]

A few ethnographic facts provide the background for my analysis. My data come from a large tribal village in southwest Iran. The three thousand villagers speak Luri, a dialect quite different from standard Persian, are Shi'i Muslims, and settled from a pastoralist-transhumant way of life about a hundred years ago. Since then, the village has had a mixed agricultural economy that includes subsistence and cash crop farming, transhumant sheep and goat herding, and dairy cows. The village is becoming increasingly dependent on income from non-farming activities, mostly wage labor, salaried jobs, and trade. The bases of the local sociopolitical life are kin groups. These were part of a tribal political organization in which subtribal chiefs and khans, wielding often ruthless power, were backed by outsiders like the shah or allied khans from other tribes, so that common people had little political autonomy and limited decision-making authority in economic and political matters. Time and again, chiefs interfered in domestic matters, commandeered services, syphoned off domestically created surplus, and even, on some infamous occasions, demanded sexual favors.

It is important to emphasize this situation: the general population, men and women, lacked political autonomy and thus a public voice in the political sense. The view from below is one in which the rifles of the khans and their retinue, and later those of government agents, directed life for most villagers. Furthermore, crowded domestic space and weak boundaries in the village (and even more so in the outposts and camps, where life is conducted in branch huts and tents), make everyday life largely public. Thus a woman churning butter at night (in a skin bag suspended on a tripod, producing characteristic slosh-bang sounds) tells everybody else in camp not only that she is working, but also how much yogurt she is processing and how much butter she is likely to yield. A woman's crying in a corner of her house, certainly a private affair, is heard, commented on, and potentially acted upon by her neighbors. Her private discomfort becomes a public event with sociopolitical consequences instigated and often negotiated later by the public. A young bride from another village, for example, who was unhappy in her in-laws' house but never had complained to others about her treatment in accordance with proper face-saving behavior, one day aired her discontent by wailing loudly, if briefly. Although the incident seemingly was ignored, within two days her father appeared with a large group of other relatives and demonstratively took her home. A long politically and economically costly negotiation began, involving a wide circle of people, until the conditions were hammered out under which the husband could take her back.

To express the scarcity of bounded space in numbers: a tent or branch hut affords about two square meters of space per person; a house in a village between two and a half and four square meters (roughly one-tenth of what we deem adequate in the United States), and in most cases between two and eight square meters per person of open porch and verandah in front of the living rooms. Although such boundaries as a reed wall, a fireplace, a pile of household goods, and a rug on the floor delineate and define space, they do nothing much to privatize that space practically. Indeed, under these circumstances open public space often is more private than domestic space. If truly secret matters must be discussed, for example, a walk is advisable—in itself, however, telling everybody else that the two walkers are up to something. In this regard the unparalleled spying abilities of children, who have the run of the neighborhood and few rules to restrain them, must be noted. Adults rely heavily on the intelligence services of their young children. One can even make the point that women, more in touch with children than men are, usually are better informed about the goings-on in the village and can extract considerable power from their knowledge if they so choose.

Finally, the machismo subculture of men, which until recently centered on hunting, war, and raiding, is an important component of the larger culture. Hunting was a men-only enterprise; except as provisioners of food, women had no part in it. (They did have a parallel activity, discussed below.) Hunting played on male prowess. It took place far from home, was dramatic, and required mastering danger, difficult terrain, and skills and sacrificing domestic (that is, female) creature comfort. Likewise, fighting and raiding were organized and carried out by men only. After kinship ties, allegiance to a successful military leader was by far the most influential social tie in a family's existence. These ties were maintained exclusively by men and were sustained by the ever-present potential for outbreaks of aggression. Yet until 1963, when the war-raiding complex came to an end with the assassination of the last paramount khan, war and aggression cognitively and practically were conditions of life women, too, had to come to terms with. In attacks and raids on their village women took up defense, hurling rocks, screaming, wielding clubs, and occasionally shooting rifles. Some stories even tell of women stealing sheep. The old village and the individual houses in it were built like forts, some with guarding towers, whose windowless walls faced the roads with slits for shooting. A walk overland was a dangerous adventure; women alone in a herding outpost in the mountains had to reckon with nighttime raids on the sheep corrals by hostile neighboring villagers.

The pacification of the tribal area by the Pahlavis ended the large-scale war-raiding activities; modern guns and high demand for game among the fast-rising population almost eliminated game animals and ended the hunting. Yet tales of bravery linger, as do a romantic propensity for the great outdoors and pride in endurance. Men were the actors here, with women in the supporting roles of admirers on whom the glory of their men "shines like sunlight," as one woman put it.

In the ethnographic setting sketched here, different historic-economic strata produced the four overlapping productive systems in which men and women move. I describe them in such a way as to highlight the vulnerability of the women's position in confrontation with the patriarchal trends mentioned above.

THE HUNTING-GATHERING PRODUCTIVE SYSTEM

In spite of agriculture and herding, until about 1960 (most likely for centuries before) at times as much as 90 percent of all food consumed was procured through gathering and hunting. Most available meat was game, highly prestigious, "healthy," and provided by men, but food collecting, done almost exclusively by women, yielded the lion's share of all available foodstuff: acorns, harvested in the outlying woods in the autumn, were labor intensively turned into flour and different kinds of breadlike starch staples; wild vegetables were dried for consumption in winter; mushrooms, edible roots, wild fruits, and berries, occasionally locusts, were harvested to augment the diet. By and large, the local cuisine revolved—and still does to some degree—around foodstuff collected in the wild. Rice and wheat were luxury staples only the rich could afford.

Women's foraging parties often last from sunup to sundown and take the women far from home into areas otherwise frequented only by hunters and men on errands in the mountains. During outings men and women perform all necessary tasks themselves: hunters do not take along women to cook for them, nor do women take along men as guides or for protection.

In the past, the women's groups on these occasions were large (up to thirty participants), made up of whoever in a general neighborhood had the time, strength, and inclination to join. Today the parties are fewer and smaller. No woman was veiled on a gathering trip in the past—dress was workaday—but now most women wear their work-hindering veil wraps and discard them later, when "nobody is looking." The atmosphere on these outings is relaxed, the hard work is performed in a spirit of fun, joke-buffered competition, even rowdyness. Interaction can best be summarized as "networking" in a socially relaxed and economically productive atmosphere. Public matters are discussed at length, ranging from critique of prominent figures like the chief to matchmaking, from reprimands for the conduct of individual men or women to venting of feelings, from giving and receiving of commiseration and advice to simple bantering. Stray men encountered by chance are dealt with from a position of strength in numbers in a largely unstructured setting and a general spirit of lightheartedness: such men are put on the defensive through jokes and teasing, or given tea, or driven away with strong language, depending on the man in question and the circumstances. Neither shyness, coyness, nor avoidance—appropriate for such occasions in the village—is necessary in the etiquette of such encounters in the mountains. This is not to say that a woman on an outing enjoys the freedom of an autonomous agent; she must observe a minimum of the decorum required in interactions with other women to whom she is either related or at least well-known. But as the composition of these groups is not kin-based by design but essentially individual and economic and organized around a specific, limited project that does not involve the observation of a full set of responsibilities (such as guarding children, feeding a husband, practicing deference rituals toward in-laws), behavior rules in effect in the village are greatly relaxed here: an elder sister-in-law, for example, who is to be treated with circumspection at home, here can be ignored or dealt with on the level of a cohort member one has known all one's life. In such informal task-centered groups, women establish their own hierarchies based on skill, personality, success, wit, wisdom, and other public virtues, and they can, if so inclined, practice social skills unfettered by the familiar confinements of male authority, domestic relationships, and the demands of young children that rule life at home.

In the women's own reports, they associate the outings predominantly with feelings of pleasure, competence, and satisfaction derived from climbing around in the mountains and bringing home heavy packs of valuable food—exertion and fatigue usually are not even mentioned. The supportive, lighthearted, and word-centered atmosphere is (in our terms) therapeutic, and the skills of leadership, task-related problem solving, decision making, arguing in large groups, exerting influence, manipulating opinions, and eliciting and offering support are practiced in a nonthreatening environment. Status obtained in these interactions and through economic success is transferred by the women into the domestic setting, at least in the form of increased assertiveness. In other words, their public (but all-women) performance carries over to the domestic (both sexes) domain.

At home, women retain full control over all gathered resources. Gathered food is considered low-status food and as such is not claimed as tribute or taxes by the chiefs; public distribution thus is not compulsory (unlike game and birds, for example, which hunters were required to share with chiefs on the threat of retribution). Women alone decide what, if any, goes to whom: they are free to keep it all in their larder, to serve it to guests, or to give it as gifts. They can (and do) use their harvest prudently to enhance their status as a good food provider to children, husband, relatives, and guests, which in turn percolates into the pool of power resources vis-à-vis other women in the domestic unit. These assets are the more important politically since women are dependent on men for all other foodstuffs, except chickens and eggs, which are always in short supply for reasons beyond the women's control. A woman who takes along on visits little bundles of wild leeks (seen drying all summer long on her flat roof) or who never runs out of wild almonds or dried blackberries enjoys the reputation of a "good" woman, one who is industrious and a talented housekeeper. To the extent that a woman's distribution of her surplus transcends the domestic circles, it creates recognition and wider reciprocal relationships—both providing additional sources of self-esteem and the social benefits that go with a good public reputation.

Compared with the social skills and political moves practiced in this setting, the dynamics of a woman's actions within the kin group proper, large as this may be and rich in women, are very different: status in a kin group is assigned to positions within a hierarchy topped and bounded by men, and each carries well-defined expected behaviors; any deviation from this order has the potential to produce conflict or else is the product of a previous conflict. Among structural near equals like sisters-in-law, the interaction is seen as competitive rather than cooperative; abusive rather than supportive; and stressful rather than relaxing. Men function as ultimate authorities in crises resulting from these interactions. Although the transfer of a woman's self-confidence and skills from the all-women's extradomestic group into the domestic one often is rich in conflicts also, our observations suggest that a woman of good repute and demonstrable success in the all-women's gathering group is more likely to succeed in her domestic group than one who has no such source of status (all other factors being about equal), if by no other mechanism than her superior bargaining position. In an argument between two sisters-in-law, for example, the point was driven home by one of them this way: "And whose wild almonds have you just been feeding to your visitors? And who carried them down from the mountains on her own back, tell me? And next time you run out of goodies for your guests don't dare come to me."

Public loci of actions for women, economic independence for women, and women's solidarity, all of which characterize gathering activities, are anathema to the principles of patriarchal orders such as are (and were) operative in Iran. As long as there was an overriding economic need for women's activities that challenged the ideal order, mechanisms were activated that made it possible to tolerate women's gathering parties: they were labeled "unimportant" (hence not taxed by chiefs); men ignored them (women did not need to ask their permission to join, or for their protection); the gathered food had neither prestige nor cash value of interest to men. But once reliable food supplies became available in the wake of such state and local developments as food imports and men's access to money (trade, wages, salaries) with which to buy food, and once the exploitation by chiefs and landlords had ended, the women's gathering activities lost their economic urgency: they became optional, if not superfluous. Acorn-flour bread, for example, is now in the village a symbol of bad, hungry days gone by—there is no need to gather acorns if one can eat wheat bread. Joining a gathering party now has the flavor of leisure-time luxury, and a risqué one at that, as it blatantly runs counter to an easily asserted ideal of domestic confinement for women. Women who ten years ago went on gathering outings as a matter of course now would not dream of joining one, nor would they allow their daughters or daughters-in-law to join one of the few small parties resisting the pressure to stay home. The danger of the wilderness, exhaustion, and health risks, the possibility of molestation by never-to-be-trusted strange men, honor easily tainted in public—notions that previously had been ignored, suppressed, or downplayed now provide powerful arguments for men and women opposed to women going out in the mountains. With the sharp decline in the incidence of women's gathering parties, a well-integrated and elaborate sphere of action for women has shrunk and a source of female autonomy has dried up.

True enough, the men's hunting sphere has shrunk even more, largely because of the near extinction of game. (For a while, the disarmament policy under Shah Muhammad Reza also severely limited local gun ownership; at the same time, however, sport hunting by outsiders finished whatever game population was left after the burgeoning local population began a massive hunting for food about 1940.) But for men, alternative ways for getting out and returning with valuables have opened up, whereas for women no alternatives to gathering have emerged.

The link between subsistence necessity and tolerance of a thriving all-women economic group activity thus made it possible to bring the whole sphere of action to an end, affirming and intensifying features of a patriarchal set, including greater economic dependence of women on men, spatial restriction, and greater isolation of women from one another.[6]

THE PASTORAL PRODUCTIVE SYSTEM

Migrating and camping units are small (up to ten tents or branch huts), organized bilaterally, and unstable. The spatial mobility of the migration, the lack of visible boundaries in and around camps, and the relative freedom of movement for women within camps—features women themselves see as desirable—are counterbalanced by the social isolation that is a function of the solitary, rhythmic chores of milk and wool processing and of the smallness of the camp group. Women say they are both free (*azad*) and lonesome (*tanha*), but less free and more lonesome than men, whose spatial and temporal parameters, compared with women's, are almost unbounded: men can leave camp any time, for days on end, and for whatever reason, whereas women can not.

In the pastoral setting the only large all-women's groups are the kin-based ones that are activated in a formal atmosphere at special occasions like weddings. Camp groups are much less stable and much smaller than courtyard-neighborhood groups (organized predominantly patrilineally) in the village. This affords camp-based women more intensive interaction with fewer women over shorter periods of time than village women enjoy, but at the expense of constant access to a wide network of interaction and information.

The obvious lack of privacy during the migration and in the camps has one major benefit for women: it gives them access to all the intelligence that can be had locally, including that gained through involuntary (and voluntary) listening to conversations among men, their own as well as occasional visitors, behind solidly symbolic but only marginally effective tent planes or branch walls. Not all women benefit equally from this opportunity, however. The information thus obtainable depends on the political standing of the men of the house: the more sociopolitically active a man is, the more opportunity his women will have to listen to discussions and to participate in decisions around his fire. No matter how bright, interested, and talented a woman might be, if her husband or father is a recluse, uninterested in the affairs of his fellow beings and the world at large, she will have little opportunity to gain knowledge or to air her own opinions and manipulate those of others. But everyday affairs concerning the camp and its members, indeed, all matters under the authority of the people themselves (rather than dictated by outsiders like chiefs, urban money lenders, and government agents) are handled with the knowledge and potential input of women. Taking charge sometimes proceeds even without men, if they happen to be absent when a decision has to be made. In a small camp of four tents in the tribe's winter quarters, for example, one midmorning the women suddenly reached the decision—on what basis remained a mystery to me—to move. The only two men in camp at the time together with all the women took down the tents and corrals and moved about an hour's distance away. In the evening the absent men, thinking they were returning home, found an empty camp site and wandered around for two hours before catching up with their people. This led to some jokes but no reprimands to the wives who had made the decision to "move the fire" without waiting for their husbands.

The fireplace (*tash*) in the tent or hut is the center for both a man's and a woman's overlapping spheres of action. The word *tash* characteristically denotes the essence of domestic security (such as when a man says "my fire is dead" as a euphemism for his wife's absence) as well as a core patrilineal unit in a political sense. As the tash is the locus of a wife's power and a husband's authority, both the woman and the man are in charge, even if this locus has different significance for each.

What any particular woman does with the knowledge she gains around her fire depends on her own personality, her aspirations, and her abilities. There are chiefs' wives at centers of intelligence and power who are, as it is said, "quiet," and others have carved an enduring place of fame for themselves in the lore of local history as intriguers, shakers, and movers of all men within their considerable sphere of power. Even women in ordinary positions have the choice either to limit their knowledge and influence to purely domestic issues or to include matters of wider economic and political portent. All information is a potential source of power—how it is used is a matter of choice. But this source of power is not granted to women legally, nor is it anchored anywhere ideologically.

Lack of privacy, of course, also subjects a woman's own actions to public comment. A woman's public and private personas are identical in the camp. To be politically useful, knowledge gained about the affairs of others has to be balanced carefully against one's own conduct.

The pastoral sphere is characterized by a division of labor in which women, as milkers and milk and wool processors, are the ones who turn most of the available surplus into valuable commodities (butterfat, cheese, rugs) through hard labor, whereas men control the distribution of these goods and their profit. Economically, women are exploited. Denied control and autonomy of decision over their products, they cannot turn their activities into sources of power, public or domestic. (There is one exception: refusing to work, as a measure of last resort. Embarrassing a husband by leaving him at the height of an argument to cope with chores that he, as a man, is not accustomed to doing does put a woman temporarily into a good bargaining position, but such extreme and upsetting gestures cannot be made often.) At best, women derive a kind of underdog satisfaction from their indispensable skills. Not surprisingly, they see their own pastoral labor as hard, endless, cheerless toil and complain about exhaustion, ill health, loneliness, and lack of comfort. Rarely does a woman protest her husband's decision to reduce the herds or to settle down. Many former herders have settled and others are settling in villages and towns where they have rights in agricultural land or access to jobs.[7] There they move in a productive sphere marked by a sedentary, agricultural, or wage-labor way of life. For those who stay with the pastoral life, the standard of living is increasing due to the higher prices their products now fetch. In the case of the relatively affluent herder, the women's lot is eased by better food and small luxuries and by labor-saving gadgets like propane-gas burners, which make obsolete the arduous task of collecting firewood, and by the use of trucks for the movement of camps and animals, which mitigates the exhausting trek of people and animals on the migrations.

In either case, however, sedentarization or pastoral affluency, women automatically become more firmly embedded in webs of male control and dependency than before. Bottled gas for cooking has to be bought (with money men control), in town (far from a woman's sphere of action), and has to be transported to camp by men, whereas firewood was collected by women at their discretion and within their radius of action space. Among nomadic pastoralists, any woman could load and unload donkeys and drive them, but only men can drive trucks.

Needless to say, male control of women's actions and the dependency of women on male services and on resources controlled by men are prominent features in the patriarchal set, as are curtailment of spatial mobility and control of access to information. Seen in historical perspective, the adaptive dynamic of the pastoral life furnishes a good example of the mutual reinforcement of androcentric structures quietly operative in the culture and of changes in socioeconomic parameters.

In such a reality, our concepts of private and public, of roles, even of higher and lower status of women, are largely irrelevant. From a general tribal Islamic and local legal point of view, women have no rights vis-à-vis men other than to expect regular sexual services and adequate livelihood and protection from their husbands.[8] Women do not inherit according to tribal custom; they do not hold offices, do not carry weapons, and are expected to perform services for the men responsible for them. Legally, a woman has no rights to any of her products, economic or reproductive. Yet, as we have seen, she does have relevant input into the system in a practical sense. This input proceeds according to such general rules of power as the interplay among personality, ambition, manipulative skills, knowledge and information about important issues; the backing by a woman's own family or by her children or others in the camp group; and her standing in the hierarchy of the women around her. In daily action within the spheres open to both men and women, these criteria are the most important ones; indeed a woman may appear to be her husband's or her sons' equal or even to be informal master of the household, without, however, any structural, legal, or ideological backing.

THE AGRICULTURAL PRODUCTIVE SYSTEM

In the tightly clustered traditional village, living rooms are arranged atop barns around courtyards populated by patrilineally related men and their families. A house is referred to by the name of the man who lives there ("the house of Ali, son of Hasan"). Save for the house or the room of the rare widow living by herself, houses are male property providing female space.

The solid appearance of substantially built mud-brick houses with well-defined areas and visible boundaries notwithstanding, the densely packed rooms offer little privacy. Comings and goings in the courtyard are noticed by all; voices carry through open doors and windows; children have unrestricted movement everywhere. In addition, flat house tops, open verandahs in front of the living rooms, doorways with views into neighbors' courtyards or the streets, and the human voice can be— and are—used effectively to appropriate extradomestic settings.

Neighbors, kin, and in-laws, the large, relatively stable network of bilateral kin groups functioning in the village create and relate news that women can plug into depending on their status in the network and on their own ambitions within the domestic sphere to which they are relegated by work, child care, and custom. A fight over the operation of a flour mill that was co-owned by a set of male cousins was strongly influenced, for example, probably even settled, by three of the cousins' wives, who thrashed the issue out among themselves. The men, I was told, had little choice in this. It can be argued justifiably that by local standards of proper conduct the women overstepped their places, probably even committed sins left and right in the process. Nonetheless, they apparently found it possible, advisable, and defensible to take these matters into their own hands; again on the practical level, they acted as role models for their daughters and other women and they got away with it.

Inasmuch as kin groups function as political bodies in which domestic politics and public politics are interconnected, women can, and usually do, have effective input in decisions and access to carriers of authority. After all, no matter how excluded she may be from public loci of political authority as defined earlier, a woman does have access to her relatives and her husband's relatives (if these are different), and these include men and women, powerful ones and weak ones. For any woman all other people in her kin network are potential sources of power and potential means to create safe spaces in which to move. A young female teacher in one of the elementary schools in the village, for example, successfully defended her refusal to comply with the new order that all female teachers had to relocate to the girls' school (which for her would have meant walking four miles every day). She pointed out that of the dozen male teachers in her school every single one was related to her and that therefore she was not among strange men. The whole village found the matter a joke, but she won her case.

In the courtyards, women usually spend the day with other women save for mealtime visits from their men (husbands, fathers, brothers, sons). Most of the quintessentially female tasks of preparing food, processing wool and milk, and caring for infants are carried out there in close proximity to other women. The spaces the women occupy, however, are feminine spaces only as long as they are not challenged by men. The appearance of men will break up a women's gathering anywhere in the house if the men want to be there. Domestic space, well-defined by walls, is more of a feminine space than any other in the village (except the bathhouse at women-only times), but it is so by virtue of occupancy by women who are taking care of male property. Dissatisfied with his wife's services, a husband can send her away at any time.

Village lanes, shops, and the surrounds of the village, especially the fields, are largely male domains. Women are by no means prohibited from being outside the house, but it is understood that they must have a legitimate reason to be out: carrying water, walking from one house to another, and performing an urgent errand are acceptable reasons; going for a walk, lingering outside one's door, and hanging around a shop are not legitimate activities and would lead to gossip and censure. Although there are stories of desperate young widows with children plowing a field, harvesting a wheat crop, or cutting grass for a cow at home, such rare occurrences were remarkable enough to be remembered for decades. Women did, however, participate more actively in the cultivation of cash crops like tobacco, opium, and sugar beets. (In other words, women can work in public-oriented crops but not in the traditional domestic-oriented ones, like wheat and barley. This is another instance where the public-private categorization creates confusion.) Men are fully in control of all agricultural crops, and tax tributes to the landlord or chief had to be paid on all agricultural products grown by men.

There were no vegetable gardens in the village until the mid-1960s, when people (men and women) started to grow potatoes, tomatoes, and some green vegetables out in the fields. Kitchen gardens near the house (a woman's agricultural domain in most parts of the world), with popular greens like onions, parsley, spinach, and dill, here are tended by men and women, and even now are found only around the most modern houses, where walls, low population density, and absence of chickens make such plantings possible—or so the people say. Women do not seem to derive any benefits from these small gardens other than the availability of greens.

The agricultural division of labor thus promotes women's economic dependence on men for staple food, reversing the order of the hunting-gathering mode of earlier and poorer times. The agricultural staple (wheat), however, unlike the acorns of old, is a prestige crop. In conjunction with the legal disenfranchisement of women mentioned above, this economic dependency, the inaccessibility of staple and prestige resources, and the denial of inheritance shares and rights of management in the agricultural setting are felt by women to strongly inhibit the generation of power.

The marked separation of domestic from extradomestic life is mitigated by the absence of all-male meeting places in the village, if one disregards the chief's house in former times: there are no coffee houses and no tradition of using the mosque or the bazaar, for example, as social centers for men's daily interactions. Intravillage public matters are discussed in the street or in one another's houses. There women can listen and, if so inclined, make themselves heard from the sidelines: the back of the room, outside the door, serving tea or a meal. Men arrive at decisions through informal discussions in consensus-among-equals fashion or through mediation, and therefore women's opinions count potentially much more than in a setting where decisions are made by men's votes or by representation. Here again, the door is wide open for women to manifest individual differences in degree of political ambition and exertion of power.

A woman's political acuity and power are partly a function of her husband's (father's, sons') political standing, inasmuch as through him she has access to larger or smaller authority networks. In turn, however, a politically astute or ambitious woman will use her network of relatives, men and women, and her information, however come by, to empower her husband or sons, thereby broadening her own power base. To understand how women actually work through and around a public system that assigns them, legally speaking, second-class status with virtually no authority at all, not even over their offspring, to create a measure of independence, impact, or self-realization, one has to focus on these dynamics. Role analyses or confrontational dichotomies like public and private alone do not afford us much insight into these processes.

An example of political maneuvering among women in the context of the brideprice illustrates this point: negotiations over the brideprice and what a bride's father does with it are not only about goods and money but also about status. Relative to the actual volume and value of the brideprice, the dowry a bride brings with her in the form of household goods and luxuries is an indication of her father's willingness and ability to back her up and to watch over her interests, and thus of his status vis-à-vis his daughter's in-laws. A stingy or poor father who keeps much of the brideprice for himself can be ignored politically by his daughter's in-laws, whereas one who gives more in the dowry than he received in the brideprice is to be reckoned with in matters to come between the two families. For years after a wedding, more or less subtly, both families attempt to gain political advantage by asserting their own generosity over the other's alleged stinginess. Both men and women engage in these games of one-upmanship, and a bride supported by her father's generosity can use his backing as a power source in her new group, which in turn benefits her father. In the king-making efforts within one of the larger and upwardly mobile families in the village, for example, one man was built up by his daughter: discussing a discord between her female cousin (her father's brother's daughter) and this cousin's in-laws, she said that her own father had out of his pocket bought a rug for his niece because her father (his own brother) was a poor man and the brideprice he had gotten had been dismally meager, too. In a one-sentence stroke, the speaker thereby expressed her father's superiority over his poorer brother (implying that he was wealthier and worthier than the brother), insinuated the low status of the niece's in-laws (they were poor or stingy), and affirmed the backing of the niece by her relatives (even her uncle is supporting her). With this pronouncement the woman herself furthermore showed that she was willing and able to assert herself and to support her father, and was counting on his powerful support. Strategies like this form a woman's position as negotiated on the ground level of day-to-day living.

In the traditional agricultural setting the women's sphere of action is severely limited spatially and economically by the division of labor and by the confinement of stable, easily gender-indexed spaces. The resulting economic dependency of women on men, however, is somewhat balanced by the women's access to a large group of people, which affords them not only more occasions for input into the discussion of the large volume of issues that emerge in the life of a populous village, but also more occasions to create mutually interdependent power relationships with a wide net of relatives. To the extent that village affairs are dealt with locally (and not, for example, in the city) and that men conduct political affairs in one another's houses (and not, for example, at the mayor's office), women at least can keep abreast of happenings and decisions that affect domestic and public conditions.

THE POST-DEVELOPMENT, POST-REVOLUTION SETTING

Over the past twenty years the effective integration of the area into the rapidly developing nation, the revolution, and the post-revolutionary policies of the Islamic Republic all have worked toward shrinking the options women have for action. Economically, increased opportunities and greater availability of food have made such activities as gathering acorns superfluous and sheep and goat herding on a small scale unprofitable. There are few gathering parties now, and few women leave the village to spend part of the year in outposts with the herds. Women have lost their productive niche as gatherers and as processors of milk and wool, and the fields and newly created orchards are a solidly male domain. Since 1979, the effective implementation of the fundamentalist doctrine of domestic confinement of women has curtailed food gathering even further. Indeed, a woman's participation in such expeditions is now used in power plays between mothers-in-law and their sons' wives and between husbands and brothers and their wives and sisters, with young women usually the losers. In other words, female groups now are confined to domestic kin groups. As the locus of decision making in public affairs has shifted from the political economic arena of domestic centers to offices, from the village to towns, and from villagers to urban bureaucrats, both men and women have lost autonomy, but unequally so. Except for teachers and the occasional female member of the Islamic village council, women generally now have much less access to public places than men do. Women's sphere of action includes fewer points of access to sources of information, decision, and power, because these centers have shifted out of reach in a spatial sense and into a kind of public arena that is dominated by male strangers speaking a different language, deriving their authority from amorphous outside agents, and depending on written communications that women cannot read. This alienation of economic and sociopolitical power makes it easy for the republic's fundamentalist ideology to realize an order in which men act as culture brokers, news agents, and sole political agents for women; in which men with the full backing of the law can assert total domestic authority over their women; in which men can usurp all nondomestic space, thus making it public in the sense that women are restricted from it; and in which men can demand a degree of compliance and subordination from their women that would have been hard to obtain without severe protest a generation ago. The paradoxical situation thus is created in which women officially have a public political vote and have access to information on the national level via television and other propaganda instruments, yet lack access to input into decisions at the local level as well as information about domestic, private affairs that affect them daily.

As mentioned above, in the wake of these effects of modernization the all-women's groups no longer are important. Pre-wedding parties have stopped completely, and the bathhouse crowd is shrinking as new houses are built with shower stalls. The only new occasion for congregation of women locally is graveyard visitation on Thursday afternoons, but this is kin-based, with a decidedly downbeat mood and a narrow field of action and purpose, and thus neither an equivalent to nor a substitute for the old gathering groups.[9]

Indeed, women in the post-modernization sphere are more isolated than they were in any other sphere, as the large courtyards break up, nuclear families move into walled-in single-family houses, and legitimate economic reasons for outings by women disappear. Because this development conforms to the Islamic patriarchal virtue of domestic confinement of women, it will be difficult to circumvent, unless the new houses in turn become centers for new courtyard-type developments in the rapidly expanding village. (There are signs to this effect.) In this case, economic necessity again will override ideological postulates without changing the androcentric superstructure.

As women move in and out of the overlapping productive systems in the course of their daily routines, they appear more or less dependent, influential, visible, strong, or whatever adjectives we might wish to try on them, according to the logic of these systems. The same woman who is moving freely far from home collecting edible thistles with other women (in the first system) can be seen the next day covered from head to toe walking self-effacingly through the main street of the village (in the fourth system) on her way to a field where, without her veil, she will pull weeds with her husband in his patch of lentils, perfectly in accordance with the requirements of the third system. Neither her gender role nor definition of public and private has shifted—the seeming inconsistency in her behavior is due to her shifting among different action spheres with their different behavior codes.

Similarly, a woman who is used to receiving and hosting passing strangers at her fire from many seasons spent in a branch hut or a tent easily may transfer this familiar practice to the village should the need arise (choosing to move in the second system), whereas a woman who never was exposed to life in a camp will not even admit a stranger to the house if she is alone, thus staying firmly in the action grid of the fourth system. The difference between the behavior of those two women is due neither to a difference in their respective roles, nor necessarily to a difference in personality or degree of piety, but rather to the difference in the respective action systems in which they move. By the same logic, however, a woman accustomed to conversing freely with strangers in a camp may choose to adopt a fourth-system mode of interaction when she is in the village and ignore the stranger completely.

Overlapping action-sphere boundaries create options for women. These options can be—and are—influenced by the all-encompassing androcentric rules asserting themselves in Iran presently. In the village, lost economic niches and heavy pressure by propaganda agents, from mullahs to revolutionary guards to schoolchildren, motivate more and more women to accept the narrowly uniform parameters of the fourth system.

In this system, a woman's role is defined in authoritative religious scriptures, and the concepts of public and private divide the world into "separate but equally important" parallel spheres in which women and men work for one another's benefit. This program has rhetorical merits, but practically it amounts to a myth, one that mystifies the fact that economically, culturally, politically, and cognitively most women have lost access to sources of power both in the domestic and in the extra-domestic sphere. They have lost this access rapidly and easily because the appearances of freedom and assertion in the past were only a function of socioeconomic circumstances and not embedded in a gender-egalitarian (not to speak of gynocentric) ideology.

Notes

1. Adele K. Ferdows and Amir Ferdows, "Women in Shi'i Fiqh: Image through the Hadith," in *Women and Revolution in Iran*, ed. Guity Nashat (Boulder, Colo.: Westview, 1983), 54–68.

2. Lois Beck, "Women among the Qashqa'i Nomadic Pastoralists in Iran," in *Women in the Muslim World*, ed. Lois Beck and Nikki Keddie (Cambridge: Harvard University Press, 1978), 351–73.

3. The Seventh Berkshire Conference on the History of Women was dedicated to the exploration of the usefulness of this dichotomy.

4. No matter how controversial, the term *patriarchy* seems to be here to stay. See Gerda Lerner, *The Creation of Patriarchy* (New York: Oxford University Press, 1986).

5. Erika Friedl, "The Division of Labor in an Iranian Village," *MERIP Reports*, no. 95 (March–April 1981): 12–18.

6. There were other traditional all-women's groups in the past, not connected with gathering but sharing similar social and psychological benefits, such as par-

ties before weddings, where in a bawdy, cathartic atmosphere women made fun of their behavior during childbirth and of sex. In another informal atmosphere, the bathhouse, ad hoc bathing groups exchanged news, discussed problems, and politicked. This was also where the most private of all entities, the body, was revealed to public scrutiny: pregnancies invariably were first noted here, and if a woman could conceal elsewhere that she had been beaten, in the bath her bruises told the tale and her condition became public. Smaller all-women's groups traditionally formed around such economic tasks as hulling rice, carding wool, and spinning, but these were conducted within the domestic sphere, were composed of neighbors who usually also were kin, and therefore operated largely according to the dynamics of the kin network.

7. Reinhold Loeffler, "Recent Economic Changes in Boir Ahmad: Regional Growth without Development," *Iranian Studies* 9, no. 4 (1976): 266–87; Loeffler, "Economic Changes in a Rural Area since 1979," in *The Iranian Revolution and the Islamic Republic,* ed. Nikki Keddie and Eric Hooglund, new ed. (Syracuse: Syracuse University Press, 1986), 91–109.

8. Guity Nashat, "Women in the Islamic Republic of Iran," *Iranian Studies* 13, nos. 1–4 (1980): 165–94; Behnaz Pakizadeh, "Legal and Social Positions of Iranian Women," in *Women in the Muslim World,* ed. Beck and Keddie, 216–26; Fazlur Rahman, "Status of Women in the Qur'an," in *Women and Revolution in Iran,* ed. Nashat, 37–54.

9. For possibilities for women's gatherings not realized in this village, see Anne H. Betteridge, "The Controversial Vows of Urban Women in Iran," in *Unspoken Worlds: Women's Religious Lives in Non-Western Cultures,* ed. Nancy Auer Falk and Rita M. Gross (San Francisco: Harper and Row, 1980), 141–58; and Mary E. Hegland (Hooglund), "Religious Ritual and Political Struggle in an Iranian Village," *MERIP Reports,* no. 102 (1982): 10–17.

12 Political Roles of Aliabad Women:

The Public-Private Dichotomy Transcended

MARY ELAINE HEGLAND

Until the mid-1960s, public and political relations in the Iranian village of Aliabad were conducted through personal
relationships. The government's hand had not spread into
rural areas: no outside political authority or police force controlled village politics. The people themselves competed for
political power and were in charge of maintaining stability.
Competition between groups resulted in violence and insecurity. One had to tie personal relations together—kin,
friends, and partners—to gather political support. Personal
and domestic relations were also public and political relations, for politics was conducted through kinship and family
relations. Although there appears to be no actual delineation
between public and private realms in this setting, there is a
strong indigenous ideology of the separation between the
domestic and private and the public and political, which
assumes women to predominate in the first and men in the
second. Why this contradiction? To what uses is the public-
private dichotomy put in this situation?[1] What are the results
of encouraging such a dichotomy? An examination of the
lives of Iranian village women of two main groups, peas-

This chapter is based on research carried out in Iran from June
1978 until December 1979. I am grateful to the following for funding
my research and writing: the Social Science Research Council and
the American Council of Learned Societies; the Anthropology department and the Southwest Asian and North African program of
SUNY, Binghamton; the Educational Foundation of the American
Association of University Women; the Center for Near Eastern and
North African Studies of the University of Michigan, Ann Arbor;
and the National Endowment for the Humanities. Research would
not have been possible without the assistance of the many Iranians I
have known since 1966 and especially the residents of Aliabad, who
befriended and taught the foreigner in their midst. The name of the
village and those of individuals have been changed to protect privacy.

215

ants and traders, during several recent periods—landlord-dominated, post-land reform, pre-revolution and revolution, and post-revolution— suggests that the public-private dichotomy as ideology and as myth has been used to contain and utilize women and their activities in political competition.

THE PUBLIC-PRIVATE DICHOTOMY AS IDEOLOGY

The public-private ideology was discernible in the village of Aliabad during my fieldwork in 1978 and 1979, more so among the womenfolk of the traders than those of the peasants.[2] Whereas peasant women did not give much attention to regulations of covering and segregation, trading womenfolk were highly conscious of adhering to modesty guidelines and prided themselves on being *mo'men* (proper and sure in their adherence to their faith). They made fun of the peasant women, whose dresses, they said, were slit down the front for nursing babies; they were not modest. The traders and their wives were usually *sayyids*, or descendants of the Prophet. Sayyids were expected to adhere more faithfully to religious ritual standards than other Muslims. In addition, traders were often *hajjis*; they had made the pilgrimage to Mecca. A few of the trading womenfolk themselves had been to Mecca, which also brought greater obligations of demonstrated religiosity, including more attention to covering and black *chadors*, or veils.

Among the trading womenfolk, the public-private ideology was apparent in words, discussion, and behavior. Women belong inside the house; inside is women's area and outside is for men. The men can be in the alleyways, or in the streets outside the village. Women are supposed to be at home. Such words as *hijab* (covering) and *daruni* (inside) versus *biruni* (outside), *khaneh* (house) and *hayyat* (courtyard) versus *kucheh* (alleyway) and *khiaban* (street), and *deh* (village) versus *biaban* (countryside) indicated the proper places for women and men.

In talking with one another women often alluded to the modesty code. One woman was especially admired by the others. They said, "She hardly ever leaves her courtyard. She's such a good Muslim, she's such a good woman." Other women halfheartedly wished they could live up to her example. Women were sometimes afraid to be seen walking, even just outside their own courtyards. One young woman was uncomfortable standing on a neighbor's roof talking, for fear that people would call her a stray—the same word used for a stray dog.

In their behavior as well as their comments, sayyid women showed a consciousness of the public-private dichotomy. One young sayyid woman was known to avoid attending weddings of anyone except her closest relatives. Sayyid women rarely watched the dancing at weddings in the open areas of the village, whereas other village residents could. (Everyone was expected to watch the dancing, whether or not they were related to members of the wedding party.) Sayyid women did not go to the mosque, where they felt they would be exposed to unknown men, but other women could attend the mosque and sit in the curtained-off area for women. Sayyid women did not come outside to watch the male mourning processions during the yearly commemorations for Imam Husain, a highly significant figure in Shi'i Islam martyred in A.D. 680. When going outside their own close neighborhood, sayyid women wore the more conservative black chador rather than a lighter printed chador that they wore nearer home and that other women wore outside the village as well. When attending weddings and mourning gatherings or going to shrines and to the cemetery, sayyid women walked with a large number of their relatives and associates to be enclosed and encapsulated in a group of women.

The trading womenfolk had internalized the directives of the public-private dichotomy, as I learned when I moved from the Lower Neighborhood, where the sayyid trading women lived, to the Upper Neighborhood in Aliabad, which was more heavily peasant. My old neighbors were extremely reluctant to come and visit me in my new home. A close friend explained, "I can't come to the Upper Neighborhood. I'd feel as if I were stealing if I went there. It would be *zesht* (socially inappropriate, ugly). I couldn't come to your courtyard because I don't have any relatives there."

Finally, realizing that their failure to visit hurt me, almost the entire social group of sayyid women came to see me, apparently finding the courage to do so only in large numbers. They knocked timidly on my door, choosing the one through the village wall rather than the door into the courtyard from an internal village alleyway. By going out the main village gateway and then coming to my outside door, they could avoid walking through the part of the village alien to them. As soon as I opened the door, the women scurried into my courtyard. They sat stiffly for half an hour, keeping their formal black chadors wrapped carefully around themselves. Each time the courtyard door opened they looked up, ready to flee into a corner should a man appear.

The sayyid women had internalized the public-private ideology; they felt shame if they went outside the parameters set by that ideology. Yet in spite of their attention, talk, and demonstrated obedience to modesty standards, it was more often the trading women rather than the peasants who left their homes and domestic work to engage in economic and political activity. In addition, all of their activity, including their domestic involvement, was relevant to politics. Their domestic and personal lives were political and part of the public world.

THE MYTH OF THE PUBLIC-PRIVATE DICHOTOMY

In spite of the attention Aliabad women, especially the sayyids and trading womenfolk, gave to the public-private ideology, this dichotomy did not accurately depict reality. The accuracy of the dichotomy can be evaluated in two ways: first, the locus of activity, and second, the realm for which a particular activity is important.

In terms of the gradation between private and public locus of activity—moving from the living room, where the family carried on all activities, to the good room, where guests were received, and on to courtyard, alleyway, close neighborhood, section, village, village land, and beyond—women certainly stayed closer to home than men did. Even here, however, a strict division between public and political versus private and domestic, with men in the former and women relegated to the latter, is not accurate. Women commonly carried on domestic chores outside of their own homes and courtyards. Without a water spigot in their own courtyard—a relatively new convenience for those fortunate enough to have one—women had to wash clothes in a stream outside the village, often draping them on graveyard stones to dry. One young woman routinely took her laundry to her mother's courtyard and stayed the day, returning in time to cook her husband's dinner. Women often took their own work to other courtyards or assisted friends and relatives. Domestic work in other courtyards was especially noticeable on the occasion of weddings, death commemorations, and other gatherings.

Women rarely went outside the village on food-gathering expeditions but often visited in other homes, shopped, went to the mosque and women's religious gatherings in homes, walked to the graveyards or village shrines, and went to Shiraz and even farther to visit relatives and shrines or to conduct other business. A number of young unmarried women stayed with relatives in Shiraz to attend high school, and others worked long hours in the carpet workshop located in the village and owned by the then village boss, Sayyid Ya'qub, and his brother. Some eleven widowed, divorced, or married women worked for pay: three kindergarten teachers (among them a young woman who stayed in Shiraz to teach during the week and returned to her parents' home on the weekends to be with her two children), a kindergarten cook, two midwives, a cloth saleswoman, a seamstress, a public bath attendant, a keeper of dairy cows and other animals, and an opium smuggler.

Animals owned or tended by a family were kept in courtyards at night, and women were active in milking and otherwise caring for cows, sheep, goats, and chickens. Although agricultural fields were off limits to women in Aliabad, women could become involved in trade. In earlier years some widows became traders to support themselves and their children, and they visited the camps of migrating Qashqa'i on business in the company of a child. Women married to traders often helped with the business. Several auxiliary shops and all the wholesale grain traders' businesses were located in homes. Women waited on customers and dealt with trading partners there or in shops outside the home in the absence of their husbands. Even the wives of opium dealers were knowledgable about prices and quality, and they interacted without reticence or embarrassment with men from outside the village, usually known to them through previous association. Several women were known as good managers and astute businesswomen.

Political and economic business was often conducted in domestic settings. In addition to being a base for trading, homes were often where men held political meetings. No buildings were designated for political activity and closed to women. There were no men's houses nor was there a bazaar area. Grocery shops were too tiny to host large gatherings. The mosque was open to women (with a curtained-off side for their use) as well as to men and was not thought appropriate in any case as a location for political activity (unless it could be defended as religious activity). Political discussion then was possible only outdoors or in homes. Reception of political dependents and partners, strategy planning and decision making among allies, gatherings of *taifeh* (kinship-based factions) members, and emergency meetings and "entrenchments" (*sangar*), or gatherings, of taifeh members following violence for mutual protection and demonstration of support all took place in homes, where women often had the opportunity to watch, listen, and even participate. If nothing else, they were present to serve tea and thus could keep up-to-date on political debates and planning.

Women carried on domestic work outside their homes and entered into economic and political affairs. Men carried on business and political activity inside their homes and, of course, entered into and influenced domestic and private affairs and were the final authorities over their wives, daughters, sisters, and even, at times, their mothers. Lines distinguishing public and political from domestic and private concerning space and activity were thus not immutable. If the spatial boundaries between public and private were erratic, the dividing line becomes all the more indistinct when we consider the realm of significance for particular activities. Because of the political system in Iran and specifically in the village of Aliabad, separating the personal and private from the political is not possible.

Political relations in Iran were based more on personal contact and

connections than on universalistic criteria. Political and economic activities depended on personal acquaintance, family connections, trust
developed through intensive social interaction, friendship, kinship, and
face-to-face contact more than on reliable institutions, legal guarantees,
and impersonal contracts. In an environment of insecurity, fluctuation,
and mistrust—both political and economic—friendship, family,
kinship, and social interaction were paramount. To elicit political support, favors, and assistance, people used the obligations, emotional
attachments, history, concern, empathy, and dependency of friendship,
kinship, association, and partnership (*sharik*), as well as visiting and
eating at one another's homes. In the absence of regular political and
economic institutions, family, kinship, and friendship could not be separated from politics. Political activity was conducted largely through
personal contacts and connections.

Such was the rule in Aliabad. At the time of my fieldwork between
June 1978 and December 1979, this large village located in southwestern
Iran contained some three thousand people. Owned throughout the
first half of this century by the powerful merchant and landowning
family of Qavams, who were based in the nearby city of Shiraz, Aliabad
was administered by local representatives of the Qavams. Such representatives were so powerful that they were called little shahs; they
enjoyed almost complete control over other villagers and even over
many surrounding regions. Both peasants and traders—adult males
were divided almost evenly between these two occupations—needed
the protection and resources available only from these representatives
of the landlord. Traders needed the assurance of protection during their
dangerous trips to Shiraz or other villages; only the landlord's representatives could send armed horsemen to accompany or rescue traders and
their goods. Peasants likewise were dependent on the representatives
for access to agricultural land under their control, protection of that land
and its produce, and security for themselves, their families, and their
property from other villagers and any attacking outsiders. With no
other alternatives to deal with danger inside and outside the village,
residents submitted to the rule of the landlord's representatives. Force,
violence, and insecurity were rampant. One's only hope was to connect
oneself to a powerful political figure.

Even the landlord's representatives were not secure in their positions. In the words of a commonly quoted proverb, "One day the saddle is on the horse; the next day the horse is on the saddle." Landlord's
representatives rose to their positions through success in trade and then
used the profits from trade to build up a following of dependents and
allies—a taifeh, or kinship-based political grouping. A political contender could provoke a series of violent confrontations with the taifeh of

an incumbent. Upon winning several such struggles, the contender, recognized to be more effective as a local strong man, would be named as the new representative by the landlord. Political and economic position rested entirely on connection with a powerful political figure and membership in or support from a large and physically powerful taifeh. Such alliance rested on intense and regular social interaction and demonstrations of closeness. For Aliabadis as well as for other Iranians, then, social interaction and personal connections were of primary significance in the political process.

In a political world where the obligations and responsibilities of intimacy were the stuff of politics, women and their activities were central to the political process.[3] Although the weight of modest behavior rested more on traders and their wives, trading womenfolk were called on to be the most active in the political process, for the traders rather than the peasants were leaders in political competition. It was a myth, then, that sayyid trading women and their activities were irrelevant to the public political arena. At the same time, the public-private ideology was instrumental in curtailing women and their activities in order to channel them into public political use.

THE PUBLIC-PRIVATE DICHOTOMY: CONTROL AND CONTAINMENT OF WOMEN

Many of the roles of women were significant for the public political realm.

Social. In a system where political alliance was demonstrated and maintained through social interaction—visiting and hosting (*raft o amad*)—the activity of women was crucial. The wives of politically important figures were extremely active in women's groups and networks. The more intense the social interaction and the closer the relationship, the greater was the obligation to show support in political struggles. Men therefore encouraged their wives to lead active social lives with the womenfolk of their political allies. Women were responsible for the seemingly endless round of events connected with the life cycle, in which they were autonomous social actors and which were sometimes only vaguely recognized by men. At weddings women were especially in evidence, often coming to the bride's and groom's homes weeks in advance to help with preparations and to join in the festivity; they also attended mourning gatherings in larger numbers and for much longer after a death than men did. Some women's gatherings had no analogue among men. Men did not attend most life-cycle events connected with preparation for marriage, pregnancy, and childbirth. Men did not frequent the cemetery on Thursday afternoons, and few men were present on the various commemorative days after a death.

Men did not go to the local shrines in groups, nor did they usually attend *rauzehs* (recitations of the stories about saints, especially related to the martyrdom of Imam Husain and his followers).[4] Men had no equivalent to the gathering for religious teaching by visitors from Maktab-i Zahra, the women's religious school in Shiraz, or to the Quran reading and explanation for females in the mosque by the visiting *mulla* from Qum, a program started before the revolution.

Women's socializing was more regular and interrupted less often than that of men. During periods of conflicts, the public bath was closed during men's hours to prevent possible outbreaks of violence. Male members of competing taifehs fled the village or stayed at home to avoid meeting enemies. Mourning ceremonies for men were cancelled during hostilities, but women's mourning gatherings continued as usual and women maintained interaction with the womenfolk of opposing taifeh to a certain extent. By maintaining social interaction with enemy factions, women could facilitate rapprochement later. Because women could be seen as somewhat removed from a conflict and because they had lower status, they were used as messengers or intermediaries in delicate sociopolitical negotiations. Women often pressured for a cessation of conflict; avowed acquiescence to the demands of their womenfolk for peace provided men with a graceful means of ending a struggle.

Men often were absent from the village, maintaining shops in other villages, on itinerant trading trips, or engaged in agricultural pursuits. Women were available in the village for the frequent, intense social interaction required to demonstrate and maintain political alliance, to which the "feminine" mode of interaction and "feminine" personality lent themselves. Women's exchanges were less formal and less dignified, covered a wider spectrum of topics—often including the personal revelations that feelings of closeness encouraged—and were more free flowing. A woman could drop in at a neighbor's without notice and chat at the doorway or squat informally with the woman of the house wherever she was without interrupting work and be on her way again in a matter of minutes if necessary. A man's visit required a more formal reception, complete with admittance to the sitting room, offering of more hospitality, and a lengthier stay. Because women did not have as much status and dignity to live up to, they were less reluctant to display their emotions and true selves.

Women maintained close contact with their own families and relatives as well as with those of their husbands. Perhaps the closest kinship tie was between mother and daughter, who usually attempted to visit each other as often as possible. The bilateral kinship system provided men with a choice of political alliance and a means of changing sides when advisable.

In a world where politics was conducted largely through kinship, the responsibility of women for the "work of kinship" put them at the center of the political process.[5] Where social relations and political alliances are one and the same, women's social activities are also political activities, whether overtly recognized as such or not and whether they take place in the "domestic" sphere or in public.[6]

Women were available for the intensive, repetitive socializing with family, kin, and neighbors necessary to maintain political connections because they were prevented from having other social contacts. Women were allowed to associate only with close kin and neighbors. Even when traveling to Shiraz, women were shrouded in veils and surrounded by a group of their regular female associates and did not make new acquaintances.

Sexual. Women's sexuality (and men's) was utilized in the political process. Girls were married to men with whom their fathers or other male taifeh members wished to make or solidify political-economic alliances. Marriages were arranged with children of the landlord's representative in a neighboring village, with trading partners, within the taifeh, between taifeh in a confederation, with tribal allies, and with religious and trading figures in Shiraz. To conserve sexuality for such purposes, the modesty code was invoked to prevent girls from meeting young men on their own and to prevent married women from coming into contact with men other than their husbands. Girls could be promised at a very early age and married by age nine, again to circumvent independent expression of sexuality. Many factors colluded to reserve women's sexuality for appropriate political alliances, including the age difference between husband and wife; the power of a mother-in-law and other female in-laws over a bride; the seclusion of women in chadors and buildings; the restriction of a bride to her house in the period before and after marriage; the failure to consider female satisfaction in intercourse; early impregnation; a hovering group of female associates; internalized socialization concerning modesty and sexual loyalty to the husband; awareness of the dire results of sexual impropriety; and lack of education, of opportunities for employment, and of independent economic means, resulting in economic dependence.[7]

Reproductive. Kin were the best raw material for creating political allies. Although even family and kin were not automatically political supporters—one had to associate with them on good, intimate terms—kin could be trusted more than non-kin. The great majority of supporters of a taifeh head were his kin. A woman's reproductive activities, then, were also political.[8] Taifeh heads often were men with a good number of sons, and daughters likewise provided a means to solidify political alliances within or outside the taifeh through marriage. Women's energies were available for reproduction because early marriage and the lack of opportunity for education and for work left them no alternatives. In addition, marriage and then children—especially sons—were the route to obtaining whatever status and prestige were available to women.

Family relations. The love, concern, care, and affection expended by women on their offspring were political investments, for the resulting affective attachments and loyalty of sons and daughters to their mothers united the taifeh and often brought sons-in-law and their relatives as allies to the taifeh. The frequent visits between mother and married daughter carried political implications, as did social relations between a woman and other members of her natal and conjugal families. Again, as a woman had no other means of achieving satisfaction, the role of mother and the loyalty and affection of her children were among the few rewards available to her.

"Domestic" labor. All domestic tasks could be political public work.[9] Providing physical care and affection for children; processing, preparing, and serving food; washing; cleaning; tending to the needs of the husband and other older males; offering hospitality; dressing attractively, especially for weddings; receiving relatives and neighbors; maintaining a harmonious household and good relations with kin and neighbors; administering weddings, mourning gatherings, religious commemorations, and ritual feasts; distributing charity; and caring for incapacitated relatives served to demonstrate and to maintain or improve the political standing of husband, family, and taifeh. A woman was not allowed to work independently to earn money, thus making her labor available for the political benefit of her family and her taifeh.[10]

Religious. Going on hajj; praying; following fasting requirements and scheduling food preparation and meals to enable other family members to do so; providing charity; achieving a reputation for piety, modesty, and goodness; hosting rauzehs; attending mourning commemorations; making vows and donating food; distributing the meat from the sacrifice of a sheep required yearly for hajjis; hosting ritual feasts and religious actors and reciters from Shiraz; attending meetings for religious education; visiting shrines; and—in the pre-revolution and revolution periods—professing revolutionary fervor and loyalty to Ayatollah Khomeini and joining revolutionary demonstrations all brought prestige to one's husband, family, and taifeh and allowed appropriate opportunities for sociopolitical interaction. Women had to be content with these religious practices since they were excluded from the men's side of the mosque, from serious study of the Quran in groups in Shiraz, and from the village male ritual commemorations for the death of Imam Husain and his family.

Verbal and intellectual. Women were more verbally gifted and active than men. Spending more time than men in the company of family, relatives, and neighbors with whom they felt comfortable and natural, less compelled by dignity to restrict themselves to "important" topics of conversation, less restrained from undignified probing and pressuring, and known to be more curious and gossipy, many women developed amazing communication and information collecting skills. Confined to their homes, women often missed the most dramatic and newsworthy events. Many women became adept at questioning and probing each available informant—their own or other children, other women, and all male visitors—to piece together what had gone on and why. Women used their verbal and intellectual skills for gathering information, spying, persuading, taunting, berating, threatening, shaming, discussing, interpreting, encouraging, and building up close sociopolitical relations. Barred from much education, from primary involvement in economic pursuits, and from political policy making, women brought their verbal and intellectual abilities to these political tasks.[11]

Emotional and moral. Women were thought to be more emotional than men, and indeed they displayed more emotion. They were expected to scream and wail, scratch their cheeks, beat their chests, and go without food and drink when in grief. In cases of injury or death due to violence, supportive women streamed to the courtyard of the afflicted person with outpourings of emotion, showing sorrow and rage. The reaction of women to what they considered wrongful deeds and their expressions of emotion were often effective in persuading men to take action and in swaying village opinion. Their attachment to fathers, brothers, and cousins could mobilize women to rally men into support or to encourage them to negotiate.

Leadership. Through their active, competent, and valuable participation in both the world of women and the world of men many trading women developed amazing presence, self-confidence, interpersonal skills, and administrative abilities. They could be assertive and outgoing, even intimidating. Their leadership qualities, strength, persuasive abilities, perceptiveness, and verbal, analytical, and managerial skills could be truly outstanding. Yet such skills and abilities in the end were used to build the position of the husband and other male relatives. Without connection to a male a woman could never maintain such an elevated position.

Symbolic. The modesty and apparent seclusion and obedience of wife and daughters brought respect to a man and to his family and taifeh. Submission of dependents and allies—whether male or female—indicated political and economic strength. Inferiors showed public deference and subservience to a powerful person no matter what their private feelings. Control over womenfolk and the ability to protect them and their modesty were signs of power, as were control over and protection of male subordinates.

Although women were to stay home, covered and modest, to bring status to a man and his political grouping, they were occasionally expected to be on public display. The formidable sight of many black chadors gliding together to a wedding, to a gathering for mourning, or to the cemetery left no doubt in the eyes of beholders of the unity, size, strength, and control of the represented taifeh. Every detail of weddings—managed by women—was discussed for weeks following to evaluate the quality, expense, and number of guests and how far they had come to attend, as well as the current status of the involved families. The bridewealth demanded of the groom and his family, the household goods bought for the bride by her father, the gifts given the bride by the groom and his family, the wedding gifts of money from guests, and the bride's clothing and makeup, in addition to the food and service, were means of creating or maintaining status.

Dancing was performed in alleyways rather than in courtyards, but even if held in a large courtyard the uninvited—male and female—watched from the rooftops. Women and girls did not wear veils during the dancing. The number of women, their wedding apparel, and the effort and enthusiasm with which they celebrated were important components of the success of the wedding and the status brought to the families. A large group of women lined up together dancing was a colorful visual indication of the size and strength of the taifeh. Especially when going to the bride's father's home to bring the bride back to the groom's home, women were expected to be noisy and enthusiastic in their ululating and singing of ditties and risqué wedding songs. Even sayyid women could become loud and raucous at such times in their determination to put on a show of unity and strength. Barred from being individuals in their own right, women were available to symbolize the status and political power of their fathers, their husbands and brothers, their families, and their taifehs.

Coping mechanisms. Given the pressures of socialization, the acceptance of the existing system as natural, their dependence and lack of alternatives, the unlikelihood of successful resistance, and the necessity of family and community approval, women in general maneuvered within accepted limits to cope with their situations. Because a woman was identified primarily with her family, to improve her own position she had basically two choices: improving her own standing within the family or improving the standing of her family.[12] One important means of escaping from the confinement of family was through developing women's networks and groups, which were themselves effective social controls over women and useful for male political maneuvering. Likewise, the satisfaction and political clout developed through motherhood and close relationships with sons and daughters, and extended to fathers and brothers, perpetuated the system rather than bringing about change. A desire to improve her situation or to seek comfort could only lead a woman to strengthen ties and work harder for her family, making her all the more valuable a commodity in politics and providing all the more reason to keep her and her work in confinement.

POLITICAL ROLES OF ALIABAD WOMEN HISTORICALLY

The roles and usefulness of women in politics varied depending on the degree of control by the central government over the villages as well as on the political use of women by each regime.

Under the Qavams. In the latter part of the last century under the Qajar dynasty, the political process in Aliabad was probably somewhat similar to that which followed under the Qavams, characterized by violence, insecurity, and competition for political leadership among successful traders and their taifehs. Women and their activities most likely were crucial in the political process then, too. After the takeover by the Qavam family, their policy of allowing the victors of political competition to be their representatives and to provide political leadership encouraged factional struggle, in which the participation of women was highly significant. Social interaction was central in maintaining political ties, and women were largely responsible for social relations.

Women's political activities were at their height during the factional competition encouraged by the Qavams before land reform in 1962. Womenfolk of the political and trading elites managed large extended households with many guests and gatherings, and they directed the activities of servants and subordinates. Seven-day wedding celebrations, a month or two of hosting religious mourning troupes and other guests, and preparing sweet bread for the entire village at the new year challenged their administrative and social skills. Intrigue, changing alliances, and conflict demanded their expertise in communication.

After land reform. The demise of local and regional centers of political power after land reform in 1962 did away with meaningful local political competition. Villagers could no longer turn against a local leader who had become too corrupt and tyrannical or who failed to serve the interests of most villagers. Local politicians acted as the arm of the central government and were not susceptible to local opinion. Factional mobilization was senseless; the village boss, Sayyid Ya'qub, would immediately call on the gendarmerie to settle any "trouble."

Factional politics declined drastically. Not one case of taifeh violence and entrenchment seems to have occurred between the mid-1960s and the revolutionary period of 1978–79. Social and religious gatherings were infrequent and less elaborate. Political relations with other regional leaders declined. Now the guests most often entertained in Sayyid Ya'qub's home were the captain and others from the nearby gendarme station. Under these conditions, neither women nor men had much opportunity for overt political activity, and women's activities declined in political significance. Status and political standing within the village were of some relevance and practical importance, and the sayyid women, especially members of the taifeh of Sayyid Ya'qub, engaged in "status-producing" and "status-maintaining" activities.[13]

Pre-revolution and revolution. With the decline during the revolutionary period in the effectiveness of the Sayyid Ya'qub administration and its backers, the gendarmerie, factional confrontation and competition were again possible. Women joined in with their traditional activities, but they also took it upon themselves to organize the first revolutionary protest in the village and participated in demonstrations in Shiraz. Men approved of such female activism; it was considered to be religious activity, which traditionally was thought to be appropriate for women. The dramatically innovative aspect of the participation of masses of Iranian women in national politics was thereby obscured; thus it was difficult to rationalize women's continued participation in public political life in Iran after the revolution.

Post-revolution. Since I did not remain in Aliabad after December of 1979, I was not able to see the effects on village life of the consolidation of power under the Islamic Republic, beyond some indications of further restrictions on the mobility of women. Centralization of power has most likely again removed the possibility of meaningful local political process and with it much of the political impact of women's activities. Such infringements of public and political life on domestic life as those described by Erika Friedl for a village some sixty miles away probably are also taking place in Aliabad (see her chapter in this volume). Now villagers with political aspirations no doubt put their efforts into currying favor with representatives of the Islamic Republic. One way to do so would be to severely enforce the segregation, invisibility, and modesty of wives daughters, sisters, and mothers.

Throughout recent history in Aliabad, the public versus private myth has obscured women's very real contribution to politics. By expanding the walls of the private domestic arena, men have utilized women's activities in a variety of political ways, such as public urban demonstrations during the Iranian revolution. Once women's political work is no longer needed, the walls can be allowed to contract again.

If one ignores the myth and looks instead at the reality of women's involvement, the centrality and political utility of women's roles become apparent. It becomes clear that domestic *is* political, that private *is* public, that all activities performed in the domestic, private realm are significant for the public and political realm.[14]

At the same time that the myth of public versus private obscures women's impact in the public political arena, the public-private dichotomy as ideology is used to restrict women and their activities. The concern for modesty, with its division of life into two spheres, is politically useful in two ways. First, hijab (covering) and segregation actually do control sexuality—which can then be put to political use. Second, the avowed concern about modesty is a reason to keep women and girls confined and thus under control. The public-private dichotomy as myth and as ideology is instrumental in structuring the walls of veils, buildings, social groups, and restrictions to dam up women and their activities as a reservoir of human labor—which can then be used in the public political realm.

Notes

1. See Rayna Rapp, "Review Essay: Anthropology," *Signs* 4 (1979): 508; Michelle Rosaldo, "The Use and Abuse of Anthropology: Reflections on Feminism and Cross-Cultural Understanding," *Signs* 5 (1980): 402 n. 20; Jane Atkinson, "Review Essay: Anthropology," *Signs* 8 (1982): 238; and Sylvia Yanagisako, "Family and Household: The Analysis of Domestic Groups," *Annual Review of Anthropology* 8 (1979): 191.

2. The traders, of course, were influenced by their contacts in the Shiraz bazaar.

3. See also Suad Joseph, "Working-Class Women's Networks in a Sectarian State: A Political Paradox," *American Ethnologist* 10, no. 1 (1986): 4.

4. For further information on rauzehs and women's religious practices, see Anne Betteridge, "Ziarat: Pilgrimage to the Shrines of Shiraz" (Ph.D. diss., University of Chicago, 1985).

5. See Micaela di Leonardo, "The Female World of Cards and Holidays: Women, Families, and the Work of Kinship," *Signs* 12 (1987): 440–53.

6. See Barbara Aswad, "Women, Class, and Power," in *Women in the Muslim World*, ed. Lois Beck and Nikki Keddie (Cambridge: Harvard University Press, 1978), 473–81.

7. See Hanna Papanek, "Purdah: Separate Worlds and Symbolic Shelter," *Comparative Studies in Society and History* 15, no. 3 (1973): 319.

8. See Julie Peteet, "No Going Back: Women and the Palestinian Movement," *MERIP Middle East Report* 16, no. 1 (1986): 20–24, 40. Honoring mothers for raising their children to become martyrs and for sacrificing their children was an important aspect of the ideology surrounding "martyrdom" during the Iranian revolution and then during the Iran-Iraq war. I remember watching television interviews even some years after the Vietnam War in which mothers proclaimed how proud

they were that their sons had died for freedom and for America and how happy they themselves were to have made such sacrifices for their country. This kind of attitude is probably widely taught in Iran and elsewhere partly to encourage mothers to give up their children.

9. See Peteet, "No Going Back."

10. Women who worked would bring great shame to the men in charge of their care; the men would be thought unable to support them, which could not be tolerated. With one exception (the opium smuggler) all the women in Aliabad who worked for money had no alternative—they did not have a male provider. Even in these cases, the sort of work available to them involved other women and was low paying and unreliable—midwifing, keeping a shrine, helping with bread baking. Few women had any real alternatives to economic dependence on a male. It is noteworthy, however, that four young women from Aliabad (and perhaps others) were teachers and thus did have a means of economic independence. See Erika Friedl, "The Division of Labor in an Iranian Village," *MERIP Reports*, no. 95 (March–April 1981): 12–18, 31.

11. With their skill at ferreting out information from a variety of sources and piecing it together to form a rich, detailed picture of events, including discussion of the differing interpretations of the various participants, and their verbal ability in conveying an almost visual account to others, women were usually better informants than men.

12. See Andrea Rugh, *Family in Contemporary Egypt* (Syracuse: Syracuse University Press, 1984), 275–89.

13. See Hanna Papanek, "Family Status Production: The 'Work' and 'Non-Work' of Women," *Signs* 4 (1979): 775–81.

14. For relevant discussion, see Azar Tabari, "The Women's Movement in Iran: A Hopeful Prognosis," *Feminist Studies* 12 (1986): 343–60; Rayna Rapp, "Family and Class in Contemporary America: Notes toward an Understanding of Ideology," *Science and Society* 42, no. 3 (1978): 278–300; Carol Delaney, "Seeds of Honor, Fields of Shame," in *Honor and Shame and the Unity of the Mediterranean*, ed. David G. Gilmore, American Anthropological Association Special Publication 22 (Washington, D.C.: AAA, 1987), 35–48; Suad Joseph, "Family as Security and Bondage: A Political Strategy of the Lebanese Urban Working Class," in *Toward a Political Economy of Urbanization in Third World Countries*, ed. Helen Safa (Oxford: Oxford University Press, 1982), 151–71; Maxine Molyneux, "Mobilization without Emancipation? Women's Interests, the State, and Revolution in Nicaragua," *Feminist Studies* 11 (1985): 227–54; Judith Tucker, "Insurrectionary Women: Women and the State in Nineteenth Century Egypt," *MERIP Middle East Report* 16, no. 1 (1986): 9–13, 34; and Sylvia Yanagisako, "Women-Centered Kin Networks in Urban Bilateral Kinship," *American Ethnologist* 4, no. 2 (1977): 207–26.

IV The Modern Arab World

13

Ties That Bound: Women and Family in Eighteenth- and Nineteenth-Century Nablus

JUDITH E. TUCKER

To study Arab women and the family in historical context, we must address three discrete problems. First, there is a dearth of studies of the family in the region from a historical perspective. With the exception of the recent work of Margaret Meriweather and Linda Schatkowski Schilcher, who have done valuable reconstructions of family patterns among the elite of Ottoman Aleppo and Damascus, there has been little significant work on family history and even less on the specifically female experience of the family.[1] Until recently, historians of Arab women have had other agendas. Women's relation to systems of production and exchange has been studied: we now have considerable information on women's active role in the endowing and managing of *waqf* property and on women as independent economic actors in trade and real estate.[2] Some historians have focused on women and politics, including women's behind-the-scenes impact through *harim* intrigues and their more visible clout in feminist movements.[3] Most recently, historians and anthropologists have tried to capture the elusive woman's voice through oral histories.[4] These approaches share a desire to redress the almost total neglect of women in writing the history of the region and to demonstrate women's economic, political, and cultural contributions.

The family, however, has received little systematic attention. This lacuna may reflect a view of the family as an unchanging instrument of oppression, as a mediator of patriarchal values, in brief, as the antithesis of women's aspirations. Although the family is an important locus of women's historical experience, study of the family was not at the top of the agenda in the "compensatory" period of Arab feminist scholarship. I think we are now entering a new period, however, when women's contributions are no longer so totally obscured, and we can turn our attention to the questions of what such a fundamental institution looked like, how it changed over time, and what part it played in mediating gender roles and relations in society.

Once we do recognize the importance of the family, how do we construct our approach to its study? There is, of course, a well-established school of family history pioneered in the European context. Largely demographic in approach, such family history asks certain basic questions of primarily quantitative data, seeking to establish the size of the household, fertility rates, marriage patterns, and so forth.[5] We certainly want to have this basic demographic data, but as women's historians we also want to ask other questions. What was the family from a woman's point of view? How did the Arab family structure gender relations? How does study of this basic social institution help us to understand changes in gender definition and the relation between gender and power over time?

How, then, do we explore this family? We do not always have the kind of source materials that have been employed in European history, and we lack detailed census data until the rather recent past. We can, however, draw on legal records, both the law as prescribed in theory and the actual practice in the Islamic courts. The plethora of marriage contracts, divorce agreements, child custody cases, and family support claims that we have for most urban areas of the Arab world in the later Ottoman period constitutes a record of how women lived their family lives. I use these in the following discussion of the family in the eighteenth and nineteenth centuries, with the knowledge that the study of other kinds of sources, including literature, popular discourse, and material culture, can add a great deal in the future to our understanding of the family.

In an attempt to understand what the family appeared to be in Nablus, we must explore a number of family relationships. What were family relationships from the woman's point of view and how did they define, control, and support her? Sociologists have seen the male patriarch as the linchpin of the family. Halim Barakat characterizes the "traditional Arab family" as "stratified on the basis of sex and age." The father of the family exercised authority and expected compliance from his wife and children, so that "according to the traditional norms, a woman commits a grave mistake by challenging her husband's authority."[6] We can examine the reality of this patriarchal family through study of the three major categories of relationship that emerge from the Islamic court records: marital relationships, parent-child relationships, and extended kin relationships. First, was the husband the primary pillar of patriarchy? To what extent did he control his wife's behavior and enforce obedience to himself and to traditional norms? Second, how did a woman's relationship with her parents and children define her reproductive roles? Did such relationships modify or circumscribe her husband's power? Third, did relations with extended kin reinforce the control of women or did they also, at times, diffuse and thus weaken this control?

Such relationships did not develop in a vacuum. The family was intimately linked to the material base and to the relations of production in Nablus society, a society based primarily on economic surplus from the land collected from a free peasantry by a small number of powerful families. The surplus was supplemented by income from long-distance trade and craft production. The center of these activities, the town of Nablus, is particularly well suited to a study of family, as family solidarity and family-based alliance played critical roles in this economic system and the political arrangements undergirding it between 1720 and 1856. As the most important market and production center in the Palestinian highlands during much of the eighteenth and nineteenth centuries, Nablus had a thriving economy and a population of 12,000 to 15,000 in 1800, diverse enough to allow us to study the family in a varied environment.[7]

Although the Jabal Nablus region, for which the town of Nablus served as both administrative and business center, remained putatively under the rule of the Ottoman Empire, Ottoman control had grown weak and indirect by the eighteenth century. The Ottoman presence in the Palestinian highlands region was limited, by and large, to an annual tax-collecting tour made by the Ottoman *wali* (governor) of Damascus. Authority on the ground had devolved into the hands of a small number of important families, members of which monopolized official posts. From their bases in the town of Nablus or in outlying village redoubts, the al-Nimrs, Tuqans, 'Abd al-Hadis, Jarrars, Jayyusis, and others acquired power at various times through their ability to employ family solidarity and patronage for influence or armed struggle when necessary. Indeed, the political narratives of the period read as Byzantine accounts of conflicts and alliances among family groups that competed to acquire, preserve, and increase their power, whether it be economic, in the form of landholdings, through control of *timars* (land grants) and *iltizams* (tax farms) or administrative, in the form of major offices, including governorships.[8] After 1856 the Ottomans attempted, with varying rates of success, to reassert more direct control in the region in keeping with the goals of the *tanzimat* period of reform and centralization.

The majority of the Nablus population did not belong to the families of wealth and power that ruled the region. In the Islamic court records from the town of Nablus, three distinct social groups emerge. First, a few ruling families, notably the al-Nimrs and Tuqans, who maintained their primary residences in the town, brought their business to the Nablus court; other ruling-group families with power bases in the countryside apparently were less apt to use the Nablus court, and the records are almost silent concerning their activities. Second, residing in the town were a larger number of merchants and artisans, whose presence reflected the importance of Nablus as a market and production center for the Palestinian highlands. In addition to trade in grain and handicrafts, Nablus was famous for its soap, which was exported as far as Egypt, Anatolia, and the Arabian Gulf. A group of merchant families that traded primarily in soap and grains prospered in the town, and the ranks of this middle social group were further swelled by tradesmen and artisans whose markets were more regional. Third, a still larger number of relatively poor families—the less affluent artisans, petty traders, service and day workers—formed the bulk of the town's working population. Family life was not necessarily constant across social groups, and we face the potential problem of dealing with a variety of family forms, from that of the ruling governor to that of the poor peddler. As we explore family relations, we can expect to encounter differences among these social groups, differences in the political and economic significance of the family, and as a result differences in gender definitions.

The primary source material for the study of the family is found in the records of the Islamic court (*mahkama shar'iyya*) in Nablus. The records are not complete for the period under discussion: only two registers (*sijills*) survive from the early eighteenth century, covering 1722 to 1729, but there is a fairly complete set of records from 1798 onward. Much of the material in the extant court records has a direct bearing on family life. The most relevant and useful documents are marriage contracts, registrations of divorce, support payments to family members (*nafaqa*), and records of partition of estates. These documents do not appear as frequently as property sales or waqf endowments: indeed, the nine sijills of the 1722 to 1729 and 1798 to 1856 period, each of which contains the minutes from 600 to 1,200 cases, recorded a total of only 107 marriage contracts, 95 registrations of divorce, and 23 cases of nafaqa. Several hundred estates were also registered: of these, I selected a random sample of 100. The modest number of documents dealing directly with family relations suggests that many marriages, divorces, and support arrangements were not registered in the court: these may well be cases that were considered particularly important or problematic.

The court did not cater only to the wealthy, however. Although the ruling group and the prosperous merchant class are overrepresented in the records, many of the poorer residents of the town also availed themselves of court services: for example, about one-third of all marriage contracts listed brides and grooms of lower-class background, and 37 of the 100 estates sampled involved modest amounts of property. Thus although court cases undoubtedly feature the more complicated or intractable situations, they do cut across class lines and enable us to form

, an idea of family life, particularly at its critical and tense moments, among all social groups. The case material also allows us to focus on relationships central to the family.

THE MARITAL RELATIONSHIP

The marital relationship was an important tie for women and men alike. This acquired form of relatedness structured basic gender relations in the family and largely determined the distribution of power at the center of family life. What features shaped this experience for women? Age at marriage, the form of marriage arrangements, the permanence or impermanence of the relationship, the number of marriages an individual might make in a lifetime, the practice of polygyny, the life expectancies of women and men, and the kinds of material ties binding the couple influenced the expectations a bride and groom brought to a marriage and described the contours of the relationship for both.

Marriage was very much a normal expectation. Indeed, out of a sample of thirty-five women who left estates to be divided by the court, only one appears not to have been married, and she probably had barely reached her majority. Saluh, who died in 1260/1854 with a modest estate composed entirely of cash, left only her mother and four young sisters.[9] Both the contents of her estate, notably the absence of the clothing and kitchen equipment possessed by married women, and the youth of her siblings (they had yet to attain puberty, the age of majority in Islamic law) suggest that Saluh died very young, before her marriage could be arranged. All the other female estates belonged to women who left husbands as heirs, or who clearly had been married and borne children at some point. In the absence of celibate communities or any possibility for independent existence, the marital state was invariably imposed on women.

Male prospects did not differ radically, although certain male careers, while not precluding marriage, at least rendered marriage less of a necessity. Out of a sample of sixty-two male estates, six belonged to men who apparently had never married. In two instances, occupations seem to have played a role in their bachelorhood. One *shaikh*, or member of the ulama, never married and left his modest estate, that of an *'alim* without important business or official connections, to his nephews.[10] Another of the bachelors was an Ottoman soldier, whose possessions, composed of weapons, clothing, and cash, testified to a life of rootless mobility.[11] In the remaining cases, youth may have been a factor but the evidence is not conclusive. In any event, men were almost as likely as women to marry at least once: Nablus was definitely a marrying society.

Precise age at marriage is impossible to determine. Marriage contracts do not specify the ages of the bride and groom, although the bride is identified as either a minor (*saghira*) or a major (*baligha*), with puberty the dividing line between legal minority and majority. Some girls were indeed married off in their minority: of 107 marriage contracts in the Nablus records, 19 recorded the marriage of prepubescent girls. Such marriages gave enormous power, at least in a legal sense, to the girl's family: the father of a minor or another close male relative, acting as her marriage guardian (*wali*), could marry her off to a "suitable" groom with a proper *mahr* (bridewealth) without consulting her. The upper and more affluent middle classes of the city were the most likely to arrange these early marriages: all but 4 of the 19 minor brides came from prosperous families. Although the child bride was clearly not the rule, a significant number of families did favor such marriages and society as a whole apparently valued young brides—the minor's mahr was invariably among the highest in her social group—which suggests that women often were married young, if not before, then shortly after, puberty.[12] The dearth of unmarried women's estates reinforces such a conclusion: a woman did not advance far into her legal majority before a marriage was arranged for her.

We have far less evidence for male age at marriage because marriage contracts do not provide information on the legal status of the groom. The minor bride, however, could be married to a man who was well established in his profession and thus certainly her senior. In 1725, one prepubescent girl, Badawiyya, was married to the court scribe, Muhammad Effendi, and the girl Amnah was married to the shaikh Sulaiman, an acknowledged religious scholar, in 1726.[13] Nablus society clearly countenanced a certain discrepancy between the ages of the bride and the groom but we cannot be sure whether such a discrepancy was the rule or was an occasional, although accepted, practice.

That minor marriage occurred at all underscores the extent to which marriage was viewed as an arrangement to be made by the families of the bride and the groom. The overlapping practices of child marriage and cousin marriage (17 out of 107 contracts) signaled the centrality of family wishes to marriage arrangements: whereas child marriage allowed for ultimate familial control, cousin marriage was arranged to preserve the integrity of property or to strengthen the solidarity of the extended family for political ends. As with child marriage, cousin marriage was more prevalent among the middle and upper classes, which had more to protect in terms of property and influence. Many upper-class brides were married off at a young age to cousins, or to men from other families with which their own families sought alliance. The political history of Nablus is paralleled by a history of strategic marriage arrangements. Of the six marriages recorded for the influential Tuqan family, members of which held important official posts in the eighteenth and early nineteenth centuries, two were made within the family circle and three united Tuqans with other families at the apex of the power structure.[14] The fine hand of family management is also evident in the utter absence of mésalliance: marriage contracts were invariably drawn up between social equals.

Once in a marriage, could a woman expect to remain with her husband permanently? Social background again played a large part. Of the 107 women whose marriage contracts were registered in the Nablus courts, 23 were clearly identified as having been married before. Among these women, 15 were of lower-class origin, testifying to the relative impermanence of marriage among the poorer sectors of the population; by contrast, only 2 upper-class brides were entering a second (or third, and so on) marriage. Depending on their social origins, then, women entered marriage with rather different expectations. The upper-class woman, whose marriage was so closely tied to family needs and politics, barring the premature death of her husband, usually could expect to spend her life in one marital relationship. The lower-class woman, however, was more apt to divorce and to embark on a second marriage.

The practice of polygyny further helps to explain this difference. Although Islamic law allows a man to take up to four wives at a time, concurrent multiple wives were not the rule: of the sixty-two men whose estates listed all surviving heirs, only ten were survived by two wives and only one by more than two. Of these polygynous men, only one or possibly two left estates reflecting lower-class economic standing: polygyny was usually reserved for the prosperous. An upper-class man in search of sexual variety or more progeny could absorb the expense of adding a wife to his household, but a poor man would be more likely to divorce his current wife and marry anew. An upper-class woman, though far more likely than her lower-class sister to remain in the same marital household, might also have to tolerate the presence of an additional wife.

Whether widowed or divorced, neither women nor men remained single for long. The inheritance records reveal striking evidence of the drive to remarry, to establish a new marital relationship to replace one that had been terminated. The vast majority of both women and men died in the marital state: 72 percent of the women with estates and 76 percent of the men left spouses behind. Only frequent remarriage could account for such figures because of relatively high rates of divorce and premature death, particularly among women. The same registers that recorded 107 marriages also recorded ninety-five divorces, which far understates the actual number. The male-initiated divorce (*talaq*), which could be pronounced at the will of the husband without recourse to legal grounds or judicial proceedings, was not ordinarily registered in the court. Because of the ease of this type of divorce, we may assume that it was the most commonly practiced form.

Four types of divorce were brought to court. A woman who wanted a judicial decree of separation (*faskh*) was obliged to state her case before the judge, either in person or using the offices of an agent, in the following manner:

> The *hurma* [woman] Amnah bint 'Ali bin Jabril al-Nabulsi, the wife of Yusif al-Zubaidi, came to the court and claimed that the aforementioned Yusif, her husband, had been absent for four years prior to this day and had left her neither nafaqa nor *kiswah* [clothes], nor a legal supporter, and there had been no news of him, she did not know his whereabouts which caused her great hardship, and she no longer had the patience to endure it. He had taken her means of support with him. So she requested from our lord the shari'a judge a faskh of the marriage so that she could marry whomever she wants once the '*idda* [waiting period] is over. He [the judge] did not just take her word for it but asked her to prove her claims with legal evidence. So she brought witnesses, the Hajj 'Ali bin Husain al-Saraji, Sulaiman bin Isma'il al-'Alul, and Mansur al-Qawwas, who testified that Yusif al-Zubaidi, the husband of the above-mentioned Amnah, had been absent for four years and had left his wife without nafaqa and a legal supporter, and there had been no news of him and no one knows his whereabouts, and no estate or money had been found which Amnah could use to support herself. Theirs was a valid, legal testimony in both form and content. Our lord the shari'a judge then asked her to take an oath by God, the mighty and merciful, that her husband did not leave her nafaqa for the period and that she deserves nafaqa, and she did so. So he then told her to be patient and wait for her husband, but she refused and insisted on an annulment. He gave her a three day period in which to reconsider, and then annulled his marriage to her on the morning of the date below after asking God's forgiveness for doing so. At that point, she requested from the judge a written document of the annulment in accordance with the *madhhab* [legal school], and he did so knowing the difference among the *imams* on this matter, and implementing the Hanafi madhhab. 25 Jumada I, 1136.

Only eleven such divorces were registered in the court: in all the cases, women obtained divorces on the grounds of desertion and their subsequent failure to receive material support from their husbands.

A woman also might promise to compensate her husband financially if he would grant her a divorce, known as *khul'*. Khul' divorce, although female initiated, required the express consent of the husband, who had to agree to the terms and actually pronounce the divorce. This type of divorce was thus available only to women whose husbands were willing to divorce them in return for some kind of compensation.[15] More than half of the divorces recorded in the court, forty-nine out of ninety-five, were of the khul' variety, according to which a woman agreed to forgo what her husband owed her: the remainder of her mahr, legally prescribed support payments (*nafaqat al-'idda*) in the post-divorce period, or even debts. Several women even made a further payment, a sort of ransom to their husbands.

Divorces that took place before consummation of the marriage were recorded in the court as well: ten such divorces, which required the groom to pay half of the stated mahr if the divorce were his desire, and none of it if he pronounced the divorce at the request of the bride, were registered in the courts.

The remaining twenty-five divorce cases were instances of male-initiated talaq, the unilateral repudiation of the wife by her husband. Such a divorce could be pronounced at any time and place by the husband, who did not need to bring it to court. Indeed, almost all the cases of talaq recorded in the court are a special variety: these conditional divorces came about after the husband had sworn that his wife would be divorced if she disobeyed his express orders; the court recorded the disobedience and the subsequent automatic divorce. Cases of talaq in which the husband simply divorced his wife without the complications of special settlements or swearing of oaths were rarely recorded. We may assume, however, that the simple form of talaq was the most common, being the easiest and most free of legal complications. The inclusion of such divorces in the records would have raised the overall number of divorces significantly. Whatever the type of divorce, the overwhelming majority of registered cases involved, not surprisingly, people of lower-class background, for whom marriage did not carry the same economic and political weight.

If divorce often terminated the marital relationship, especially in poorer circles, so did the premature death of a young wife. Early marriage and the risks of childbearing took their toll on women: the resulting difference between female and male life expectancies is striking. Although the inheritance records never give age at death, we do have evidence provided by surviving relatives. More than half (53 percent) of the women who left estates were survived by at least one parent, a derailing of the normal life cycle that suggests high mortality in the childbearing years. By comparison, only 18 percent of male estate holders were survived by one or both parents. Similarly, more than half of all deceased mothers left children who were all minors. The estate of Safiyya, daughter of al-Sayyid Khadr, was typical.[16] She left her meager possessions, some jewelry, clothes and household goods worth 249 *ghurush*, and the remainder of her mahr and other debts owed by her husband totaling 452 ghurush, to be divided according to Islamic law among her husband, her mother and father, and her minor son. Nor did status provide a bulwark against early death. Salha, daughter of the Hajj Mustafa al-Sadr, left her property—the jewelry, clothes, and household goods of an affluent middle-class woman—to her husband, al-Sayyid Ahmad, her minor daughter, and her father, the Hajj Mustafa.[17] Men did not necessarily live to a ripe old age, but they were far more likely than women were to outlive their parents.

The marital relationship, vulnerable as it was to premature death and frequent divorce, was bolstered in some cases by the development of material ties in the guise of formal loans. Of the sample one hundred estates of men and women, fifteen recorded outstanding loans of money, in all cases owed by the husband to his wife.[18] Such debts could be substantial: one poor man died owing his wife 500 ghurush, impossible to repay from his paltry estate of 364 ghurush.[19] Among the prosperous middle class as well, wives might lend substantial sums to their husbands, perhaps for business ventures: one merchant owed his wife more than 11,000 ghurush at the time of his death.[20] Such indebtedness reinforced marital ties by binding the husband to his wife in an immediate material sense. Debts could also inhibit divorce: all such obligations, formal loans as well as the balance of the mahr, could be called in if the husband initiated a divorce.

The complexity of the marital relationship derived, therefore, from a number of factors. Tight family control over marriage arrangements, often manifested in early age at marriage and marriage to relatives, removed all choice of partner from the bride and groom and tended to encourage the marriages of young and inexperienced girls in particular. Such control was especially important to families of standing and means, who strove to preserve their position and property through strategic marriage. In these circles the marital relationship, although possibly polygynous, was viewed as fairly permanent: some guarantee of the stability of the relationship was essential to its value as a way of forging alliances. Among the lower classes the marital relationship was more temporary: many marriages ended in divorce. Death, and in particular the premature death of a young woman of childbearing years, crossed class lines to terminate marriages among all social groups. Married young without any claim to her husband's affections, a woman might depend on her family's, and her groom's, interest in the marriage to bolster her position. In addition, loaning money to her husband could provide her with a certain material leverage. Other relationships were crucial, however, in the overall definition of a woman's place in the family.

PARENTS AND CHILDREN

The relationship between parents and children was defined by legal rules and social customs as a permanent and central one, composed of material and emotional obligations and attachments. Socially constructed definitions of the relationship were refined, of course, by the physical realities of the time. Maternal and infant mortality in particular set harsh limits on the ability of parents and children to fulfill mutual obligations, and in some cases even jeopardized the possibility of having such a relationship at all.

How many children survived the perilous first years of life? Men married later, sometimes practiced polygyny, and lived longer than women, and thus tended to leave larger numbers of children behind: the fifty-six men who married left a total of 187 children, or an average of 3.3 children apiece. Many women, thrust early into marriage and childbearing, undoubtedly died in childbirth or of its complications: indeed, the thirty-seven married women studied here left 68 children, only 1.5 apiece. Most men fathered four or fewer surviving children (see table 13.1). Larger families were rare: four of the fifty-six men left seven or more children, and only one man produced ten survivors. Women left far smaller families behind: nineteen, more than half of the thirty-seven married women, died leaving only one or no living children, and no woman's estate named more than five children. We have every reason to suspect that these families would be even smaller if we could count the children who survived to adulthood. For men and women alike, more than half of their surviving children were legal minors, still in the hazardous zone of childhood with its special vulnerability to death from disease.

The relatively small number of surviving children inevitably modified the prescribed legal and social obligations of the relationship. Parents and children were bound, under law, by a set of mutual material responsibilities. Islamic law insists on the partition of an estate among specified legal heirs in precise proportions; the ability to make bequests is very limited. Children were the most important of the parents' legal heirs: depending on the number and relationship of other surviving heirs, children would typically receive anywhere from half to the entire estate of their parents. When a child predeceased his or her parents, the parents' share of the child's estate was less but still substantial, usually anywhere from one-sixth to one-half, again depending on other eligible heirs. The hurma Hajjiyya, for example, left an estate of 1,196 ghurush. Once funeral expenses and court costs of 207 ghurush were deducted, the re-

Table 13.1: Number of Living Children at Time of Parent's Death
(data from estates of single men and women excluded)

Number of Children	Male Estates (N = 56)	Female Estates (N = 37)
0	4	4
1	9	15
2	7	9
3	11	3
4	11	4
5	5	2
6	5	0
7	2	0
8	1	0
9	0	0
10	1	0

Total number of children from male estates: 187
Total number of children from female estates: 68

maining 989 ghurush was to be divided among her husband (one-fourth), her mother (one-sixth), and her minor son (the remainder, or seven-twelfths).[21] If neither of the deceased's parents was living, the children of the deceased inherited a larger portion. Amun left an estate of 4,530 ghurush, which included her inheritance from her father, a sum of 1,206 ghurush. Once funeral and court costs of 805 ghurush were paid, a quarter of the remaining 3,725 ghurush went to her husband and the rest was divided equally among her four children.[22] Whereas mothers and fathers were entitled to equal shares in their children's estates, sons inherited twice as much as daughters: Sara's net estate of 1,335 ghurush was divided in the following manner: 334 to her husband, 250 each to her daughters Safiyya and Saluh, and 501 to her son, Musa.[23] Inheritance law thus spun a web of material ties between parents and children, giving each a substantial claim to the other's property. Although we cannot be sure that the letter of the law was always observed, especially in the case of female heirs, the Nablus records are free of any female protests about disinheritance.

Not only were parents and children reciprocal heirs, but they also, according to the law, owed each other material support when necessary during their lifetimes. Islamic law imposes the duty of providing support (nafaqa) for the poor on certain of their relatives: parents and children, when they attain their majority, are legally bound to support each other should the need arise. Although much of this support undoubtedly was delivered without any recourse to the courts, certain problematic cases were brought to the *qadi* for discussion and registration. A husband and father had to support his children: should he fail to do so, his wife could come to court to request the judge's intercession. One Muhammad told the judge he would pay his wife and children the money for a proper level of daily support and buy his children clothing when necessary.[24] As the case gives no context for the unusual extraction of this commitment, we can only assume that Muhammad's wife failed to persuade her husband to fulfill standard familial duties and had finally resorted to the court to secure an unequivocal statement of his obligations. A woman might also go to the court on her behalf and that of her children when a husband's long absence left them without support. In these instances, the intent was to record her husband's ultimate responsibility for a set amount of support. The court might then authorize the wife to borrow the necessary money, on the understanding that her husband would be responsible for its repayment, as in the following case:

> The shari'a judge imposed nafaqa, clothing, house rent, toiletries, soap, bread, oil, and other things, and the rest of her legally prescribed needs, for the hurma Amnah bint Darwish al-Ghazawi on the date below, and two *qita' misriyya*. He permitted her father Darwish to borrow the money, and the debt incurred will be owed by her husband, Ahmad bin Subah, who was away from the city and had left her with neither nafaqa nor anything else, nor had he delegated a legal provider for her in the prescribed legal fashion. Recorded at the beginning of Rabi' I, 1138.

A woman named Khadija and her daughter also were left without any support from a missing husband, so Khadija asked the judge for a nafaqa award that would cover the costs of their rent, clothing, food, drink, soap, and toiletries.[25] Khadija was responsible for borrowing the awarded amount, but her husband could be charged for it when, and if, he returned.

Mothers were not liable for nafaqa payments. Although a woman might keep children, particularly young children, in her care (*hidana*) during the absence or after the death of her husband, she was not responsible for material support. Indeed, her role consisted of overseeing the expenditure of nafaqa payments to the children made by others. She might pay the costs of support herself with the expectation of being reimbursed by her children when they reached their majority, or she might collect the money from relatives of her husband.[26] Such a burden could, however, prove formidable. Lutfiyya, a poor woman, cared for two young sons, Bakr and 'Asad, after their father died. On the basis of the court-awarded nafaqa of 30 *fidda misriyya* daily, during the course of about two and a half years she spent 675 ghurush for their upkeep. Whereas she was able to collect 275 ghurush from her late husband's estate for nafaqa, the remaining 400 ghurush had come out of her own pocket. With no responsible relatives in a position to help, she finally had to surrender the children to her late husband's sister, who agreed to take them without nafaqa.[27] According to the law, such was the solution: if the deceased father's family was too poor to make nafaqa payments, it had the option of taking custody of his children instead.

Once children reached majority, they in turn assumed legal responsibility for the support of destitute parents. The fairly short life expectancy and the no doubt strong social pressures to assist parents help explain the near absence of litigation concerning this issue: the Nablus records of 1720 to 1858 reveal only one instance where parents resorted to the court to force their grown children to support them. The Hajj 'Abd al-Ghani [?] al-Fatayir and his wife Mas'uda asked the judge to impose nafaqa payments on their two grown sons of 5 ghurush daily, or 150 ghurush a month. In agreeing to their request, the judge noted that children were obliged to support poor parents, even those capable of working, and that any child who could afford to pay the alms tax (zakat) should pay the awarded nafaqa.[28] For both parents and children, gender played a large role in defining responsibilities. Material support was legally required and expected only from men: neither mothers nor daughters bore financial responsibility for their children or parents. Such a definition of material responsibilities buttressed a patriarchal system in which continuation of the family name, loyalties, and property devolved largely on male descendants.

What effect might this critical difference have had on the valuation of male and female children? We have only indirect evidence here, but men who wanted a son or sons seem to have been more predisposed to take a second wife. Of the ten deceased men with two wives, four had daughters only, one had seven daughters and one son, and one had two daughters by his first wife and a daughter and three sons by his second. These six polygynous men may have been concerned, first and foremost, with the number of surviving male children. Any preference for male children was not translated into obvious differential treatment of infants, however. If girl children were less welcome and useful than boys, they did not receive less food or less care, judging from mortality rates. The 100 combined male and female estates record 255 surviving children, of whom at least 136 were girls. In spite of the greater strength and durability of the legal relationship between parents and male children, boys were not favored to such a degree that they survived infancy in greater numbers than girls did.

In general, class differences seem to have had little impact on most

Table 13.2: Number of Living Children by Size of Estate (in *ghurush*) (male and female estates combined)

Number of Children	Size of Estates		
	1–1,000	1,000–10,000	10,000+
0	3	5	0
1	13	10	0
2	5	10	1
3	5	6	2
4	6	7	1
5	3	2	1
6	2	3	0
7	0	2	0
8	0	2	0
9	0	0	0
10	0	1	0

features of the parent-child relationship. Men and women of different classes had roughly similar numbers of children, although wealthier families did tend to be a bit larger (see table 13.2). Affluence proved no barrier to maternal mortality: the women of the prosperous middle class were just as likely to die in their childbearing years as were lower-class women; the estates of those who died leaving children in their minority ranged in size. The one striking class difference appears in the cases of nafaqa awarded to children or parents. Of nine such cases, eight named poor and untitled people; only one case, that of a woman awarded nafaqa for the care of four minor children by her deceased husband, involved a middle-class ulama family. The entire problem of nafaqa did not, in general, touch the more prosperous, whose resources allowed for the care of all family members without resort to litigation.

OTHER RELATIONS OF KIN

Although most inheritance and nafaqa arrangements gave the marital or the parent-child relationship the greatest weight, other forms of relatedness also entailed real rights and responsibilities. A woman's relationship with her brother, for example, could be very close and dependent, especially if their father was dead. Brothers, in the absence of a father, acted as guardians or as agents for their sisters' marriages: in the 107 marriage contracts, brothers acted as guardians of minors four times and as agents for women in their majority seven times. Since many of these women were marrying for a second or third time, their relationship with their

brother was an enduring one that they could return to between marriages. A brother might also be assigned responsibility for the care of his
orphaned minor siblings. He was not expected, however, to spend his
own money for their care: whatever he had to disburse was to be repaid to
him by his siblings when they came of age.[29] Infrequently, if a man died
without surviving children, his siblings, including sisters, might inherit
part of his estate. Such was the case when a man died leaving a wife,
mother, sister, and two brothers, all of whom were legitimate heirs.[30]

These lifelong bonds of protection, support, and material claims lay at
the heart of the social value attached to the brother. Mary Eliza Rogers
relates a story she heard of a woman who sought out Ibrahim Pasha,
governor of the region during the Egyptian occupation of Palestine. Having told Ibrahim that three men of her family—her husband, her brother,
and her eldest son—had been taken for the army, the woman pleaded for
the release of one. Which do you want? asked Ibrahim. My brother, she
said, for I might find another husband, I have younger sons, but if my
brother dies he cannot be replaced.[31] If a brother provided protection, the
policing of sexual behavior was also his responsibility. Although the
Nablus sources remain silent on a brother's role in enforcing women's
obedience to norms and in punishing transgressions, later work on Palestinian society stresses the extent to which fathers and brothers were
expected to intervene should a woman commit any offense. Sexual transgressions, including the crime of elopement, were punishable by death at
the hands of the brother.[32] Such an execution was not ordinarily recorded, either as crime or punishment, presumably because of its extra-
legal but nonetheless widely accepted status.

Another legally recognized, although somewhat less important, relationship was that between grandparents and grandchildren. Limited life
expectancy meant that not many grandparents survived to take on responsibility for their grandchildren. Nonetheless, there are a few cases of
grandparents involved in nafaqa arrangements. Salaha, for example,
raised her son Rajab's daughter. Even though the court had awarded her
two qita' misriyya daily from Rajab, she agreed to waive payments and
raise her granddaughter at her own expense.[33] In another instance, a
man took responsibility for his minor granddaughter; in his case, his
expenses would be met from the money she had inherited.[34] Equally rare
was the reverse situation, in which a man assumed responsibility for a
grandparent. In one lone case, an elderly destitute woman was awarded
nafaqa payments from her grandson.[35] Although law and society thus
recognized special ties of mutual responsibility between grandparents
and grandchildren, these were rarely activated.

A stronger relationship that was more frequently activated was that
between children and their aunts and uncles, particularly on the father's

side. As in most patrilineal societies, children belonged to their father and his family, the members of which bore material responsibility for them. Although, as we have seen, young children might remain temporarily in their mother's care after the death of their father, the father's family was responsible for providing material support and paternal uncles acted as the child's legal guardians. If the father's family could not afford the nafaqa payments, they could, instead, take custody of the children themselves. Salha's seven children were taken from her care and placed in the keeping of their father's sisters, whose brother was poor and could not afford to pay Salha the awarded nafaqa.[36] Even if the nafaqa could be paid, the mother might lose custody to the father's family for a number of reasons. First, under the Hanafi law applied in Palestine, boys at age seven and girls at age nine could be removed from their mother's custody and given to the father's family. Second, a mother's remarriage to any "stranger" who was not a close relative of the children meant that the children must leave her house. Finally, a woman could be declared an unfit mother if she did not give the children proper care. It is not surprising, therefore, to find minor children in the care of their paternal aunts and uncles.[37] In these cases, nafaqa was awarded for a different reason: money spent on their care by paternal relatives was a debt incurred by the children, which they were obligated to repay when they reached adulthood. Although legal guardianship and eventual custody of children devolved on paternal relatives, in their absence a maternal uncle might become the guardian and supporter of his sister's child.[38]

Thus whereas many prevailing social and economic arrangements stressed the marital tie and the bonds between parents and children, a number of legal and social obligations widened the family circle to include other kin—siblings, grandparents, aunts, and uncles. Although these types of relations appeared to be of lesser intensity than those women formed with husbands and children, they constituted an important second tier of affective family ties to which women could turn, especially in times of trouble. That the court was sometimes used, particularly by the poor, to activate these relationships, however, points more to their weakness than to their strength: legal obligations had to be activated when social custom and pressure proved insufficient, as apparently they sometimes did among the poor. The wealthier and more powerful members of Nablus society, however, enjoyed resources that rendered recourse to the court unnecessary, either because individuals did not require material support or because, when needed, it was automatically provided by kin.

In our exploration of the kinds of social relations within the family that defined and elaborated gender, the production of female gender proved to be a complex and variegated process. The court material does not suggest a crude patriarchy in which an all-powerful male head of family imposed absolute submission on women, be they wives or daughters; rather it suggests that women's lives encompassed a number of affective family relationships. Certainly the marital relationship appears to have been the most significant: most women were married young and were bound to their husbands by a number of economic and social ties. The husband did enjoy the right to demand obedience and submission from his wife as part of the legal definition of marriage rights and obligations.[39] Such legal enshrinement of a husband's patriarchal control was modified in practice, however, by the kinds of leverage a woman might exercise through control of her mahr and other capital, and more important for our purposes, through the relationships she maintained with other family members. Other affective relations—with her parents and children, her brothers and sisters, her grandparents, her aunts and uncles—provided her with both material and moral support from a wider family circle. The ongoing involvement and interest of a number of family members diffused her husband's control and protected her against an overly imperious, neglectful, or abusive husband.

Still, the family setting did emphasize, at least initially, the role of a female in biological reproduction: married young, women often perished in their early childbearing years as a result of the perils of frequent pregnancies at a young age. To the extent that many women did not survive the years of early matrimony, their lives were almost completely colored by the view of female gender as tied to motherhood and service to a husband. For the woman who escaped maternal mortality, however, the possibility of divorce and second marriages, the ability to amass some capital through mahr payments and inheritance, and the activation of a support network of parents, children, brothers, and aunts and uncles all lessened her subjugation to her husband. The normative female was certainly an obedient wife and a mother first and foremost, but she was also a member of a larger family with very real claims to support and protection from its members, claims that could grow in importance and complexity if she survived her childbearing years.

Subtle differences in definitions of female gender can also be detected between different classes in Nablus society. In upper-class circles, where marriage tended to be viewed as a more permanent arrangement, a woman's relationship with her husband loomed large as a lifetime affair, thus highlighting her role as a wife. Indeed, the absence of any evidence in the courts that upper-class women turned to other family members in times of need suggests either that they were more enclosed in the world of their marriage and less likely to activate other relationships, or that upper-class families provided support as a matter of course without recourse to litigation. Because of the importance of marriage alliances to the social and political life of the times, we suspect that parents, brothers, sisters, uncles, and aunts did indeed maintain an active interest in a woman's marital situation. In lower-class circles, however, the issue is clearer: women used the courts to activate networks of kin support, particularly critical in a milieu where marriage was viewed as less permanent and many women's ties to their husbands were loosened by the probability of serial marriage. In both cases, the image of husband as unbridled patriarch exercising absolute power over his wife does not jibe with the evidence for complexity of family relations. Various studies tell of the normal progression of wives from young brides dominated by mothers-in-law to increasingly respected mothers of growing sons.

Clearly we need to explore the contours of the family further as it developed in the Middle East, taking into account the ways in which the institution evolved in articulation with the level and organization of production in the society. The substantial issues of such context and change in the development of the family lie outside the scope of this chapter, but our understanding of the position and power of women in Middle Eastern societies needs a systematic exploration of how changes in family arrangements structured gender relations in society as a whole.

Notes

1. See Margaret Meriweather's forthcoming book on family and society in Ottoman Aleppo, and Linda Schatkowski Schilcher, "The Lore and Reality of Middle Eastern Patriarchy," *Die Welt des Islams* 28 (1988): 496–512.

2. See Gabriel Baer, "Women and Waqf: An Analysis of the Istanbul Tahrir of 1546," *Asian and African Studies* (Jerusalem) 17, nos. 1–3 (1983): 9–28; Ronald C. Jennings, "Women in the Early Seventeenth Century Ottoman Judicial Records: The Sharia Court of Anatolian Kayseri," *Journal of the Economic and Social History of the Orient* 28 (1975): 53–114; Abraham Marcus, "Men, Women and Property: Dealers in Real Estate in Eighteenth-Century Aleppo," *Journal of the Economic and Social History of the Orient* 26 (1983): 137–63; and Judith E. Tucker, *Women in Nineteenth-Century Egypt* (Cambridge: Cambridge University Press, 1985).

3. Margot Badran, "Dual Liberation: Feminism and Nationalism in Egypt, 1870s–1925," *Feminist Issues* 8 (1988): 15–34; Fanny Davis, *The Ottoman Lady: A Social History from 1718 to 1918* (Westport, Conn.: Greenwood, 1986).

4. See, for example, Nayra Atiya, *Khul-Khaal: Five Egyptian Women Tell Their Stories* (Syracuse: Syracuse University Press, 1982); Elizabeth W. Fernea, ed., *Women and the Family in the Middle East* (Austin: University of Texas Press, 1985); Fatima Mernissi, *Doing Daily Battle: Interviews with Moroccan Women* (London: Women's Press, 1988); and Rosemary Sayigh, *Palestinians: From Peasants to Revolutionaries* (London: Zed, 1979).

5. See, for example, Richard Wall, Jean Robin, and Peter Laslett, eds., *Family Forms in Historic Europe* (Cambridge: Cambridge University Press, 1953). For a

discussion of feminist concerns in Western family history, see Joan Kelly, "Family and Society," in her *Women, History and Theory* (Chicago: University of Chicago Press, 1984), 110–53.

6. Halim Barakat, "The Arab Family and the Challenge of Social Transformation," in *Women and the Family in the Middle East,* ed. Fernea, 31–32.

7. For a discussion of the demographics of Nablus in this period, see Beshara Doumani, "Merchant Life in Ottoman Palestine: Jabal Nablus and Its Hinterland, 1800–1860" (Ph.D. diss., Georgetown University, 1990).

8. For accounts of the political history and administration of Jabal Nablus, see Ihsan Nimr, *Ta'rikh Jabal Nablus wa'l-Balqa'* (Nablus: al-Matba'a al-Ta'awuniyya, 1975), vol. 1; Amnon Cohen, *Palestine in the Eighteenth Century: Patterns of Government and Administration* (Jerusalem: Magnes, 1973), 164–69, 301–6; Miriam Hoexter, "The Role of the Qays and Yemen Factions in Local Political Divisions," *Asian and African Studies* (Jerusalem) 9 (1973): 249–311; Mordechai Abir, "Local Leadership and Early Reforms in Palestine, 1800–1834," in *Studies on Palestine during the Ottoman Period,* ed. Moshe Ma'oz (Jerusalem: Magnes, 1975), 284–310; and Alexander Schölch, "The Decline of Local Power in Palestine after 1856: The Case of 'Aqil Aga," *Die Welt des Islams* 23–24 (1984): 458–75.

9. Mahkama Nablus (M.N.), sijill (s.) 12, p. 113. Estates with minor heirs had to be registered in the court. The estates of women without minor children, therefore, may well be underrepresented in the records. Since the legal heirs of unmarried women could include minor siblings, nephews, or nieces, these estates also would be registered on a mandatory basis.

10. M.N., s. 9, p. 250.

11. M.N., s. 12, p. 29.

12. For an expanded discussion of age at marriage, see Judith Tucker, "Marriage and Family in Nablus, 1720–1856: Towards a History of Arab Muslim Marriage," *Journal of Family History* 13 (1988): 165–79.

13. M.N., s. 4, pp. 201, 331.

14. M.N., s. 4, p. 11; s. 4, p. 11 (second case), s. 4, pp. 127, 254, s. 7, p. 349.

15. We have little information on the frequency of khul' divorce, which did give women some control within a marriage. We suspect, however, that khul' divorce was not uncommon: in nineteenth-century Egyptian court records, khul' divorces occur with some frequency. See Tucker, *Women in Nineteenth-Century Egypt,* 54.

16. M.N., s. 9, p. 4

17. M.N., s. 9, p. 3.

18. M.N., s. 9, pp. 4, 16, 26, 41, 70, 73, 78, 82, 125, 149, 169, 324, s. 12, pp. 75, 53, 97.

19. M.N., s. 9, p. 149.

20. M.N., s. 9, p. 41.

21. M.N., s. 9, p. 50.

22. M.N., s. 9, p. 154.

23. M.N., s. 9, p. 3.

24. M.N., s. 11, p. 112.

25. M.N., s. 4, p. 254. Other similar cases include M.N., s. 4, p. 237, and s. 10, p. 173.

26. M.N., s. 5, pp. 29, 93.

27. M.N., s. 11, p. 156.

28. M.N., s. 12, p. 354.

29. M.N., s. 9, p. 69.

30. M.N., s. 9, p. 118.

31. Mary Eliza Rogers, *Domestic Life in Palestine* (London: Bell and Daldy, 1862), 272–73. The same story, in the context of a different war and a different army, was still popular in the late 1920s, as recorded in Hilda Granqvist, *Marriage Conditions in a Palestinian Village* (New York: AMS Press, 1975), 2:253.

32. See Granqvist, *Marriage Conditions* 2:219, 255.

33. M.N., s. 4, p. 82.

34. M.N., s. 5, p. 171.

35. M.N., s. 5, p. 150.

36. M.N., s. 5, pp. 62–63. A similar case, in which the children were awarded to their father's sister, was recorded in s. 11, p. 156.

37. M.N., s. 4, p. 99, s. 11, p. 119, s. 12, p. 7.

38. M.N., s. 4, p. 291.

39. See John Esposito, *Women in Muslim Family Law* (Syracuse: Syracuse University Press, 1982), 23.

14

The House of Zainab: Female Authority

and Saintly Succession in Colonial Algeria

JULIA CLANCY-SMITH

Nineteenth-century visitors to the Rahmaniyya *zawiya* (sufi lodge) in al-Hamil, Algeria, were inevitably surprised by its appearance. Located in the arid reddish foothills of the Saharan Atlas, the town clings to the side of a mountain, its highest point formed by the square white minaret of the mosque adjoining the Rahmaniyya establishment. The sufi center was of relatively recent construction, having been founded only in 1863. By the last decade of the nineteenth century, it claimed thousands of followers in Algeria and the Maghreb who were spiritual clients of al-Hamil's head *shaikh*, Sidi Muhammad b. Abi al-Qasim, and later of his daughter, Lalla Zainab.[1]

The town's prominence as a pilgrimage site and educational center was the work of Sidi Muhammad (1823–97), a powerful saint, mystic, and scholar.[2] By the eve of the shaikh's death, a group of buildings surrounded his family residence and the mosque: a library boasting an unusually rich collection of manuscripts, guest houses for pilgrims and travelers, a children's school (*kuttab*), a meeting room for sufi devotions, and lodgings for older students attending the *madrasa* (theological seminary).[3] At any given moment, several hundred students, instructed by full-time professors, studied at the Rahmaniyya establishment. This contrasts with the situation in other parts of Algeria under the Third Republic, which neglected or limited Muslim education for political as well as economic reasons.[4]

The zawiya's activities were not restricted to education, however. Those in need, the poor, the disinherited, and even fugitives from French justice found shelter in al-Hamil, which was able to provide a multitude of social services because of its remarkable prosperity. The monetary worth of the center's holdings in 1897—gardens, land, flocks, mills, cash, and so on—has been evaluated at 2.5 million francs, a

254

huge sum for the period in view of the general impoverishment of the Muslim Algerians.[5] In addition, the sufi center employed a small army of people to carry out its charitable works and to supervise its numerous *hubus* (*waqf*, or pious endowments) properties, mainly devoted to agriculture or pastoral production. The day-to-day administration of the zawiya thus required substantial managerial skills as well as bookkeeping to monitor incoming revenues, mainly in the form of pious offerings by the shaikh's religious clients.

On 2 June 1897, Sidi Muhammad b. Abi al-Qasim died, to the eventual consternation of local French authorities in the nearby Bureau Arabe in Bou Saada, some twelve kilometers to the north of al-Hamil. Throughout his tenure as head shaikh, Sidi Muhammad had carefully eschewed political activities, refusing to be drawn into anticolonial rebellions led by Rahmaniyya notables in other areas of Algeria.[6] Because of this, the al-Hamil center was regarded favorably by the colonial regime, which explains the zawiya's affluence and its ability to flourish in an era when many other sufi establishments and their elites were under attack.[7] Local military officials had assumed that the headship of al-Hamil would pass uncontested to the deceased shaikh's nephew, Muhammad b. al-Hajj Muhammad, who was Sidi Muhammad b. Abi al-Qasim's closest male associate and, more important, well disposed toward France. Calm assurance soon gave way to dismay in French circles. The matter of spiritual succession unleashed a bitter struggle that divided not only the shaikh's family but also his far-flung religious clientele, threatening the political calm of a sensitive region in the Sahara. Colonial officials had failed to take Lalla Zainab (c. 1850–1904), the daughter of Shaikh Muhammad, into account.

From 1897 until her death in 1904, Lalla Zainab directed the Rahmaniyya zawiya herself, assuming the heavy responsibilities for education and social welfare in al-Hamil. She did this in spite of intense opposition from the Bureau Arabe officers in Bou Saada, who were backing her male cousin's claims to the post of head shaikh. Zainab's tenure in office raises a multitude of questions. Who was she, what was her story, and what does Zainab tell us about relations between colonizer and colonized, between men and women in late-nineteenth-century Algeria? More generally, what can we learn from Lalla Zainab about the involvement of North African Muslim women in sufi orders or in other manifestations of "popular religion" within the context of European systems of domination? How typical or atypical was she of other women and of other saints and sufis? Before examining Zainab's story, a brief overview of women's participation in the North African *tariqas* (sufi orders) will place her story in a larger cultural and historical context.

WOMEN, SUFIS, AND SAINTS

Most studies of Muslim women begin by evoking their status as defined in Quran and the holy law. Patriarchy, which shaped male and female roles and often legitimized them through appeals to the law and to sacred texts, is also cited. Yet recent research has effectively demonstrated that women's social place in Muslim societies varied considerably over time and space. Adjustments must be made for such important structural determinants as class, ethnicity, and modes of production as well as historical circumstances. Prior to the modern Salafiyya movement of reformed Islam, the most visible manifestation of female religiosity was women's active involvement in saint veneration or mysticism or both. Although there are some recent studies of present-day female involvement in saint cults, pilgrimage centers, and sufi orders, women's association with these important communal religious and sociocultural activities in the past has received relatively little scholarly attention.[8] Indeed the path to mysticism for Muslim women seems to begin and end with Rabi'a al-'Adawiyya, who died in Basra in A.D. 801.

Aside from the empirical matter of women's relation to popular Islam, the existence of revered female mystics and saints raises an additional theoretical issue tied to the public-private dichotomy, now under intense scrutiny and refinement.[9] Did the borders, at times fluid, defining sacred and profane spaces and activities influence the contours of gender-based boundaries informed by various systems of patriarchy? Conversely, how did gender influence the domain of the sacred? Some of these issues can be addressed by using the experience of North African women in the past century as case studies.

In the Maghreb, some of the North African tariqas permitted women members a measure of institutionalized collective participation in Islam as locally lived and received, notably the Tijaniyya and the Rahmaniyya orders. In the nineteenth century, there appear to have been relatively large numbers of female Rahmaniyya members. This was in part because the Rahmaniyya claimed the single largest following among the Algerian orders and also because of certain doctrinal tenets of the order and its founder, Sidi Muhammad b. 'Abd al-Rahman al-Azhari (died c. 1793—94).[10] Statistics for female membership are somewhat difficult to obtain, and mainly come from colonial sources. Louis Rinn estimated that in the commune of Akbou (in the Kabylia) there were some four thousand women Rahmaniyya members during the 1880s; wherever their numbers were sufficient, women had their own female *muqaddamat* (circle leaders).[11] A 1913 study from the Awras (Aurès) Mountains revealed that one small oasis in the region of Tkout counted three times as many female Rahmaniyya members as male initiates.[12]

The voices of ordinary women in the past were muted or silent about the meaning that sufism held for them in their daily lives. An anecdote from nineteenth-century Algeria, however, indicates that tariqa membership was a source of immense pride for women, particularly in confrontations with more powerful forces. A Bureau Arabe official in Batna reported in 1849 that an Algerian woman had come to him to lay forth a grievance and demand that justice be done. Encountering a dilatory response, the woman then threatened the colonial officers in the following manner: "If you do not listen to me, I will go and complain to Sidi 'Abd al-Hafiz [shaikh of the Rahmaniyya zawiya of Khanga Sidi Naji]. . . . I am a sister of the Rahmaniyya."[13]

Several of the nineteenth-century Rahmaniyya *ijazas* (diplomas) specifically mention initiation rites (*talqin*) for female *murids* (aspiring sufi adepts) performed by male shaikhs; in other cases, women sufis were allowed to initiate other women into the tariqa.[14] Many of the initiation ceremonials—the recitation of certain prayers, the state of ritual purity, and the engagement or pact (*'ahd*)—were the same for men and women. When the *'ahd* ceremony was performed by a male shaikh, however, it was subject to the principles governing sexual segregation. Thus the male muqaddam arranged the women in front of him, and instead of placing his palm upon that of the female murid so as to engage the thumbs (as was done for men), she held one end of a long cloth in her right hand and the muqaddam held the other end. Another method to avoid physical contact between the sexes during the engagement ritual was to place a bowl of water between the muqaddam and the neophyte. Each then immersed the index finger of the right hand into the bowl and, with closed eyes, recited certain prayers together. Finally, as was true for men, the initiation ceremony was concluded by the whispering of secret instructions to the female novice, although these instructions were simplified for women.[15]

The experience of ordinary women in the tariqas raises in turn the issue of females who were themselves saints or sufis or who enjoyed an elevated socioreligious status by virtue of kinship in sufi or saintly families.

Among the Ait Isma'il of the Jurjura Mountains in the Kabylia, the Rahmaniyya order's original geographical matrix, we find several instances of women assuming leadership roles, at least temporarily. In 1836–37, bitter disagreements erupted over the matter of succession to the headship of the central zawiya. The widow of the deceased shaikh, Lalla Khadija, herself a powerful saint, not only directed the sufi center for several years but also on her own initiative resolved the dispute to the satisfaction of all by 1842. Although the Kabyles appear to have been quite amenable to her de facto administration of the zawiya, Lalla Khadija's activities were subject to one gender-based restriction—she did not actively engage in Rahmaniyya missionary work outside the region.[16] Rinn suggests that there was also gender-based opposition to her spiritual authority by some Rahmaniyya muqaddams who directed secondary zawiya. During Khadija's five-year administration, various sufi subalterns were negligent in remitting revenues back to the central zawiya from places outside of the Jurjura. This is somewhat ambiguous, however, since provincial sufi deputies often behaved this way toward male shaikhs whose authority was either contested or waning.[17]

In the next decade, Lalla Khadija's eldest daughter, who was the spouse of the current head Rahmaniyya shaikh, emerged in a leadership role during the French assault on the Jurjura Mountains between 1856 and 1857. Lalla Fatima not only organized armed resistance to the colonial army but also fought alongside her male counterparts in defense of Kabyle independence. In addition, Lalla Fatima appears to have been the first to initiate women into the tariqa as "sisters" and to authorize female sufi circle leaders, or muqaddamat.[18]

In the Algerian Sahara at the end of the nineteenth century, two women from sufi lineages assumed the direction of a desert sufi center. After the death of Sidi Mabruk b. 'Azzuz sometime before 1895, his co-wives, Mabruka and Khadija, took over the daily administration of the Rahmaniyya zawiya in al-Aghwat (Laghouat). They received pious offerings from religious clients performing the *ziyara* (local pilgrimage to a sufi or saint's shrine, often accompanied by donations) and provided the requisite hospitality—food and shelter—to those visiting the center from outside the immediate area. It should be noted, however, that the spiritual affairs of the al-Aghwat center were handled by a male Rahmaniyya notable residing in the oasis of Tulqa in the Ziban.[19]

Other Muslim women—and even European women—did temporarily assume leadership roles in some North African orders.[20] This was frequently the result of unusual circumstances, however, such as internecine quarrels among the tariqa's male elite, the disorders of colonial conquest, or the absence of male family members to carry on the work of a particular sufi center or saint shrine.[21]

The case of Lalla Zainab differs somewhat from these examples. Her tenure came after the political upheavals of the early colonial period had ended for the most part. The native Muslim population of fin de siècle Algeria was more or less resigned to the unpleasant realities of French rule. Although rebellious activity had not entirely been suppressed, revolt had given way to passive or more subtle forms of resistance by the 1890s. Moreover, Zainab's assumption of responsibility for both the spiritual and the social welfare functions of the al-Hamil zawiya did not follow a period of contention over leadership, but rather triggered a struggle for spiritual power from which she eventually emerged victorious. And a suitable male successor to Zainab's father had been waiting patiently in the wings for some time prior to the shaikh's death—his nephew, Muhammad b. al-Hajj Muhammad.

ZAINAB BINT SHAIKH MUHAMMAD B. ABI AL-QASIM, C. 1850–1904

During her lifetime and after, Zainab was venerated as a pious, learned woman and a saint by a large number of followers, both male and female. Although part of her socio-spiritual capital was clearly inherited from her father by virtue of kinship, Zainab expanded that fund of popular veneration through her own actions and activities. And she did so in spite of— or perhaps because of—opposition from colonial officials and from some of her male counterparts within the Rahmaniyya hierarchy.

Knowledge about Zainab's early years is extremely scanty. There is some biographical material, published and unpublished, devoted to her father, but Zainab is conspicuous for her absence in the Arabic texts. In one case she is referred to simply as the shaikh's "bint saliha" (virtuous daughter) with no further elaboration on her life.[22] Most of our documentation comes from unpublished French archival sources dating from the 1897–99 period, when Zainab's headship of the zawiya was opposed by local colonial officials. Thus, aside from a few quite sympathetic travelers' accounts by Europeans who had met personally with Zainab—among them, the notorious Isabelle Eberhardt (see below)—much of our information about her comes from her opponents.[23]

Zainab was born in al-Hamil around 1850, soon after her father had arrived in the oasis to establish the madrasa, but before he became a Rahmaniyya shaikh, which occurred in the following decade. Zainab's family enjoyed two significant sources of socio-spiritual authority. First in importance was that her father claimed to be from the Prophet's lineage, which bestowed an eastern Arab ancestry on the clan. Second, however, Shaikh Muhammad was the descendant of al-Hamil's saintly founders, who had emigrated several centuries earlier to the Bou Saada region from elsewhere in North Africa and created the village by performing a miracle.[24] Yet sharifian descent and maraboutic origins were not necessarily sufficient to establish a reputation for holiness and a popular following. Piety, learning, good deeds, and miracles were also required. In the course of her lifetime, Zainab constructed her own saintly persona, which not only outlived her but also completely overshadowed her successor—and rival—at the Rahmaniyya zawiya, Muhammad b. al-Hajj Muhammad.

Zainab appears to have spent most, if not all, of her early life in the oasis of al-Hamil. This changed after her father's death in 1897, when the demands of running a complex sufi center as well as of combating her enemies in French officialdom required Zainab to travel extensively. In accordance with the custom of endogamy among North African saintly sufi clans, Shaikh Muhammad b. Abi al-Qasim had taken several wives from religious families in the area. In addition, he concluded strategic marriage alliances with the "aristocratic" Muqrani clan from northeastern Algeria and with other distinguished families. These liaisons brought a large measure of social mobility and prestige, but apparently did not produce any surviving male heirs.[25]

From a young age, Zainab was taught by her father, himself a scholar of distinction. The shaikh took the matter of Zainab's education very seriously since she had attained an advanced level of instruction and was well versed in the books and manuscripts housed in the zawiya's library. She was quite learned in the Quran and hadith; her erudition was appreciated by her father's disciples and enhanced the "already great prestige she enjoyed" in the community as the shaikh's daughter. One source claims that Sidi Muhammad "had trained her from childhood to fill the role that awaited her."[26]

Zainab was raised in the *harim* of the shaikh's residence, which housed some forty women, including the shaikh's mother and his sister. Because the divorced wives of saintly and sufi figures were normally not permitted to remarry, at the time of the shaikh's death several women who had been repudiated remained under his care, in addition to his legal wives. Other women, deprived of male or family protection, resided in the zawiya and were generously provided for by Muhammad b. Abi al-Qasim. After his death, Zainab assumed the role of protector for the harim's women, shielding them in at least one instance from harassment by local French officials.[27]

The sufi residence provided shelter to a number of people besides the women of the harim. Political refugees from the 1864 revolt of the Sidi Aulad Shaikh (in western Algeria) and from the 1871 Muqrani uprising (in northeastern Algeria) were accorded asylum in al-Hamil together with their families.[28] These refugees may have provided Zainab with information about the workings of the colonial regime elsewhere in Algeria. When she took over the zawiya in 1897, Zainab was surprisingly conversant with the ways of the infidels—a knowledge she could not have acquired otherwise since there were no Europeans residing in the oasis.

Thanks to geographical isolation and to the absence of European settler communities in the Sahara, the oasis of al-Hamil was spared undue interference by the colonial order. Thus Zainab had few prolonged contacts with the French prior to 1897. Moreover, the prosperity of the zawiya served as a buffer against the harsh social conditions and political repression experienced by Muslims in northern Algeria. Although Sidi

Muhammad's professed neutrality had won him special treatment by French officials, the region was under military control and visitors to the al-Hamil zawiya were required to obtain permits from army officers in Bou Saada.[29] Yet direct intervention in the Rahmaniyya center was negligible as long as Sidi Muhammad b. Abi al-Qasim was alive. Once Zainab assumed control of the zawiya, colonial interference increased markedly, mainly because she was a woman.

Shaikh Muhammad centralized the administration of the sufi center's numerous properties and complex affairs within his own hands. Nevertheless, he apparently kept Zainab informed of financial and other operations, viewing her as a confidante and perhaps as his successor. After Sidi Muhammad's death, his daughter was the individual most knowledgeable about the past and present social services offered to the community by the Rahmaniyya zawiya. Zainab returned her father's affections, describing him as leading an exemplary life, moved by a love for others; she cited "his pity for the disinherited, his generosity, his great theological knowledge, disinterest in the things of this world, and his scrupulous observance of Muslim law in all matters."[30]

In spite of having a number of suitors, Zainab at some point decided to take a vow of celibacy and remained unmarried at her death. Her virginity, asceticism, simplicity of manners, and utter devotion to the needy brought her popular veneration as a saint in the Sahara. Moreover, when Zainab was in her late twenties, her father drew up a hubus document that indicated the shaikh's respect for his daughter. In the 1877 document Sidi Muhammad stated that his substantial possessions—land, houses, fields, gardens, valuable household items, and so forth—were constituted as hubus "in favor of his daughter Zainab and other children of either the masculine or female sex." Any male heirs were to receive, as was customary, double the share of the inheritance that females received. Zainab, however, was singled out specifically to receive a "portion equal to male" offspring, although her renunciation of the pleasures of marriage meant that Zainab would have no heirs to complicate the matter of inheritance.[31] Twenty years later, Zainab relied in part on this document to advance her claims against those of her cousin.

"A DANGEROUS WOMAN"

As Muhammad b. Abi al-Qasim's health began to deteriorate, French officials in the local Bureau Arabe pressed him to publicly designate a successor. The shaikh demurred until the eve of his death. Under heavy pressure from the commanding officer, Captain Crochard, whose official mission was to force the Rahmaniyya leader to select someone compatible with French interests, Sidi Muhammad finally named his nephew,

Muhammad b. al-Hajj Muhammad. His choice was made known in a letter to military officers in the Bou Saada office dated March 1897. Nevertheless, the shaikh took no action to change the content of the 1877 hubus document, and French officials were unaware of its existence until the headship of the Rahmaniyya zawiya became a matter of dispute. Whether Zainab knew of her father's letter to the Bureau Arabe designating her cousin as head shaikh is uncertain. Later, however, she based her grievances against the Bureau Arabe in Bou Saada in part on this letter, which may have been elicited from Muhammad b. Abi al-Qasim when he was ailing and his faculties declining.[32] By the summer of 1897, the stage was set for a confrontation.

Zainab's objections to Muhammad b. al-Hajj Muhammad's bid for the directorship of the Rahmaniyya zawiya were twofold: her cousin's impious behavior, which made him unworthy to succeed her father; and more important, the specious nature of his claims as a legitimate successor, meaning that Zainab (and others in the Rahmaniyya hierarchy) rejected the nomination letter submitted by her father to Captain Crochard. When Zainab's cousin tried to assert his authority in al-Hamil, she took the keys to the various buildings and to the zawiya's coffers to prevent him from assuming control over the sufi center. She also forbade the zawiya's students and staff to obey his commands and wrote letters to subordinate Rahmaniyya muqaddams discrediting her cousin's claims. With al-Hamil's educational and devotional facilities off limits to him, Muhammad b. al-Hajj Muhammad attempted to create a counterfollowing among some of the zawiya's clients by establishing a rival school outside the village. A little less than a year after the dispute broke out, he had attracted only a small group of some thirty students to his side.[33]

Nevertheless, the struggle between Zainab and her cousin did provoke divisions among her father's religious followers and the various tribes in the Sahara. Zainab's bold actions presented Sidi Muhammad b. Abi al-Qasim's closest spiritual associates with a rather serious dilemma. She had declared that any Rahmaniyya brother who joined her cousin's side "could no longer hope to see the door of Lalla Zainab's [zawiya] open to him."[34] Although some of her father's disciples believed Muhammad b. al-Hajj Muhammad to be the legitimate successor, they hesitated to openly disavow Zainab because of their great respect for her. Significantly, Muslim Algerians' objections to Zainab's administration did not necessarily revolve around the issue of gender. Some Rahmaniyya notables opposed both Zainab's and her cousin's claims, maintaining that succession to al-Hamil should alternate between Shaikh Muhammad's lineage and another prestigious Rahmaniyya sufi clan in the oasis of Aulad Jallal.[35]

Thus, for many Rahmaniyya members, the disagreement over Sidi

Muhammad b. Abi al-Qasim's spiritual heir was not—as far as we know—primarily framed in terms of proper gender roles or boundaries. Rather it was local colonial officials who were the most vehemently opposed to Lalla Zainab. Being a woman, they argued, she would be a weak, pliable instrument in the hands of anti-French forces, "people of intrigue and disorder."[36] Predictably, colonial officers in Bou Saada portrayed Zainab's actions as the consequence of female conspiracies within the zawiya's harim, instigated by her women companions, whose families had sought asylum there from French justice. Captain Crochard thus maintained that:

> the two daughters of the former bash-agha of the Majana, who . . . believed that [Zainab's cousin] was hostile to them and would neglect their interests, began to create problems, adversely influencing the daughter of the deceased shaikh. The bash-agha's wives and daughters are friends of Lalla Zainab and portrayed Muhammad b. al-Hajj Muhammad as an ambitious man who wanted to control the material possessions of the zawiya in order to seize the deceased shaikh's worldly goods.[37]

By the time that Crochard was writing this, he had largely failed in his mission to "arrange" for a docile and pro-French male to succeed Muhammad b. Abi al-Qasim. More serious, however, was that Zainab had brought a formal grievance to those at the pinnacle of authority in French Algeria. Thus Crochard's vilification of Lalla Zainab reflects his own precarious position within the colonial bureaucracy; in effect, Crochard may have risked losing his command because of the actions of a "rebellious woman."[38]

The death of her father and Crochard's efforts to undermine her authority brought Zainab a greatly expanded public role as director of the zawiya. Realizing the threat to her administration posed by authorities in Bou Saada, Zainab decided to outmaneuver her opponents. In August 1897 she engaged the legal services of a French lawyer in Algiers, Maurice Ladmiral, who was at the court of appeal in the capital. Ladmiral presented Zainab's case to the procureur général of the republic, the highest office within the colonial system of justice. The matter was then brought to the attention of the governor-general of Algeria and the commanding general of the province. In a letter to Governor-General Jules Cambon (1891–97), General Meygret informed his superior that Zainab's complaint "contains allegations of a very grave nature" regarding the conduct of the heads of the Bou Saada office.[39]

Here it should be noted that, upon his nomination as governor-general, Cambon had attempted to soften the regime's rather hostile stance toward the Algerian sufi orders and to establish cordial relations with the leaders of the "great brotherhoods," the Qadiriyya, Tijaniyya, and Rahmaniyya.[40] The intervention of the local Bureau Arabe into the affairs of a "friendly" sufi center such as al-Hamil was viewed with displeasure in Algiers. Zainab's actions had, therefore, thrown the colonial administration into a certain amount of disarray.

By doing this, Zainab also checkmated Crochard's move to put her cousin into the office of head shaikh in al-Hamil. Moreover, she had done so entirely within the prevailing system of colonial justice, displaying a remarkable grasp of how that system functioned. Between 1897 and 1899, Zainab thus was locked in a struggle with two men, her paternal uncle's son and Crochard. To his superiors Crochard naturally portrayed Muhammad b. al-Hajj Muhammad in glowing terms—as a faithful, upright individual concerned only for the zawiya's welfare and the security of France. Other French officials, however, had earlier expressed somewhat different opinions of Zainab's cousin, who was described as "of average intelligence, ambitious, haughty, and prone to excess."[41] These evaluations were shared not only by Lalla Zainab but also by the inhabitants of al-Hamil, who viewed Muhammad b. al-Hajj Muhammad as "miserly and worldly," traits that were incompatible with popular veneration and support for a sufi leader.[42] Zainab's determined struggle against her own cousin was therefore based on realistic fears that his administration might prove detrimental to the zawiya's interests and to the continuation of her father's work.

Zainab met with her nemesis, Crochard, on several occasions during 1897, engaging him in rather heated face-to-face confrontations over the matter of the zawiya's headship. The issue involved more than spiritual authority, for the division of the zawiya's properties among Sidi Muhammad's heirs was also at stake. In the course of one of their meetings, Crochard scored a minor victory by bringing Zainab to his office against her will. She had attempted to deal with him on her own turf, by obliging Crochard to call at her residence in Bou Saada, and thus on her own terms. Having failed at this, Zainab informed the Bureau Arabe authorities that the letter of nomination obtained under duress from her father was "apocryphal." They in turn accused her of being "une fille insoumise," a rebellious daughter who ignored the last wishes of her father.[43] More telling were Crochard's concluding remarks, which reveal the frustration experienced by those ostensibly in control of the local Muslim population: "This affair demonstrates that Zainab is a dangerous woman whose intrigues and activities should be closely surveyed. She knows that a woman is always treated with circumspection and she takes advantage of this in order to cause problems for the local [colonial] authority which she believes is favoring her cousin in the matter of succession."[44]

The next rounds, however, were won by Zainab. By the end of 1897, General Meygret recommended to Jules Cambon that the colonial regime refrain from further interference in the al-Hamil dispute, leaving Zainab in control of the zawiya. Although she was left more or less in peace as shaikha, at least one more attempt was made to undermine her authority. In 1899 an Algerian by the name of Sa'id b. Lakhdar requested that the Bureau Arabe in Bou Saada take action on his behalf against the Rahmaniyya establishment. Lakhdar, who was mentally deranged, maintained that Zainab's father had owed him the completely outrageous sum of 2.2 million francs. In addition, Sa'id ibn Lakhdar claimed that the shaikh had named him as his *khalifa,* or successor! Local officials, who seemed eager to entertain Lakhdar's clearly fraudulent claims— perhaps out of spite—contacted Zainab about Lakhdar's complaint, demanding an explanation.[45]

Lalla Zainab deftly refuted all of Lakhdar's allegations by relying on Muslim law and customary practices, French legal procedures, and her own highly developed powers of reasoning. Among other things, she observed that "there is no native Algerian in all of our region who has ever possessed over two million francs in specie."[46] Moreover, the sum of money claimed by the plaintiff was not recorded in the zawiya's financial registers, nor did Lakhdar have a written receipt of deposit from Shaikh Muhammad. Finally, Zainab pointed out the irrational nature of the complaint brought against both the Rahmaniyya center and its female director:

> Sa'id ibn Lakhdar says that he deposited this sum of money with my father. Assuming that the sum was in cash, [the plaintiff] would have had to transport a heavy load of specie, requiring enormous numbers of donkeys to deliver it to the zawiya . . . the claims of this person have no foundation . . . however, one should see in this affair the hand of someone other than Lakhdar who is a tool for those who hate us and who are intent upon the ruin and loss of the zawiya.[47]

Zainab's written rebuttals to the authorities are a tour de force of argumentation; her letters reveal not only a complete familiarity with the colonial regime—and the mentality of Algeria's French masters—but also a profound sense of strategy. Moreover, her intimate knowledge of the details of Sa'id ibn Lakhdar's financial relations with her father indicate that Sidi Muhammad had kept his daughter informed of the zawiya's banking operations.

It was during this incident that Lalla Zainab emerged as the protector of the harim's female residents. Still pressing his financial claims, Sa'id b. Lakhdar next sought to force the wives of Shaikh Muhammad to travel together to Algiers to the tomb-shrine of Sidi 'Abd al-Rahman al-Azhari, the Rahmaniyya's founder. There, the women—some ten in number— were to take an oath swearing that they knew nothing of the sum of money owed, according to Lakhdar, by their deceased spouse. Lakhdar's demands caused distress among the zawiya's female inhabitants. Once more, Zainab skillfully refuted the legality of this demand, by appeals to both Islamic law and French justice. If need be, she said, she would take an oath on the tomb of Sidi 'Abd al-Rahman—an extremely serious act in the eyes of Muslims—but the harim's women were not parties to the dispute and were not to be disturbed.[48]

THE SHAIKHA AND THE "PASSIONATE NOMAD"

In 1902 a rather improbable relationship developed between Lalla Zainab, by then regarded as a *murabita*, or living saint, and Isabelle Eberhardt (1877–1904), the "passionate nomad." Isabelle was the illegitimate daughter of a Russian nihilist and an aristocratic German woman. Her childhood and upbringing in Europe were wildly eccentric, predisposing Isabelle to unconventional behavior throughout her life. In 1897, the year of Shaikh Muhammad b. Abi al-Qasim's death, Isabelle and her mother moved to Algiers to escape personal tragedy and social ostracism in Europe. Once in Algeria, Isabelle continued her study of Arabic and of Islam, eventually converting to Islam as well as joining the Qadiriyya sufi order. In 1902 she married an Algerian Muslim named Sliman, a soldier in the colonial army, thereby acquiring French citizenship.[49]

Isabelle aroused a great deal of overt hostility among colonial officials and in European settler society, in part because of her evident sympathy for Islamic and Arab culture. Her disorderly conduct—an undisguised fondness for drugs and alcohol, illicit sexual liaisons, and dressing as a native Algerian male—also caused dismay in French circles. (The Muslim Algerians, in general, were much more tolerant of Isabelle's scandalous ways.) In addition, Isabelle, as was true of so many Europeans in this period, was fascinated by the Sahara, since as she put it: "in the really Arab towns like the ksours [oases] of the south, the poignant and bewitching atmosphere of the land of Africa is quite tangible."[50] This attraction, and Isabelle's forays into the desert, alarmed some military officials. By 1900 the Sahara was in a state of political unrest due to French thrusts into Morocco via southwestern Algeria. A few years later Gen. Hubert Lyautey attempted to exploit Isabelle's knowledge of the desert as part of his policy of *pénétration pacifique*.[51]

It is uncertain how or when Lalla Zainab and the Rahmaniyya center first came to Isabelle's attention. Following Shaikh Muhammad's death in

1897, large numbers of pilgrims gathered at his tomb in the zawiya's mosque, seeking the saint's blessings. By this time too, Zainab's reputation for sanctity and miracles had spread far beyond the confines of al-Hamil; many believed that she had inherited her father's *baraka* (blessing). Women, both native Algerian and French, brought their ailing children to Zainab, who had the ability to cure. The shaikha was "spoken of with awe and reverence throughout every corner of Algeria where the khouans [sufi members] of the Rahmanya were to be found."[52] Isabelle therefore may have heard about Zainab from fellow Muslims in Algiers or from pilgrims. By then suffering from chronic malaria, syphilis, and perhaps anorexia, Isabelle was bent on pursuing some vague mystical vocation. In the summer of 1902, she traveled from Algiers to Bou Saada expressly to visit Lalla Zainab at the zawiya.

Arriving at the oasis in July, Isabelle found that Zainab was away on some unspecified mission. When the long-awaited meeting between the two women did take place, it had an enormous impact on Isabelle, who recorded their visit in her dairy. Apparently Isabelle bared her soul to Lalla Zainab, describing at length the details of her tormented life, to which the shaikha listened with evident sympathy. Zainab even assured the European woman of her undying friendship, approving of Isabelle's spiritual quest.[53] In turn, Isabelle left a valuable and moving account of the female saint and sufi, whom she described as dressed in the simple white costume of the Bou Saada region: "Her face, tanned by the sun because she travels frequently in the region, was wrinkled. She is nearly fifty years old. Her eyes are kindly and in them burns a flame of intelligence, though veiled by a great sadness. Everything—her voice, her mannerisms, and the welcome she accords to pilgrims—expresses a profound simplicity."[54]

According to Isabelle's account, Shaikh Muhammad b. Abi al-Qasim had designated Zainab to succeed him, educating her in the manner "of the best of his students" in preparation for a role that was vastly different from that normally reserved for ordinary Algerian women. Zainab was clearly in control of the zawiya and of those affiliated with the Rahmaniyya establishment in al-Hamil. "More so than any other of the sufi centers, Zainab's zawiya is a refuge for the poor who come here from all over."[55] Isabelle noted that Lalla Zainab's health was declining. She suffered from a painful throat disease that made talking difficult and rendered her voice hoarse; their conversations were interrupted by a "harsh cough that shook [Zainab's] frail body, fragile as that of a child under its burnous and veils."[56] A lifetime of fasting and asceticism had left its mark on the shaikha; Isabelle was correct in anticipating Zainab's approaching death.

In spite of the brevity of their first encounter, the two women took to one another, and Zainab in turn confided in Isabelle. With tears in her eyes, she told her European visitor: "My daughter . . . I have devoted my entire life to doing good for the love of God. Yet, there are men who refuse to recognize the good that I have done for them. Many hate and envy me. And yet, I have renounced all in life: I never married, I have no children, no joy."[57] The next year Zainab again welcomed Isabelle, who by now clearly viewed the Algerian woman as her spiritual mentor as well as her dearest female friend. Isabelle wrote in her dairy that "each time I see Lalla Zaynab, I experience a sort of rejuvenation. . . . I saw her yesterday twice in the morning. She was very kind and gentle towards me and expressed joy at seeing me again."[58] By this time, the friendship developing between the two women was known to colonial authorities.

The French military had been discreetly surveying Zainab's activities in al-Hamil since 1897 and monitoring Isabelle's movements as well, although rather less discreetly. Isabelle's second journey to al-Hamil in 1903 was tracked by the colonial police, who gathered information about the meetings at the zawiya. The two women's relationship was deemed of enough political interest that the new governor-general, Charles Jonnart, urged the commanding general of the province of Algiers to discover the "subjects of the two women's conversations."[59] It was only with the first publication of Isabelle's diary in 1923, however, that their conversations became known.[60]

The two women did not see each other again after 1903. The next year brought Isabelle's death in a desert flash flood at 'Ain Sefra, where the French army was poised to move into Moroccan territory. Lalla Zainab also died in 1904 and was buried in the family cemetery in al-Hamil, where her tomb-shrine became the object of veneration for pilgrims. Her cousir Muhammad b. al-Hajj Muhammad accordingly assumed control of the zawiya—seven years later than he had anticipated. Although he was now the head shaikh of a large and prestigious Rahmaniyya center, he was never highly regarded by the zawiya's clientele; Zainab's saintly reputation completely overshadowed his.

On the eve of World War I another European woman, Helen C. Gordon, visited al-Hamil. A decade had passed since Zainab's death, but her memory remained vividly alive among the villagers and sufi initiates: "So beneficent had been her sway, so charitable was she that her memory is still green in the hearts of her people, and by children her name is spoken as one would whisper that of a revered saint, with awe and to bear witness to the truth of some statement."[61]

Zainab's story does not end here, however. An American woman artist, Kate Delas, recently traveled through the oasis and found that people there continue to talk about Zainab. Based on what she heard from al-Hamil's inhabitants, Delas was able to draw a portrait of the shaikha.[62] In independent postcolonial Algeria, Zainab remains the stuff of legends and lore; and in spite of the terrible upheavals of the revolution, the zawiya still stands today.

Women in colonial societies were under a form of dual control composed of two intersecting systems of patriarchy, one indigenous, the other foreign and European. It is within these systems of domination that Zainab's story must be considered. As a woman, Lalla Zainab was in theory subject to the restrictions of a doubly patriarchal society. Yet she was popularly regarded as a saint, a mystic, and a learned woman, in addition to enjoying membership in a prestigious sufi lineage. Acquired and inherited spiritual authority, and the immense social value placed on the gift of baraka, made Zainab an extraordinary woman. As such, she could move without censure outside of the gender boundaries constructed by her own culture and also defy, with relative impunity, those imposed by the colonial order.

By virtue of saintliness, she acquired freedoms in native Algerian society not normally the prerogative of ordinary women. More significantly, Zainab confronted French officials with a boldness not readily accorded to many Muslim men. She thus perceived, and used to advantage, the weak points within the colonial system of domination—particularly the absence of effective mechanisms to deal with unsubmissive Muslim women. Zainab did this openly and consciously in order to carry on her father's work of cultural survival for the Algerian community, which also entailed defying the wishes of some Muslim males.

In her diary, Isabelle pointed out the importance of Zainab's life and the need to study the shaikha's story.[63] At the same time, Isabelle's much more flamboyant life and equally sensational death have perhaps drawn attention away from Zainab, at least among Europeans. One reason that Isabelle was able to move so freely about colonial Algeria was her androgynous behavior. Isabelle "combined transvestism with Don Juanism."[64] She was both male and female, yet neither, and thus rejected sexual and gender boundaries. Zainab in no way repudiated the norms and conventions of her Arabo-Berber Muslim culture, which provided a religious and social space for female religiosity, particularly within the idioms of sufism and saint cults. Nor did she assume the headship of the zawiya by adopting a male guise or masculine attributes. Unlike Isabelle, Zainab did not dress like a man, and she expressed female chagrins and desires to Eberhardt during their first meeting in 1902, especially the emotional deprivation she felt at being childless.

Lalla Zainab's decision to remain celibate was an important component of her saintly persona; it also relieved her of conjugal duties and the distractions of child rearing, allowing her to devote all her energies to the

zawiya and to the needs of its numerous religious clients. Although unmarried women were normally considered inferior in status to married
women—remaining as "bint" all their lives—Zainab's vow of celibacy, as
a spiritual act, conversely brought immediate prestige.[65] In addition,
Zainab was a "producer" of baraka, and that role brought her into the
public domain as dictated by popular religiosity. Yet the shaikha also
expanded her public activities to reach beyond the demands associated
with administering a sufi center. After her father's death, she traveled
and paid visits to colonial officials as part of her campaign to retain control
of the zawiya.

Conflicts over spiritual hegemony within, or among, the elites of the
North African brotherhoods were not uncommon at the end of the nineteenth century. French authorities frequently intervened to back one side
or another so as to ensure social order and political control. Zainab's
victorious struggle against both the French hierarchy and her own cousin
appears unique in the annals of colonial Algerian history. This
uniqueness may, however, be due in part to the lack of research devoted
to the experiences of Algerian women, whether ordinary or extraordinary beings, in the past century.

Notes

1. For information on the Rahmaniyya zawiya in al-Hamil, see Archives du
Gouvernement Général de l'Algérie, Dépôt d'Outre-Mer, Aix-en-Provence (hereafter cited as AGGA), 16 H 8, "Notice sur l'ordre des Rahmanya," 28 June 1895, and
2 U 20, 2 U 21, and 2 U 22; Muhammad 'Ali Dabbuz, *Nahdat al-Jaza'ir al-haditha wa
thauratuha al-mubaraka*, 2 vols. (Algiers: Imprimerie Coopérative, 1965); and Abu
al-Qasim Sa'adallah, *Ta'rikh al-Jaza'ir al-thaqafi* (Algiers: Société Nationale d'Edition et Diffusion, 1981).

2. On the life of Shaikh Muhammad b. Abi al-Qasim, see Dabbuz, *Nahda* 1:52–
53; Muhammad al-Hafnawi, *Ta'rif al-khalaf bi rijal al-salaf* (1907; reprint, Tunis: Dar
al-Maktaba al-'Atiqa, 1982); and AGGA, 16 H 8, 2 U 20, 2 U 21, and 2 U 22.

3. AGGA, 16 H 8, "Notice sur l'ordre des Rahmanya," 28 June 1895; René Basset,
"Les manuscrits arabes de la zaouyah d'el-Hamel," *Giornale della Societa Asiatica
Italiana* 10 (1896–97): 43–97.

4. Yvonne Turin, *Affrontements culturels dans l'Algérie coloniale: Ecoles, médecines,
religion, 1830–1880* (Paris: Maspero, 1971); Charles-Robert Ageron, *Les Algériens
Musulmans et la France (1871–1919)*, 2 vols. (Paris: Presses Universitaires de France,
1968).

5. Ahmed Nadir, "La fortune d'un ordre religieux algérien vers la fin du XIXe
siècle," *Le mouvement social*, no. 89 (1974): 59–84. Nadir's study is the only recent
one devoted to the Rahmaniyya center in al-Hamil; see also Youssef Nacib,
Cultures oasiennes (Paris: Publisud, 1986).

6. For a fuller account of Shaikh Muhammad b. Abi al-Qasim and his relations

with the colonial regime, see Julia Clancy-Smith, "The Shaikh and His Daughter: Coping in Colonial Algeria, c. 1830–1904," in *Struggle and Survival in the Modern Middle East, 1750–1950*, ed. Edmund Burke III (London: I. B. Tauris and Berkeley: University of California Press, 1991); for the political activities of some Rahmaniyya leaders, see Julia Clancy-Smith, "Saints, Mahdis, and Arms: Religion and Resistance in Nineteenth-Century North Africa," in *Islam, Politics, and Social Movements*, ed. Edmund Burke III and Ira M. Lapidus (Berkeley: University of California Press, 1988), 60–80.

7. Ageron, *Les Algériens Musulmans;* Julia Clancy-Smith, "In the Eye of the Beholder: The North African Sufi Orders and the Colonial Production of Knowledge, 1830–1900," *Africana Journal* 15 (1990); 220–57.

8. See, for example, Daisy Hilse Dwyer, "Women, Sufism, and Decision-Making in Moroccan Islam," in *Women in the Muslim World*, ed. Lois Beck and Nikki Keddie (Cambridge: Harvard University Press, 1978), 585–98; Nancy Tapper, "Ziyaret: Gender, Movement, and Exchange in a Turkish Community," in *Muslim Travellers: Pilgrimage, Migration and the Religious Imagination*, ed. Dale F. Eickelman and James Piscatori (London: Routledge, 1990), 236–55; the articles in *Women in Islamic Societies*, ed. Bo Utas (London: Curzon, 1983); Jane I. Smith, ed., *Women in Contemporary Muslim Societies* (Cranbury, N.J.: Associated University Presses, 1980); and a particularly fine account of present-day Algerian women and popular religion by Willy Jansen, *Women without Men: Gender and Marginality in an Algerian Town* (Leiden: E. J. Brill, 1987).

9. See, for example, Michelle Zimbalist Rosaldo and Louise Lamphere, eds., *Women, Culture, and Society* (Stanford: Stanford University Press, 1974), and works, published and unpublished, by Mary Hegland; see also Caroline Walker Bynum, Stevan Harrell, and Paula Richman, eds., *Gender and Religion: On the Complexity of Symbols* (Boston: Beacon, 1986).

10. On the Rahmaniyya and its founder, see al-Hafnawi, *Ta'rif*, 457–74, and Sa'adallah, *Ta'rikh* 1:514–16; see also Julia Clancy-Smith, "The Saharan Rahmaniya: Popular Protest and Desert Society in Southeastern Algeria and the Tunisian Jarid, 1750–1881" (Ph.D. diss., University of California, Los Angeles, 1988), and Clancy-Smith, "Between Cairo and the Algerian Kabylia: The Rahmaniya Tariqa, 1715–1800," in *Muslim Travellers*, ed. Eickelman and Piscatori, 200–216.

11. Louis Rinn, *Marabouts et Khouan: Etude sur l'Islam en Algérie* (Algiers: Jourdan, 1884), 473, 479.

12. AGGA, 16 H 2, "Renseignements sur les ordres religieux," 1903.

13. This incident was reported by Captain Marnier in AGGA, 16 H 2, on 1 Aug. 1849; Marnier also observed that "there are many woman members of the Rahmaniyya in the region of Batna." Nevertheless, there were many more males than females.

14. AGGA, 16 H 8, "Renseignements politiques," 1895; Octave Depont and Xavier Coppolani, *Les confréries religieuses musulmanes* (Algiers: Jourdan, 1897), 388; Edmond Doutte, *L'Islam algérien en l'an 1900* (Algiers: Mustapha, 1900), 72.

15. AGGA, 16 H 8, "Notice sur l'ordre des Rahmanya," 28 June 1895.

16. AGGA, 16 H 1, "Notice sur l'ordre religieux de Sidi Mohammed ben Abd-er-

Rahman," 1849; Edouard de Neveu, *Les Khouan: Ordres religieux chez les Musulmans de l'Algérie* (Paris: Guyot, 1846), 118–19; Marthe and Edmond Gouvian, *Kitab Aayane al-Marhariba* (Algiers: Imprimerie Orientale, 1920), 145–46.

17. Rinn, *Marabouts*, 457.

18. Gouvian, *Kitab*, 146.

19. AGGA, 16 H 8, "Renseignements politiques," 1895.

20. Auguste Cour, "Recherches sur l'état des confréries religieuses musulmanes dans les communes de Oum el Bouaghi, Ain-Beida, Sedrata, Souk Ahras, Morsott, Tebessa, Meskiana, et Khenchela, en novembre 1914," *Revue africaine* 62 (1921): 299.

21. Aurélie Picard (1849–1933), for example, dominated the Algerian Tijaniyya from 1883 until her death, and Emily Keene was "Sharifa" of the sufi order of Wazzan; on these women, see Ursula K. Hart, *Two Ladies of Colonial Algeria: The Lives and Times of Aurélie Picard and Isabelle Eberhardt*, Ohio University Monographs in International Studies, no. 49 (Athens: Ohio University, 1987), and Emily, Shareefa of Wazan, *My Life Story*, ed. S. L. Bensusan (London: Arnold, 1911).

22. Dabbuz does not mention Zainab in *Nahda*, although he discusses her father at length and her cousin as well; Muhammad al-Hafnawi, who studied at the al-Hamil zawiya under Zainab's father, mentions Lalla Zainab merely as "virtuous daughter" in *Ta'rif* (p. 352). There may be a lack of material on Zainab in the Arabic sources because Muhammad b. al-Hajj Muhammad, Zainab's first cousin and rival, wrote the most comprehensive history of al-Hamil and a biography of Shaikh Muhammad b. Abi al-Qasim, still in manuscript form, which has been invariably relied upon by subsequent writers.

23. The sole published article of recent date devoted to al-Hamil is Nadir's "La fortune," which mentions Zainab only in passing since the real focus of the study is the zawiya's holdings and monetary worth. The zawiya of al-Hamil is closed to researchers at the present time.

24. AGGA, 16 H 8, "Notice sur l'ordre des Rahmanya," 1895; Dabbuz, *Nahda*.

25. The report in AGGA 16 H 8 ("Notice sur l'ordre des Rahmanya," 1895) notes that a local maraboutic notable from the Bou Saada region incurred Sidi Muhammad b. Abi al-Qasim's wrath by daring to marry a former wife of the great sufi leader. By taking the shaikh's divorced spouse into his own household, the local marabout was attempting to assert his spiritual equality vis-à-vis the leader of al-Hamil. On the shaikh's socially strategic marriages, see Jacques Berque, *L'intérieur du Maghreb, XVe—XIXe siècle* (Paris: Gallimard, 1978), 419–23.

26. AGGA, 16 H 8; Cecily Mackworth, *The Destiny of Isabelle Eberhardt* (London: Quartet, 1977), 157.

27. On the harim, see AGGA, 16 H 8. Gustave Guillaumet, *Tableaux algériens* (Paris: Plon, 1891), 119–26, describes a visit to the zawiya's harim by a group of French ladies in the 1880s. The author, meeting Zainab at her father's residence, noted her physical appearance: "His only daughter [was] a saintly creature whose face was marked by smallpox and decorated with small tattoos" (p. 121). AGGA, 16 H 61 (report of 29 Sept. 1899) contains information concerning Zainab's assumption of her father's role as protector of the zawiya's women (see below).

28. AGGA, 16 H 8 (1895).

29. Clancy-Smith, "Shaikh"; Mackworth, *Destiny*, 155.

30. AGGA, 16 H 61 (29 Sept. 1899).

31. An exact French translation of the hubus document dated 31 Aug. 1877 is in AGGA, 16 H 61 (3 Sept. 1897); an Arabic version is in 2 U 22.

32. AGGA, 16 H 61 (10 Mar. 1897).

33. AGGA, 16 H 8 (report of 21 Mar. 1898).

34. Ibid.

35. Ibid. Muhammad b. Abi al-Qasim had inherited the *baraka* of the Rahmaniyya leader of the Aulad Jallal zawiya in 1862 upon Shaikh Muhammad al-Mukhtar's death. This, in theory, established a precedent for alternating spiritual succession between the sufi-saintly lineages controlling the two sufi centers, a principle observed by other branches of the Rahmaniyya.

36. AGGA, 16 H 8, 16 H 61.

37. AGGA, 16 H 61.

38. Ibid.

39. Ibid.

40. Ageron, *Les Algériens Musulmans* 1:478–527.

41. AGGA, 16 H 8.

42. Helen C. Gordon, *A Woman in the Sahara* (New York: Frederick Stokes, 1914), 78.

43. AGGA, 16 H 61 (22 Oct. 1897).

44. Ibid.

45. AGGA, 16 H 61 (29 Sept. 1899) contains a French translation of Zainab's letter to the commandment of Bou Saada. The original Arabic letter is in 2 U 22.

46. Ibid.

47. Ibid.

48. AGGA, 16 H 61 (12 Dec. 1899) and 2 U 22, contain letters from Zainab. An oath taken on the tomb of the saintly founder of the Rahmaniyya order was regarded not only as a legally binding act but also as a religiously based affirmation of the veracity of an individual's statement.

49. The literature, both colonial and recent, devoted to Isabelle Eberhardt is too extensive to be cited here. The information on Isabelle contained in this chapter is drawn from Mackworth's *Destiny;* Hart's *Two Ladies;* Annette Kobak's *Isabelle: The Life of Isabelle Eberhardt* (New York: Alfred A. Knopf, 1989); and Isabelle Eberhardt, *Lettres et journaliers,* ed. Eglal Errera (Arles: Editions Actes du Sud, 1987); see also the review article by Margot Badran, "Deserts of the Heart," *Women's Review of Books* 5 (December 1987): 7–8, and Julia Clancy-Smith, "The 'Passionate Nomad' Reconsidered: A European Woman in Algérie française (Isabelle Eberhardt, 1877–1904)," in *Complicity and Resistance: Western Women and Imperialism,* ed. Nupur Chaudhuri and Margaret Strobel (Bloomington: University of Indiana Press, 1992).

50. Kobak, *Isabelle*, 190.

51. Ibid., 207–30; Hart, *Two Ladies*, 98–101. Lyautey engaged Isabelle's services in 1903 as the French army was moving into the Colomb-Béchar region on the border between Morocco and Algeria. He did this not only because of Eberhardt's familiarity with the desert, but also because of her friendship with Lalla Zainab.

The shaikha of the al-Hamil zawiya was in turn "close to the sheikh of Kenadsa," who was the head of the strategically placed Ziyaniyya sufi center just within Moroccan territory. Lyautey was at this time courting the head shaikh of Kenadsa as part of his plan for penetrating the sharifian state; see Kobak, *Isabelle,* 221.

52. Isabelle and her mother rented a house in Bône in 1897, which was located near a Rahmaniyya zawiya. Gordon, *A Woman,* 77; Mackworth, *Destiny,* 155–56.

53. Eberhardt, *Lettres,* 189.

54. Ibid.

55. Ibid.

56. Mackworth, *Destiny,* 158.

57. Eberhardt, *Lettres,* 189.

58. Ibid., 203.

59. Kobak, *Isabelle,* 191.

60. Isabelle Eberhardt, *Mes journaliers,* preface by René-Louis Doyon (Paris: La Connaissance, 1923).

61. Gordon, *A Woman,* 77.

62. This information was kindly provided by Kinza Schuyler, who now has the "portrait" of Lalla Zainab painted by Kate Delas.

63. Eberhardt, *Lettres,* 189.

64. Gabriele Annan, "Roughing It," *New York Review of Books* 35 (22 Dec. 1988): 3.

65. Amal Rassam, "Women and Domestic Power in Morocco," *International Journal of Middle East Studies* 12 (1980): 119–37.

15

The Making and Breaking of

Marital Bonds in Modern Egypt

BETH BARON

Debate rocked elite circles in Egypt in 1904 when Safiyya 'Abd al-Khaliq al-Sadat, a notable's daughter, married Shaikh 'Ali Yusuf, editor of the nationalist paper *al-Mu'ayyad*, against her father's wishes. Having initially agreed to the betrothal of his daughter to Yusuf, al-Sadat then postponed the wedding. After four years of waiting, Safiyya consented to marry Yusuf at the home of a relative, for under Islamic law she was of age and able to contract a marriage herself. When al-Sadat learned of the event, however, he took the case to the *shari'a* (Islamic law) court, petitioning for an annulment. He argued that according to Hanafi law (the school officially recognized by the Ottoman government), there was a lack of *kafa'a* (suitability) in this match. Although the Hanafi school is liberal in allowing a mature woman freedom to choose her husband, it is strict in evaluating suitability, stipulating that the man must be equal to the woman or her family in wealth, occupation, lineage, piety, and other attributes; as such, Hanafi law gives the guardian the right to challenge a match. Al-Sadat won the court case after widely publicized and highly controversial proceedings. In the end, however, the parties were reconciled, al-Sadat accepted Yusuf as a son-in-law, and Safiyya returned to the husband of her choice.[1]

This story illuminates certain aspects of turn-of-the-century Egyptian society. It shows, for example, shifting class boundaries. Born in relative poverty in an Upper Egyptian village, Yusuf had become a successful journalist in Cairo, amassing considerable wealth. Yet journalism was not exactly an esteemed profession, particularly to such notables as al-Sadat, who traced his lineage to the Prophet Muhammad. Yusuf's first wife had shared his "humbler" origins. Through this second marriage he hoped to raise his social status and gain greater respectability.

Yet this is not just a story about 'Ali Yusuf and class; it is also a story about Safiyya al-Sadat and marriage. She consented to marry against her father's will, corresponded with Yusuf to arrange the marriage, and refused to return to her father's house during the trial, insisting on staying with a third party instead. In attempting to marry the man of her choice, Safiyya demonstrated remarkable tenacity. This story suggests that a new notion of marriage—a union of choice based on mutual consent and affection—had surfaced in turn-of-the-century Egypt.

In looking at Western family history, Lawrence Stone has argued that the issue of "the timing and nature of family change from the traditional to the modern" is of crucial importance. He characterized this transition by (1) the weakening of the bonds of kinship; (2) a greater emotional bonding between spouses, as marriage becomes "a matter of free choice based on personal affection and sexual attraction rather than the result of a mercenary arrangement made between the parents," with a concomitant increase in the demand for divorce as an escape from unsatisfying relationships; and (3) a change in attitudes toward children.[2] This chapter focuses on the second set of factors (marriage) in Egypt. Robert Springborg has warned against dichotomizing arranged and free-choice marriages for Egypt. He suggests that "marriages should be seen on a continuum, ranging from those entirely arranged by the parents and family elders," in which the partners have no say and have not met, to those "that are totally the product of the partners' instigation." The concept of continuum proves useful, for the arranged marriage of today (in which a couple that has been introduced meets frequently before marriage) is not the arranged marriage of earlier generations.[3] The goal here is to trace movement along this continuum.

For most Egyptians, marriage is contracted according to Islamic law. A normative Islamic marriage pattern emerged in the early centuries of Islam that permitted men up to four wives and unlimited concubines and made divorce easy for men but quite difficult for women.[4] This legal structure, combined with the wider social structure, discouraged strong marital bonds, putting the patriarch rather than the couple at the center of the family. Yet within the parameters established by law, in different times and places, and among various strata, marital relations have developed in diverse ways.[5] Here the specific concern is to trace the marriage patterns of middle- and upper-class urban Egyptians in the nineteenth and twentieth centuries.

Edward Lane gave a rich description of practices in the 1830s in *An Account of the Manners and Customs of Modern Egyptians*. In looking at various strata in towns and cities, Lane found arranged marriages, based on a brideprice, of couples who did not meet until the wedding ceremony. Some brides were as young as twelve or thirteen and few older than sixteen. Incidences of polygyny were rare, perhaps one in twenty, and according to Lane occurred more often among the "lower orders" than the upper ones. Middle- and upper-class men, however, frequently had concubines in addition to wives. Lane found rampant male-initiated divorce and maintained that "there are certainly not many persons in Cairo who have not divorced one wife, if they have been long married."[6]

More than a century later urban marriage patterns in Egypt had changed significantly. Leila el Hamamsy wrote in the 1950s that "the trends are towards a higher age of marriage among educated women. Especially for those who want to attend the university, marriage may have to wait until they reach the twenties. . . . Many of them would like to choose their own husbands . . . [and] want to marry men closer to their own age."[7] In the 1980s Andrea Rugh observed that rational and romantic approaches to marriage were still frequently at odds among the urban lower classes.[8] But the ideal of companionate marriage had spread among the urban middle and upper classes. Though marriages might still be arranged in these strata by family or friends, the couple usually met before marriage as young people increasingly looked for love matches.

When did companionate marriage emerge in Egypt? Sources from the 1870s on show reformers criticizing marital and divorce practices and promoting a new vision of conjugal relations, which paved the way for new legislation in the 1920s. During this period urban middle-class and upper-class Egyptians proved increasingly receptive to the idea of marriage based on mutual affection. This was primarily a consequence of internal changes in Egyptian society rather than a product of European example.

LOVE AND MARRIAGE

Nineteenth-century Egyptians were heirs to medieval Arabic poetry and prose rife with stories of romance. One recurrent theme was that of chaste love: In "Majnun and Laila," for example, conditions conspired to prevent the couple from consummating their love through marriage.[9] In any case, many medieval writers held that union spoiled love, maintaining that it thrived better before or outside of marriage. These writers developed a "copious vocabulary" for love, and tended to use 'ishq, hawa', and hubb interchangeably, though the first two terms sometimes suggested lust and usually referred to greater intensities of love.[10] Modern writers preferred the more moderate word hubb, emphasizing emotional bonds and deemphasizing physical passion in their attempts to couple love and marriage.

Love and marriage were the themes of many plays by the Egyptian writer Ya'qub Sanu', who staged some of his dramas in Cairo in the early

1870s and is credited with the founding of modern Arabic theater. His play *Bursat Misr* (The stock market of Egypt) relates the story of a banker who promises his sixteen-year-old daughter Labiba to a man she does not love, disregarding her love for a less wealthy man. In the play *al-'Alil* (The sick man), a father pledges his young daughter Hanim to the man who heals him, unaware that she has been exchanging love letters with a young man named Mitri. In yet another play, *al-Sadaqa* (Friendship), the orphan Warda vows to marry her cousin Na'um, but when Na'um's letters stop coming from England where he is studying, her aunt tries to persuade her to marry another suitor. Dealing with the lives of middle- and upper-middle-class Egyptians, these plays end happily as love triumphs over all obstacles, especially family opposition. Audiences of diverse backgrounds responded enthusiastically to these plays, indicating support for the idea of love as the basis of marriage.[11]

Turn-of-the-century writers echoed this idea. Sa'diyya Sa'd al-Din, an Egyptian Muslim woman writing under the pseudonym Shajarat al-Durr, stressed the companionate as well as the romantic dimensions of love. Noting that a wife is the partner of a man in his life, she implied that marriage should be monogamous, emotionally fulfilling, and long lasting. A few years later the Syrian immigrant writer Niqula Haddad linked love and marriage in a book by that title, *al-Hubb wa'l-zawaj* (Love and marriage).[12] During this period there was an outpouring of romantic literature in Egypt, including translations of European works and original Arabic short stories and narratives. One of the earliest Egyptian novels, *Zainab*, written by Muhammad Husain Haikal and published in 1914, deals with love. It focuses on the peasant woman Zainab, who loves a poor peasant named Ibrahim but is forced to marry someone wealthier. When Ibrahim is sent away, she succumbs in despair to sickness and death. Meanwhile, the landowner's son Hamid searches for love among peasant and city women, yet fails to find it. According to Charles Smith, the central issue of *Zainab* is "that of love, *hubb*, and the impossibility of its fulfillment in Egypt." Haikal argued that true love, as opposed to physical passion (*hawa'*), would not be realized until women were educated and transformed from emotional to more rational beings.[13]

The idea that marriage should be based on love seemed to be spreading, at least among the urban middle and upper classes. Malak Hifni Nasif, a female essayist who wrote under the name Bahithat al-Badiya, claimed that women were no longer satisfied only with clothes and food like "one of the servants of the house," but wanted "marital happiness more than previously," for they had learned that there is no reason to live together "if love is not the basis of a couple's relations."[14] Male and female writers of various backgrounds pushed companionate marriage as an alternative to arranged marriages based solely on economic calculations.

THE CONTRACT

In Islamic law marriage is a contract. The groom is responsible for the *mahr* (bridewealth), paid directly to the bride, with some portion deferred in case of divorce or death.[15] Once married, the husband is required to provide adequate maintenance (food, clothing, and housing) for his wife and their children. In return, the woman promises obedience. Marriage was arranged through negotiations between families, who bargained over the bridewealth and other details. Through advantageous alliances families sought to improve their economic position, cement political ties, or enhance their social prestige. In short, the marriage system operated according to market principles, to the detriment of some women. "If she is poor, he does not want her, and if she is rich, he wants her money," wrote Malak Hifni Nasif.[16]

Since the financial underpinnings of marriage were clear, changes in the economy invariably had an impact on marital agreements in particular and on marriage patterns in general. For the growing middle class, Egypt's entry into the world market resulted in greater preoccupation with capital and consumption as the country became a market for European manufactured goods. A few writers in the early 1900s bemoaned this situation, where money had become the "all and all" and marriages based on "true lasting love" were rare.[17] Greater financial risks and gains raised expectations for the mahr. Some men, particularly those who worked for the government, claimed that their salaries were not high enough to enable them to save money. Hence they appeared to be "fleeing from marriage."[18]

Financial problems plagued the marital agreements of non-Muslims as well as Muslims. Among Egyptian Copts and Jews the woman's family was responsible for the dowry, sometimes providing the groom with enough capital to start a business. Yet in turn-of-the-century Egypt fathers seemed "unable to raise what the groom demands," preventing or postponing some marriages.[19] Expectations for the bridewealth and the dowry were probably rising in a period of unprecedented speculation and prosperity at the end of the nineteenth and beginning of the twentieth century. Then the 1907 economic crisis sent shock waves through the marriage market, adversely affecting marital plans. Writers, especially those of the newly emerging middle class, criticized the emphasis placed on the financial considerations of marriage. They set out to reform the business of arranging marriages, urging a shift in focus from the economic to the emotional compatibility of a couple, which meant allowing couples to meet before marriage.

PREMARITAL MIXING

In the early nineteenth century agents and agencies helped parents or parties to arrange marriages. In Cairo, for example, marriage bureaus located partners for clients through a network of representatives in public baths and slave markets. The marriage broker still appears in the twentieth century, for example, in Naguib Mahfouz's *Midaq Alley,* set in 1940s Cairo.[20] According to Islamic law an arranged marriage could not proceed until a girl had given her consent, though until a girl reached puberty (the age of majority, set at no less than nine and presumed by age fifteen), she did not have the right to voice approval or disapproval. This meant that a girl was given a description and a name. Lack of response was interpreted as acceptance, or a negative response was overruled and girls were forced to marry against their will. Social critics called for more informed choices, suggesting that the prospective bride and groom be allowed to meet after their engagement and before marriage.[21]

A couple became engaged when parents, guardians, or representatives had agreed to the mahr and read the opening verse of the Quran together. Still, unless they were related (in which case they probably knew one another), they could not meet, even in the company of others. Many held that Islamic law forbade premarital meetings. Others maintained that custom, not law, prohibited engaged men and women from meeting. The Islamic reformer Muhammad 'Abduh argued that all schools permitted it.[22] A few Muslims initiated premarital contacts in enterprising ways. One man placed an advertisement in a newspaper calling for a young Muslim woman to exchange letters with him, his only stipulation being that she not be over twenty. Seventeen women responded, indicating that young people were attempting to communicate with one another.[23]

Observers pointed to changing patterns among Copts, who had recently permitted couples to meet before marriage. The patriarch encouraged this mixing in an 1895 encyclical letter to his clergy, instructing them to ensure that mutual knowledge and consent existed before performing the marriage ceremony.[24] Copts were probably more open to supervised premarital mixing because they did not have the options of polygyny or easy male divorce. (Marriages could be dissolved upon conversion of a spouse, a tactic occasionally used, or annulled; but divorces were granted only on grounds of insanity or infertility.)

As Egypt was transformed from a family-centered society with little geographical or social mobility into a more mobile society with a growing bourgeoisie, love matches became more accepted, particularly among the urban middle and upper classes. Some men and women began to meet before marriage to determine affinity and romantic possibility, but not yet challenging parental prerogatives.[25]

RAISING THE AGE AT MARRIAGE

After the marriage contract was finalized (the offer to marry was accepted in front of two male witnesses), the event was usually publicized by a wedding procession and party. Among the upper strata this celebration increasingly incorporated Western food, fashion, and drink, reflecting some degree of Westernization and changing values.[26] In whatever way they celebrated, women in turn-of-the-century Egypt seemed "pre-destined" for marriage, for "sooner or later, with very rare exceptions," they were "subject to this natural law," in the words of Alexandra Avi-erino, owner of the journal *Anis al-jalis*.[27] But was it sooner or later?

Lane reported in the 1830s that most women married at age twelve or thirteen and few later than sixteen. In late-nineteenth-century Egypt, early marriage was still common, particularly in the countryside. Some parents used early marriage to safeguard against illicit sexual activity; others to force a desired match. By the early 1900s these unions were viewed by many as dangerous and were blamed for a range of psychological and physiological problems. Malak Hifni Nasif observed that many girls who married at a young age developed "diseases of the nerves (hysteria)." Doctors also documented the medical consequences of early marriage, showing difficult and fatal deliveries.[28]

As a result of their growing awareness of the harm of early marriages, reformers tried to prevent them, appealing to the different religious authorities in Egypt. The Coptic patriarch supported this drive and refused to issue a marital license before a girl reached the age of sixteen and a boy twenty.[29] Yet Muslim authorities could find no basis in Islamic law to justify the establishment of minimum age limits. (The Prophet Muhammad had married 'A'isha when she was about six and consummated the marriage a few years later.)[30] Legislators and administrators tried different tactics. A Muslim deputy introduced a bill into the legislative assembly in 1914 that attempted to fix the marriage age at sixteen, but it was defeated. A few years later administrators amended the penal code to treat consummation of marriage with a child under twelve as rape, though the marriage itself was considered valid.[31] Then, in 1923, the Egyptian Code of Organization and Procedure for Shari'a Courts required that all marriages be registered in order to make legal claims and directed the courts not to hear claims of marriage if the bride was under sixteen and the groom under eighteen at the time of the contract. Furthermore, officials would not conclude or register a marriage contract between couples who had not reached these ages. Although such regulations did not void child marriage per se, they did discourage it.[32]

The legal attempt to raise the age at marriage mirrored a trend already under way. Qasim Amin, the author of several books on women and society, noted in 1900 that the average age at marriage was generally between twenty and thirty, whereas in the past it had been at maturity or before.[33] Statistics confirm this impression. The 1907 and 1917 censuses show that most girls married between the ages of twenty and twenty-nine, and the number of girls who married before this—the overwhelming majority of whom were fifteen to nineteen—was less than 10 percent of the female population.[34] Many young men, particularly professionals of the new middle class, postponed marriage until they had earned degrees, found employment, and saved money, and many now wanted educated wives. Young women entered the new state and private schools in growing numbers, putting off marriage until they finished school.[35] Influenced by a combination of medical, economic, and educational considerations, women and men in the early 1900s were marrying at later ages.

Reformers also condemned the related practice of marrying young women to older men. Though the censuses give little indication of how often this occurred, the much higher proportion of widowed or divorced women over fifty (60 percent in 1907) to widowed or divorced men (10 percent) suggests that older men who remarried chose younger wives.[36] Many Egyptians maintained that a husband should be ten to twenty years older than his wife, but extreme gaps seemed improper.

The practice of marrying young girls to older men occurred among rural inhabitants as well as among urban elites. Al-'Afaf carried the story of the forced marriage of a twenty-year-old educated Cairene woman, former secretary of a women's organization. "Without any shame" her father and uncle decided "to sell her like a commodity" to a wealthy man of eighty. She became distressed and "cut off her hair in despair"; after the marriage she attempted suicide by throwing herself in the path of a train. The editor of al-'Afaf used this story to illustrate the injustice of marrying a young girl or woman to an older man, or any man, against her will.[37]

The ideal of companionate marriage based on mutual affection and physical attraction implied marriage between adults relatively close in age who sought a consensual and monogamous union. A clear trend toward later marriage among the elites had begun, as had efforts to bridge the age gap and to ensure consent. To what extent had multiple partners, one of the main obstacles to the new marital ideal, been eliminated?

TOWARD MONOGAMY

According to Islamic law a Muslim man could take up to four wives, provided that he treated them equally (a stipulation that was morally but not legally binding). At the same time, he could enjoy innumerable concubines, female slaves who served as sexual partners. In the second half of the nineteenth century female slaves were still purchased in Egypt, including the highly prized Circassians. Free women decried the "army of Circassians" that had conquered Egypt, "emerging victorious with the best of our men."[38] In 1877 the Anglo-Egyptian Convention outlawed the slave trade, and in the following decades female slavery disappeared. Yet concubinage, in any case, may have been losing ground as the ideal of companionate marriage began to spread in some circles. Here Ottoman attitudes present certain parallels. In looking at the literature of Ottoman male reformists after 1860, Deniz Kandiyoti found "a rejection of the slave girl . . . and a hankering for more companionate and romantic relationships" as a persistent theme.[39]

Did wives replace concubines as partners, causing an upsurge in polygyny? The 1907 census reported 6 percent more married women than men, which was taken to be a rough estimate of the rate of polygyny. This corresponds to Lane's estimate in the 1830s of one marriage in twenty as polygamous.[40] Though it is difficult to know how much this figure had fluctuated in the interim, the elimination of concubinage does not seem to have caused an increase in the rate of polygyny. Rather, the demise of slavery strengthened the institution of marriage and served as a necessary first step toward the ideal of monogamy.

Although only a small minority of Egyptian marriages were polygynous, the threat hovered over all women married to Muslim men, for they could take additional wives at any time for any reason. Some men became impatient when their wives did not conceive or produce sons in particular. Other men planned second marriages to younger women. One woman told a reporter from al-'Afaf that she had lived with and loved her husband for many years, but that he had married a poor girl whom she took in as a servant. The first wife then asked for a divorce.[41] Second wives were usually seen as intruders and cannot have enjoyed the competition for the resources and attention of a shared husband.

Some women found divorce preferable to polygyny. "The first is pain and freedom, and the second is pain and fettering," wrote Malak Hifni Nasif.[42] Yet a divorce under such circumstances was contingent on a husband's approval, which was not always given. As a result, many women felt trapped. A few killed husbands who took second wives; some killed themselves. In one report from Port Said, a soldier's wife set herself on fire, "saying in her last breath that she committed suicide because she was unable to continue near her co-wife."[43]

Reformers used the press and the podium to mobilize public opinion against polygyny. Although attitudes began to change among certain strata, legislation on this issue lagged as many Muslims continued to hold as basic the right to four wives. A committee appointed in 1926 to recommend reforms in the laws of marriage and divorce proposed a series of articles limiting polygyny. But these articles were excluded from the 1929 reform law at the personal decision of King Fuad, in part because polygyny was practiced mostly by peasants and therefore justified on the grounds of its impact on the birthrate and the economy.[44] In any case, the flip side to polygyny was easy divorce, making serial wives a viable alternative to concurrent ones.

DISSOLVING A MARRIAGE

As expectations for emotional fulfillment in marriage increased in Christian countries, so, too, did demands for ending dissatisfactory relationships. This meant expanding grounds for divorce, and in the process deconsecrating marriage.[45] By contrast, divorce was already legal under Islamic law, for marriage was a contract that could be voided. According to Hanafi law, a man could divorce his wife at will for whatever reason without appearing in court. A woman, however, had few options for dissolving a union. She could apply for judicial annulment on the grounds of her husband's impotence, and upon reaching puberty a child bride could repudiate a marriage not contracted by her father or grandfather.[46] Deserted, abused, and simply unhappy wives had little recourse to divorce if their husbands would not consent. The challenge in Egypt in the early twentieth century became one of striking a balance: expanding women's grounds for divorce while limiting men's abuse of it.

Social critics first set out to document the results of the powerlessness of women to leave their husbands. In one case reported in the press, a woman from Bani Suwaif who could not get a divorce from her husband killed him with the help of her cousin (who in the course of the crime confessed his love for her). The two were caught after the body was discovered; she was sentenced to twelve years in prison and he to death. In another case, a father of five spent his wife's savings on prostitutes and gambling, and when she attempted to leave threw her from the window of their third-story apartment. Other abused wives took their own lives. One Cairene woman who had become "debilitated by her husband's treatment . . . and had given up all hope of deliverance from him" swallowed a fatal dose of carbolic acid.[47]

Stories such as these generated debate about the need to expand women's grounds for divorce. One woman told a reporter that she believed "a young woman should be granted freedom in separating from a husband" but was clearly looking for ways to reconcile Islamic law with contemporary women's expectations. Some Egyptians argued that Islamic law already protected women, by giving them the right to stipulate grounds for divorce in conditional clauses in their marriage contracts, providing that their husbands agreed. Yet not many women knew that they had this right or thought to use it on the eve of marriage, and in any case some jurists considered these clauses invalid and nonbinding.[48]

Calls to grant women wider grounds for divorce, and to guarantee that their separation did not hinge on a husband's approval, prior or otherwise, culminated in new legislation. A 1920 law that was supplemented in 1929 recognized four new conditions for judicial relief: if the husband had a chronic or incurable disease, failed to provide maintenance, deserted his wife, or maltreated her, she could apply to a court for dissolution of the marriage.[49] Part of a general reform of marriage and divorce law that drew on the different Islamic law schools and minority opinions within them, these articles sought to terminate unions that did not conform to the emerging ideal of companionate marriage. Yet efforts to limit men's arbitrary ability to divorce their wives at will outside the court proved less successful.

ATTEMPTS TO RESTRICT REPUDIATION

Unilateral divorce empowered men, for it could be used as a threat to modify a wife's behavior or as a punishment to teach her a lesson. In most cases it was reversible: a husband could take back his wife during the waiting period (a few months set aside to see if she was pregnant) without negotiating a new contract. Even after one or two divorces, the couple could remarry. However, a third divorce or triple *talaq* (the oath of divorce pronounced three times in a row) was final and irreversible. Hanafi law was strict in this regard, considering a formula of divorce valid, whether pronounced under duress or intoxification, as a threat or an oath, in anger or in jest.[50]

This created hardships for women who wanted to return to their former husbands. One twenty-five-year-old woman in this predicament asked a religious scholar for advice. She had lived with and loved her husband, by whom she had two children, until he had pronounced a triple talaq. Now he wanted her back, but she did not know what to do.[51] According to the law, whether or not her husband had intended to divorce her, he had pronounced the formula and therefore the divorce stood. Only if she contracted a marriage with another man, consummated it, and he then divorced her could she remarry her first husband.

Yet an interim marriage contracted for this purpose was illegal, though not unknown. Reformers recognized that some legal change was needed in this area.

Most wives were not taken back, and they left with their possessions and the deferred portion of the bridewealth. A divorced wife did not receive any maintenance after the waiting period, though if she had small children in her care she was supposed to receive money for them. Many women returned to their families, but this was not always possible.[52] The plight of divorced women, who often had no legitimate way to support themselves, led reformers to call for more work opportunities for women.

Divorce seemed widespread to early-twentieth-century observers. Men repudiated women for "weak reasons or none at all."[53] Yet to measure the frequency of divorce during this period is difficult. Censuses listed divorced women as widows, and shari'a court records were not necessarily accurate or comprehensive. In 1903, for example, the courts of Egypt recorded 176,474 marriages and 52,992 divorces—more than two divorces for every seven marriages, or a divorce rate of 30 percent. These figures, however, did not necessarily reflect remarriages for which no new certificate of marriage was needed and other marriages and divorces escaped the notice of the courts.[54]

Whatever the figures, reformers found the number of divorces excessive and sought to discourage unjust and unnecessary divorce. They condemned men for repudiating older wives and wives who had not produced male children. They also pointed out that the threat of divorce—not only the act itself—was harmful. "Shajarat al-Durr" argued that divorce caused a "lack of trust in a Muslim woman's heart" and forced her "to use deceit, lies, and cheating" to please her husband. Yet she did not call for elimination of divorce altogether, the absence of which "would also have been damaging when the couple is unable to harmonize in life and love."[55]

The 1929 Law of Reforms in Marriage and Divorce dealt with certain aspects of male divorce. It stipulated that divorces pronounced under compulsion or while intoxicated (but not those made in jest) were invalid; so, too, were oaths and utterances not intended to lead to divorce; finally, almost all pronouncements of divorce were considered single and revocable.[56] The new law cleared up certain difficulties, but did not greatly restrict unilateral male divorce. In the meantime, reformers tried to modify behavior by publicizing the problems caused by easy divorce.

In the Muslim Middle East, marriage has always been a contract that could be voided. The debate surrounding divorce in early-twentieth-century Egypt was an attempt to infuse that contract with greater meaning. Men had to be more committed to marriage and prevented from repudiating wives at will. Women had to have more freedom to leave unsupporting, diseased, or abusive husbands. It proved easier to expand women's grounds for judicial divorce than to limit male prerogatives. Yet demands for female-initiated divorce and reforms in this area should not be taken as a sign of the decline of marriage or of the family. Rather they should be seen as part of the effort to strengthen the couple and place it at the center of the family, as well as further proof of the emerging ideal of companionate marriage.

The ideal of companionate marriage began to spread in Egypt in the early twentieth century among the urban middle and upper classes. Essayists, dramatists, and novelists all argued for the need to make love a cornerstone of marriage. At the same time young people asked to meet before marriage to determine compatibility. For a variety of reasons men and women married later, a delay that created the possibility for greater intellectual and emotional affinity, raised expectations for the relationship, and probably decreased fertility. Though polygyny remained a threat to many and a reality for a few, concubinage had been eliminated. Female-initiated divorce became accessible in certain situations, whereas male repudiation was slightly curtailed. Taken together the evidence suggests that the marital ideal was in flux, moving along a continuum from arranged marriages toward ones of greater choice.

The question of agency remains. What propelled the movement? Were the urban middle and upper classes drawn toward companionate marriage as a Western idea, or were other factors at work? Egyptian writers rarely pointed to Western marital relations as a model, for many felt that Western family ties were eroding and should definitely not be emulated.[57] Instead, indigenous economic developments, social changes, ideological debates, and legal reforms all combined to reshape conjugal relations. Other aspects of family life were probably undergoing parallel transformations. In this regard it would be helpful to study changes in the bonds of kinship and in attitudes toward children during the same period.[58] A shift from patriarchal to conjugal family may have begun, marking the origins of a modern family type in Egypt.

One final question: What happened to Shaikh 'Ali Yusuf and Safiyya al-Sadat, the couple who had married against her father's wishes and had fought him in court to stay together? Though they remained married until Yusuf's death in 1914, theirs was not in the end a harmonious union.[59] Selecting one's partner did not guarantee marital success, nor did it necessarily promise more happiness than an arranged marriage. Still, unions of love and choice were increasingly favored by young people.

Notes

1. Esther Moyal, "al-Sayyid 'Abd al-Khaliq al-Sadat wa karimatuhu," *al-'A'ila* 3, no. 11 (1 Aug. 1904): 83–84; Ahmad Baha' al-Din, *Ayyam laha ta'rikh* (Cairo: Kitab Ruz al-Yusuf, 1954), 1:47–61; Abbas Kelidar, "Shaykh 'Ali Yusuf: Egyptian Journalist and Islamic Nationalist," in *Intellectual Life in the Arab East, 1890–1939*, ed. Marwan R. Buheiry (Beirut: American University of Beirut Press, 1981), 18.

2. Lawrence Stone, "Family History in the 1980s: Past Achievements and Future Trends," in *The New History: The 1980s and Beyond*, ed. Theodore K. Rabb and Robert I. Rotberg (Princeton: Princeton University Press, 1982), 72–73, 83. Other scholars reject the "traditional to modern" typology, preferring the "patriarchal to nuclear" paradigm. See Linda Schatkowski Schilcher, "The Lore and Reality of Middle Eastern Patriarchy," *Die Welt des Islams* 28 (1988): 496–512. Schilcher suggests that patriarchy can be "a family pattern linked to a particular family's own development cycle" and locates the advent of this pattern in early modern times.

3. Robert Springborg, *Family, Power, and Politics in Egypt: Sayed Bey Marei —His Clan, Clients, and Cohorts* (Philadelphia: University of Pennsylvania Press, 1982), 29–30.

4. See Leila Ahmed, "Women and the Advent of Islam," *Signs* 11 (1986): 665–91.

5. See, for example, Judith E. Tucker, "Marriage and Family in Nablus, 1720–1856: Toward a History of Arab Marriage," *Journal of Family History* 13, no. 2 (1988): 165–79. Tucker shows the variety of marriage patterns among women of different classes in the Palestinian town of Nablus.

6. Edward William Lane, *An Account of the Manners and Customs of the Modern Egyptians* (London: Ward, Lock, 1890), 141–74.

7. L. S. el Hamamsy, "The Changing Role of the Egyptian Woman," in *Readings in Arab Middle Eastern Societies and Cultures*, ed. Abdulla M. Lutfiyya and Charles W. Churchill (Paris: Mouton, 1970), 597–98.

8. Andrea B. Rugh, *Family in Contemporary Egypt* (Syracuse: Syracuse University Press, 1984), 107–47; see also Edwin Terry Prothro and Lutfy Najib Diab, *Changing Family Patterns in the Arab East* (Beirut: American University of Beirut Press, 1974).

9. J. C. Burgel, "Love, Lust, and Longing: Eroticism in Early Islam as Reflected in Literary Sources," in *Society and the Sexes in Medieval Islam*, ed. Afaf Lutfi al-Sayyid-Marsot (Malibu, Calif.: Undena, 1979), 91–93.

10. Lois Anita Giffen, *Theory of Profane Love among the Arabs: The Development of the Genre* (New York: New York University Press, 1971), 83–96, 129.

11. Matti Moosa, "Ya'qub Sanu' and the Rise of Arab Drama in Egypt," *International Journal of Middle East Studies* 5 (1974): 422–33; Shmuel Moreh, "Ya'qub Sanu': His Religious Identity and Work in the Theater and Journalism, according to the Family Archive," in *The Jews of Egypt: A Mediterranean Society in Modern Times*, ed. Shimon Shamir (Boulder, Colo.: Westview, 1987), 111–29.

12. Shajarat al-Durr, "al-Talaq wa ta'addud al-zaujat," *Anis al-jalis* 1, no. 7 (1898): 206. Shajar al-Durr was the name of a medieval woman ruler in Egypt,

which in contemporary popular writing is usually rendered Shajarat. Niqula Haddad, *al-Hubb wa'l-zawaj* (Cairo: al-Matba'a al-'Umumiyya, 1901).

13. Charles D. Smith, "Love, Passion and Class in the Fiction of Muhammad Husayn Haykal," *Journal of the American Oriental Society* 99, no. 2 (1979): 251; Muhammad Husain Haikal, *Zainab* (Cairo: Maktabat al-Nahda al-Misriyya, 1914).

14. Malak Hifni Nasif [Bahithat al-Badiya], *al-Nisa'iyyat* (Cairo: Matba'at al-Jarida, 1910), 3–4.

15. The term *bridewealth* seems more appropriate than *brideprice*, for the money went to the bride and not to her family, at least in theory. See Jack Goody, "Bridewealth and Dowry in Africa and Eurasia," in *Bridewealth and Dowry,* ed. Jack Goody and S. J. Tambiah (Cambridge: Cambridge University Press, 1973), 1–58.

16. Nasif, *al-Nisa'iyyat,* 57.

17. Rosa Antun, "al-Zawaj al-sa'id," *al-Sayyidat wa'l-banat* 2, no. 11 (1906): 307.

18. "Al-Zawaj," *Anis al-jalis* 1, no. 12 (1898): 383–88; "Kaifa natazawwaj wa kaifa na'ish," *Anis al-jalis* 2, no. 9 (1899): 343–47.

19. Regina 'Awwad, "al-Zawaj," *al-Sa'ada* 1, no. 3 (1902): 51; see Mark Glazer, "The Dowry as Capital Accumulation among the Sephardic Jews of Istanbul, Turkey," *International Journal of Middle East Studies* 10 (1979): 373–80.

20. Nadia Tomiche, "Egyptian Women in the First Half of the Nineteenth Century," in *The Beginnings of Modernization in the Middle East,* ed. William R. Polk and Richard L. Chambers (Chicago: University of Chicago Press, 1968), 179; Naguib Mahfouz, *Zuqaq al-midaqq* (Cairo: Maktabat Misr, n.d.); *Midaq Alley* (Washington, D.C.: Three Continents Press, 1981).

21. See, for example, "al-Mar'a al-muslima fi Misr," *Anis al-jalis* 5, no. 2 (1902): 980–81.

22. Ibid.; see Muhammad 'Abduh, *al-A'mal al-kamila li'l-Imam Muhammad 'Abduh,* ed. Muhammad 'Imara (Beirut: al-Mu'assasa al-'Arabiyya li'l-Dirasat wa'l-Nashr, 1972) 2:68–77.

23. "Al-Mar'a al-misriyya," *Anis al-jalis* 6, no. 9 (1903): 1546–54.

24. E. L. Butcher, *Things Seen In Egypt* (London: Seeley, 1910), 50–51.

25. "Al-Mar'a al-wataniyya," *al-Sufur* 3, no. 140 (24 Jan. 1918): 2–3.

26. Fatima Rashid, "al-Afrah," *Tarqiyat al-mar'a* 1, no. 7 (1908): 98–101; Malak Hifni Nasif, "al-A'ras," *Anis al-jalis* 7, no. 7 (1904): 1872–75.

27. Alexandra Avierino, "L'enseignement de la jeune fille," *Le Lotus* 2, no. 1 (1902): 20.

28. Lane, *Manners and Customs,* 143; Nasif, *al-Nisa'iyyat,* 32; A. C. McBarnet, "The New Penal Code: Offenses against Morality and the Marriage Tie and Children," *L'Egypte contemporaine* 10, no. 46 (1919): 383.

29. Butcher, *Things Seen in Egypt,* 50–51.

30. Nabia Abbott, *Aishah: The Beloved of Mohammed* (Chicago: University of Chicago Press, 1942), 6–7.

31. Anna Y. Thompson, "The Woman Question in Egypt," *Moslem World* 4, no. 3 (1914): 266; McBarnet, "New Penal Code," 382–86.

32. J. N. D. Anderson, "Recent Developments in Shari'a Law III," *Muslim World* 41, no. 2 (1951): 113–15; John L. Esposito, *Women in Muslim Family Law* (Syracuse: Syracuse University Press, 1982), 52.

33. Qasim Amin, *al-Mar'a al-jadida* (Cairo: Matba'at al-Sha'b, 1900), 98.

34. Ministry of Finance, *The Census of Egypt, 1907* (Cairo: National Printing Department, 1909), 92; Ministry of Finance, *The Census of Egypt, 1917*, vol. 2 (Cairo: Government Press, 1921); McBarnet, "New Penal Code," 383.

35. Nabawiyya Musa, *al-Mar'a wa'l-'amal* (Alexandria: al-Matba'a al-Wataniyya, 1920), 42–43; Elizabeth Cooper, *The Women of Egypt* (New York: F. A. Stokes, 1914), 169. See Alexandra Avierino, "Matlab jadid," *Anis al-jalis* 2, no. 5 (1899): 173, for one group of bachelors who vowed to marry only educated women.

36. *Census of Egypt, 1907*, 92.

37. Sulaiman al-Salimi, "Rufaqa' bi'l-qawarir," *al-'Afaf* 1, no. 36 (17 Oct. 1911): 7. Al-Tayyib Salih describes the violent outcome of one such marriage in rural Sudan in his novel *Mausim al-hijra ila al-shamal* (Cairo: Dar al-Hilal, 1969), published in English as Tayeb Salih, *Season of Migration to the North*, trans. Denys Johnson-Davies (London: Heinemann, 1969).

38. Nasif, *al-Nisa'iyyat*, 14. For more on slavery and its demise, see Ehud Toledano, *The Ottoman Slave Trade and Its Suppression, 1840–1890* (Princeton: Princeton University Press, 1982), 179–84; and Judith E. Tucker, *Women in Nineteenth-Century Egypt* (Cambridge: Cambridge University Press, 1985), 191–93.

39. Deniz Kandiyoti, "Slave Girls, Temptresses, and Comrades: Images of Women in the Turkish Novel," *Feminist Issues* 8, no. 1 (1988): 40.

40. *Census of Egypt, 1907*, 91; Lane, *Manners and Customs*, 167.

41. Zakiyya al-Kafrawiyya, "Ma wara' al-khudur," *al-'Afaf* 1, no. 19 (17 Mar. 1911): 2.

42. Nasif, *al-Nisa'iyyat*, 29.

43. Sulaiman al-Salimi, "Qatilat zaujiha," *al-'Afaf* 1, no. 34 (4 Aug. 1911): 14–15; al-Salimi, "al-Maut wa la al-darra," *al-'Afaf* 2, no. 52 (9 Feb. 1914): 8.

44. Anderson, "Recent Developments III," 124–26. At the time, overpopulation had not yet become an issue of concern in Egypt.

45. See Roderick Phillip, *Putting Asunder: A History of Divorce in Western Society* (Cambridge: Cambridge University Press, 1989), and a review of that book by Lawrence Stone, "The Road to Polygamy," *New York Review of Books* (2 Mar. 1989): 12–15.

46. J. N. D. Anderson, "Recent Developments in Shari'a Law V," *Muslim World* 41, no. 4 (1951): 271; Esposito, *Muslim Family Law*, 17, 53.

47. Sulaiman al-Salimi, "La tuharrijuha," *al-'Afaf* 2, no. 64 (19 June 1914): 6; al-Laqita [the Orphan], "Qatil zaujatihi," *al-Jins al-latif* 12, no. 3 (1919): 99–104; al-Salimi, "Rufaqa' bi'l-qawarir," *al-'Afaf* 1, no. 35 (13 Oct. 1911): 7; al-Salimi, "Ittaqi Allah ya rajul," *al-'Afaf* 1, no. 29 (9 June 1911): 15.

48. Zakiyya al-Kafrawiyya, "Jam'iyya li-tahsin al-azya'," *al-'Afaf* 1, no. 26 (12 May 1911): 13–14.

49. Anderson, "Recent Developments V," 278–88; Esposito, *Muslim Family Law*, 53–54.

50. Anderson, "Recent Developments V," 271–77.

51. "Su'al wa-jawab," *al-'Afaf* 1, no. 17 (3 Mar. 1911): 1.

52. See, for example, al-Salimi, "al-Mar'a al-mankuba," *al-'Afaf* 1, no. 34 (4 Aug. 1911): 14.

53. Alexandra Avierino, "al-Zawaj wa'l-talaq," *Anis al-jalis* 7, no. 8 (1904): 1914.

54. "As in India, it was thought advisable not to show divorced persons separately from widowed" (*Census of Egypt, 1907,* 91). Great Britain, Public Record Office, Foreign Office 407/163, no. 4, Cromer to Lansdowne, Cairo, 26 Feb. 1904, "Annual Report of 1903." After 1897, documentation was needed to make claims concerning marriage and divorce, thereby increasing incentive to record changes in marital status.

55. Al-Durr, "al-Talaq," 203–6; see also Nasif, *al-Nisa'iyyat,* 60.

56. Anderson, "Recent Developments V," 271–87; Esposito, *Muslim Family Law,* 58–59.

57. See Beth Ann Baron, "The Rise of a New Literary Culture: The Women's Press of Egypt, 1892–1919" (Ph.D. diss., University of California, Los Angeles, 1988), chap. 9.

58. On parent-child relations in an earlier period, see Avner Giladi, "Concepts of Childhood and Attitudes towards Children in Medieval Islam," *Journal of Economic and Social History of the Orient* 32, no. 2 (1989): 121–52.

59. Kelidar, "Shaykh 'Ali Yusuf," 20.

16 Artists and Entrepreneurs:

Female Singers in Cairo during the 1920s

VIRGINIA DANIELSON

Female professional musicians, often singers, have been at the forefront of musical life in the Arab world historically. As in other societies, however, concepts about musical accomplishment, as well as music criticism and commentary, often written by men, have generally been constructed so as to exclude women from the category of truly skilled and "serious" musicians. Accounts of musical life have focused only infrequently on women. Unlike their male counterparts, female performers have rarely been identified by their full names. Too often they have been confused with dancers or prostitutes, especially by foreign observers.[1]

The development of commercial entertainment in Egypt during the early twentieth century offered new opportunities for women, which they readily accepted. In Cairo, a center for Arab musical life, female professional singers assumed roles in commercial recording, musical theater, music hall performances, and public concerts as these media developed in the late nineteenth and early twentieth centuries. Ali Jihad Racy noted the "expanding role of women in post–[World War I], Egyptian urban music" in commercial recording during the first decades of the twentieth century, and women's activities extended into all venues of commercial entertainment, even into management, generally the province of men.[2] The concurrent emergence of many specialized magazines and newspaper columns dealing with theater and music and of the memoir as a popular literary genre during the 1920s allowed female singers to be seen

Research for this chapter was conducted in Egypt during 1982–83 and 1984–86, when I collected data about the lives of more than fifty female singers working in Cairo between 1850 and 1930. I am grateful to the Fulbright-Hayes Doctoral Dissertation Abroad Fellowship program for its generous support.

more clearly as both artists and entrepreneurs. This chapter presents a view of the lives of some of these women, including the young Umm Kulthum, and their roles in the cultural life of the society and, to some extent, as public figures communicating with an ever-growing audience via the nascent mass media.

MUSICAL LIFE IN NINETEENTH-CENTURY EGYPT

Documentation for musical life in nineteenth-century Egypt is not readily available, but it is clear that musical entertainment accompanied special occasions such as saints' days, weddings, and holidays of all sorts throughout the country. The performers at these events were sometimes local people, frequently professional in the sense that they were recognized for unusual musical skill and compensated for their performances, sometimes very well, regardless of whether musical performance constituted their only occupation. Some were full-time entertainers.[3] Many traveled from the capital to the countryside or from town to town, by invitation, to perform at special events. Although ostensibly private, these occasions in fact usually involved whole communities, including those who could not themselves afford to hire musicians. Singers also performed in coffee houses under the patronage of the management or those patrons who could offer gifts.

Women performed in most of these contexts. They recited the Quran, usually for other women, and sang religious repertories professionally. Best known during the nineteenth century was al-Hajja al-Suwaisiyya, an Egyptian from Suez whose brother, husband, and son performed with her as accompanists. She appeared wearing a *malaya* (a long black wrap), head covering, and face veil. From her home region of Suez she moved to Port Said and eventually to Cairo, where she sang regularly at the coffee house called Monsieur Antoine near the 'Ataba in the center of the city.[4]

The female professional singers of Cairo during the nineteenth and early twentieth centuries were usually identified as *'awalim* (s. *'alima*). They maintained their own trade guild (*ta'ifa*) and performed under contract to individual patrons for specific occasions. Most of the 'awalim about whom information is available were born in Egypt, often to working-class families in Cairo. Although some were Christian and others Jewish, the majority were Muslim. Most of them married tradesmen from their family neighborhoods and continued to perform after marriage. In some cases other members of the women's families were also musicians or singers, including husbands and daughters. Al-Hajja Huda, for example, leader of the guild of 'awalim in the early twentieth century, was born in 1880 in the Muski area of Cairo. The daughter of a miller, she also married a miller to whom she bore three daughters and a son. All three daughters later became 'awalim.[5] Among the most fondly remembered of the 'awalim was Bamba Kashshar (d. 1917), the daughter of al-Shaikh Muhammad Kashshar of Hayy al-Sha'rani in Cairo. Three of her nieces—Fathiyya, Mufida, and Ratiba Ahmad—became famous professional singers during the 1920s.

The most accomplished singers were in great demand, held in high esteem, and able to profit handsomely from the money given them by audience members. The gifted few attracted the patronage of elite families, including the royal family, who supported a number of 'awalim, actually taking the women into the household. European visitors observed singers in these elite contexts and noted that excellent singers won great acclaim and were literally showered with money. In the homes to which Edward Lane was invited, "they sit in one of the apartments of the hareem, generally at a window looking into the court. The wooden lattice-work of the window, thought too close to allow them to be seen by persons without, is sufficiently open to let them be distinctly heard by the male guests sitting in the court or in one of the apartments which look into it."[6] Georg Ebers wrote, "Here, as in Europe, among these favoured mortals, the women hold their own against the men in number and estimation."[7] Unquestionably the most famous was Almaz, who attracted the patronage of Khedive Isma'il. A talented young woman born to a Lebanese family in Alexandria, Almaz performed professionally for private parties and was compared favorably with the best singers, male and female, of her day. She married her principal competitor, 'Abduh al-Hamuli, reputed to be the best male singer of his century.[8] Almaz and the other court singers led prosperous lives in opulent circumstances as long as their talents lasted. When they aged and their voices failed, they relied on marriages or work in the less rarified surroundings of the music hall to sustain themselves. Their careers were extraordinary compared with those of most other singers.

Public commercial entertainment establishments proliferated in urban areas during the nineteenth century. The development of the Azbakiyya Garden brought with it restaurants and open-air music halls. The area of Azbakiyya had long been a gathering place for entertainment; after Friday prayers in the early sixteenth century, animal tamers and public games could be seen there. By the nineteenth century, the center of the Prophet's birthday celebration was Azbakiyya. After the arrival of the French, "local Christians and Europeans . . . started taverns, restaurants, and cafes in the European style" in the area.[9] The Garden itself included cafes and "kiosks," where European and Egyptian music was performed, and eventually housed Sala Santi, one of Cairo's foremost music halls of the early twentieth century.

A theater district grew up in the area, which featured European productions, annual seasons at the Opera House (with "closed boxes for Moslem ladies"), and Arabic adaptations of European plays as well as original Arabic theater. Performances by local singers during the intermissions became standard, and many young singers began their careers in this manner.[10]

Commercial entertainment spread to Raud al-Faraj, located on the banks of the Nile northwest of the Azbakiyya area. During the first quarter of the twentieth century, such stars as Fatma Rushdi, Na'ima al-Masriyya, and Ratiba Ahmad began careers in Cairo or spent the waning years of their careers in the theaters and music halls of Raud al-Faraj.[11] Small theaters also appeared in the so-called popular quarters of Cairo. Muhammad 'Abd al-Wahhab began his career there, and Umm Kulthum, among many others, sang public concerts at the small theaters when she moved from her village to Cairo in the early 1920s.

Activities such as commercial recording accelerated after the end of World War I. The 1920s were a relatively prosperous time in Egypt during which commercial entertainment of all sorts was well supported. The professional guild of female singers who contracted for specific occasions largely gave way to singers (and actresses) who contracted by themselves or through theatrical agents with institutions such as theatrical companies, recording companies, and theater management for seasons or years at a time. By the beginning of World War I, few old-style 'awalim remained. Some of the older singers made the transition from one milieu to the other, and newcomers launched themselves immediately into the commercial enterprise.

FEMALE SINGERS IN EARLY TWENTIETH-CENTURY CAIRO

Tauhida and Na'ima al-Masriyya represented the older generation of singers in the 1920s. Tauhida, an immigrant of Syrian extraction, began her career as a singer and dancer working in the Azbakiyya area. She married an Egyptian Greek, who opened the club Alf Laila wa Laila especially for her, where she was the featured singer from 1897. After he died she continued to own and manage the business until her death in 1932. Tauhida made few, if any, commercial recordings, but as an accomplished singer and 'ud player, she retained a loyal, if relatively small, audience.[12]

Raised in a lower-middle-class neighborhood in Cairo, Na'ima al-Masriyya became a professional singer to support herself following a divorce. At first she sang with two neighborhood women for local weddings. As her reputation spread, she moved to music halls in the provincial cities of Egypt, then to Raud al-Faraj, and finally to the main theater district. By 1927 she had purchased her own casino, the Alhambra, which she managed herself, appearing as the star singer and planning the other entertainment.

Musical theater had become increasingly popular in Egypt and was probably the most popular type of theatrical production in the Arab world, for as was commonly said, more than plot or production, the audience came to see a singing star. Since the mid-1910s, following the successful performances of Munira al-Mahdiyya (c. 1895?–1965), musical theater had been an important venue for female singers. Born in the provincial town of Zaqaziq and educated at a convent school there, as a child Munira al-Mahdiyya sneaked out of her house at night to hear the popular singer al-Lawandiyya. Munira eventually left home to pursue a career in Cairo, and by 1913 she was singing nightly at the famous coffee house Nuzhat al-Nufus. She later sang at the Alhambra and the Eldorado and was one of very few women to make commercial recordings at that time. After the British authorities closed Nuzhat al-Nufus, Munira, with the help of director 'Aziz 'Id, joined a theatrical company. In about 1915 she became a member of the troupe headed by Salama Hijazi, who had established musical theater as a popular art in Egypt. With the onset of his final illness, she performed the male roles written originally for Hijazi to great acclaim and subsequently formed her own company, performing roles written especially for her. Her company frequently performed nationalistic songs that were summarily censored by British colonial authorities. These incidents increased Munira's popularity and led to the slogan "Hawa' al-hurriyya fi Masrah Munira al-Mahdiyya" (There is love of freedom in the theater of Munira al-Mahdiyya).[13]

Munira personally assumed management responsibilities for her troupe, negotiating with theater owners, composers, lyricists, and singers, planning schedules and meeting payrolls, as well as performing herself. She occasionally hired an artistic director to help with these tasks, but inevitably rejected his judgment in favor of her own and resumed decision making herself. She was a great entertainer, on stage and off. Her theater and home became gathering places for many notable politicians and journalists of the day. Sa'd Zaghlul and Husain Rushdi Pasha were among her admirers. A strong personality, she was a pioneer among women in commercial recording and musical theater.

Public concerts emerged as a new and attractive mode of entertainment. Fathiyya Ahmad (1898?–1975), a talented and successful singer in musical theater, left that stage in 1925 to devote herself to public concerts and private parties in order to exercise greater control over her repertory.

Fathiyya was the daughter of a Quran reciter and the niece of 'alima Bamba Kashshar. She began her theatrical career in about 1910, with the companies of Najib al-Rihani and Amin Sidqi. She enjoyed great success in musical theater and recorded extensively. A relatively quiet personality, Fathiyya Ahmad kept her personal life from the newspapers. She married a well-off landowner in the early 1920s and left professional life for several years beginning in 1929 to have children. When she returned in 1931, she appeared regularly as the featured star at a music hall owned by Badi'a Masabni, and she assumed the management of the hall when Badi'a toured.[14] A gentle and dignified woman and accomplished singer, she performed professionally until about 1950.

Badi'a's music hall, or *sala*, was a landmark in the entertainment business of Cairo.[15] Born in Syria in the 1890s, Badi'a worked as a singer and dancer in music halls in Syria, the Levant, and Egypt, supporting herself with the proceeds of her work and the assistance of a series of wealthy lovers. She moved to Cairo in 1921 and quickly became the star of Najib al-Rihani's theatrical troupe. She married al-Rihani in 1923, then left him and his troupe in 1926. Using her accumulated cash, she opened her own music hall, Sala Badi'a. It was an immediate and sustained success and drew rave reviews until she retired from the business in the 1940s.

Sala Badi'a featured a varied program designed around a single female singing star. Badi'a hired performers and trained her own dancers. She constantly sought new entertainment and afforded first opportunities to singers Laila Murad, Farid al-Atrash, Najat 'Ali, and Nadira. Badi'a instituted a weekly matinee for women only, which was quickly imitated by other music halls and theatrical companies. She was tireless in overseeing her sala. The success of Sala Badi'a prompted other singers, including Mari Mansur, Fatma Qadri, 'Aliyya Fauzi, Ansaf, Ratiba Rushdi, and others, to open their own music halls.[16]

A determined business woman and colorful personality, Badi'a was the subject of many stories. It was said that she would argue with a waitress, a singer, or even a customer over a single piaster. On one occasion, she reportedly threatened to shoot any editor who published compromising information about her varied, and in many respects unfortunate, background. Her divorce from al-Rihani remained a topic of gossip for years: Badi'a initiated the separation while on tour with al-Rihani's troupe in North Africa. Having discovered al-Rihani with a French actress, she said nothing, but packed her bags and left town in the middle of that night, leaving the troupe without a star and, according to her note, leaving al-Rihani to his French woman.[17]

Unquestionably the most important singer of the century, Umm Kulthum began her career in Cairo during the 1920s in the shadows of Munira, Fathiyya, and Badi'a and in the environment they had collectively fashioned. Umm Kulthum was born to a poor village Quran reciter who augmented his income by singing for weddings and holidays in the area near his village in the eastern Delta. Realizing his daughter's talent at an early age, he took her along with his son and nephew to perform with him. She soon became the family star. After several years of increasing and lucrative opportunities, the family moved permanently to Cairo to advance Umm Kulthum's career.[18]

Like other singers in Cairo, Umm Kulthum gained access to performance opportunities with the help of mentors, usually male, who were often musicians or well-to-do audience members. Hers included the religious singer al-Shaikh Abu al-'Ila Muhammad, the composer Zakariyya Ahmad, and the poet Ahmad Rami. Abu al-'Ila introduced Umm Kulthum to Rami (who would write more than half of the lyrics she sang during her career), and Rami in turn introduced her to the array of literati and politicians who formed his acquaintance. She was aided by elite families, including the 'Abd al-Raziqs and the family of Amin al-Mahdi, at whose homes she performed. Medhat Assem, then a young boy who was taken by his mother to visit the 'Abd al-Raziqs, described Umm Kulthum's appearance there as follows:

> The ladies were in one room and Umm Kulthum was singing. She was probably invited because someone of the 'Abd al-Raziq family heard her in one of the villages in which they owned land. She wore a yellow dress of the plainest sort and a black head covering. After she sang the ladies literally pushed her into the men's salon to sing for them. Umm Kulthum was all alone and terrified. All the heads of state were there, as they gathered at the house to talk politics, current events, literature and so on. In the beginning the guests turned away from her to conversations with their neighbors. But her voice had hardly left her throat when conversations stopped and a deep silence fell on the place for several seconds. Umm Kulthum sang religious words. . . . The audience turned their attention to her and requested many repetitions and returns. The 'Abd al-Raziqs invited Umm Kulthum more than once to sing in their home, and this opened the doors of other houses to her.[19]

Such invitations enhanced her reputation generally.[20]

Umm Kulthum was initially viewed as countrified, unsophisticated, and unschooled. "She sang old songs in the style of the saints' day celebrations, accompanied by her father and a chorus made up of turbanned religious men," according to composer Muhammad al-Qasabji. For those prepared to honor tradition, she was "a beautiful country girl . . . [who] stood among her family in the clothes of a Bedouin man; she sang vintage Egyptian music, consisting of religious songs. She raised her angelic voice calling forth in it the voices of the authentic religious Egyptian people." For others, she was "a tradition-bound imitation" with a strong but unruly voice and little knowledge of art.[21] Most abhorrent was her accompanying ensemble of male vocalists, her father and relatives from her village, men of modest talent who were viewed as old-fashioned and completely unsophisticated: "Do you know anyone who does not complain about their presence around her in this contemptible manner which invites only disgust, especially when they raise their ugly voices roaring like the sound of a camel screaming in distress. . . . What is even more ridiculous is that, when people clap for Umm Kulthum, one of them stands up, in all his repulsiveness, smiling and saluting the audience. . . . Such dull baseness ruins art."[22]

An ambitious woman, Umm Kulthum was not content to occupy the marginal position accorded female reciters of the Quran and religious singers. She learned new musical styles and practices, copied the manners of the elite of the city, and eventually replaced her father's ensemble with professional instrumental accompanists. Opportunities to sing in Cairo increased for Umm Kulthum between 1917 and 1922. Her early engagements consisted of appearances at small nightclubs outside the main theater district, small concerts in the working-class areas near the Husaini mosque, performances between the acts of plays in the large theaters, and informal gatherings and prenuptial parties at or near the homes of wealthy families. These were typical opportunities for a newcomer. She later moved to such major music halls as Sala Santi and eventually booked herself into the larger theaters, including the largest, Azbakiyya Theater, which seated about eight hundred people.

Her father made the business arrangements for her concert appearances through theatrical agents. Usually a series of concerts was booked and advertised at once. The agent arranged advertising, rented the premises or settled a fee with club managers, and paid Umm Kulthum, after taking a percentage for himself. Like almost every other entertainer in Cairo, Umm Kulthum complained vociferously about the agents' efforts to increase their shares of the profits. Unfortunately, her father was not particularly savvy in business matters, and eventually (by about 1928) Umm Kulthum assumed personal control of her contracts and finances.

Umm Kulthum preferred to sing two public concerts per week during the season, three if necessary, and she augmented this schedule with one or two private parties. Like other singers, she experienced bad seasons, as indicated by the following: "To induce people to come to her concerts, promoters have also billed 'the astonishing man who eats 300 eggs, 50 pieces of bread, and 10 jars of pickles.' . . . The name of Umm Kulthum used to be enough."[23] When her revenues were lower than usual in 1927–

28 (a difficult season for many entertainers), she performed more frequently and scheduled public concerts in provincial cities—Luxor, Asyut, al-Minya, Bani Suwaif, and Alexandria. While in a city, she would give one or two public concerts and also perform at the homes of the local elite. Like other traveling female stars, she was generally invited to stay at one of these homes, typically the town house of a wealthy landowner such as Islam Pasha in Bani Suwaif or Muhammad Bey Sha'rawi in al-Minya.[24]

It was in the realm of commercial recording that Umm Kulthum experienced the success that sustained her during her early years in Cairo. Recordings had been extremely popular in Egypt since 1904 and were played throughout the country on gramophones in coffee houses or in the houses of well-to-do villagers whose neighbors were invited to listen. Recording companies, although usually conservative and disinclined to chance a new singer, were also eager to capture as large a share of the market as possible.[25] Thus Odeon Records recruited Umm Kulthum in 1923 and between 1924 and 1925 released fourteen songs sung by Umm Kulthum and written by composers on retainer to the company. The discs were recorded in groups of five to ten, each batch governed by its own contract.

Umm Kulthum's first records were an immediate success and sold completely in a short time. The large volume of sales surprised recording executives as well as the singer herself, who had declined to accept a percentage of sales in favor of a very modest fee paid at the time of recording. She later attributed the large sales to her long years performing throughout the eastern Delta, where she was better known to a wider audience than the urban singers were: "Everyone from the countryside in whose home or at whose wedding I sang, bought my records in order to be able to say to his friends, 'Come and listen to the girl who sang at my daughter's wedding.' "[26]

Most singers sold their recordings for a flat fee, leaving all rights to profits to the recording company. Others took a percentage of sales, usually 3, 5, or 10 percent, occasionally more, payable to the artist during her lifetime and to her estate after death. The percentage of sales option could be very profitable, but like most female singers Umm Kulthum was wary of such contracts and changed her mind only after suffering substantial losses with flat fees. Following her initial success, Umm Kulthum negotiated the highest recording fee in Cairo c. 1924, £E50, or about $250 per side.[27] Mansur 'Awad, the new director of Odeon's principal competitor, Gramophone Records, lured Umm Kulthum away from Odeon Records in 1926 with an even larger contract, which also secured her annual income, an unusual feat in the volatile entertainment business. The contract provided that Umm Kulthum receive an annual retainer of

£E2,000 and £E80 per recording, rising to £E100 per disc in 1927, whereas other stars made £E10 to £E50 per disc without an additional retainer.[28]

The terms of Umm Kulthum's contract, which allowed her to choose her own accompanists and to exercise final judgment on the release of the songs, were the best in Egypt. Her success in commercial recording was critical, for it stabilized her uncertain income at an early stage and thus permitted her to exercise greater choice in performing opportunities thereafter. Combined with her artistic accomplishments, her success in commercial recording cemented a perception of her as "the best" singer and afforded her great freedom in the further development of her career.

COMMON GROUND

Contrary to the popular wisdom that female singers were foreign or non-Muslim, most of the female singers working in Cairo between 1850 and 1930 were native Egyptians and most were Muslim. Occasionally they came from families in which other members were also musicians or singers, but such was not the norm. Almost all for whom data are available were born to lower-class families, and success in entertainment offered them a means of upward mobility economically and, to some extent, socially.

Most of the singers eventually married. The 'awalim about whom information is available married tradesmen from their natal quarters. The later generation of singers usually married into a higher economic stratum than their own, espousing titled landowners or upper-middle-class professionals such as doctors and lawyers. Divorces or multiple marriages figured in the lives of some: Munira al-Mahdiyya married and divorced at least five different men; Ratiba Ahmad, according to one journalist, set records for marriages and divorces.[29] Many, however, remained married to the same man all their lives.

Blatantly immoral conduct clearly was not tolerated from star female singers. Badi'a Masabni's series of lovers was public knowledge and drew occasional negative comment. Ratiba Ahmad was castigated for her habitual rowdiness and public drunkenness. Whereas a strong, outgoing, fun-loving personality was rewarded, some semblance of decent public behavior was also expected. Prostitution as such was associated with a lower echelon of entertainer and in most instances, not surprisingly, was a last resort.

The commercial environment presented more problems for the entertainers than did private homes and community gatherings: audiences were larger and often unknown to the singer, alcoholic beverages were sold, and patrons were occasionally rowdy. In some cases, singers employed by the music halls and cafes were required to socialize or drink

alcohol with patrons. Tauhida, for instance, after much negotiation reportedly signed a contract stipulating that she could not be compelled to
sit with customers or to drink more than five glasses of cognac in one
evening.[30] Journalists ruefully reported occasions on which audience
members tried to embarrass performers or compel them to sing only
requests. A reviewer in 1922 deplored an incident at a concert by the then
new singer, Umm Kulthum. Having accepted an audience request, the
"sweet young singer" was interrupted by a "harsh voice" from the balcony commanding her to stop the song and sing another instead. In spite
of protestations from the partisans of the initial request and Umm
Kulthum's promise to sing the second request after she finished the first,
the group in the balcony began "screaming, whistling and clapping until the place was in disorder and the audience upset, and the cry 'Long live
the people—Down with Umm Kulthum!' became 'Long live "This is the
night of a lifetime" [the first song]—Down with "It is impossible for me
not to love"' [the second], and so on until the curtain fell. Then the yell-
ing and screaming only increased." Later that month, Umm Kulthum reluctantly sang "You hurt me, my cousin," which was requested, in the
opinion of the reviewer, only to embarrass her; her cousin, to whom she
was believed to be betrothed, was one of her accompanists at the time.
When Fathiyya Ahmad performed in the provincial city of al-Minya in
1927, her performance was disrupted by two local prostitutes who made
"suggestive gestures" to men in the balcony. In the 1930s, when she was
managing a music hall herself, Fathiyya complained that, whereas
drunken patrons were bad enough, even some of the dancers in the show
were drunk. Asmahan frequently recalled the bad days of her early career
in music halls by complaining about the behavior of drunken audiences.[31] Although such incidents were occasional, difficult audiences
afflicted almost every female singer, compelling each to find a way to deal
with them. A common strategy was to "pack" the audience with a large
coterie of one's own supporters, who would loudly voice approval of the
singer and handle problematic patrons themselves. These cliques of supporters (or "courts" as they came to be known) brought their own problems, as the singers insisted they be admitted free of charge, a practice
objectionable to owners and other patrons alike. The behavior of these
enthusiasts was occasionally theatrical and distracting in itself. One of
Fathiyya Ahmad's "court," for instance, moved by her performance, was
reported to have blown "resounding kisses to each of his table companions, and then to everyone else he recognized in the room."[32]

All of the women mentioned here commanded a great deal of money.
A conservative estimate of Umm Kulthum's income in 1926–27 would be
well over £E5,000 (or $25,000), and Fathiyya Ahmad's about £E2,200
($11,000). Female concert singers generally made more than actresses or

singers in plays and bore fewer expenses, because makeup and sometimes costumes were paid for by the individual performer. Women's fees
were roughly equal to men's for concerts and recordings and sometimes
higher.[33]

Women pursued careers in this difficult arena for the rewards they
believed could be obtained: recognition of their artistic talent, personal
fame, and fortune. A number of them succeeded in attaining their goals
by dint of artistic creativity, good business sense, and careful negotiation
of the difficult and demanding career path. In addition to their artistic
contributions, these women had a lasting impact on the role of women in
the public eye in Egypt.

Although their individual approaches to their careers were different,
these women were generally ambitious and hard working, and they invested a great deal of energy and effort into ensuring artistic and commercial success. Although their financial rewards were great, their schedules
were not easy. During the season most of them worked at least three and
often five nights per week, performing on stage for periods of three to five
hours. Days were spent planning upcoming events, courting journalists,
and for such women as Badi'a Masabni and Munira al-Mahdiyya, managing the business of a music hall and theatrical troupe, respectively. During the summers most of the women toured and planned the following
year's commitments. Efforts were made in the off season as well to remain
in the public eye.

Most of the female stars eventually assumed the management of their
own careers and money, seeking the counsel of others but retaining the
ultimate decision making. Stars such as Umm Kulthum, Munira al-
Mahdiyya, and Badi'a Masabni became competent business people and
developed reputations as tenacious negotiators. Most of the female stars
deliberately built up savings accounts, and many invested in residences
and other real estate.[34]

Male and female singers, as well as actors, actresses, and dancers,
occupied relatively low social positions. Marriage into the elite classes
was almost impossible. Egyptian feminist Huda Sha'rawi initially declined even to permit her photograph to appear in the then-theatrical
magazine Ruz al-Yusuf, for fear that she might be associated with
actresses. The prevailing attitude had two aspects: one was the belief that
musical performance was an unworthy use of time. When Zakariyya
Ahmad, for instance, announced his intention to compose music for the
theater, his father's response was "What! You're the son of educated
religious men and you're going to become one of those whose lives
[consist of] 'Oh my night, oh my eyes'?!"[35] Another was the association
of entertainment, particularly commercial entertainment, with such vices
as prostitution, drunkenness, gambling, consumption of drugs, and un-

dignified public display. The area of Azbakiyya had long included taverns and brothels, and the resulting problems for performers have already been noted. The presence of foreign soldiers in Egypt exacerbated the situation, as these men, alone on holiday in the city, had plenty of money and few constraints. It was generally believed that their behavior encouraged vice and, in turn, corrupted Egyptian youth.[36]

At the turn of the century, female singers were commonly associated with "light" entertainment. Their repertories were depicted as musically and textually simple, lacking both serious poetic content and sophisticated musical composition. Whereas Lane found a number of female singers to be "learned," they were generally viewed as unskilled compared with their male counterparts and overlooked altogether in serious discussions of music. In his turn-of-the-century book on music, Kamil al-Khula'i ignored female singers entirely, except to comment on their "complete ignorance" of the principles of their art.[37] Women were associated with a genre of song called the *taqtuqa*, a strophic piece in colloquial Arabic dealing with coquetry or other common amorous themes. By contrast, the classical *qasida* was considered to be a male genre, optimally a musically sophisticated rendition of a literary text containing allusions to Arabic literature or to historical and religious events.[38] In fact, a number of female singers were credited, however grudgingly, with having mastered the repertory of sophisticated song ordinarily associated with their male counterparts. Almaz was the most famous of them, and others included Waduda al-Manyalawiyya, Sakina Hasan, al-Sitt Nuzha, al-Hajja al-Suwaisiyya, Asma' al-Kumsariyya, and Munira al-Mahdiyya.[39]

By virtue of their achievements, the women who engaged in commercial entertainment demanded and were accorded a measure of public respect. Led by Umm Kulthum and Fathiyya Ahmad, and built on the memories of notable 'awalim such as Almaz and religious singers such as Sakina Hasan, these women raised the visibility of female singers and firmly established them in the public eye as respectable individuals and accomplished artists. Throughout her long career, Umm Kulthum exhibited a dignified demeanor, and she is widely credited today with having raised the level of respect for female singers generally.

The commercial enterprises of recording and radio and the performers who engaged in them had a dramatic effect on the musical life of Egypt. Because phonograph players and radios were shared and were frequently found in such ordinary places as coffee houses and grocery shops, the commercial music produced and performed in Cairo reached all parts of the country, and eventually all of the Arab world. The impact of the singers, especially those cognizant of their larger audience, extended well beyond their immediate listeners; they became familiar figures throughout Egypt.

Women singers seized the opportunities commercial entertainment offered. They were able to do so because Egyptian society had for years enjoyed and supported female singers, and the male owners of the nascent commercial institutions, seeking the largest possible share of the market, were willing to exploit the women's talents. Not content with this alone, female stars took matters into their own hands, managing their careers and owning their establishments. Umm Kulthum eventually assumed positions of leadership and control on the governing board for music programming for radio, as seven-term president of the musicians' union, and on federal commissions for funding of musical activity. Umm Kulthum in particular, but other female singers as well, set standards of public behavior for entertainers by carrying concepts of dignity familiar to many ordinary Egyptian women into the domain of commercial entertainment. Using the opportunities available to them, the female singers of Egypt attained the fame and fortune they sought and, along the way, implanted an image in the public eye of the female singer as a talented and accomplished individual.

Notes

1. In Egypt, the word *musician* (*musiqi*, f. *musiqiyya*) refers to an instrumentalist; singers are designated by a variety of different terms, including *mutrib* (f. *mutriba*) and *mughanni* (f. *mughanniyya*). For the purposes of this chapter, I have adopted the English usage, which subsumes singer as a type of musician. The relative importance of the singer compared with instrumentalists is a long-standing feature of Arab musical life. See, for instance, Habib Hasan Touma, "History of Arabian Music: A Study," *World of Music* 22 (1980): 72; also Kamal al-Najmi's "Umm Kulthum al-khalida wa mustaqbal al-ghina' al-'arabi" (The eternal Umm Kulthum and the future of Arabic song), *al-Kawakib* (25 Feb. 1975). Research on the roles of female singers during the Umayyad and Abbasid periods is currently being conducted by Suzanne Meyers Sawa (see her "Role of Women in Musical Life: The Medieval Arabo-Islamic Courts," *Canadian Woman Studies* 8 [1987]: 93–95). The anonymity of female singers in Tunisia's history is discussed by L. Jafran Jones, "A Sociohistorical Perspective on Tunisian Women as Professional Musicians," in *Women and Music in Cross-Cultural Perspective*, ed. Ellen Koskoff (Urbana: University of Illinois Press, 1989), 69–83. Hiromi Lorraine Sakata notes "the common tendency in many societies to ignore the contributions of women and to allow them to go unrecognized because so often the cultural definitions of music and musician focus solely on male traditions" ("Hazara Women in Afghanistan: Innovators and Preservers of a Musical Tradition," in *Women and Music*, ed. Koskoff, 94). See also Jennifer Post, "Professional Women in Indian Music: The Death of the Courtesan Tradition," ibid., esp. 97–98.

2. Ali Jihad Racy, "Musical Change and Commercial Recording in Egypt, 1904-1932" (Ph.D. diss., University of Illinois, 1977), 193.

3. The best surveys of nineteenth-century musical life are Ali Jihad Racy, "Music in Nineteenth-Century Egypt: An Historical Sketch," *Selected Reports in Ethnomusicology* 4 (1983): 157–79, and Habib Hasan Touma, "Die Musik der Araber im 19. Jahrhundert," in *Musikkulturen Asiens, Afrikas, und Ozeaniens im 19. Jahrhundert* (Regensburg: Gustav Bosse, 1973), 49–71. See also Sarah Graham-Brown, *Images of Women* (New York: Columbia University Press, 1987), chap. 6. In the 1907 and 1917 censuses for Egypt numerous individuals in every part of the country identified themselves as professional musicians, singers, dancers, and music teachers. Nizarat al-Maliyya, *Ta'dad sukkan al-qutr al-Misri fi sana 1325 hijriyya—sana 1907 miladiyya* (Cairo: al-Matba'a al-Amiriyya bi-Misr, 1909); Egyptian Ministry of Finance, Statistical Department, *The Census of Egypt Taken in 1917*, 2 vols. (Cairo: Government Press, 1920).

4. Fikri Butrus, *A'lam al-musiqa wa'l-ghina' al-'arabi* (Stars of Arabic music and song) (Cairo: Al-Hai'a al-Misriyya al-'Amma li'l-Kitab, 1976), 92; Raja' al-Naqqash, "Aswat atrabat ajdadana" (Voices that charmed our grandparents), in *Lughz Umm Kulthum* (The secret of Umm Kulthum) (Cairo: Dar al-Hilal, 1978), 153.

5. Butrus, *A'lam al-musiqa*, 125.

6. Edward William Lane, *An Account of the Manners and Customs of the Modern Egyptians Written in Egypt during the Years 1833–1835* (The Hague: East-West Publications, 1978), 494, see also 355.

7. Georg Ebers, *Egypt: Descriptive, Historical and Picturesque*, trans. Clara Bell (London: Cassell, Petter, Galpin, 1883), 2:312, 314; see also Lucie Duff Gordon, *Letters from Egypt* (1865; reprint, London: Virago, 1983), 20; and Muhammad Mahmud Sami Hafiz, *al-Musiqa al-misriyya al-haditha* (Modern Egyptian music) (Cairo: Maktabat al-Anjlu al-Misriyya, 1982), 9.

8. Butrus, *A'lam al-musiqa*, 61–62.

9. Doris Behrens-Abouseif, *Azbakiyya and Its Environs*, Supplement aux *Annales Islamologiques*, Cahier no. 6 (Cairo: Institut Français d'Archéologie Orientale, 1985), 76, see also 25.

10. Karl Baedeker, *Egypt and the Sudan: Handbook for Travellers*, 6th ed. (Leipzig: Baedeker, 1908), 37, also 32 and 47, and 7th ed. (1914), 37. Cf. an account written by J. W. McPherson in 1902: "Sabry had tickets for the Ezbekieh Gardens where an unique kind of Gala was proceeding. We stayed there until midnight listening to Native and European singing, watching Turkish sword-dancing and sham fighting and innumerable shows" (Barry Carman and John McPherson, *Bimbashi McPherson: A Life in Egypt* [London: British Broadcasting Corporation, 1983], 36). According to Baedeker's 1908 and 1914 guidebooks, "cafes in the European style, at which beer and other beverages are obtained, abound in and near the Ezbekiyah; none of them are suitable for ladies." Almaz and 'Abduh al-Hamuli sang during entr'actes, popularizing the practice. Mahmud Kamil, *al-Masrah al-ghina'i* (Cairo: Dar al-Ma'arif, 1977), 12.

11. *Ruz al-Yusuf*, no. 107 (24 Nov. 1927), 20; *al-Sabah*, no. 188 (2 May 1930), [5] and [40]; "Hikayat Fatma Rushdi" (The story of Fatma Rushdi), *al-Fanan*, no. 2 (4 Dec. 1962), 27–29; "Fathiyya Ahmad," *al-Kawakib* (5 Dec. 1978), 34–35.

12. *Ruz al-Yusuf,* no. 74 (31 Mar. 1927), 13, no. 237 (29 Aug. 1932), 24–25; Mahmud Kamil, *Muhammad al-Qasabji* (Cairo: Al-Hai'a al-Misriyya al-'Amma li'l-Kitab, 1971), 147; Ahmad Abu al-Khidr Mansi, *al-Aghani wa'l-musiqa al-sharqiyya baina al-qadim wa'l-jadid* (Oriental songs and music, ancient to modern), 2d ed. (Cairo: Dar al-'Arab li'l-Bustani, 1965–66), 185–86; al-Naqqash, "Aswat," 154–55.

13. *Al-Masrah,* no. 27 (24 May 1926), 23; *Ruz al-Yusuf,* no. 83 (9 June 1927), 11, no. 48 (29 Sept. 1926), 15, no. 176 (10 June 1930), 24.

14. *Ruz al-Yusuf,* no. 240 (18 Sept. 1932), 18, no. 272 (1 May 1933), 30; *al-Masrah* (14 June 1926), 25.

15. *Sala,* meaning literally "hall," was a term applied to places of entertainment that featured musicians, singers, dancers, and variety acts, and where drink and often food were served. One sat at small tables, in a style similar to that of a Western nightclub. Such places were also called clubs (*klub, nadi*) or casinos (*kazinu*), although gambling was not necessarily available.

16. *Al-Masrah,* no. 48 (22 Nov. 1926), 16, in which the author claimed that Badi'a "proved again that women can do and obtain what they want"; *al-Sabah,* no. 105 (1 Oct. 1928), 11; *Ruz al-Yusuf,* no. 40 (4 Aug. 1926), 6–7, no. 74 (31 Mar. 1927), 18, no. 111 (Dec. 1927), 17-18, no. 164 (18 Mar. 1930), 17, no. 176 (10 June 1930), 17, no. 77 (17 June 1930), 17, no. 178 (24 June 1930), 16, no. 219 (25 Apr. 1932), 21, no. 234 (8 Aug. 1932), 26. The music halls were usually situated in older theaters, such as the Biju Palace, which were rented on short-term leases by the singer or by a financial backer on her behalf. Most closed after two years or less.

17. In her memoirs, Badi'a told of being sexually assaulted as a young girl. The resulting scandal led her mother to move the family from its village. Nazik Basila, *Mudhakkirat Badi'a Masabni* (The memoirs of Badi'a Masabni) (Beirut: Dar Maktabat al-Haya, n.d.); see also *Ruz al-Yusuf,* no. 97 (15 Sept. 1927), 12; and Mahmud Rif'at al-Muhami, ed., *Mudhakkirat Badi'-Khairi: 45 sana taht adwa' al-masrah* (The memoirs of Badi' Khairi: 45 years under the lights of the theater) (Beirut: Dar al-Thaqafa, n.d.), 118.

18. Most information about Umm Kulthum's life presented here has been gleaned from a survey of Egyptian periodicals from 1924 to 1975 and from personal interviews with her associates and family. The most useful larger biographical works are Muhammad al-Sayyid Shushah's *Umm Kulthum: Hayat Nagham* (Umm Kulthum: A life of song) (Cairo: Ruz al-Yusuf, 1976); Ni'mat Ahmad Fu'ad's *Umm Kulthum wa-'asr min al-fann* (Umm Kulthum and an era in art) (Cairo: Al-Hai'a al-Misriyya al-'Amma li'l-Kitab, 1976); and Umm Kulthum's memoir, as told to Mahmud 'Awad, *Umm Kulthum allati la ya'rifuha ahad* (The Umm Kulthum nobody knows) (Cairo: Mu'assasat Akhabar al-Yaum, n.d.), which has been translated into English in Elizabeth W. Fernea and Basima Bezirgan, eds., *Middle Eastern Muslim Women Speak* (Austin: University of Texas Press, 1977).

19. Personal communication from Medhat Assem, 28 Jan. 1986.

20. Among the important relationships of mentors to young musicians were: theatrical director 'Aziz 'Id and young actresses Ruz al-Yusuf, Munira al-Mahdiyya, and Fatma Rushdi; composer and theatrical entrepreneur Salama Hijazi and Munira al-Mahdiyya; politician and orator Fikri Abaza and young singer Najat 'Ali; poet laureate Ahmad Shauqi and his friends among Egyptian politi-

cians such as Makram 'Ubaid, and singer-composer Muhammad 'Abd al-Wahhab; composer Daud Husni and singers Fatma Sirri and Asmahan; pianist-composer Medhat Assem and aspiring singer Farid al-Atrash; and poet 'Abbas al-'Aqqad and singer Nadira. Familial relationships among musicians were less common; the principal support system and means of entrée into commercial entertainment was the mentor-newcomer relationship. These relationships also demonstrate the strong and sometimes personal connections between musicians and influential members of the elite, a significant aspect of musical patronage in Cairo even in the commercial environment.

21. "Dhikrayat ma'a al-Qasabji" (Memories with al-Qasabji), based on interviews with him in 1955, al-Kawakib (11 Feb. 1975), 33–35; Husain Fauzi, in Wada' 'an Umm Kulthum (Farewell to Umm Kulthum), ed. Muhammad 'Umar Shatabi (Cairo: Al-Markaz al-Misri li'l-Thaqafa wa'l-A'lam, 1975), 55; al-Masrah, no. 24 (3 May 1926), 15, no. 29 (7 June 1926), 20.

22. Al-Masrah, no. 26 (17 May 1926), 15.

23. Ruz al-Yusuf, no. 31 (2 June 1926), 12.

24. Ibid., no. 115 (21 Feb. 1928), 16, no. 119 (29 Mar. 1928), 16, no. 125 (1 May 1928), 19, no. 141 (28 Aug. 1928), 17, no. 145 (22 Jan. 1929), 17; al-Sabah, no. 67 (9 Jan. 1928), 4. Cairene singers toured in Syria and Palestine, North Africa, and even South America, especially during the summer months, and their recordings were marketed in these places as well.

25. Racy, "Musical Change," 126–27, 129.

26. Quoted in Fu'ad, Umm Kulthum, 98; see also 'Awad, Umm Kulthum, 62–64.

27. By way of comparison, Columbia Records paid Bessie Smith, one of their top artists, $150 per side in 1923. See Chris Albertson, Bessie (New York: Stein and Day, 1982), 45.

28. Ruz al-Yusuf, no. 48 (29 Sept. 1926), 14–15. Umm Kulthum's contract in 1928 dollars would amount to about $10,000 per annum in retainers and $400-$500 per disc recorded. By comparison, Bessie Smith's second contract with Columbia in 1926 specified $200 per usable side (for at least twelve and up to as many discs as she chose to record in that year) with no retainer (Albertson, Bessie, 98).

29. Ruz al-Yusuf, no. 185 (30 Aug. 1930), 18.

30. Fu'ad, Umm Kulthum, 58.

31. Al-Kashkul al-musawwar, no. 57 (18 June 1922), 6, no. 58 (25 June 1922), 4; al-Sabah, no. 28 (11 Apr. 1927), 14; Ruz al-Yusuf, no. 260 (6 Feb. 1933), 28–29; Muhammad al-Taba'i, Asmahan tarwi qissataha (Asmahan tells her story) (Cairo: Mu'assasat Ruz al-Yusuf, 1965), 45–46.

32. Ruz al-Yusuf, no. 243 (9 Oct. 1932), 28.

33. My estimate of Umm Kulthum's income includes £E1,660 for two public concerts weekly during a season lasting from October through May; £E960 for one private party weekly during the same season; £E2,000 annual retainer from Gramophone Records; and £E80 for each of about ten new records; for Fathiyya's, £E600 from recordings, £E500 from touring Syria, about £E600 from appearances at Sala Badi'a during an abbreviated season, since she spent two months in Syria, and perhaps another £E500 from private parties.

34. Fatma Sirri and Badi'a Masabni had large bank accounts. Tauhida owned a

music hall and several residential buildings. 'Aziza Amir purchased rental property in fashionable Garden City. Umm Kulthum bought land in her home village.

35. Zakariyya's father was referring to a common text for vocal improvisation, *Ya lail, ya 'ain* (quoted in 'Awad, *Umm Kulthum*, 47). Sha'rawi's action was reported in *al-Masrah* (31 May 1926), 4. Condemnation of music altogether on orthodox Islamic religious grounds was uncommon in Egypt. A good discussion of the prevailing view of music held by the religious establishment in Egypt appears in Kristina Nelson, *The Art of Reciting the Qur'an* (Austin: University of Texas Press, 1985), chap. 3.

36. Nahid Ahmad Hafiz summarized commonly felt sentiments when she wrote that Cairo during the colonial period "was a place of many vices, for example gambling, licentiousness, usury, drunkenness, drugs and prostitution, all of which resulted from colonialism" "Al-Ughniya al-misriyya wa-tatawwuruha khilal al-qarnain al-tasi' 'ashr wa'l-ashrin" (Egyptian song and its development during the nineteenth and twentieth centuries) (Ph.D. thesis, Helwan University, 1977), 216.

37. Lane, *An Account*, 355; Kamil al-Khula'i, *Kitab al-musiqa al-sharqiyya* (Oriental music) (Cairo: Matba'at al-Taqaddum, c. 1904), 91.

38. Racy, "Musical Change," 53, 200–3; Hafiz, *al-Musiqa*, 9.

39. Racy, "Musical Change," 48–49, 201; Mansi, *al-Aghani*, 173–74, 180; Butrus, *A'lam al-musiqa*, 85–86.

17 Biography and Women's History:

On Interpreting Doria Shafik

CYNTHIA NELSON

This chapter addresses the issue of shifting boundaries between self and other as this occurs in the process of interpreting the life of an Egyptian woman. It also raises certain
epistemological and methodological questions concerning
women's experience and women's history in the Middle
East. What are the presuppositions underlying the biog-
rapher-memoirist relationship in writing a woman's life?
What is the nature of interpretive inquiry followed by the
biographer as she attempts to recover and reconstruct
knowledge of the other, primarily through personal documents we call memoirs? How do such attempts to recover
women's voices and women's lives inform contemporary
feminist discourse on the Middle East?

Tentative answers to these questions emerge from my experience writing the biography of Doria Shafik. An Egyptian
woman best known nationally and internationally during
the 1940s and 1950s as a militant feminist, she fought for
women's full political equality until she was put under house
arrest in 1957 for her strong protests against Gamal Abdel
Nasser's regime and her demands for the restoration of democracy in Egypt. She spent the remaining eighteen years of
her life in veritable seclusion before leaping to her death from
her sixth-floor apartment in Cairo on 20 September 1975.

Many scholars have argued recently that there is and can
be no neat and simple divide between the factual and the
fictional, whether in autobiography, biography, or ethnography, for each of these forms of discourse is dependent on the
transforming creating medium of the writer and her states of
consciousness.[1] Biography then becomes a process of "constructing the other," in which the story that emerges reflects
the biographer's mode of organizing, her translation and
"reading" of the many levels of experience embodied in
those memoirs and personal documents where the encoun-

310

ter takes place. What those levels of experience are and how they are woven into the biographer's story constitute the methodology of the work. I do not presume to "explain" Doria Shafik's life, but rather to try to "grasp" it—perhaps only fleetingly—in the context of its various levels of meaning. The connection between us, then, is that of the impact of one humanity on another.

My first encounter with Doria Shafik occurred in the summer of 1983 in Cairo, when her two daughters presented me with a gift of five volumes of her collected poems.[2] At that moment I had no intention of writing her biography. It was only later (1984–85), while teaching at the University of California at Santa Cruz, that I met Akram Khater, a young Lebanese graduate student who took an independent study with me on the history of women's movements in the Middle East. From those readings and discussions my curiosity was sufficiently aroused that I felt a serious biographical study of Doria Shafik was not only relevant to a number of my own intellectual interests but also, given the sparse mention of her in the literature, long overdue. Returning to Egypt in the spring of 1985, I broached the idea in a letter to her daughters expressing my desire to undertake a biographical study of their mother:

> Through those verses which I have read, I have heard a voice, that despite its Egyptian roots in the desert and the Nile, despite its confrontation with a history that was not mine, despite its own unique biographical trajectory, has touched me by its paean to solitude. I have wanted to know more about the life behind that voice, particularly since there seems to be a "conspiracy of silence" concerning her role in the struggle for women's rights in the Egyptian women's movement of the 1940's and 1950's. Emma Goldman once wrote: that the real revolutionist—the dreamer, the creative artist, the iconoclast in whatever line—is fated to be misunderstood, not only by her own kind but often by her own comrades. That is the doom of all great spirits: they are detached from their environment. Theirs is the lonely life—the life of the transition stage, the hardest and most difficult period for the individual as well as for a people. In many ways Doria Shafik personifies that life of the transition stage. Through undertaking to write her biography we can explore the intersection of self and society.[3]

Their response was and continues to be both enthusiastic and encouraging. And it is thanks to their trust that Doria Shafik's personal memoirs and unpublished papers have been generously shared. From that time until the present Doria Shafik and I have been engaged in a process of "constructing the other." We have met in that interstitial space shared by those who have crossed the boundaries of each other's culture.

There are several reasons, blending the personal and professional dimensions of my self, why the life of Doria Shafik is particularly interesting. Paramount is the woman herself: complex, contradictory, and controversial. She grew up in a very modest and traditional middle-class family in the provincial Delta towns of Tanta and Mansura during a period when Egypt was in the throes of great internal turmoil following World War I, embodied in the 1919 revolution. During the 1920s and 1930s, when for women of her class background endowed with intelligence, ambition, and beauty there were few outlets from the constraints of tradition except through education, Doria exploited that avenue to the fullest and obtained her doctorate from the Sorbonne in 1940.[4] But her ultimate ambition was to enter the public and political domain. And it was within the context of post–World War II Egypt that Doria Shafik was able to catapult herself into national and international prominence. As an intellectual she represented a model radically different from Huda Sha'rawi as a leader of the women's movement in Egypt.[5] Doria began her career as an inspector of French-language teaching in the secondary schools of Egypt, then turned to journalism before emerging as the militant leader of a self-conscious feminist struggle for women's full participation in the political life of her country. Her public career ended in 1957 when, in her quixotic public defense of liberal democracy, she pitted herself against Nasser at a time when "populism" had become the dominant political ideology of the majority of the Egyptian people.

Married to a brilliant and socially prominent lawyer and the mother of two beautiful and talented daughters, Doria Shafik also pursued a public career as a poet, publisher, and political activist. By 1945 she was the owner and editor-in-chief of the French literary and cultural magazine *La femme nouvelle* (The new woman) and the founder of two Arabic magazines: *Bint al-Nil* (Daughter of the Nile), a woman's magazine oriented to the emerging middle class, and *Katkut* (Little chicken), one of the first children's magazines published in the post–World War II period. She also established a feminist union and a political party under the name of Bint al-Nil, through which she challenged the bastions of male authority under both pre-revolutionary and revolutionary regimes. She fashioned her feminist consciousness through activism: storming the Egyptian Parliament; attempting to run illegally for parliamentary elections; staging sit-ins to protest the British occupation; and undertaking hunger strikes. She expressed her feminist vision through writing. Between 1944 and 1955 Doria Shafik published seven books in French and Arabic, including two volumes of poetry, one novel, and four books dealing with Egyptian feminism.[6] She was invited to lecture on the Arab women's struggle to audiences in Europe, the United States, India, and Pakistan. Her protest against the erosion of democracy under Gamal Abdel Nasser led to her house arrest in 1957. Although she was politically and socially secluded from public life thereafter until her death in 1975, her name still evokes strong reactions in Egypt.[7]

Within the post–World War II context of social and political upheaval, Doria Shafik attempted to shape a new woman's consciousness in Egypt on several fronts: first, through the pages of her magazines; second, through her feminist organization and political party; and finally, through her books on the history and political situation of Egyptian women. At the same time that she was engaged in this "feminist struggle" she was also developing a reputation among the francophiles of Egypt as a woman of impressive aesthetic sensibility, both as the editor-in-chief of the prestigious cultural and literary magazine *La femme nouvelle* and as a poet, described by Pierre Seghers "as that instant of splendid gravity, an exceptional being of *meditation* and *action*, a bearing, an allure that passed through Time."[8] The dynamism and tension among these interlocking and sometimes contradictory strands and demands in her life—the cultures of the East and the West, the languages of Arabic and French, the meditative mode of the poet and the activist mode of the feminist, the exigencies of domestic and public responsibility—contribute to her fascination.

In spite of a growing interest in and literature on women and women's movements in Egypt and the Middle East,[9] there is a surprising lack of attention to the post-World War II period. The recovery of Doria Shafik's life may shed light on both the historical period and the women's movement.

THE HISTORICAL CONTEXT OF THE WOMEN'S MOVEMENT IN EGYPT

Women's active participation in the political life of Egypt has a long history. Most contemporary scholars associate the beginnings of an authentic Egyptian women's movement with the 1919 revolution. Although earlier writings by Egyptian women reflect a concern with nationalism, it was only in the 1920s when Huda Sha'rawi broke with the Wafd that the women's movement turned away from nationalist politics.[10] Many writers recount the accomplishments of the Egyptian Feminist Union (EFU), established by Sha'rawi in 1923, as examples of feminist struggle. Similarly, these writers date the demise of the movement to the period between the late thirties, with the onset of World War II, and 1947, when Sha'rawi died.[11] The period 1945–59 is usually overlooked in analyses of the women's movement in Egypt. Yet, I would argue, it was then that the women's movement came of age, in the sense that: (1) it experienced a diversification in ideology, tactics, and goals; and (2) it began to transcend its elitist origins and membership. Moreover, in this post–World War II period the women's movement consciously shifted away from being a welfare-oriented, mostly philanthropic activity, to a more politicized movement that linked the struggle for women's full participation in the decision-making processes to such political and social concerns as the nationalist movement and class struggle. Generally, the women's movement in Egypt went through two main phases. The first started between 1919 and 1923 with the founding of the EFU by Huda Sha'rawi. This phase continued up to the end of the "liberal experiment" in Egypt around the late 1930s.[12] During World War II feminist activity in Egypt was almost nonexistent and only came to life again in 1945. This was the beginning of the second phase in the history of the Egyptian women's movement, which was characterized by a more radical approach and which ended in 1959 when the state under Nasser clamped down on any independent political action.

Throughout the first phase (1923–39) in the history of the Egyptian women's movement there was a definite separation between the social and the political issues in society. The EFU viewed the social problems of Egypt (bad health conditions, poverty, prostitution, and illiteracy) not as the results of a specific socioeconomic structure, but rather as caused by the neglect of the state in its responsibilities toward the people. The EFU argued that the state had a responsibility to maintain the morality of the nation, as well as its welfare, although it defined women's issues from the narrow and class-based perspective of upper-class women. Its appeal was thus limited, and its goals were not derived from a real understanding of the situation of most women in Egypt. To some extent it followed, in this regard, the political practices of most parties in Egypt during the 1920s and 1930s, which regarded politics as the prerogative of the educated elite. In confronting social problems, however, even from the heights of the elite, the EFU was bringing into the political arena, albeit indirectly, the idea of the social responsibility of the state to the people.

By the end of World War II hard economic realities and the obvious corruption and inadequacy of the ancien régime (the monarchical system under King Faruq) provided impetus for a general radicalization of Egyptian politics. The women's movement experienced a similar transformation. In this heated environment many young Egyptian feminists came of political age and became involved in the struggle for women's rights. They were convinced that the tactics of the EFU were as outdated as its goals. No longer was the establishment of a health clinic or the distribution of charity, according to the new feminists, an adequate solution to social problems, nor did equal rights mean simply access to education. During this postwar period other voices—those of a younger and more radical generation of Egyptian women—began shaping a different public discourse on the goals of the feminist movement. Reflecting the liberal ideology of the modern secularists was the voice of Doria Shafik, whose rhetoric and activism centered on attaining the full political and legal rights of women. There were also voices of the progressive left, such as Inji Aflatun, whose rhetoric and activism followed the Marxist argument that the socioeconomic class system underlying the oppression of women had to be changed. The Islamic conservatives opposed both of these tendencies over the question of women's rights. The men of religion vehemently criticized the more visible "modernist" Doria Shafik, perceiving her claims as the most direct threat to conservative Islamic values and tradition. In short, the women's movement became much more politicized and overtly political in its demands.[13]

It is precisely in the context of the events erupting in Egypt following World War II, particularly the struggle for national independence from British occupation, that we can best understand Doria Shafik's role in the history of Egypt.

MEMOIRS

Since it is through her memoirs that we can explore how Doria Shafik perceived and experienced her own life situations as well as the historical conditions that fostered her political consciousness and action, it is important to understand how these memoirs came to be written. Doria Shafik wrote three different versions of her memoirs during the last twenty years of her life. These are not so much separate and distinct stories as they are three different angles of vision of the same life story. The first version was begun in 1955 in response to a specific request from the editor of the then Harper and Brothers Publishers for Doria to write her "personal story that would give you the opportunity to say all the things you believe in and are working toward in your public life." For various reasons the project was unfinished, and in the fall of 1956 the Suez War erupted and all correspondence between Harper and Doria ceased. The second version was begun following her dramatic protest against Nasser and subsequent house arrest in 1957. These memoirs were written in French, the medium of her poetic and literary expression, under conditions of political and social confinement and "official" condemnation.

Over the next sixteen years of solitude and semiseclusion until her tragic death in 1975, Doria Shafik continued to explore the "profound meaning of my own existence" through the act of writing.[14] I wondered why it was that she wrote the final version of her memoirs during this period. "In order to see clearly into myself. In sounding the Past, the Present will be brought to view and then I may look to the Future with more clarity. Writing this book will help me to be aware of the essential meaning of the events surrounding me."[15]

These three manuscripts are the different voices of a self creating and re-creating, what Phyllis Rose would call a personal mythology: "that highly personal configuration of significance by which a person views his own experience."[16] By reading back and forth among these different voices I begin to see how each reveals as well as conceals something that expands and enriches my understanding of the whole person. They also help me grasp the significance of other materials concerning the trajectory of her life and the historical context, thus revealing how knowledge is constructed through a process of dialogue not only between Doria Shafik and her own self-reflections, but also between her reflections and those of her biographer. Through this dialogue the biographer attempts to discover how self and society intersect. By following Doria Shafik's own quest for meaning within a society from which she always felt estranged, we catch a glimpse of Egypt in a time of stress and transformation, "the life of the transition stage."

INTERPRETING DORIA SHAFIK

Doria Shafik always perceived her own life as intimately connected to and influenced by those explosive social and political transformations that her country had to suffer. As she wrote in her memoirs, "My life began with the First World War and ever since has been a continual struggle." The official records give her year of birth as 1908, but this fact tells us less about Doria Shafik's perception of herself and her world than does her metaphorical association of life "beginning" with World War I. From this period onward, an old order was crumbling in the face of increasing discontent over how Egypt was to be governed. It was a historical moment that witnessed the appearance of the nationalist leader Sa'd Zaghlul, the Wafd, and the rise of the Egyptian nationalist movement, which erupted into the revolution of 1919; the emergence of an authentic Egyptian women's movement under the banner of Huda Sha'rawi; the creation of Egypt's first constitution and the experiment with liberal democracy that led to the struggles between the palace, the Wafd party, and the British over who controlled the reins of power; the rise of Islamic fundamentalism under Hasan al-Banna; the outbreak of World War II and the postwar struggle for independence from colonial rule; the unfolding of the Cold War between Russia and the United States; the Palestinian question and the creation of the state of Israel with the subsequent Arab-Israeli wars; the Egyptian revolution of 1952 and the rise to power of Nasser; the Baghdad Pact and the Bandung Conference of 1955; the rise of the nonaligned movement; and the Suez crisis of 1956.

Throughout this period Doria Shafik's life unfolded. Born on 14 December 1908 in the home of her maternal grandmother in Tanta, Gharbiyya, she was the third child and second daughter of the six children of Ratiba Nasif Qassabi Bey and Ahmad Chafik Sulaiman Effendi. The titles bey and effendi distinguish the class backgrounds of her parents. Doria's mother belonged to a high-status rural notable family (bey), but her mother's mother, widowed and having failed to produce any male heirs, lost control over her share of the inheritance to her uncle and grand-uncle,[17] leaving Ratiba without wealth of her own. Doria's father came from a petty bourgeois background and worked as a civil engineer for the Egyptian government. Marriage between such distinct social classes was very unusual during this period, but because Ratiba Nasif had no wealth and was under the guardianship of her uncle, she was married off into the effendi class. Doria spent the earliest years of her childhood in Mansura, where her father had a job as a civil engineer and which she remembered with great nostalgia. When she reached primary school age she was separated from her parents and sent to live with her grandmother in Tanta, where she completed her primary education in the well-known French mission school, Notre Dame des Apôtres. A few years later, when Doria was barely thirteen, her mother died in childbirth. This was the single most devastating experience of her childhood and created a sense of loss and abandonment that stayed with her throughout her life. As she recounts in her memoirs: "The loss of my mother left a wound so huge that it marked the whole of my life. As an outlet for my despair and desolation I concentrated all my energy into reading and studying. The result was that I progressed so rapidly that I found myself in the same class as my sister."[18]

She obtained her certificate from the preparatory school of St. Vincent de Paul in Alexandria, where she had gone to live with her father and brothers after her mother's death. Her elder sister, Sorayya, who was married and raising their younger sister, Laila, also lived in Alexandria. At that time there was no girls' lycée (French secondary school) in Alex-andria, and Doria's father could not afford to send her to the boarding school in Cairo. But Ahmad Chafik,[19] a self-educated and pious Muslim whom Doria often compared to Balzac's self-sacrificing Père Goriot, strongly supported his daughter's precocious intellectual talents. He al-lowed her to prepare for her examinations at home under the guidance of male tutors, among them a Belgian who taught philosophy at the boys' lycée. It was thanks to his intellectual encouragement and the moral and financial support of her father that Doria, at the age of sixteen, was the youngest to sit and successfully pass the examinations for the French baccalauréat in June 1925, achieving the second highest score in the coun-try. Doria's ambitions to continue her education finally evoked the sup-port of Huda Sha'rawi, who secured for her a scholarship from the Minis-try of Education to attend the Sorbonne. In August 1928, Doria left alone for Paris and spent the next four years studying for her diploma of state in philosophy. She returned to Egypt in the summer of 1932, hoping to reconcile her own ambitions with the country she loved but from which she felt estranged. She taught at the newly opened girls' lycée in Alexandria[20] for a couple of years, but because of some unhappy circumstances centering on family and social pressures to marry, she returned to Paris in 1936 to pursue her ultimate goal of "obtaining the highest degree in the world." While there she met her cousin, whom she had known during her childhood years in Tanta but with whom she had lost contact after the death of her mother. He was on scholarship from King Fuad I University (now Cairo University), studying for his doctorate in law at the University of Paris. What began as a casual meeting between relatives who had been childhood friends and now were strangers together in a foreign culture quickly developed into a whirlwind courtship of love and marriage. Through her own free choice and without dowry (she accepted a symbolic 25 piasters) or parental approval, Doria Shafik and Nur al-Din Regai were married in 1937, the same year the young King Faruq married Safinaz Zulfiqar, the popular Queen Farida. After completing their doctoral theses, Nur and Doria returned to Cairo on the eve of the outbreak of World War II in Europe. Doria wanted very much to teach philosophy at the University of Cairo but was refused by the dean of the Faculty of Arts, Ahmad Amin, on the grounds that because of "her beauty and modern style she was not suited to instruct young men." She returned to the Ministry of Education and worked as the inspector of French language throughout the secondary schools of Egypt for the duration of the war years. Also during this period she gave birth to her two daughters, Aziza in 1942 and Jihan in 1944.

But Doria did not feel that she had fulfilled her ambition. Eager to be more actively involved in public affairs, Doria began searching for an outlet and in 1945, through a connection of her husband's, was offered the position of editor-in-chief of a new magazine to be founded by Princess Chewikar, the ex-wife of King Fuad and founder of the benevolent association La Femme Nouvelle.[21] Doria comments in her memoirs that she was not altogether happy in that milieu and became sensitive to popular criticism that she must be in the pay of foreign powers since she was writing a magazine in French. It was then that she decided to launch her own Arabic-language magazine, *Bint al-Nil*, through which she continued to champion the equal rights of women. Finally, signaling her impatience with the prevailing complacency of the government toward women's political and legal rights, Doria Shafik took the decisive step in March 1948 of establishing her Bint al-Nil Union on behalf of the complete emancipation of Egyptian women. The factors that led to this decision were her experiences as the owner and editor-in-chief of her magazines,

La femme nouvelle and *Bint al-Nil* and the death of Huda Sha'rawi in December 1947.[22]

The letters from readers in response to the column "Let Bint al-Nil Solve Your Problems" made Doria Shafik acutely aware that "nearly all of the difficulties facing Egyptian women centered around polygamy and hasty divorce by men without protection for women and children."[23] Initially she tried to help these women on a case-by-case basis through the creation of an employment bureau in her Bint al-Nil office. She tried to find work for the young and healthy and referred the old and indigent to friends who worked in the various benevolent associations whose specific aims were to provide public assistance. But it was quickly evident to her that this strategy was addressing only a "small section of the millions of women suffering from the same injustice." She attempted to enlist the support of male members of Parliament to elaborate laws guaranteeing women family security. But nothing was done. As she states in her memoirs:

> It was obvious to me that women representatives were essential in Parliament. They must not only be present in the legislative chambers when laws concerning them are legislated; but also they must be involved in writing the laws. It would be the only answer to the problem of formulating laws that really did further the cause of women. It was not surprising that the only two bills presented in 1923 by Huda Sha'rawi (one for limiting polygamy and the other for curbing easy divorce) had long been forgotten; while all other laws concerning men were developing and improving according to their growing needs. Women as half the nation had to be represented in Parliament, and justly protected. But why should men alone represent their nation? Women should have an equal say in the laws that ultimately affect them and their children. The only solution was to build up a Feminist Union to demand political rights for women.

With this objective in view the Bint al-Nil movement was launched. Doria Shafik was convinced that she was not creating just another women's association but initiating a new and invigorated Egyptian feminist movement, whose primary purpose at its inception was to proclaim and claim the full political rights of women. By this act Doria Shafik was openly asserting her leadership of a moribund movement, which she felt had been ineffective and inadequate to reach this ultimate goal since the death of Huda Sha'rawi. In addition, by addressing herself to middle-class women and their problems, Bint al-Nil Union reflected a departure from the earlier elitist women's organizations, like the Egyptian Feminist Union and the plethora of social welfare associations. In purpose and constituency Bint al-Nil was attractive to a growing middle-class youth coming out of the national universities, and in its organization and extension throughout Egypt was aiming to be much broader in its membership than the EFU.

Many young women students and graduates were attracted to Bint al-Nil Union because it provided an alternative to the older EFU. A look at the roster of its members or at the photographs of its meetings shows many young faces and names that are Egyptian, as opposed to those of Turkish origin, and without "Hanim" (elite Turkish title for women) preceding them. These women were seeking to define a new position for themselves in Egyptian society that would take them beyond the boundaries of house and marriage and into the realm of public life and work.

Governed by an executive committee composed of middle-class professional women, Bint al-Nil Union focused its goals on three main objectives: (1) to establish the constitutional and parliamentary rights of the Egyptian woman in order to defend the laws guaranteeing those rights; (2) to diffuse cultural, health, and social services among poor Egyptian families through the promotion of literacy programs and the creation of small industries to augment their earnings; (3) to call attention to the conditions of these families, especially maternal and child care, through the full use of all mass media, conferences, and editorials and to adopt every means that would guarantee their protection and support. Thus the demand for political rights was followed by an extensive plan of social reform which began with a campaign against illiteracy among adult women. Bint al-Nil founded centers in Cairo, Alexandria, and several provincial towns throughout the Delta where women were taught the rudiments of reading and writing, some elementary hygiene, and trades they could work at in their homes to augment family income.[24]

How did Doria Shafik and her Bint al-Nil Union appeal to the various social classes within Egyptian society during this period? Shafik was of that generation of young middle-class women who received their education at French religious mission schools. The contradictions within her own provincial middle-class background and her liberal education helped convince her that Egyptian women would be able to break the chains of tradition only when they had access to decision-making positions within society. This would come through obtaining their full political rights, which would allow women not only to vote but also to be elected into the spheres of institutionalized power, that is, the Parliament. In this stance Doria Shafik took the liberal ideology of the EFU one step further, becoming more militant in her reformist ideas and action than Huda Sha'rawi. One also must understand that Doria Shafik thought of herself as the symbol of the new Egyptian woman emerging after World War II—highly educated, articulate, internationalist, urbane,

attractive, and elegantly well dressed. She presented herself, quite inten-
tionally, as different from the secluded, traditionally clad, silent majority
of Egyptian women. Militant while remaining feminine ("our feminism is
entirely feminine"), Shafik was out to conquer the male elite sphere of
politics. At the beginning of her career she might have defended the
upper classes as the "natural" rulers of Egypt, particularly since she
worked closely with Princess Chewikar and Princess Faiza on the magazine *La femme nouvelle*. By the end of the 1940s, however, she was definitely becoming one of the leading spokespersons for the middle class,
which she considered eligible to rule.

Education, public health, and change in the family status law were just
as important in the eyes of Doria Shafik and other middle-class women
who joined her as they had been for the earlier feminists.[25] But politics
was their dominant concern, especially for a class that did not own the
means of production and thus did not exercise much control over the
process of decision making. The only route to power, given that birth and
money were the prerogatives of the elite, was parliamentary politics.
Thus Shafik directed most of her energy toward that goal. Her demands
before and after the 1952 revolution were for the rights of women, at least
educated ones, not only to vote but to run for public office as well. The
demonstrations, newspaper articles, lectures, and hunger strikes were
all for the sake of getting access to the voting booth and to Parliament.

The two magazines that Doria Shafik published and edited displayed
her changing feminist and political consciousness during this period.
Prior to 1948 her editorials in *Bint al-Nil* were basically an extension of the
moral feminism of the EFU, although in the voice of a different class. After
1948 she shifted toward a more radical demand for equal rights. The titles
of the two magazines, *The New Woman* and *Daughter of the Nile*, embody
this development in feminist discourse and vision. The new woman assumes the presence of the old woman, and provides a dichotomy between the old and the new. A reading of both magazines gives one the
idea that Shafik's new woman, as well as that of other members of the
Bint al-Nil Union, is one of the secular liberal middle class who dresses in
affordable, fashionable elegance, exercises to maintain a healthy
youthfulness, and raises her children the modern, that is, Western way.
Bint al-Nil's modern woman is as aware of the politics of the world as she
is of dinner etiquette. Although the magazine did not actively call for
women to go out and work or deal with peasant and working-class wom-
en's lives and issues, it did concentrate on the special problems of emerging middle-class women—as homemakers, wives, and mothers—as well
as those of professional, educated, and working women. Its readership,
which also extended outside of Egypt, was primarily made up of these

"new" middle-class women and their families. It was primarily through *Bint al-Nil* that Shafik's feminist platform and ideology reached beyond Egypt's borders to other Arab countries.[26]

By replacing the vague title *The Egyptian Woman* of the magazines of the EFU[27] with the more specific title *Daughter of the Nile*, Shafik was symbolically excluding identification with the Turko-Circassian elite and appealing specifically to women of Egyptian background. At the same time her title did not refer to any specific class of Egyptian women, whether rural or urban, Copt or Muslim. In an atmosphere of highly charged nationalist discourse that emphasized the dichotomy between Egyptian and foreigner, this title implied a rejection of the view that her vision of society and women's position within it was "foreign." In other words, with the symbolic title *Daughter of the Nile* Doria Shafik was not only attempting to claim leadership of the women's movement from the EFU but also asserting her own Egyptian identity.[28]

Other evidence suggests that Doria Shafik, through the Bint al-Nil Union, wanted to lead a total movement toward full political participation for women, but attempts to unify with other women's groups to achieve this objective proved illusory in the long run. One of Doria Shafik's first moves following the establishment of Bint al-Nil Union was to travel to Zurich to affiliate her union with the International Council of Women (ICW).[29] On 30 March 1949 *La Bourse egyptienne* reported the alliance of two feminist parties—the Egyptian Feminist party and Bint al-Nil (to be called collectively the National Council of Women in Egypt)—to represent Egypt within the International Council of Women. The inability of the leaders to agree on fundamental issues, not to mention the structural difficulties raised by such a merger, precluded the success of such an alliance. Consequently Fatma Nimat Rashid declared her "withdrawal of the National Feminist Party from the ICW" on 20 February 1950 in a statement to *Le journal d'Egypte*. The Bint al-Nil Union announced itself, thereafter, as the National Council of Women in Egypt—Bint al-Nil and from then on gathered momentum over the issue of full political rights for women. At the same time, however, Doria Shafik continued to be the focus of critical attacks from both the left and the right within Egypt. One leader of the Muslim Brothers, Muhammad Fahmi 'Abd al-Wahhab, impugned her motives for affiliating with the ICW, calling it a "movement of mutiny against the morals and traditions of Islam" and suggesting that she was playing into the hands of Western colonialism and Zionism. But Doria Shafik was not deterred, and in 1955 she tried to establish a new and broader-based Arab feminist union that would follow the one established in 1944 by Huda Sha'rawi. But she met with resistance, both from those who identified strongly with the EFU and the memory of Huda Sha'rawi[30] and from the progressive forces, who never felt comfortable with Shafik's liberal ideology, particularly at a time when Nasser was establishing his own brand of Arab socialist solidarity.

There were moments, however, when Bint al-Nil and the other women's organizations came together over women's rights. In February 1951 Doria Shafik organized a mass rally at the American University in Cairo. As she describes in her 1955 memoirs: "My strategy was to unite the largest number of women regardless of their ideologies or their particular relation to Bint al-Nil, in order to build one front. We would invade the Parliament with the objective of demanding our political rights and at the same time prove to society the solidarity of all women in this demand and thus create a major social repercussion."

Nearly fifteen hundred women marched the few blocks to Parliament to "take it by storm." This demonstration evoked satirical comment from Shafik's critics, who found it inconceivable that Ceza Nabarawi, "spiritual daughter" of Huda Sha'rawi, would participate with Shafik, whom she disliked intensely.[31] More strident reaction against Shafik came from the conservative Islamic organizations. Following both the storming of Parliament and Shafik's attempts to run for political office, the issue of women's rights became newsworthy and a veritable tirade erupted. In 1952 Akhir Sa'a published a series of polemical exchanges between members of different Islamic organizations and Doria Shafik. Under the banner "Islamic Congress against Bint al-Nil: Islamic Organizations Rise to Resist the Feminist Danger," we read:

Eastern women have become fond of imitating Western women. Employing women in public work stimulates their emancipation from the bonds of men. If a woman is economically independent, she will refuse to submit to the man and will neglect her home and children. The result will be the breakdown of family unity and the resultant breakdown of society. When she demands the right of suffrage she contradicts nature!!! Recently an adventurous movement has begun which defies the limits set by God and dares to challenge Islamic beliefs, thus creating a serious danger to the nation. This devilish movement is made up of women who are not attached to their homes and do not carry out family duties such as taking care of their husbands and children. They are inspired by imperialistic foreign influences which are moving against our religion and social system. Our reputation shall be ruined, as this movement proclaims principles that are obviously contradictory to Islam—that is, the restriction of divorce and polygamy. Therefore the General Association of the Islamic Organizations of Egypt requests his Majesty: (1) to abolish women's organizations that call for participation in politics; (2) to force Muslim women to return to their homes and tables with the necessary legal codes to protect them from corruption; [and (3) to strictly impose the veil.][32]

In her rebuttal, "One Woman Against the Flood," Doria Shafik answered:

> I have never known of a cause opposed by such insults, attacks, lies and silly thoughts as the cause of women. Only its opponents have been heard. And people listen to them as if they alone were the leaders of guidance and minarets of right religion. The makers of these anecdotes have closed their eyes to the facts: the education of girls at a university is a fact; the employment of women in public service is a fact; and women's constitutional rights is a problem that will be solved in spite of the opposition, the meetings, the insults and accusations because it is a logical and just cause supported by the merciful and generous religion of Islam. Our cause is destined ultimately to be achieved, in spite of their futile objections.

Following the storming of Parliament, Doria Shafik focused her struggle almost exclusively on obtaining full political rights for women.[33] In October 1951 she formed a Bint al-Nil political party composed mostly of university students, which men as well as women joined. In March 1952 she submitted her registration papers to run for election to the Egyptian Parliament, although there was no official recognition of women's suffrage. After she was refused she filed suit before the State Council to amend the election law. On 23 July 1952 the revolution took place, and Doria Shafik was optimistic that "the leaders of the Egyptian Revolution would in time realize the second revolution, no less important than the first, that of giving women an equal say in the laws of the country." And she waited. Even after the Bint al-Nil political party was abolished along with all other political parties in 1953, Doria Shafik continued to expect that the issue of women's political rights would receive attention. She grew impatient, however, with the lack of government action and "when on 12 March 1954, I read that the Constitutional Assembly would convene with no mention in the newspaper that women would take part I felt women's rights were in danger. I decided to play the last card. I decided to go on a hunger strike to death for women's full political rights."[34]

And, indeed, at noon that day at the Egyptian Press Syndicate, Doria Shafik began her hunger strike in which she was joined by eight other women, "not only to protest the omission of women's political rights in the new provisional constitution of the Revolution but also to underscore the strength of the democratic trend and its roots in the popular consciousness that could no longer tolerate to be patient about rule with no parliament, no constitution and no freedom."[35] It ended when Muhammad Naguib (then president of Egypt) promised to give her petition serious consideration. This act brought Doria Shafik and her feminist struggle national and international publicity. She received cables from more than fifty Arab, Western, and Third World women's organizations as well as from individuals supporting her actions. Several of these organizations invited Shafik to present lectures on the theme "The Arab woman in contemporary politics." In October 1954 she left for a three-month lecture tour around the world. Her first stop was the United States, at the invitation of the American Friends of the Middle East, which led to Harper and Brothers' suggestion that she write her autobiography. In 1956 women's right to vote became Egyptian law, but Doria felt that the law equivocated by stipulating that women had to apply in order to vote, which would discriminate against women by requiring them to demonstrate their literacy (a condition not required of men). She publicly protested, which further alienated her from the Nasser regime.

During the later 1950s, when Nasser's regime was consolidating power, the issue of women's rights was subsumed under the goals and aspirations of the new socialist state. Political parties, the press, and women's organizations were superseded by a larger state-controlled system. Within this historical context Doria Shafik took her final public stance—not for women's rights, not for national liberation, but for what she believed was the broader issue of human rights. On Wednesday, 6 February 1957, she walked into the Indian Embassy, having announced to the press that she was "going to hunger unto death as a protest against the infringement of my human freedom on two fronts—the external: (1) the Israeli occupation of Egyptian land, and the internal: (2) the onset of dictatorship that is leading Egypt into bankruptcy and chaos."[36] This was to be her final political protest. Nasser placed her under house arrest, withdrew her civil rights, and ordered her name banned from public print. Her former comrades within the Bint al-Nil Union forced her resignation.[37]

Ceza Nabarawi and Inji Aflatun drafted and circulated a petition entitled "Egyptian Women Condemn the Position of Doria Shafik." Although the document bore the names of twenty-seven women representing more than a dozen different women's groups, professions, and syndicates, it was never published. Essentially it denounced Shafik's actions as counterrevolutionary:

We the Egyptian women are astonished by Mrs. Doria Shafik's statement and we declare our severe disapproval of her act that distorted the reputation of the Egyptian Women's movement abroad. This movement entered into a new phase after the rise of our national revolution in 1952 and after the Egyptian woman got her political rights in the new constitution. Therefore our women's movement became a people's movement apart from the individual leadership that is built on personal propaganda.

This totally unsympathetic response to Shafik's dramatic act underscores the deep-seated opposition to her not only among the progressive left but also among many secular Nasserites. From their point of view Shafik was too ideologically committed to Western bourgeois values of liberal humanism with its emphasis on social and legal reform based on a democratic system of parliamentary government—a system that in Egypt had allowed uncontrollable power to fall into the hands of the few. Whereas the leftist progressive women were organizing people's resistance groups among the lower classes within the orbit of the general revolutionary struggle against imperialist domination, class hierarchy, and economic inequality, Doria Shafik was championing values of individual freedom expressed in the feminist struggle for "political rights." Through the pages of her *Bint al-Nil* editorials, Shafik was openly hostile both to communism and to what she believed was the rise of dictatorship. She consciously avoided joining any political party or social movement except her own Bint al-Nil party, which many considered ineffectual and futile in the face of the national anti-imperialist struggle facing Egypt (the Israeli occupation of Arab land after the 1956 Suez War). Her open challenge to Nasser during this most critical phase of the Cold War era when Egypt was under attack by the Western imperialists was interpreted by her opponents as direct evidence of "playing into the hands of the enemy." As the petitioners asked: "Wouldn't it have been more proper for Mrs. Doria Shafik to show her jealousy about the 'liberation of the country' by participating in the women's resistance committees during the Tripartite treachery by our enemy against Egypt our cherished country instead of remaining in complete isolation?"

Ironically, this political stance of remaining apart led to her final isolation—house arrest and then self-imposed seclusion. Within a few months her magazine had been destroyed along with her personal papers and files, and Doria Shafik disappeared from public life until her tragic death on 20 September 1975 brought her name for the last time onto the front pages of the Egyptian press.

To conclude this chapter, let us return to our original question: what theoretical contribution can the attempts to recover women's voices and women's experiences make to contemporary feminist discourse on women in the Middle East? Recently Arab and non-Arab feminist scholars have begun to call for a different focus on Middle Eastern societies. This is a call to those doing research on Middle Eastern societies not merely to include a paragraph or two on the generic category "women," but to begin to reinterpret society from a new perspective, one that is not dominated by patriarchal notions of power and action in society. Doing research on women thus becomes a way of deconstructing dominant patriarchal social science theories and notions of historical relevance, including certain presuppositions about feminism and Islam. It is in this context that I see the relevance and importance of discovering and recovering the hidden voices of Middle Eastern women, such as Doria Shafik, to examine how particular conditions of women's lives have fostered different kinds of political consciousness and action in the shaping of recent Egyptian history. Several themes emerging from our brief excursion "interpreting Doria Shafik" argue for the relevance of memoirs to the construction of women's history in the Middle East.

The first centers on an issue that not only dominated Doria's thought and political activism but also seems to plague feminist scholars today: the compatibility of Islam and feminism. Some contemporary Arab feminist scholars argue that if any significant advance is to be made in the status of women, there must be a complete severance of Islamic tradition from the issue of the position and status of women. A truly decisive breakthrough will depend on the reassertion of a secular culture that seems today everywhere under siege. "If feminism is defined as a struggle against every inherited tradition and instinctive value informing relations between men and women, Arab feminism has yet to emerge into the light of day."[38]

Embedded in that position is a presupposition of a negative and binary opposition between Islam and women: that Islamic tradition is some static, monolithic cause contributing universally to female oppression throughout Middle Eastern societies. And it denies the validity of the subjective experiences of Middle Eastern women struggling to find meaning in a world structured as much by economic, political, and cultural factors as by religion. Just as there is "at heart of the feminist project, East and West, a desire to dismantle the existing order of things and reconstruct it to fit one's needs, there is also a difference among feminists, East and West in the grasp they have on the existing order and the tools they use to dismantle it."[39]

Doria Shafik's experience is instructive in this context, for in many ways her entire life represented a continual revolt against the view of Islam as some immutable Fate constraining women either to accommodate or to apostatize. Her feminist struggle was aimed at dismantling a political and legal system that kept women apart from the centers of power. She viewed her radical, militant strategy as compatible with a secular Islamic value system reflecting the continuity of thought of those ardent secular liberals of an earlier generation, Qasim Amin and Taha Husain.[40]

Another theme discussed among contemporary feminists and reflected in Doria Shafik's life is the role of the woman intellectual in bringing about change in society. Doria Shafik was trying to forge a public political space for women on different grounds than those of women leaders who came before her. She challenged dominant Islamic ideology, and by her own personal example she tried to redefine women's own conceptions of themselves and their place in the wider political system. This is still a burning issue within the Arab Islamic East. As Sidonie Smith has recently commented: "Suspended between culturally constructed categories of male and female selfhood, women, particularly the literate and educated, would have discovered a certain fluidity to the boundaries of gender. These sliding spaces of ideology and subjectivity she would have negotiated in greater or lesser degrees of conformity and resistance."[41] Doria Shafik was an educated woman who could visualize the broader context of her historical situation. She was a nonconformist who could "break out of the mold." In that context, Doria believed the educated woman had an important role to play as a force in bringing about new synthesis or harmony in society, not only between men and women—her vision of feminism and the feminist project was not of a continuous struggle between men and women but rather of their harmony, understanding, and cooperation—but also between the classes. She argued that educated women could erase the class differences in Egypt by spreading ideas of the women's movement beyond the elite to the rest of the Egyptian women. Thus middle-class women, as intellectuals, were to be the mediators not only between the sexes but also between the estranged classes of Egypt. These women would create national unity. Nationalism and feminism were fused in Doria Shafik's vision, and as an intellectual she reflected the romanticism and rationalism inherent in the liberal and bourgeois ideology of middle-class women more than the political consciousness of either the communist left or the fundamentalist right.

A final theme emerging from her memoirs and relevant to contemporary feminist discourse on the Middle East is the whole question of the authenticity and relevance of an Arab or Egyptian feminism itself. There are those who would argue that Egyptian feminism is nothing more than an imported ideology, and that Doria Shafik was more European than Egyptian. Historically, Egypt after World War II was a society in fermentation struggling to change. There were many radical forces on both the left and the right—the Communists, the Socialists, the Muslim Brothers, the New Wafd—trying to mobilize the masses. Doria Shafik appeared on the scene fervently believing in two goals: the modernization of Egyptian society following the chaos of World War II; and changing the status of Egyptian women as a strategy toward achieving this modernization. It is true that in her dress and physical appearance Doria Shafik appeared the epitome of the Westernized Egyptian woman, but her objectives and her commitment to free herself and her society from the "chains of the past" were authentically Egyptian, grounded in the cultural roots of her past as well as in the present realities of her own society. That the rank and file of Egyptian women could not identify with her was as much a consequence of her own personality—her public image—as it was of her message. Her public persona was daring, proud, self-centered, and strong willed. She has been variously described as the "perfumed leader"; a "radical"; a "danger to the Muslim nation"; a "militant feminist"; the "beautiful leader"; a "taste of candied chestnut"; the "woman of the 88 eyebrows"; a "traitor to the Revolution"; the "only Man in Egypt." As one prominent Nasserist journalist for *al-Ahram* recently confided: "Doria Shafik emphasized the 'modernistic' in her appearance but what she was saying was right and we students at university supported her. She was out of tune with her times."[42]

From the perspective of this chapter it is useful to see feminism in the context of specific Egyptian historical circumstances that shaped the ideologies and strategies of particular Egyptian women in their search for explanations to the contradictions that they had experienced in their own lives. These conditions were not so much imported as they were the result of an actual historical encounter between Egypt and the West. This opened up the possibilities of choice for an increasing number of women from middle-class backgrounds and led to the conviction that women could be an important force for changing oppressive and unjust conditions within their own society. As such, feminism in its Egyptian context became a conscious strategy to obtain more rights within specific historical realities. In other words, the choice of feminism by some women was a conscious decision and a tactic that they knew would bring them into direct conflict with their own society. And some women, like Doria Shafik, paid a heavy price for their commitment. What this interpretation offers to those contemporary feminists looking for "women" to "write her self" is the recognition that Doria Shafik had a voice in shaping a feminist discourse and practice at a certain moment in Egyptian history when women were redefining themselves in the face of changing realities. But we also hear through those memoirs and poetry the echoes of another voice, etched in pain and loneliness, which reverberates "the life of the transition stage, the hardest and most difficult for the individual as well as for a people."[43]

Notes

1. Stephen Oates, ed., *Biography as High Adventure* (Amherst: University of Massachusetts Press, 1986); Marc Pachter, ed., *Telling Lives: The Biographer's Art* (Philadelphia: University of Pennsylvania Press, 1981); Johannes Fabian, *Time and the Other: How Anthropology Makes Its Object* (New York: Columbia University Press, 1983); James Clifford and George E. Marcus, eds., *Writing Culture: The Poetics and Politics of Ethnography* (Berkeley: University of California Press, 1985); George E. Marcus and Michael M. J. Fischer, *Anthropology as Cultural Critique: An Experimental Moment in the Human Sciences* (Chicago: University of Chicago Press, 1986).

2. *Larmes d'Isis* (Tears of Isis) and *Avec Dante aux enfers* (I–IV) (With Dante in hell) (Paris: Pierre Fanlac, 1979).

3. Author's letter to the daughters, 14 Feb. 1985.

4. Doria Shafik was one of the first Egyptian women to receive a doctorat d'état in philosophy from the Sorbonne. She wrote two theses: *L'art pour l'art dans Egypte antique* (Art for art's sake in ancient Egypt) and *La femme et le droit religieux de l'Egypte contemporaine* (Women and religious law in contemporary Egypt) (both published Paris: Paul Geuthner, 1940).

5. I consider Doria Shafik an intellectual not only because she self-consciously set about to question those social, cultural, and legal traditions she viewed as oppressive and inimical to the full equality of women in her society, but also because she engaged, more directly than the women of the previous generation, in the intercultural political discourse surrounding feminism and Islam.

6. *La femme nouvelle en Egypte* (The new woman in Egypt) (Cairo: Schindler, 1944); *Tatawwur al-nahda al-nisa'iyya fi Misr* (The development of women's renaissance in Egypt), coauthored with Ibrahim 'Abduh (Cairo: Maktabat al-Tawakkul, 1945); *La bonne aventure* (The good adventure) (Paris: Pierre Seghers, 1949); *L'esclave sultane* (The sultan's slave) (Paris: Editions Latines, 1952); *al-Kitab al-abyad li-huquq al-mar'a al-siyasiyya* (The white book on the political rights of women) (Cairo: Maktabat al-Sharqiyya, 1953); *L'amour perdu* (The lost love) (Paris: Pierre Seghers, 1954); *al-Mar'a al-misriyya min al-fara'ina ila al-yaum* (The Egyptian woman from the Pharaohs until today), coauthored with Ibrahim 'Abduh (Cairo: Matba'at al-Misr, 1955). Ibrahim 'Abduh was the founder of the Department of Journalism at Cairo University and its leading professor from the 1930s until the 1952 revolution.

7. Following the presentation of my paper on Doria Shafik at an international colloquium in Cairo in 1985, an angry debate among several Egyptian participants erupted over Shafik's role in the history of the women's movement in Egypt. One person (a leftist) suggested that Doria Shafik was a traitor to the revolution and did not merit a biography. See Cynthia Nelson, "The Voices of Doria Shafik: The Shaping of a Feminist Consciousness," *Feminist Issues* 6, no. 2 (1986): 15–31.

8. Personal communication from Seghers to the daughters following Shafik's death. Pierre Seghers was her friend and mentor and the publisher of her poetry.

9. Leila Ahmed, "Feminism and Feminist Movements in the Middle East," in *Women and Islam*, ed. Aziza al-Hibri (New York: Pergamon, 1982); Lois Beck and Nikki Keddie, eds., *Women in the Muslim World* (Cambridge: Harvard University Press, 1978); Elizabeth W. Fernea and Basima Bezirgan, eds., *Middle Eastern Muslim Women Speak* (Austin: University of Texas Press, 1977); Mervat Hatem, "The Enduring Alliance of Nationalism and Patriarchy in Muslim Personal Status Laws," *Feminist Issues* 6, no. 1 (1986): 19–43; Thomas Philipp, "Feminism and National Politics in Egypt," in *Women in the Muslim World*, ed. Beck and Keddie, 277–94; Earl Sullivan, *Women in Egyptian Public Life* (Syracuse: Syracuse University Press, 1986).

10. The Wafd (delegation) is the name of the first organized mass party in Egypt, founded by Sa'd Zaghlul in 1918. Sha'rawi headed the women's committee within this party.

11. Arslan Bohdanowicz, "The Feminist Movement in Egypt," *Islamic Review* 8 (August 1951): 24–33; Ijlal Khalifa, *al-Haraka al-nisa'iyya al-haditha* (The modern women's movement) (Cairo: Dar al-Kutub, 1973); Amal Kamil al-Sabaqi, *al-Haraka al-nisa'iyya fi Misr ma baina al-thauratain 1919 wa 1952* (The women's movement in Egypt between the two revolutions 1919 and 1952) (Cairo: Hai'at al-Kitab al-'Amma, 1987); Kumari Jayawardena, "Reformism and Women's Rights in Egypt," in *Feminism and Nationalism in the Third World*, ed. Kumari Jayawardena (London: Zed, 1986), 43–56.

12. This term is used by Afaf Lutfi al-Sayyid Marsot in her history of this period, *Egypt's Liberal Experiment* (Berkeley: University of California Press, 1977).

13. See Akram Khater and Cynthia Nelson, "al-Harakah al-nissa'iyah: The Women's Movement and Political Participation in Modern Egypt," *Women's Studies International Forum* 2, no. 5 (1988): 465–83; and Selma Botman, "The Experience of Women in the Egyptian Communist Movement, 1939–1954," *Women's Studies International Forum* 11, no. 2 (1988): 117–26.

14. She was to pen seven volumes of poetry, another novel, and several philosophical and political essays, as well as numerous translations of sections of the Quran into English and French. She learned Italian in order to read Dante in the original.

15. Unpublished memoirs, 1975. This last version was in English, her least comfortable language. One might speculate that she wrote in this language as another intellectual challenge to herself.

16. Phyllis Rose, *A Woman of Letters: A Life of Virginia Woolf* (New York: Harcourt and Brace, 1978), 9.

17. When wealth meant land it was not uncommon for a male to assume responsibility for the management of the woman's property, especially if the woman was unmarried, widowed, or illiterate. See Judith E. Tucker, *Women in Nineteenth-Century Egypt* (Cambridge: Cambridge University Press, 1985). This was not formal disinheritance, which would have been illegal under Islamic law, but rather a de facto control over the woman's wealth, which in the case of Doria Shafik's grandmother ultimately led to its alienation. Because of his great wealth,

Doria's grand-uncle was elected senator to the first Parliament of Egypt in 1924, representing the Wafd party from Tanta.

18. Unpublished memoirs, 1975.

19. The different spelling of the last name is linked to this period of Doria's life. Doria's dearest friend, whose last name was Soriatis, was frightened about the school preparatory examinations. As seating for the exam was alphabetical, Doria changed the spelling of her name from Chafik to Shafik so that she could sit near her friend to offer moral support.

20. Following Doria's outstanding performance and the pressure from other families, the French decided to open a girls' lycée in Alexandria.

21. Many Egyptians with whom I spoke believe that, after having been divorced by Fuad for not producing a male heir, Chewikar took her revenge by initiating Faruq into his life of corruption and dissipation. After the death of Chewikar in 1947, Princess Faiza, who had assumed the leadership of the benevolent association, agreed that Shafik should assume the ownership and the responsibility for the complete production of the magazine. From that moment until its demise in the early fifties, many, both in Egypt and in Europe, regarded *La femme nouvelle* as a literary and cultural magazine of the highest caliber. The magazine was oriented toward the French-speaking elite of both Egypt and the West and focused its articles on the art, poetry, literature, and history of Egyptian culture.

22. That Huda Sha'rawi died on Doria Shafik's thirty-ninth birthday was interpreted by her imaginative and poetic mind as a symbol of the mystical bond between them, signifying that Doria had a special mission to continue the work of her childhood heroine and benefactor.

23. Unpublished memoirs, 1955.

24. By 1952 thirty such centers were in operation and, according to one of the members of Bint al-Nil Union, there were nearly eighty by 1954. The provincial centers were run by local committees affiliated with the Bint al-Nil central committee in Cairo, which was in charge of determining policy. Each local committee had its own elected officers, and an annual report on activities and budget was forwarded to Cairo. Graduates of the center's training programs automatically became members of the movement. Interview with Ragia Raghib, 4 June 1986.

25. See Shafik and 'Abduh, *Tatawwur,* chap. 5, on the importance of education as a means of liberating women from the shackles of ignorance and male domination.

26. *Bint al-Nil's* monthly circulation often reached or surpassed five thousand copies. Informants from Iraq, Jordan, Palestine, and Lebanon remembered reading not only *Bint al-Nil* but also Shafik's children's magazine, *Katkut.*

27. The Egyptian Feminist Union published two magazines entitled *The Egyptian Woman*—one in French, *L'Egyptienne,* and one in Arabic, *al-Misriyya.*

28. In her poetry and her memoirs she often used the image of the river to express the spiritual affinity she felt toward the Nile.

29. The ICW was founded in 1888 in Washington, D.C., and is the oldest and perhaps largest feminist organization in the world, represented by "national councils composed of national and local women's organizations. It serves as a

medium for consultation among women on those actions necessary to promote the welfare of mankind, the family, children, and the individual, advises women of their rights and their civic, social, and political responsibilities, works for the removal of all that restricts women from full participation in life, and supports international peace and arbitration." See *Bibliography of International Organizations* (1986), 300.

30. Letter from Ibtihaj Qaddura to Hawa Idriss, the young cousin of Huda Sha'rawi, 14 Dec. 1955.

31. Ahmad al-Sawi, *al-Ahram*, 20 Feb. 1951.

32. This plea to the government to actively forbid women's organized activity demanding their rights was sent to King Faruq and signed by Liwa Sulaiman 'Abd al-Wahhab Sobol, head of the Union of Muslim Associations. Among other signatures on the petition were those of Shaikh 'Ali al-Mansuri, representative of the Muslim Brothers, and Muhammad Fahmi 'Abd al-Wahhab, who also wrote the article "Relation between the Feminist Movement in Egypt and British Imperialism."

33. The exceptions were Bint al-Nil's joining a mass protest march in November 1951 against the British occupation of Egypt, particularly the massacre of Egyptian resistance forces in the Canal Zone, and a symbolic boycott of Barclay's Bank—just two days before the burning of Cairo in January 1952.

34. Unpublished memoirs, 1955.

35. Editorial in *Bint al-Nil* (April 1954), 3.

36. Unpublished memoirs, 1975.

37. Several informants expressed to me their belief that the regime "forced" these women's organizations to publicly condemn Shafik's action.

38. Mai Ghoussoub, "Feminism—or the Eternal Masculine—in the Arab World," *New Left Review* 161 (1987): 18.

39. Marnia Lazreg, "Feminism and Difference: The Perils of Writing as a Woman on Women in Algeria," *Feminist Studies* 14, no. 1 (1988): 81.

40. See Shafik's thesis *La femme et le droit religieux* (1940), as well as her early essay "Une petite mot," *L'Egyptienne* 4, no. 38 (1928): 12–14, for insight into her views about Islam.

41. Sidonie Smith, *A Poetics of Women's Autobiography* (Bloomington: Indiana University Press, 1987).

42. Personal communication from Ahmad Baha al-Din.

43. Quoted in frontispiece to Candace Falk, *Love, Anarchy, and Emma Goldman: A Biography* (New York: Holt, Rinehart and Winston, 1984).

Contributors

NERMIN ABADAN-UNAT was professor of political science at Ankara University until her retirement and is now associated with Bosporus University, Istanbul. She is author of *Women in the Developing World: Evidence from Turkey* and editor of *Women in Turkish Society.*

LEILA AHMED is associate professor of women's studies and director of Near Eastern area studies at the University of Massachusetts, Amherst. She is author of *Women and Gender in Islam: Historical Roots of a Modern Debate.*

BETH BARON is assistant professor of history at City College, City University of New York. She has written articles on Egyptian society and politics and is currently working on a book on women, culture, and the press in Egypt.

JONATHAN P. BERKEY is assistant professor of religion at Mount Holyoke College. He is author of *The Transmission of Knowledge in Medieval Cairo: A Social History of Islamic Education.*

JULIA CLANCY-SMITH is assistant professor of history at the University of Virginia. She is author of numerous articles on North African history, including chapters in *Islam, Politics, and Social Movements* and *Muslim Travellers: Pilgrimage, Migration, and the Religious Imagination.*

VIRGINIA DANIELSON is project administrator for a bibliographic project at Harvard University's Eda Kuhn Loeb Music Library. She has completed a doctoral dissertation on Umm Kulthum, the Arab world's most famous modern singer. She has published and lectured on the subjects of Arabic song, tradition and music in Islamic religious expression, and women in musical life in the Middle East.

ERIKA FRIEDL is professor of anthropology at Western Michigan University. She is the author of *Women of Deh Koh: Lives in an Iranian Village.*

MARY ELAINE HEGLAND is assistant professor of anthropology at Santa Clara University. Her works include *Religious Resurgence: Contemporary Cases in Islam, Christianity, and Judaism* (editor, with Richard Antoun) and articles on revolution, religion, women, and local politics in Iran.

DENIZ KANDIYOTI is senior lecturer in the social sciences division, Richmond College, Surrey, England. She is the author of *Women in Rural Production Systems: Problems and Policies* and editor of *Women, Islam and the State.*

NIKKI R. KEDDIE is professor of history at the University of California at Los Angeles. Among her books are *Roots of Revolution: An Interpretive History of Modern Iran* and *Women in the Muslim World* (editor, with Lois Beck). She is the editor of the new multidisciplinary journal, *Contention: Debates in Society, Culture, and Science.*

HUDA LUTFI is associate professor of Middle Eastern history at the American University in Cairo, Egypt. She is author of *al-Quds al-Mamlukiyya: A History of Mamluk Jerusalem Based on the Haram Documents.*

CYNTHIA NELSON is professor of anthropology at the American University in Cairo, Egypt. She has published articles on women and politics in several journals, including *American Ethnologist* and *Women's Studies International Forum,* and edited *The Desert and the Sown.*

CARL F. PETRY is associate professor of Middle Eastern history at Northwestern University. He is author of *The Civilian Elite of Cairo in the Later Middle Ages* and is currently writing a book on the political economy of Egypt prior to the Ottoman conquest. Petry serves on the executive board of the American Research Center in Egypt.

DONALD QUATAERT is associate professor of history and director of the Southwest Asian and North African program at the State University of New York at Binghamton. His books include *Social Disintegration and Popular Resistance in the Ottoman Empire, 1881–1908* and *The Ottoman Empire: Its Society and Economy, 1300–1914* (associate editor, with Halil Inalcik, editor).

PAULA SANDERS is assistant professor of history at Rice University. She has published articles on Fatimid ceremonial and historiography and has recently completed the book *Ritual, Politics, and the City in Fatimid Cairo.*

DENISE A. SPELLBERG is assistant professor of history and Middle East studies at the University of Texas at Austin. She has also taught in the Women's Studies and Religion Program at Harvard Divinity School. Her work on gender and Islamic history has been published in *Muslim World* and *Literature East and West.*

JUDITH E. TUCKER is associate professor of history at Georgetown University. She is author of *Women in Nineteenth-Century Egypt* and of numerous articles on women and the family in eighteenth- and nineteenth-century Egypt and Palestine. She is also a contributing editor of the *Middle East Report.*

Index